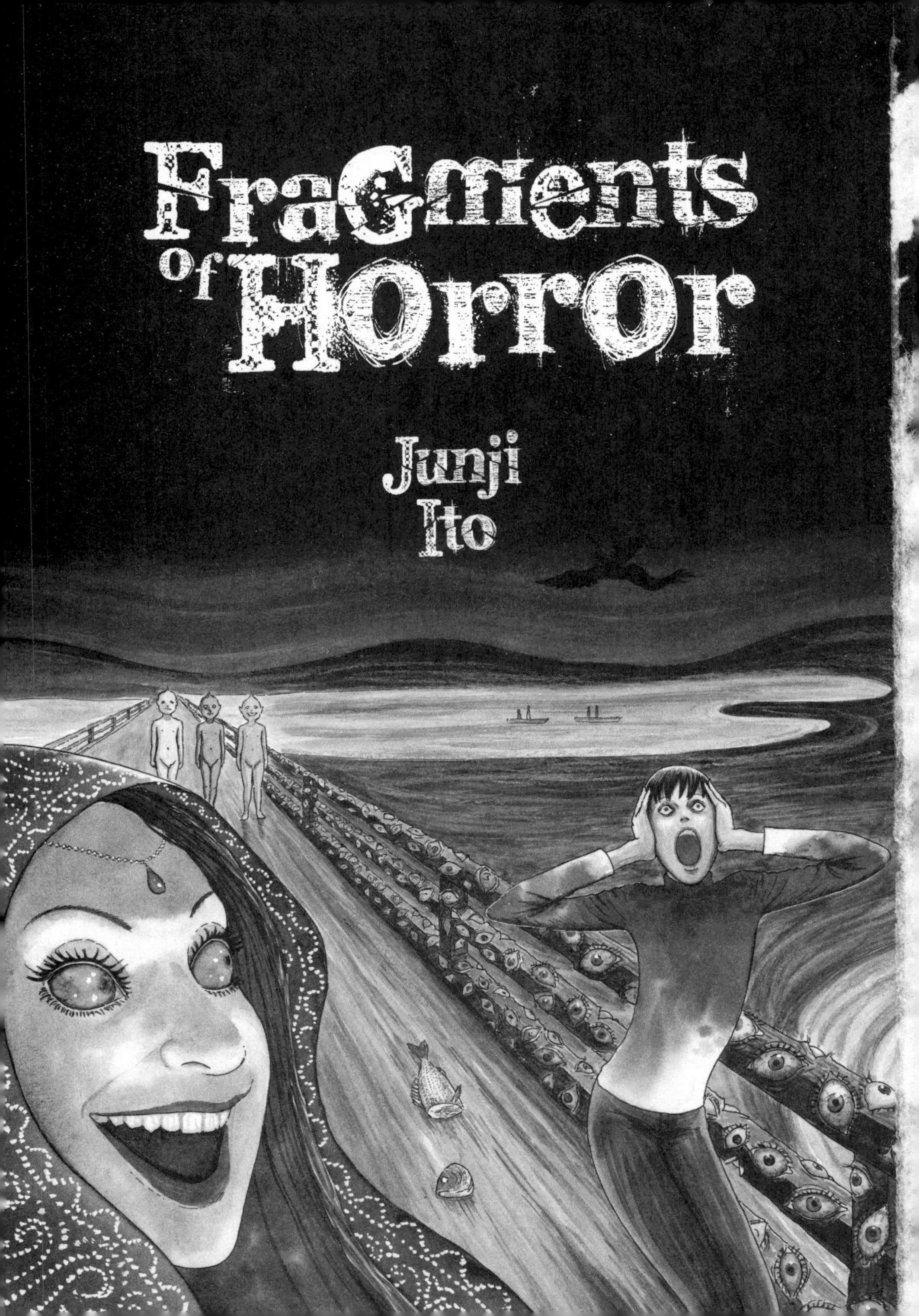
Fragments of Horror
Junji Ito

contents

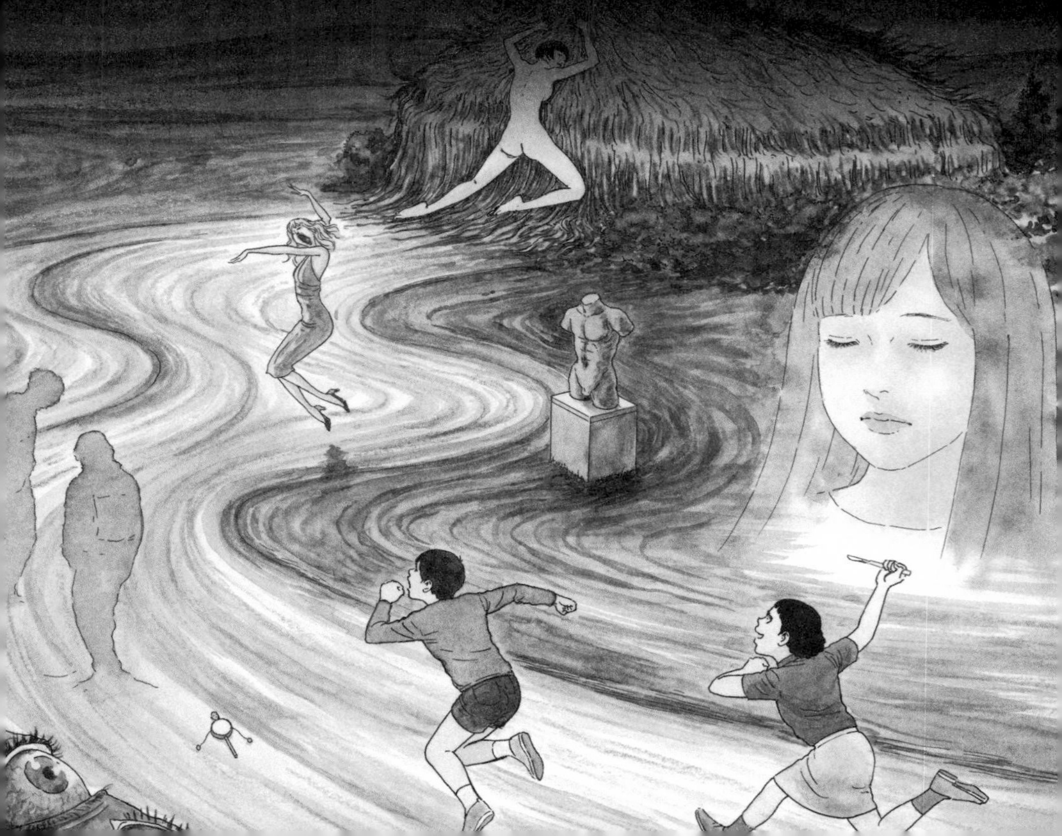

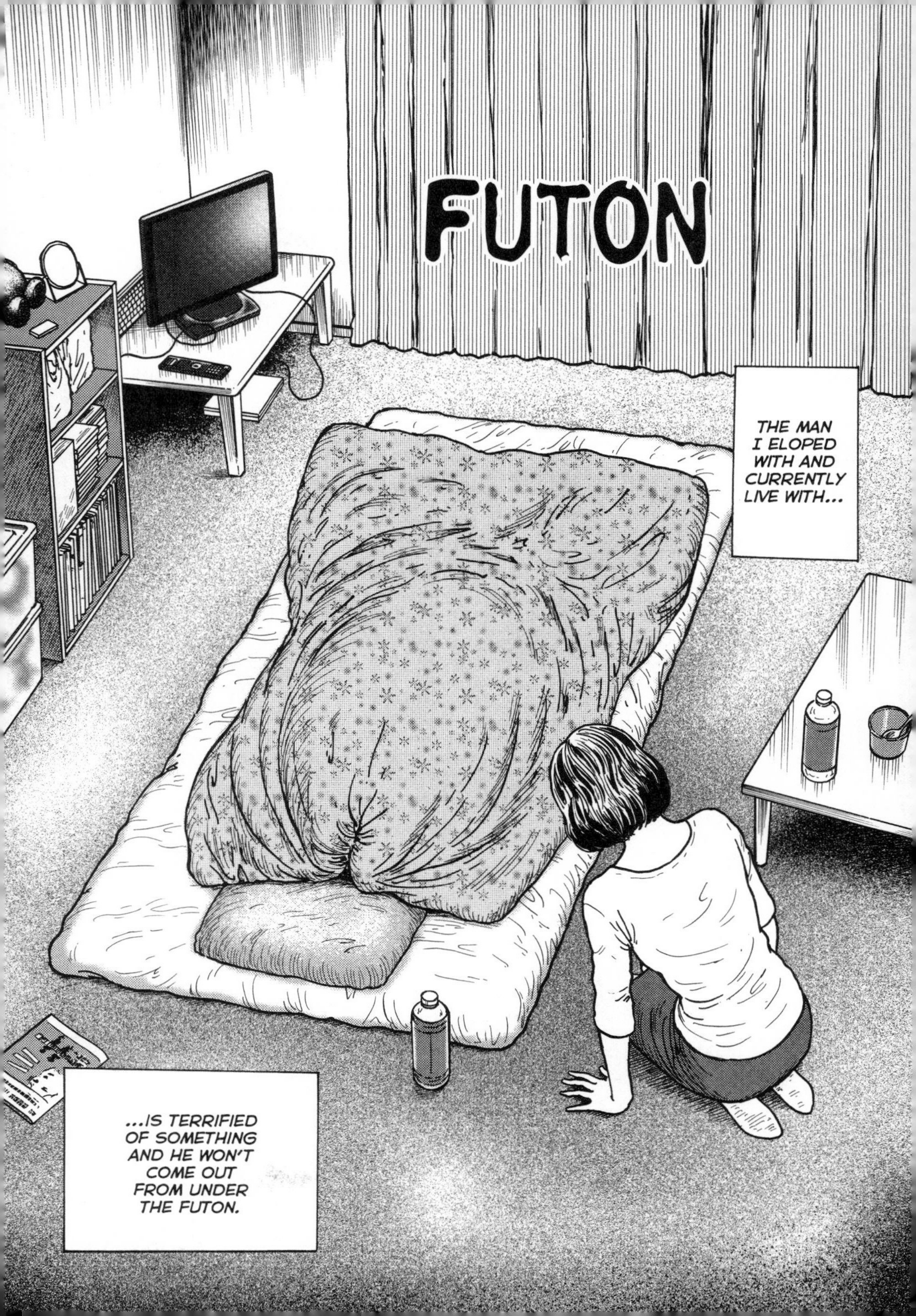
FUTON
THE MAN I ELOPED WITH AND CURRENTLY LIVE WITH...
...IS TERRIFIED OF SOMETHING AND HE WON'T COME OUT FROM UNDER THE FUTON.

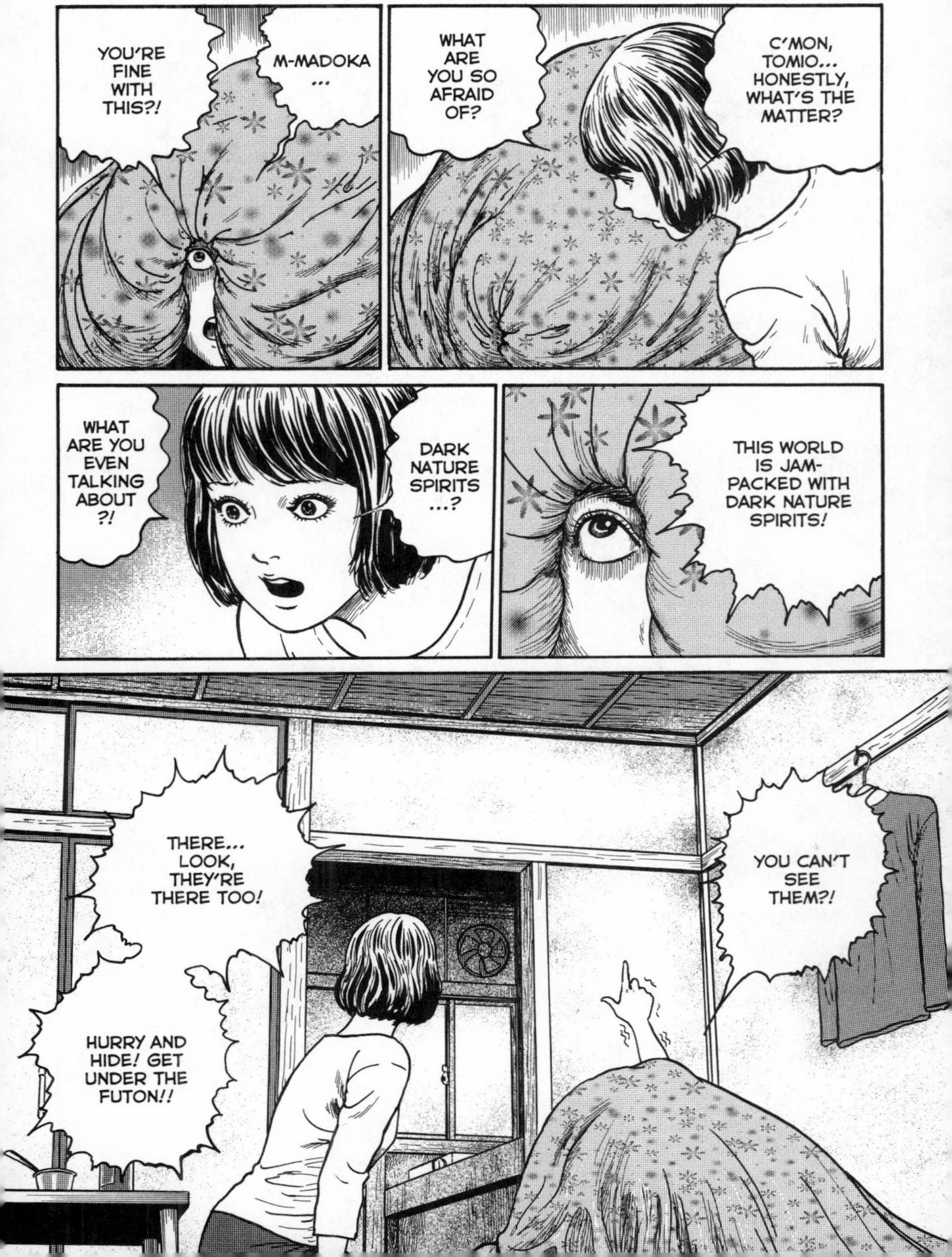
C'MON, TOMIO... HONESTLY, WHAT'S THE MATTER?
WHAT ARE YOU SO AFRAID OF?
M-MADOKA...
YOU'RE FINE WITH THIS?!
THIS WORLD IS JAM-PACKED WITH DARK NATURE SPIRITS!
DARK NATURE SPIRITS...?
WHAT ARE YOU EVEN TALKING ABOUT?!
YOU CAN'T SEE THEM?!
THERE... LOOK, THEY'RE THERE TOO!
HURRY AND HIDE! GET UNDER THE FUTON!!

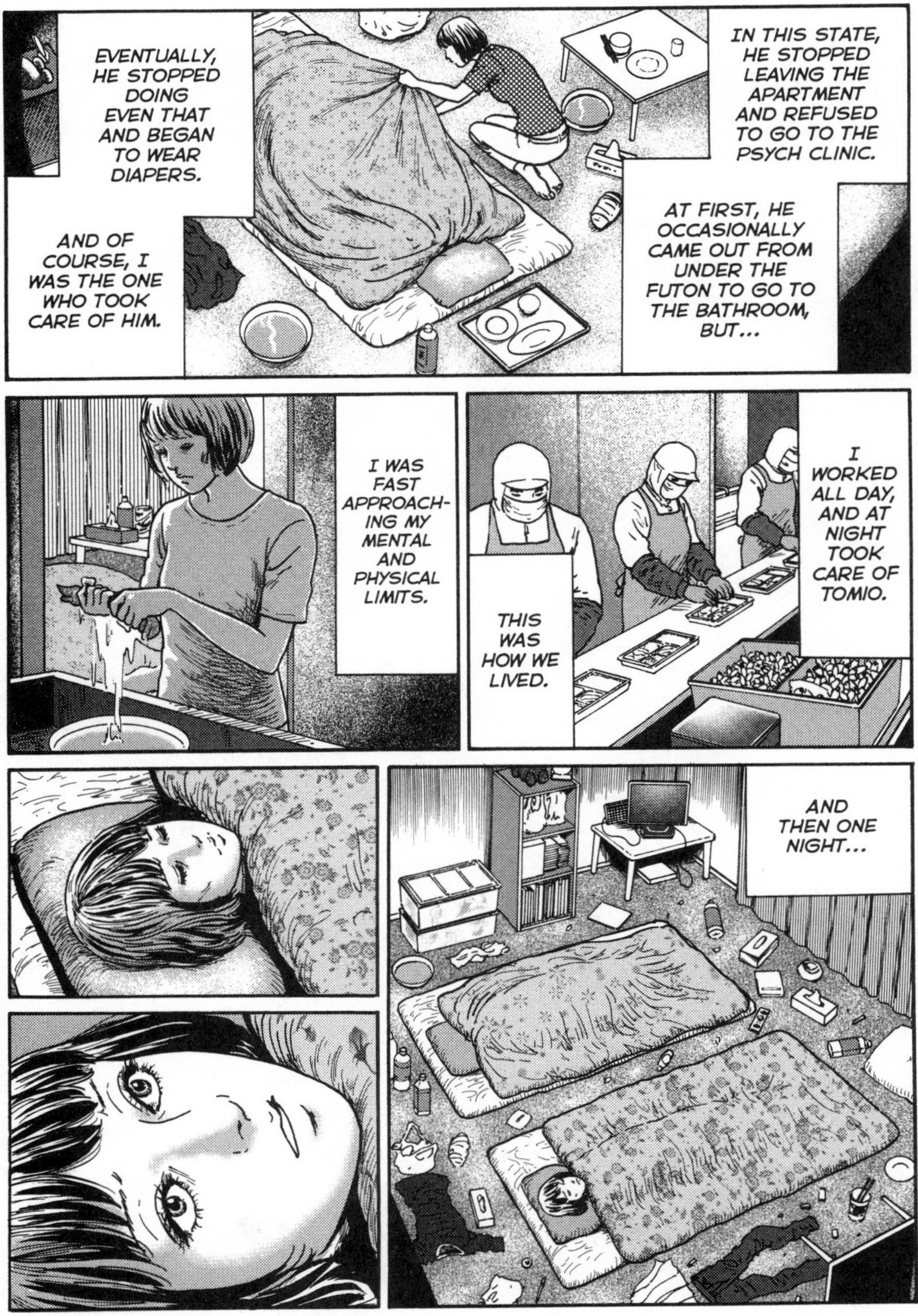
IN THIS STATE, HE STOPPED LEAVING THE APARTMENT AND REFUSED TO GO TO THE PSYCH CLINIC.
AT FIRST, HE OCCASIONALLY CAME OUT FROM UNDER THE FUTON TO GO TO THE BATHROOM, BUT...
EVENTUALLY, HE STOPPED DOING EVEN THAT AND BEGAN TO WEAR DIAPERS.
AND OF COURSE, I WAS THE ONE WHO TOOK CARE OF HIM.
I WORKED ALL DAY, AND AT NIGHT TOOK CARE OF TOMIO.
THIS WAS HOW WE LIVED.
I WAS FAST APPROACHING MY MENTAL AND PHYSICAL LIMITS.
AND THEN ONE NIGHT...

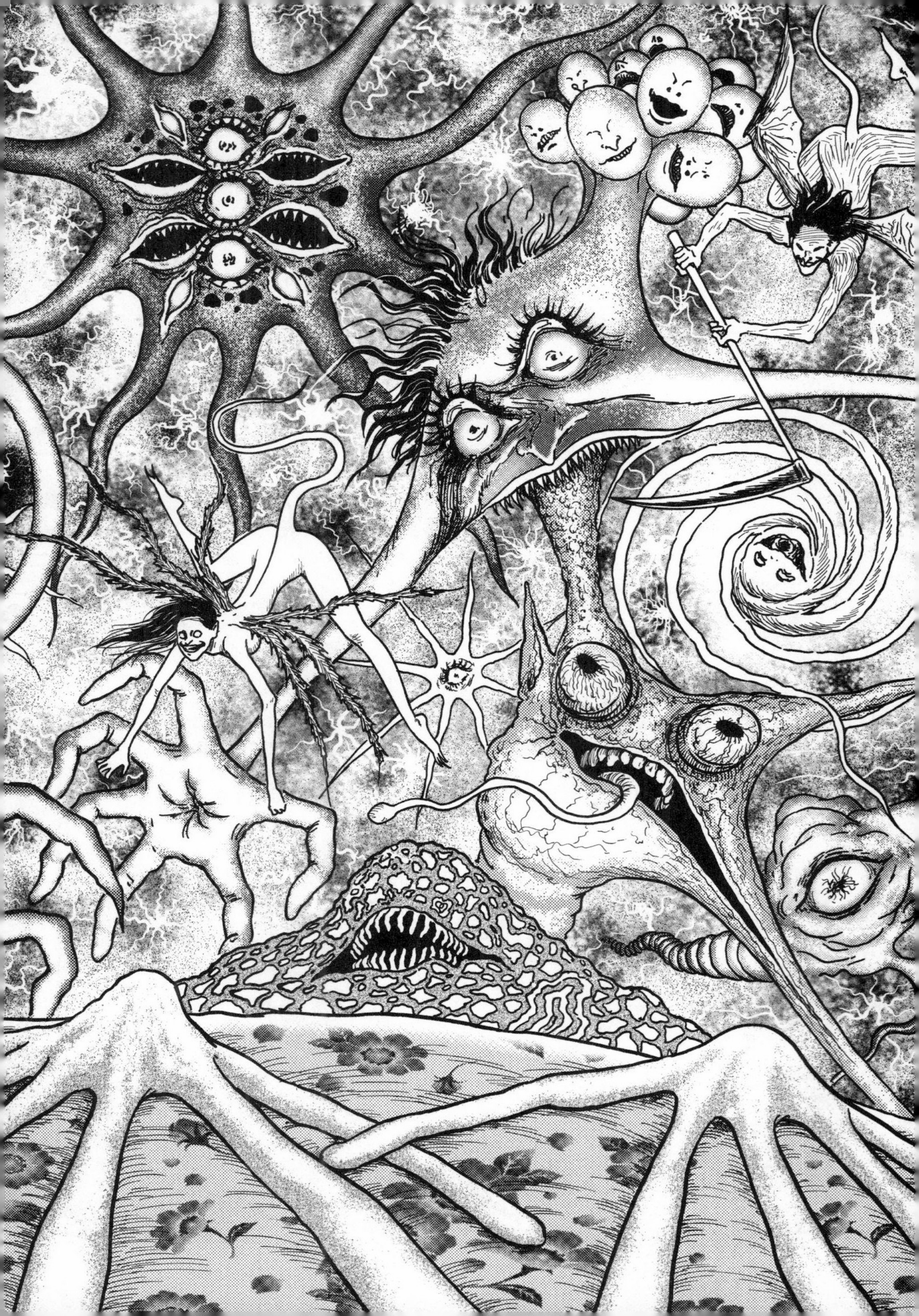

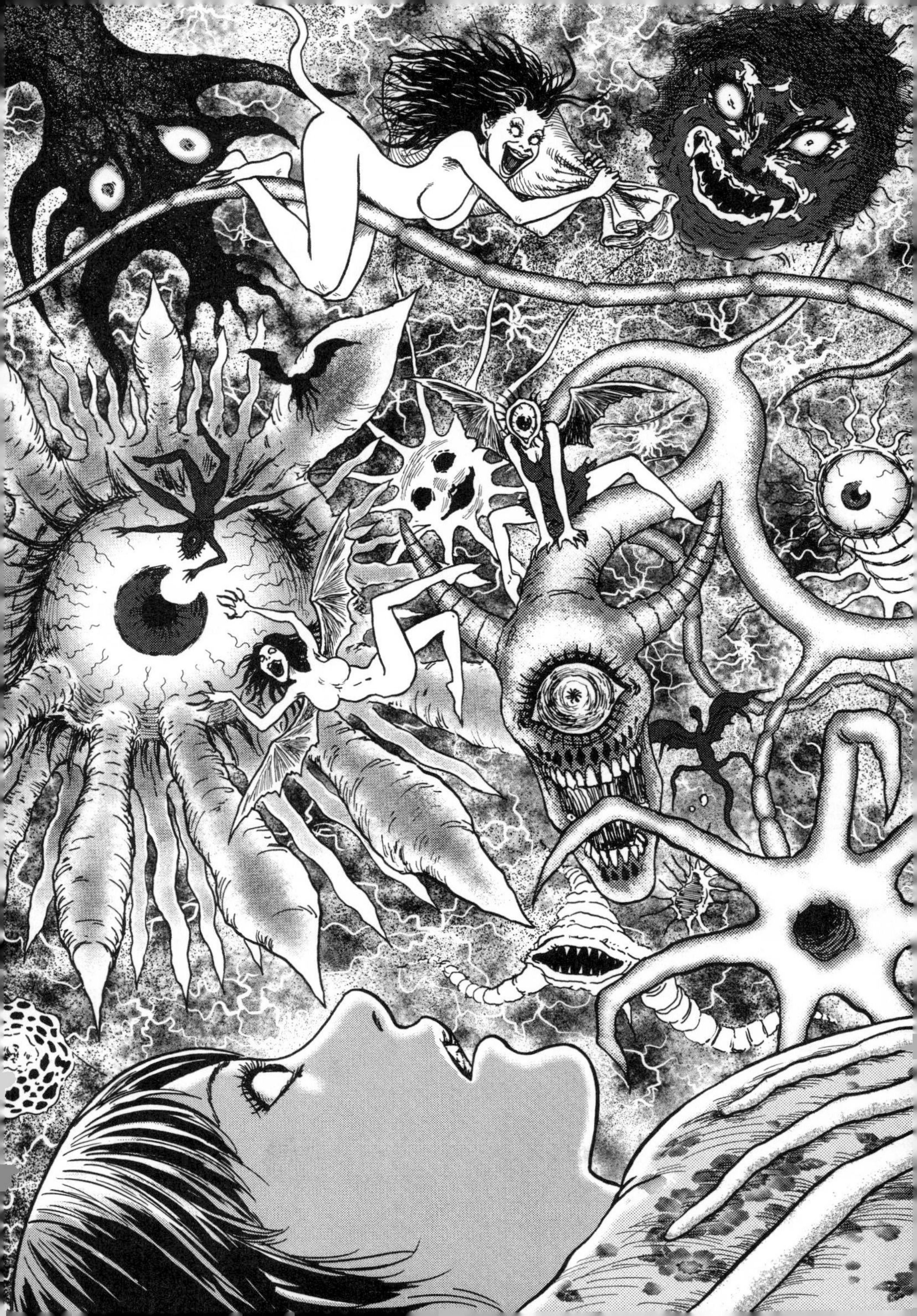

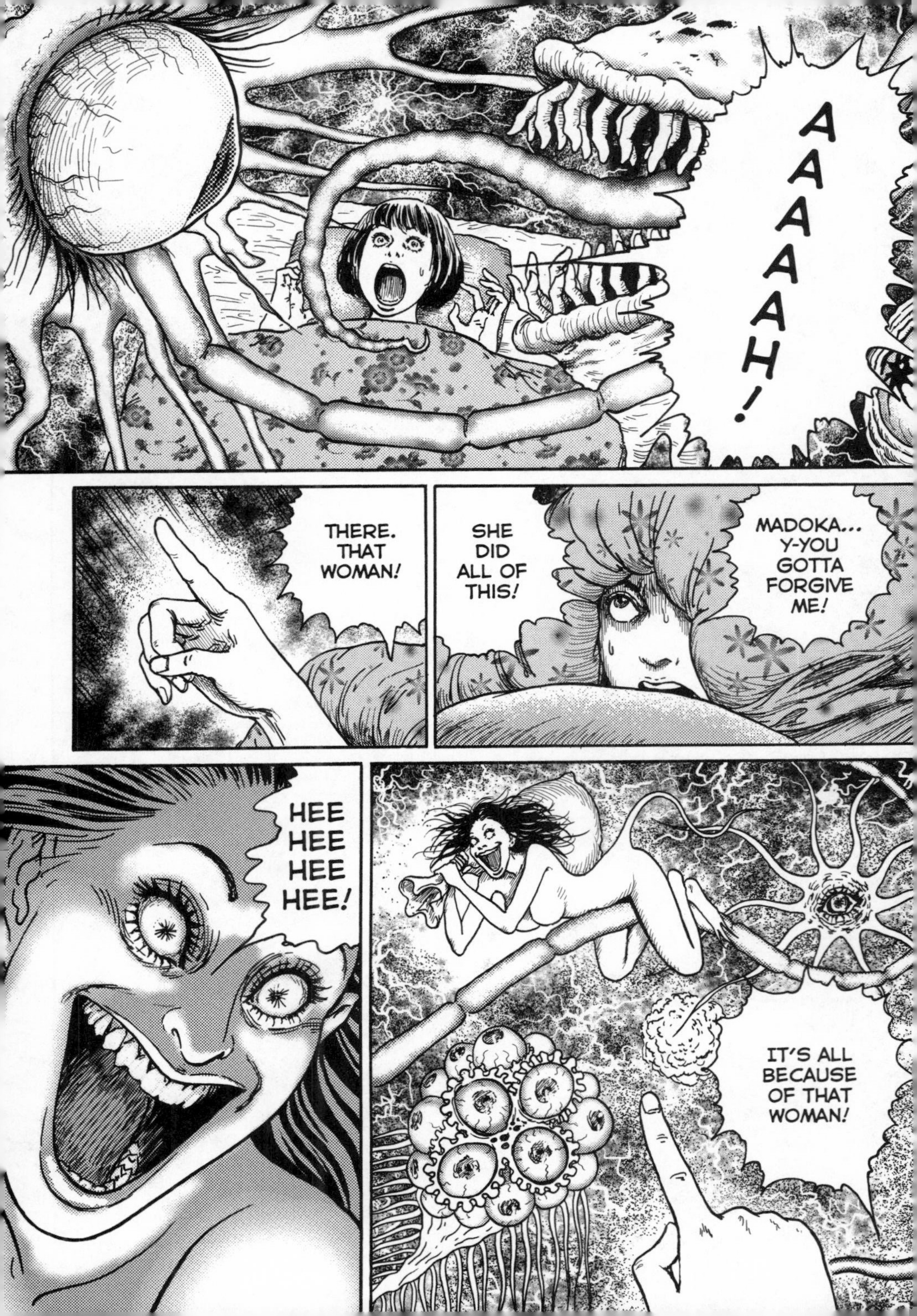
AAAAAAH!
MADOKA... Y-YOU GOTTA FORGIVE ME!
SHE DID ALL OF THIS!
THERE. THAT WOMAN!
IT'S ALL BECAUSE OF THAT WOMAN!
HEE HEE HEE HEE!

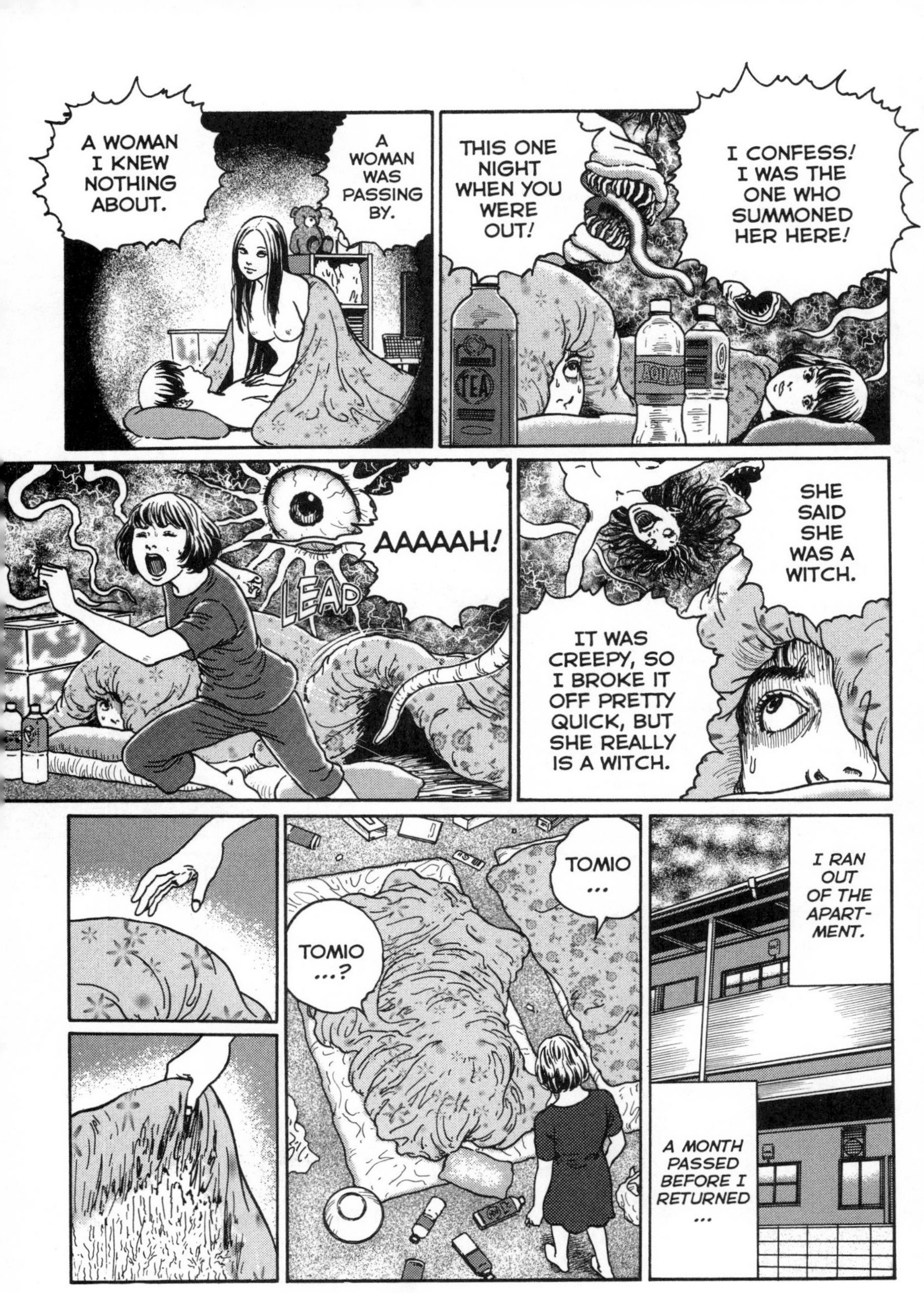
I CONFESS! I WAS THE ONE WHO SUMMONED HER HERE!
THIS ONE NIGHT WHEN YOU WERE OUT!
A WOMAN WAS PASSING BY.
A WOMAN I KNEW NOTHING ABOUT.
SHE SAID SHE WAS A WITCH.
IT WAS CREEPY, SO I BROKE IT OFF PRETTY QUICK, BUT SHE REALLY IS A WITCH.
AAAAAH!
LEAP
I RAN OUT OF THE APART-MENT.
A MONTH PASSED BEFORE I RETURNED ...
TOMIO ...
TOMIO ...?

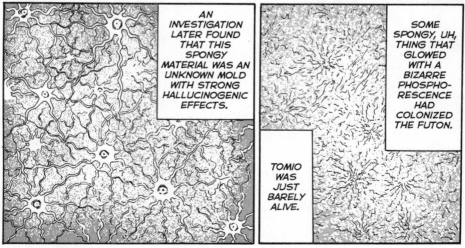

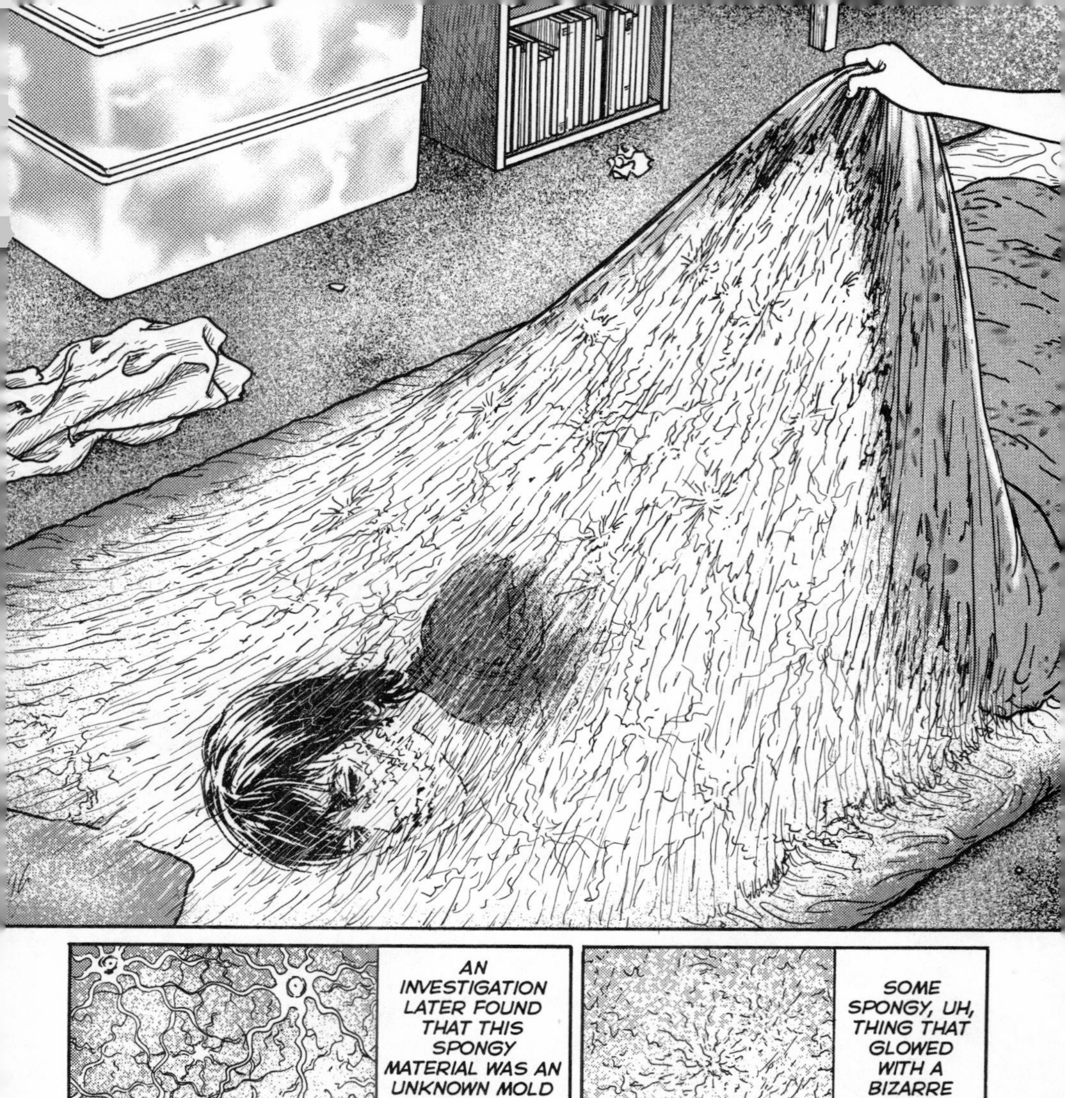
SOME SPONGY, UH, THING THAT GLOWED WITH A BIZARRE PHOSPHO-RESCENCE HAD COLONIZED THE FUTON.
TOMIO WAS JUST BARELY ALIVE.
AN INVESTIGATION LATER FOUND THAT THIS SPONGY MATERIAL WAS AN UNKNOWN MOLD WITH STRONG HALLUCINOGENIC EFFECTS.

FUTON/END

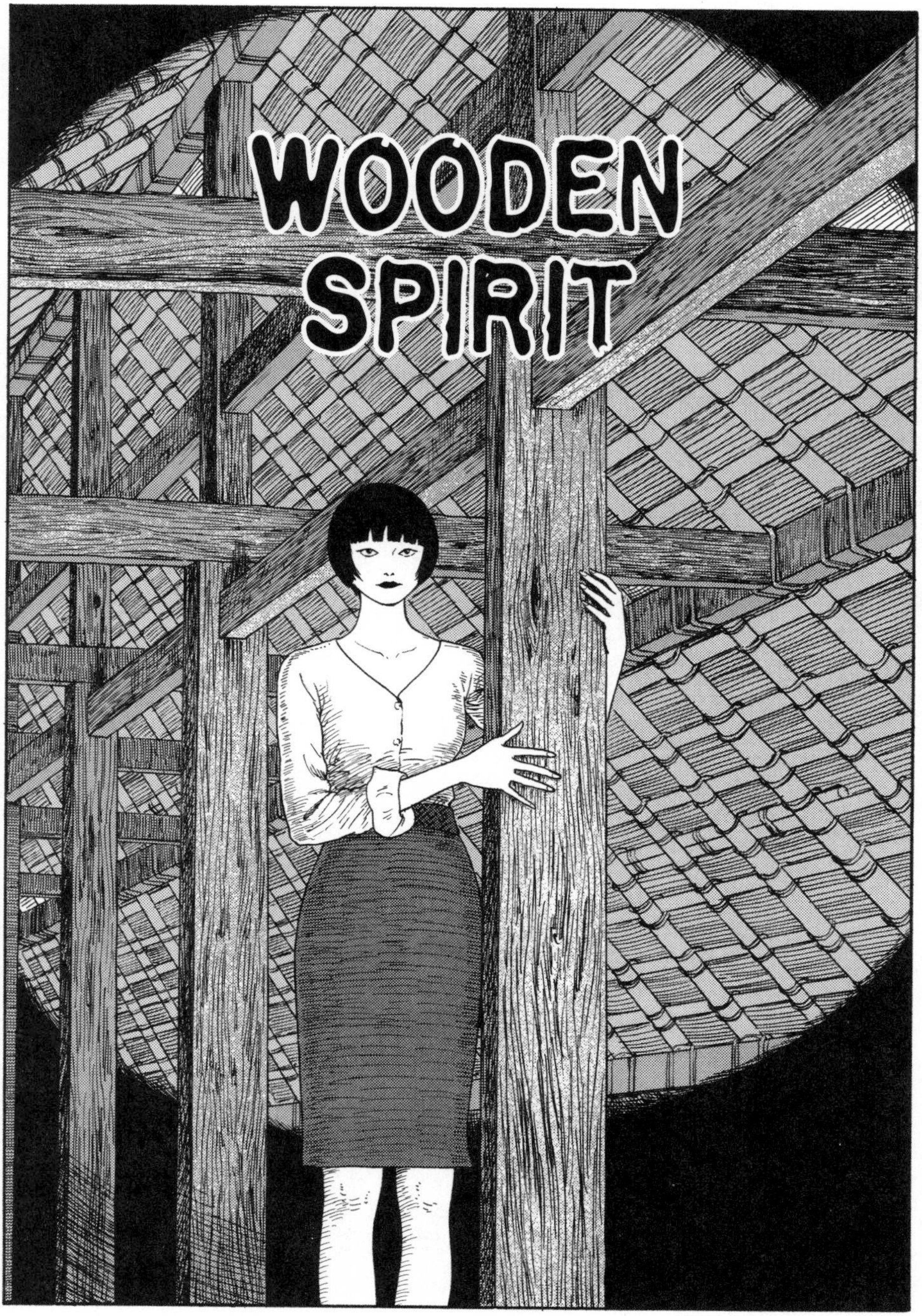
WOODEN
SPIRIT

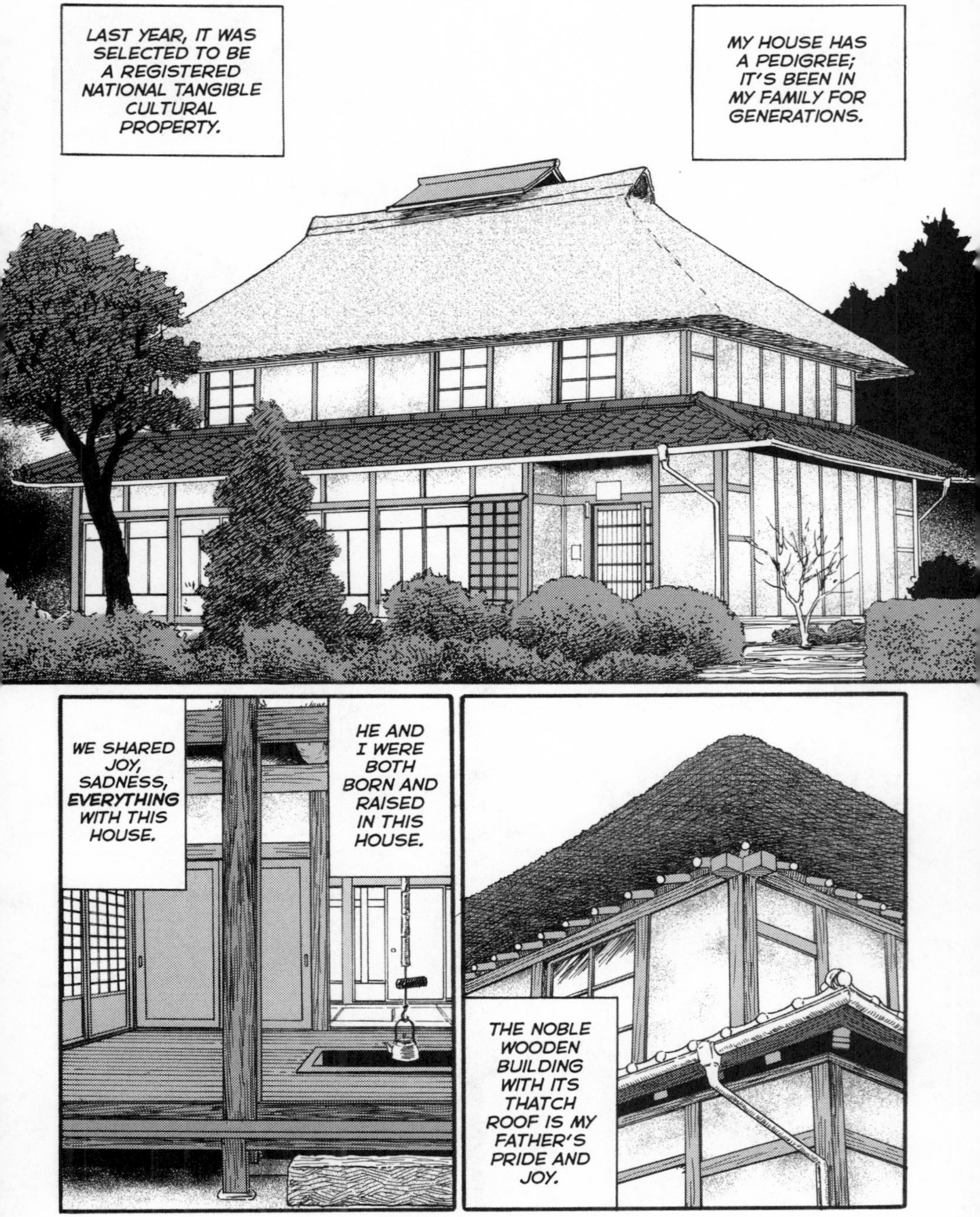
MY HOUSE HAS A PEDIGREE; IT'S BEEN IN MY FAMILY FOR GENERATIONS.
LAST YEAR, IT WAS SELECTED TO BE A REGISTERED NATIONAL TANGIBLE CULTURAL PROPERTY.
THE NOBLE WOODEN BUILDING WITH ITS THATCH ROOF IS MY FATHER'S PRIDE AND JOY.
HE AND I WERE BOTH BORN AND RAISED IN THIS HOUSE.
WE SHARED JOY, SADNESS, **EVERYTHING** WITH THIS HOUSE.

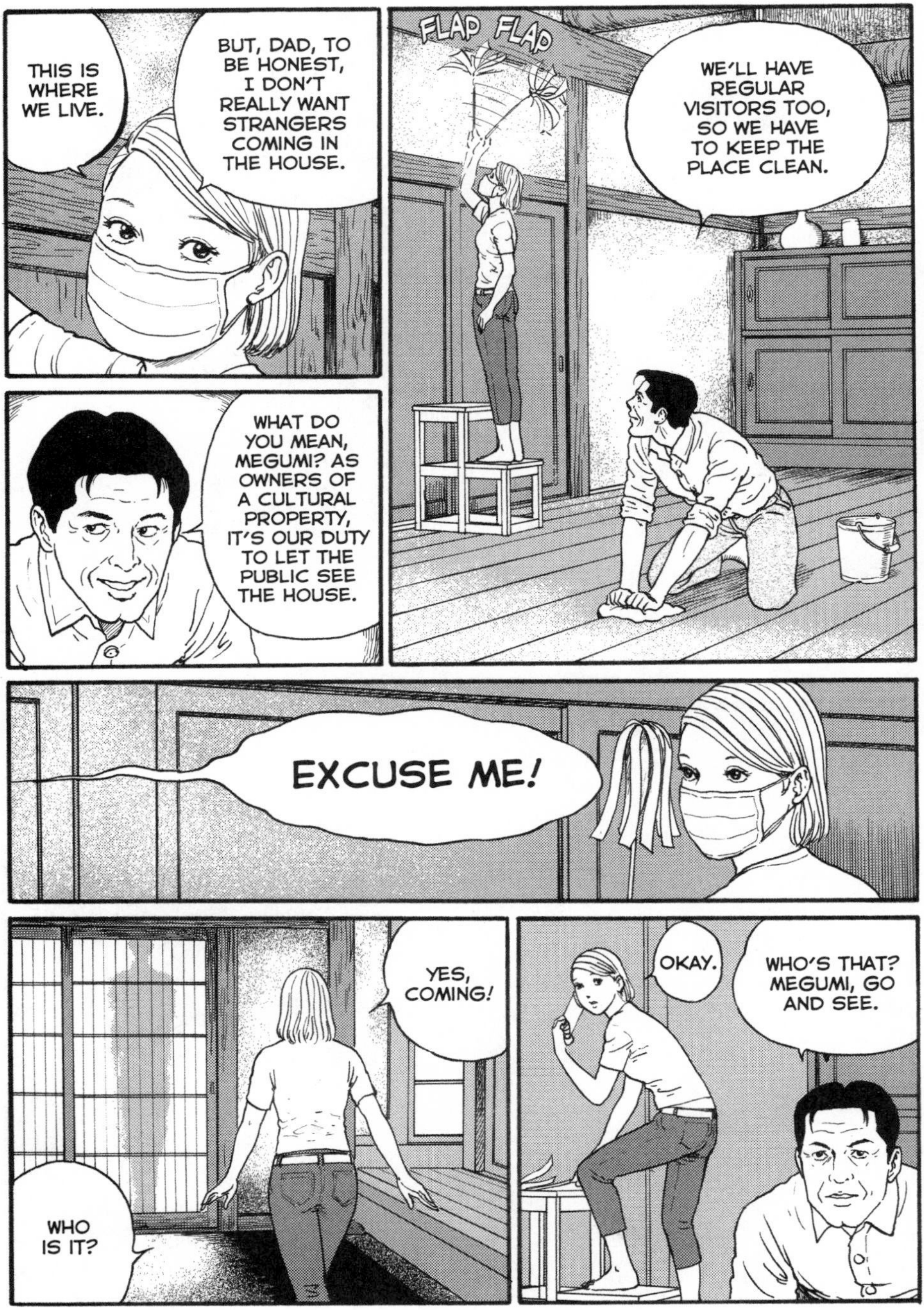
FLAP FLAP
WE'LL HAVE REGULAR VISITORS TOO, SO WE HAVE TO KEEP THE PLACE CLEAN.
BUT, DAD, TO BE HONEST, I DON'T REALLY WANT STRANGERS COMING IN THE HOUSE.
THIS IS WHERE WE LIVE.
WHAT DO YOU MEAN, MEGUMI? AS OWNERS OF A CULTURAL PROPERTY, IT'S OUR DUTY TO LET THE PUBLIC SEE THE HOUSE.
EXCUSE ME!
WHO'S THAT? MEGUMI, GO AND SEE.
OKAY.
YES, COMING!
WHO IS IT?

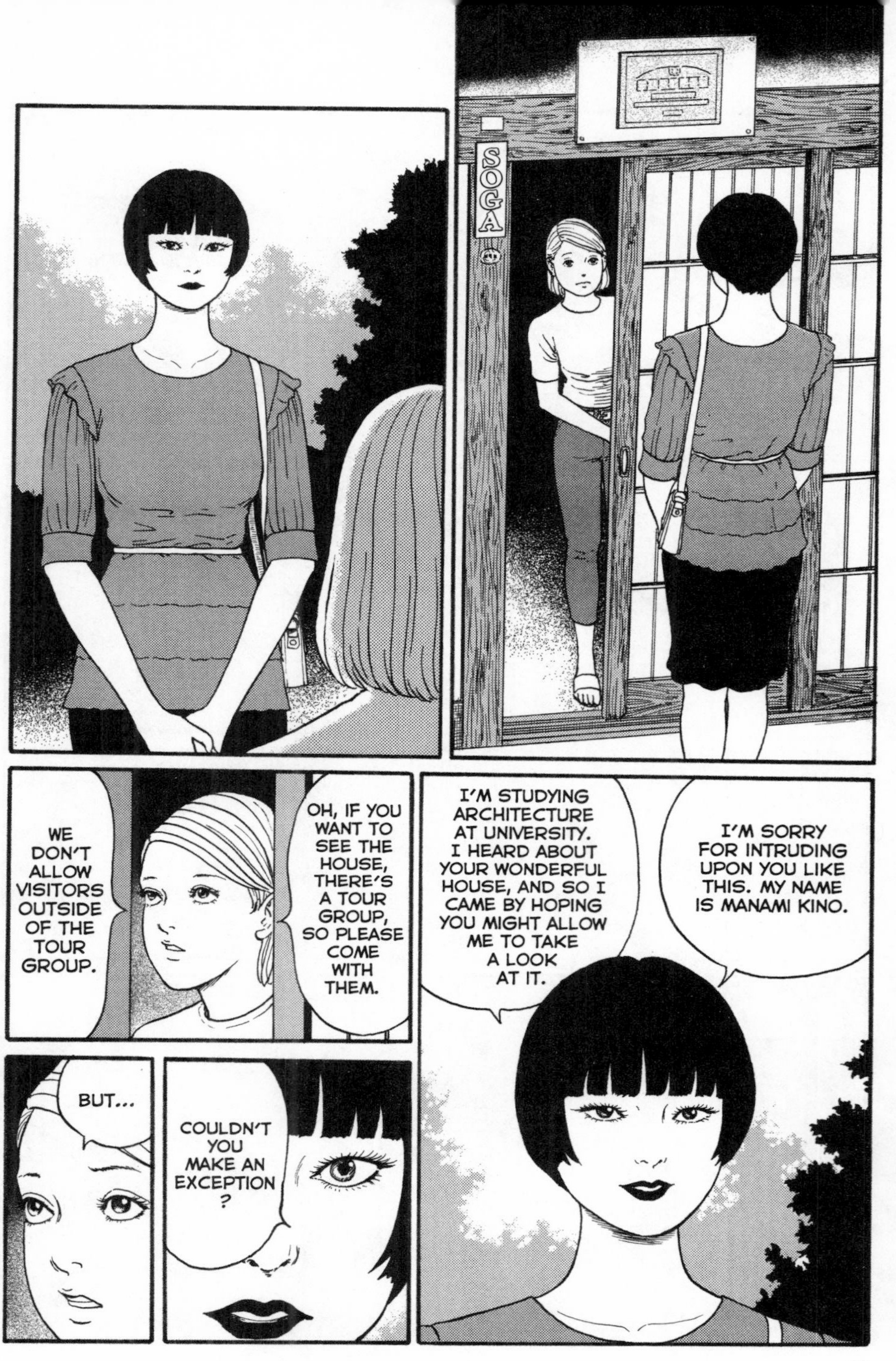
SOGA
I'M SORRY FOR INTRUDING UPON YOU LIKE THIS. MY NAME IS MANAMI KINO.
I'M STUDYING ARCHITECTURE AT UNIVERSITY. I HEARD ABOUT YOUR WONDERFUL HOUSE, AND SO I CAME BY HOPING YOU MIGHT ALLOW ME TO TAKE A LOOK AT IT.
OH, IF YOU WANT TO SEE THE HOUSE, THERE'S A TOUR GROUP, SO PLEASE COME WITH THEM.
WE DON'T ALLOW VISITORS OUTSIDE OF THE TOUR GROUP.
COULDN'T YOU MAKE AN EXCEPTION ?
BUT...

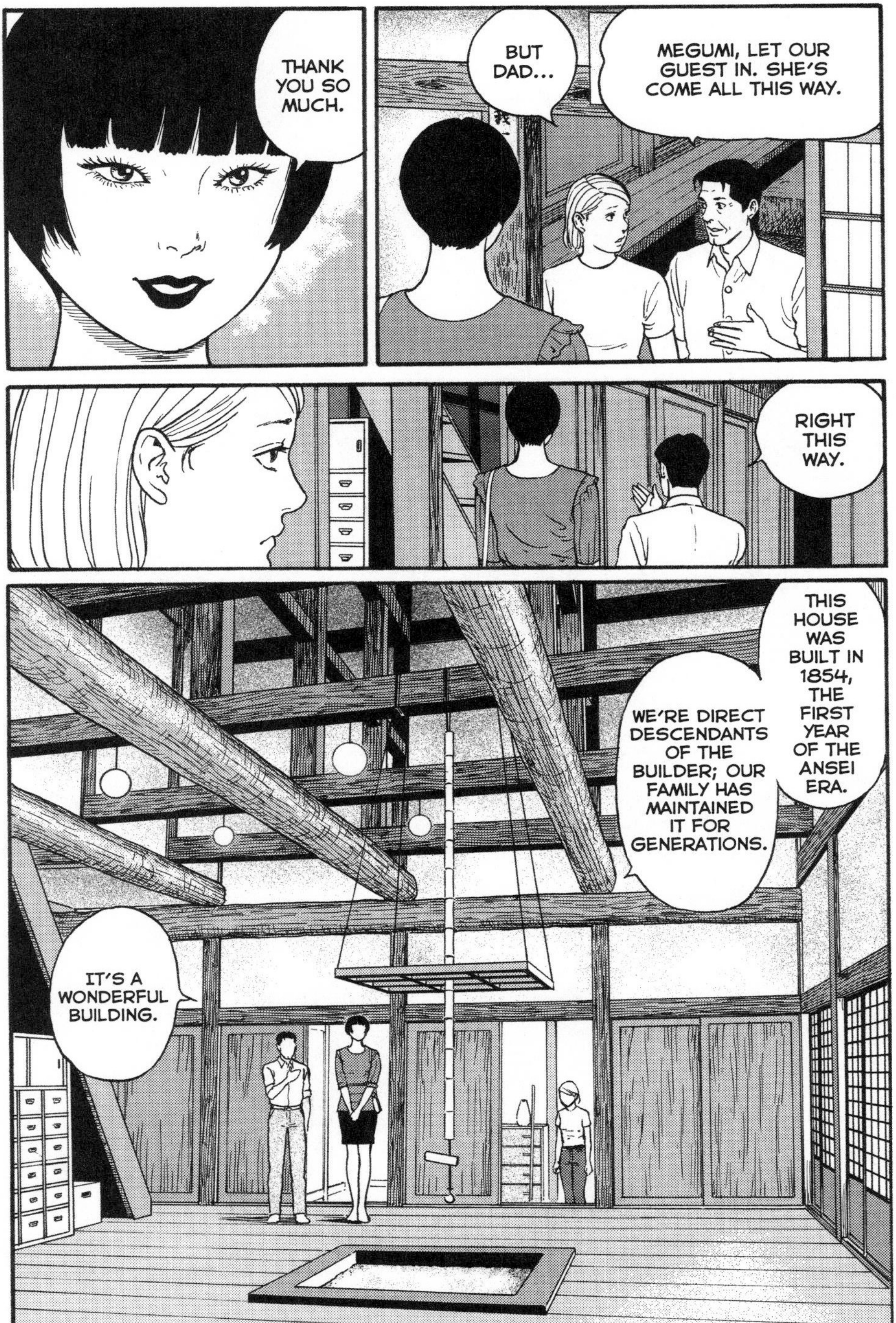
MEGUMI, LET OUR GUEST IN. SHE'S COME ALL THIS WAY.
BUT DAD...
THANK YOU SO MUCH.
RIGHT THIS WAY.
THIS HOUSE WAS BUILT IN 1854, THE FIRST YEAR OF THE ANSEI ERA.
WE'RE DIRECT DESCENDANTS OF THE BUILDER; OUR FAMILY HAS MAINTAINED IT FOR GENERATIONS.
IT'S A WONDERFUL BUILDING.

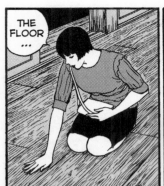

THIS PILLAR ...
THE WALLS ...
THE FLOOR ...
THEY'RE VERY SEXY.
...?
AND I CAN FEEL A MASCULINE STRENGTH IN THE JOISTS IN THE CEILING.
SOMEHOW, I GET CHILLS LOOKING AT THEM.

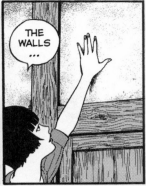

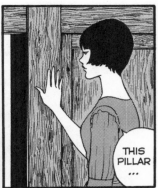

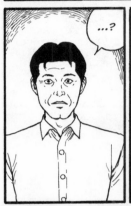

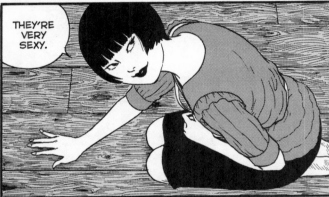

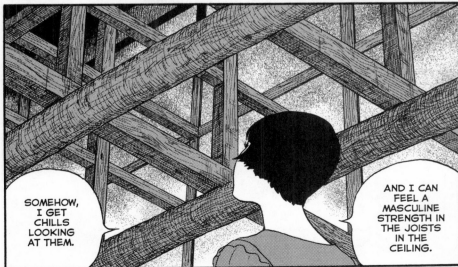

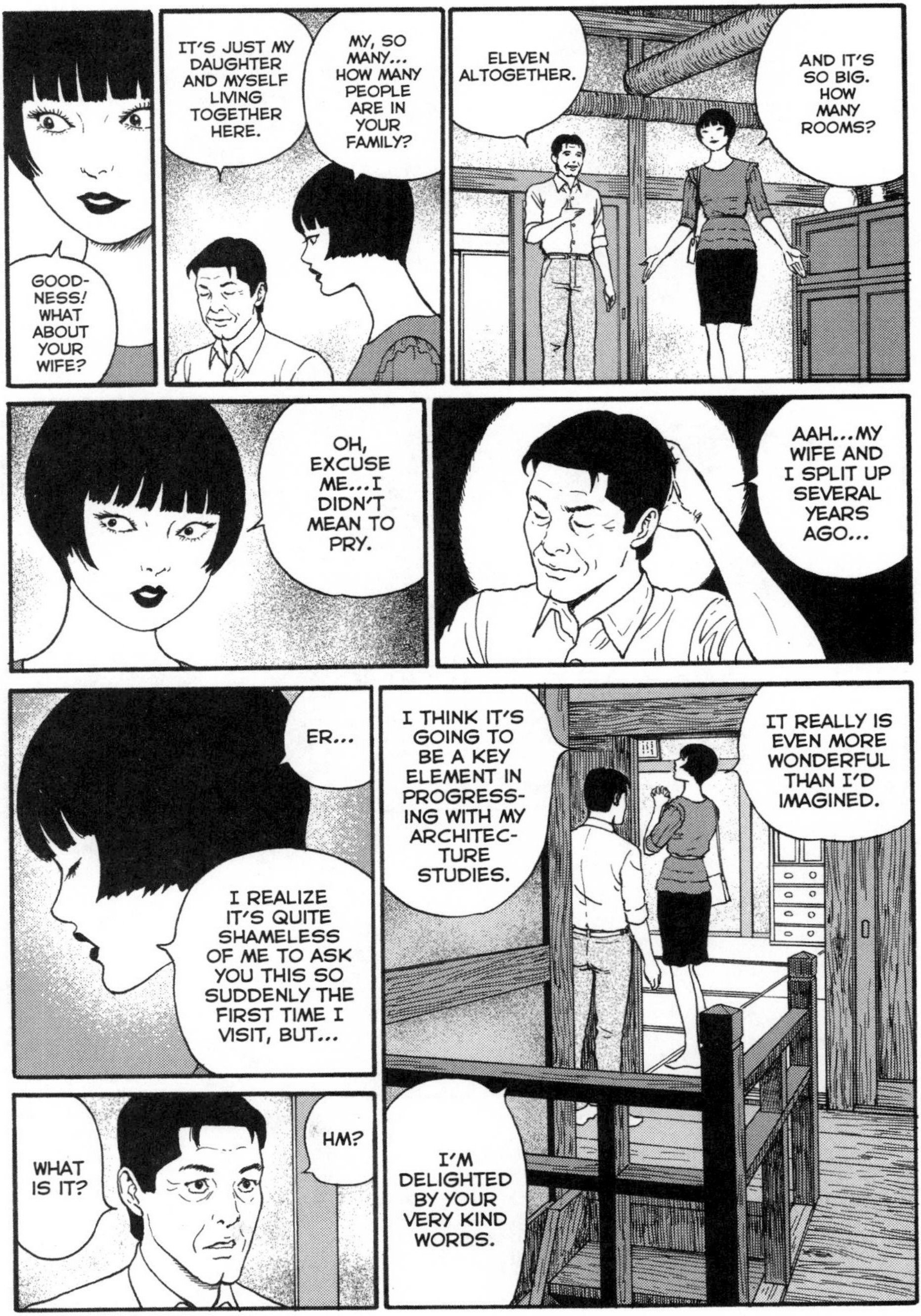
AND IT'S SO BIG. HOW MANY ROOMS?
ELEVEN ALTOGETHER.
MY, SO MANY... HOW MANY PEOPLE ARE IN YOUR FAMILY?
IT'S JUST MY DAUGHTER AND MYSELF LIVING TOGETHER HERE.
GOOD-NESS! WHAT ABOUT YOUR WIFE?
AAH...MY WIFE AND I SPLIT UP SEVERAL YEARS AGO...
OH, EXCUSE ME...I DIDN'T MEAN TO PRY.
IT REALLY IS EVEN MORE WONDERFUL THAN I'D IMAGINED.
I'M DELIGHTED BY YOUR VERY KIND WORDS.
I THINK IT'S GOING TO BE A KEY ELEMENT IN PROGRESS-ING WITH MY ARCHITEC-TURE STUDIES.
ER...
I REALIZE IT'S QUITE SHAMELESS OF ME TO ASK YOU THIS SO SUDDENLY THE FIRST TIME I VISIT, BUT...
HM?
WHAT IS IT?

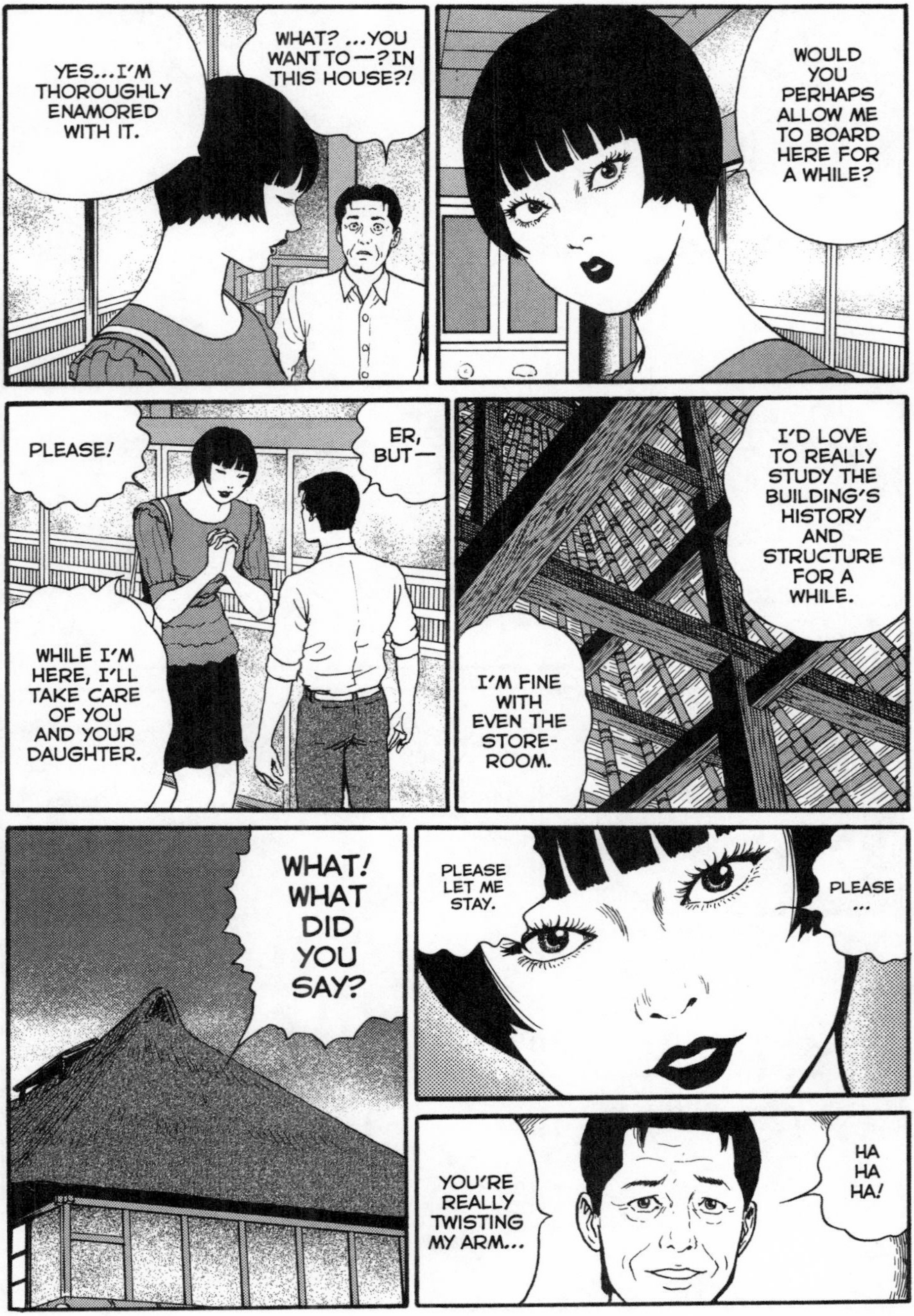
WOULD YOU PERHAPS ALLOW ME TO BOARD HERE FOR A WHILE?
WHAT? ...YOU WANT TO—? IN THIS HOUSE?!
YES...I'M THOROUGHLY ENAMORED WITH IT.
I'D LOVE TO REALLY STUDY THE BUILDING'S HISTORY AND STRUCTURE FOR A WHILE.
I'M FINE WITH EVEN THE STORE-ROOM.
ER, BUT—
PLEASE!
WHILE I'M HERE, I'LL TAKE CARE OF YOU AND YOUR DAUGHTER.
PLEASE ...
PLEASE LET ME STAY.
HA HA HA!
YOU'RE REALLY TWISTING MY ARM...
WHAT! WHAT DID YOU SAY?

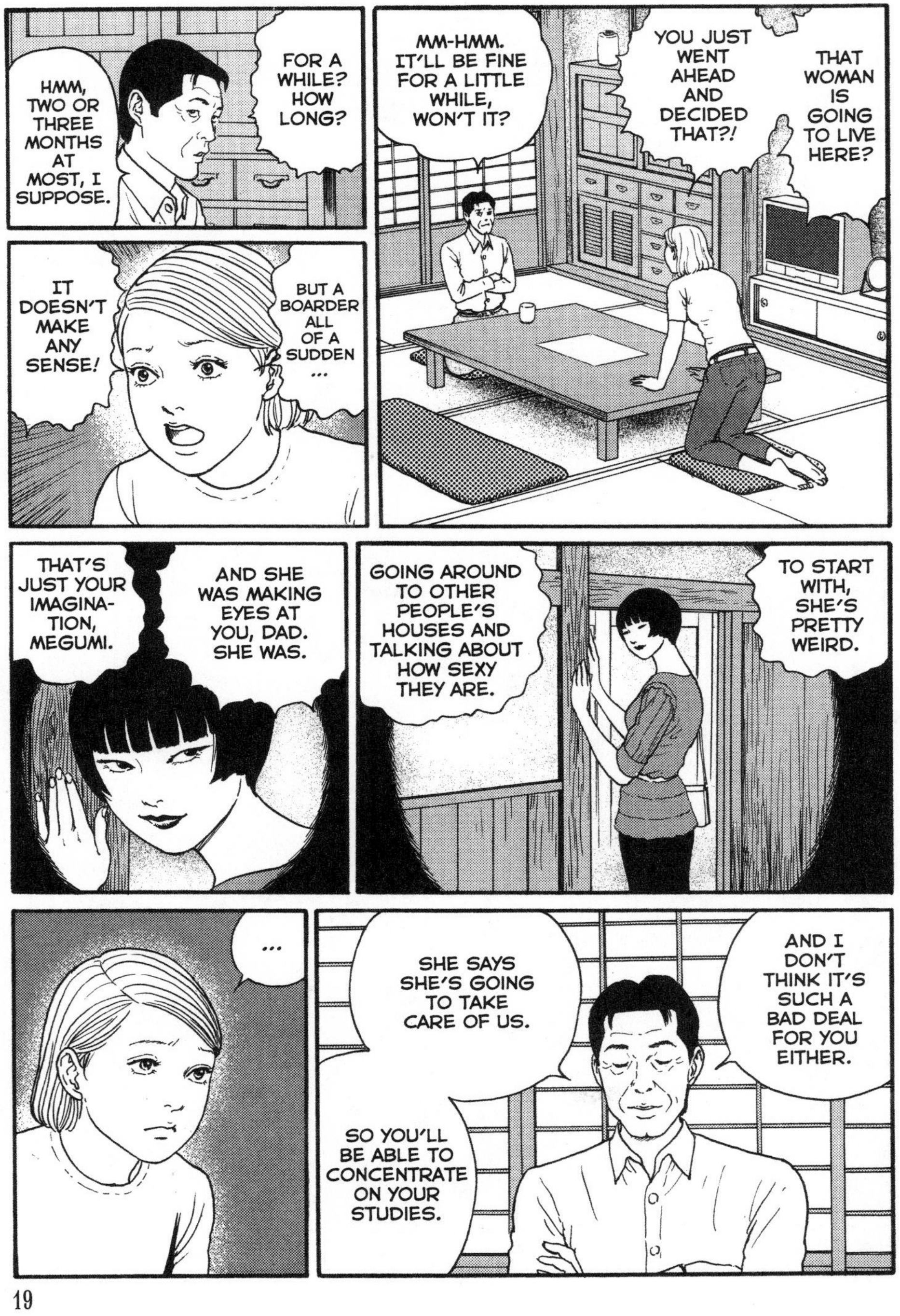
THAT WOMAN IS GOING TO LIVE HERE?
YOU JUST WENT AHEAD AND DECIDED THAT?!
MM-HMM. IT'LL BE FINE FOR A LITTLE WHILE, WON'T IT?
FOR A WHILE? HOW LONG?
HMM, TWO OR THREE MONTHS AT MOST, I SUPPOSE.
BUT A BOARDER ALL OF A SUDDEN ...
IT DOESN'T MAKE ANY SENSE!
TO START WITH, SHE'S PRETTY WEIRD.
GOING AROUND TO OTHER PEOPLE'S HOUSES AND TALKING ABOUT HOW SEXY THEY ARE.
AND SHE WAS MAKING EYES AT YOU, DAD. SHE WAS.
THAT'S JUST YOUR IMAGINATION, MEGUMI.
AND I DON'T THINK IT'S SUCH A BAD DEAL FOR YOU EITHER.
SHE SAYS SHE'S GOING TO TAKE CARE OF US.
SO YOU'LL BE ABLE TO CONCENTRATE ON YOUR STUDIES.
...

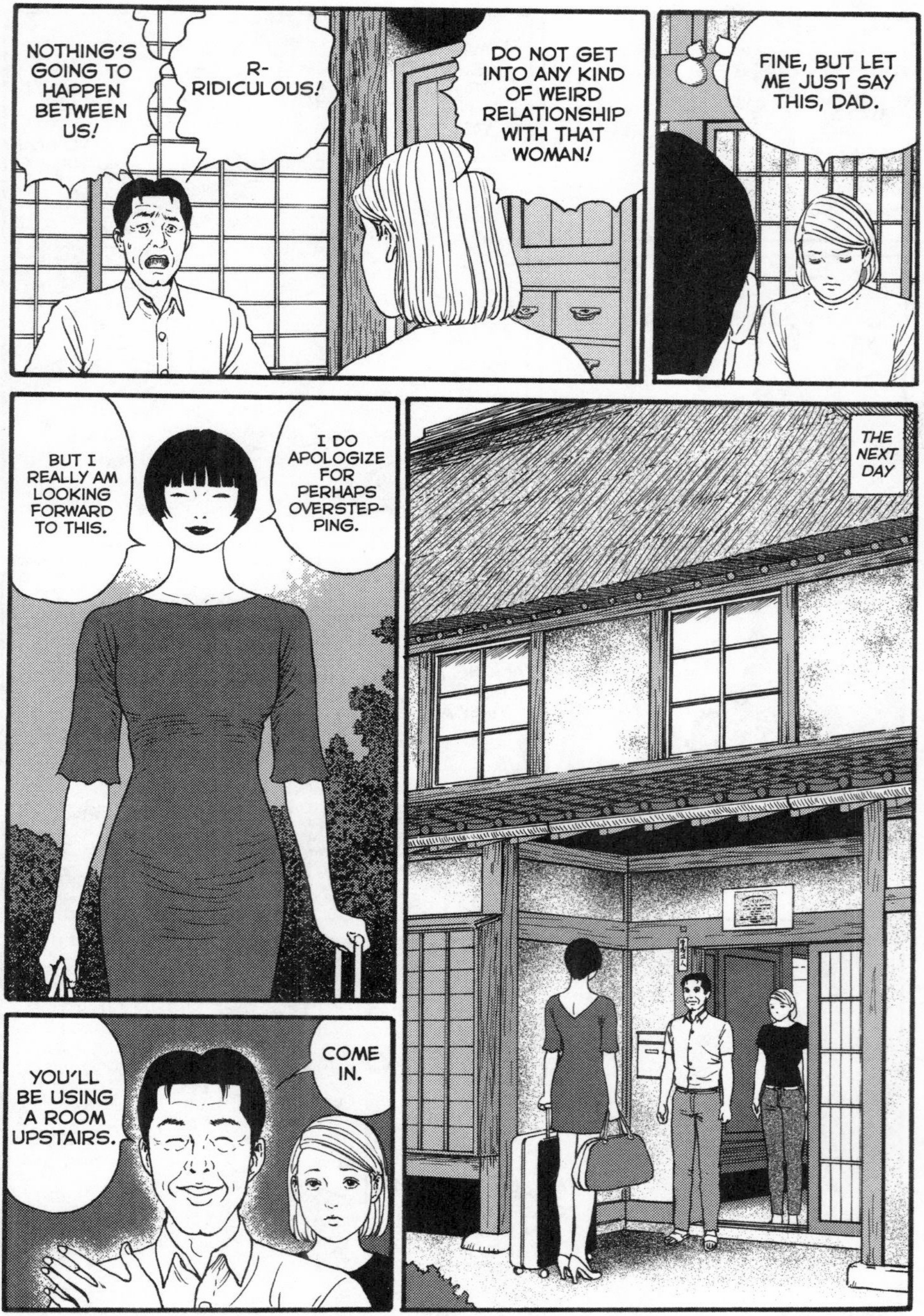
FINE, BUT LET ME JUST SAY THIS, DAD.
DO NOT GET INTO ANY KIND OF WEIRD RELATIONSHIP WITH THAT WOMAN!
R- RIDICULOUS!
NOTHING'S GOING TO HAPPEN BETWEEN US!
THE NEXT DAY
I DO APOLOGIZE FOR PERHAPS OVERSTEP-PING.
BUT I REALLY AM LOOKING FORWARD TO THIS.
COME IN.
YOU'LL BE USING A ROOM UPSTAIRS.

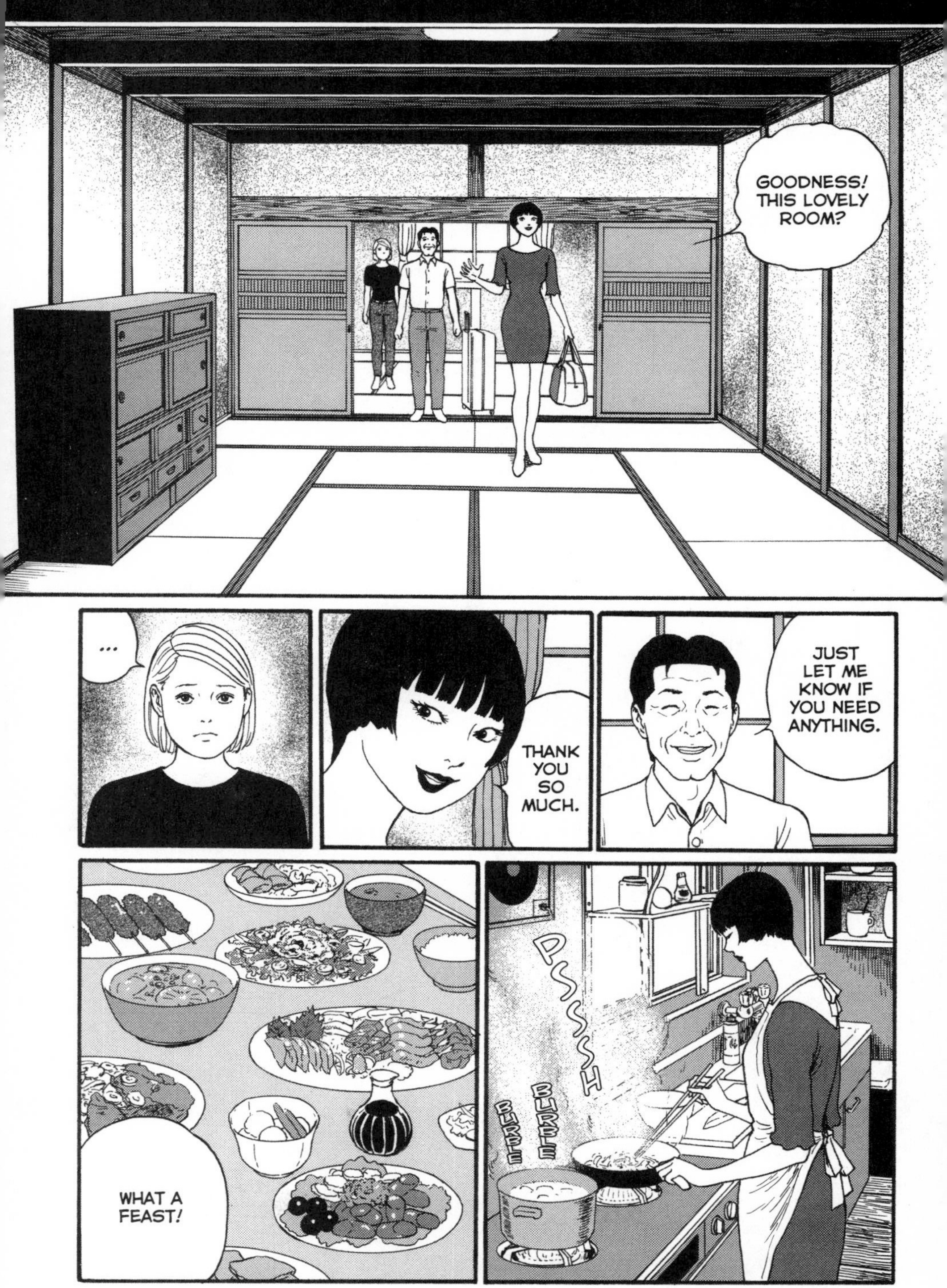
GOODNESS! THIS LOVELY ROOM?
JUST LET ME KNOW IF YOU NEED ANYTHING.
THANK YOU SO MUCH.
...
PSSSH
BURBLE
BURBLE
WHAT A FEAST!

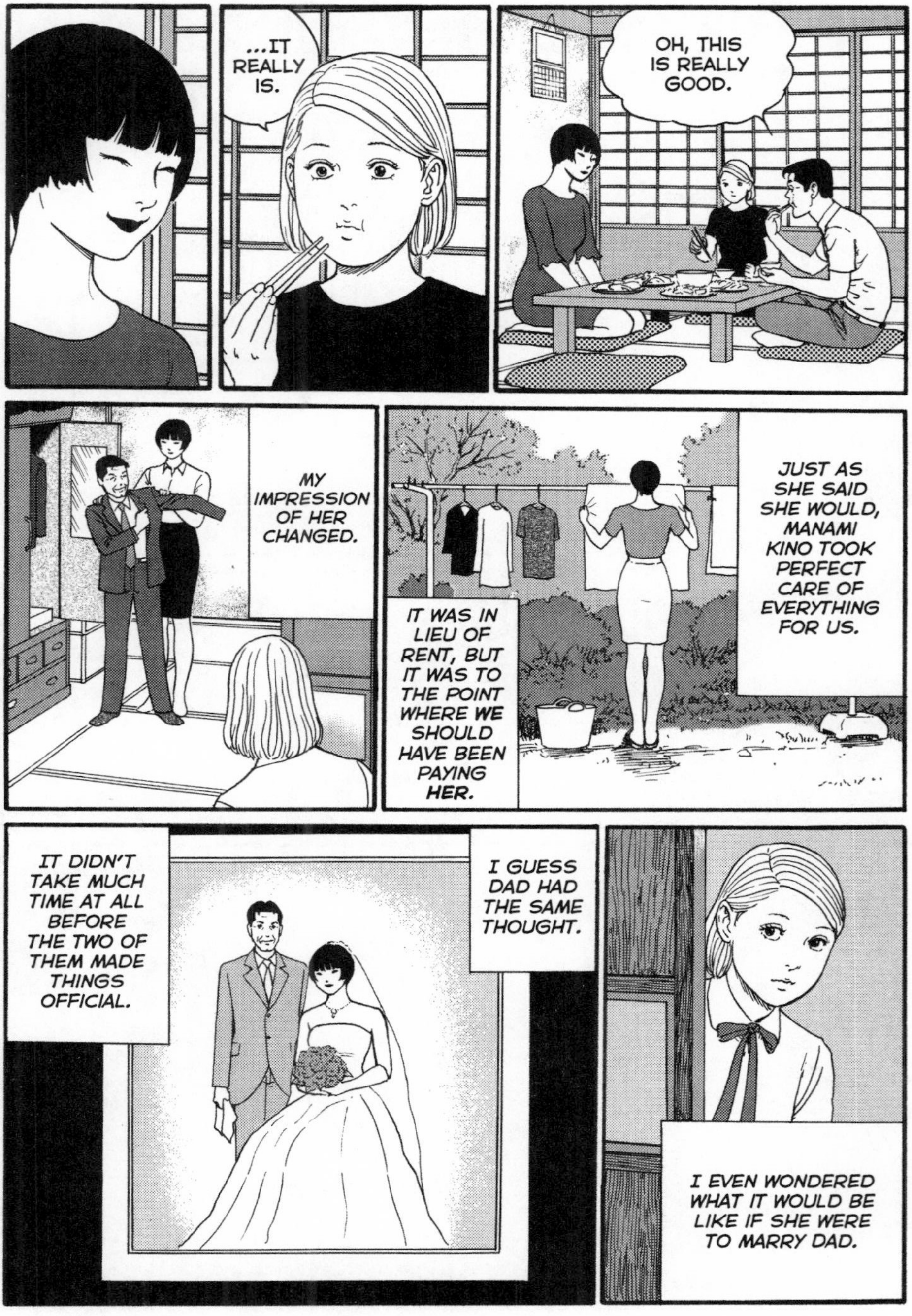
OH, THIS IS REALLY GOOD.
...IT REALLY IS.
JUST AS SHE SAID SHE WOULD, MANAMI KINO TOOK PERFECT CARE OF EVERYTHING FOR US.
IT WAS IN LIEU OF RENT, BUT IT WAS TO THE POINT WHERE WE SHOULD HAVE BEEN PAYING HER.
MY IMPRESSION OF HER CHANGED.
I EVEN WONDERED WHAT IT WOULD BE LIKE IF SHE WERE TO MARRY DAD.
I GUESS DAD HAD THE SAME THOUGHT.
IT DIDN'T TAKE MUCH TIME AT ALL BEFORE THE TWO OF THEM MADE THINGS OFFICIAL.

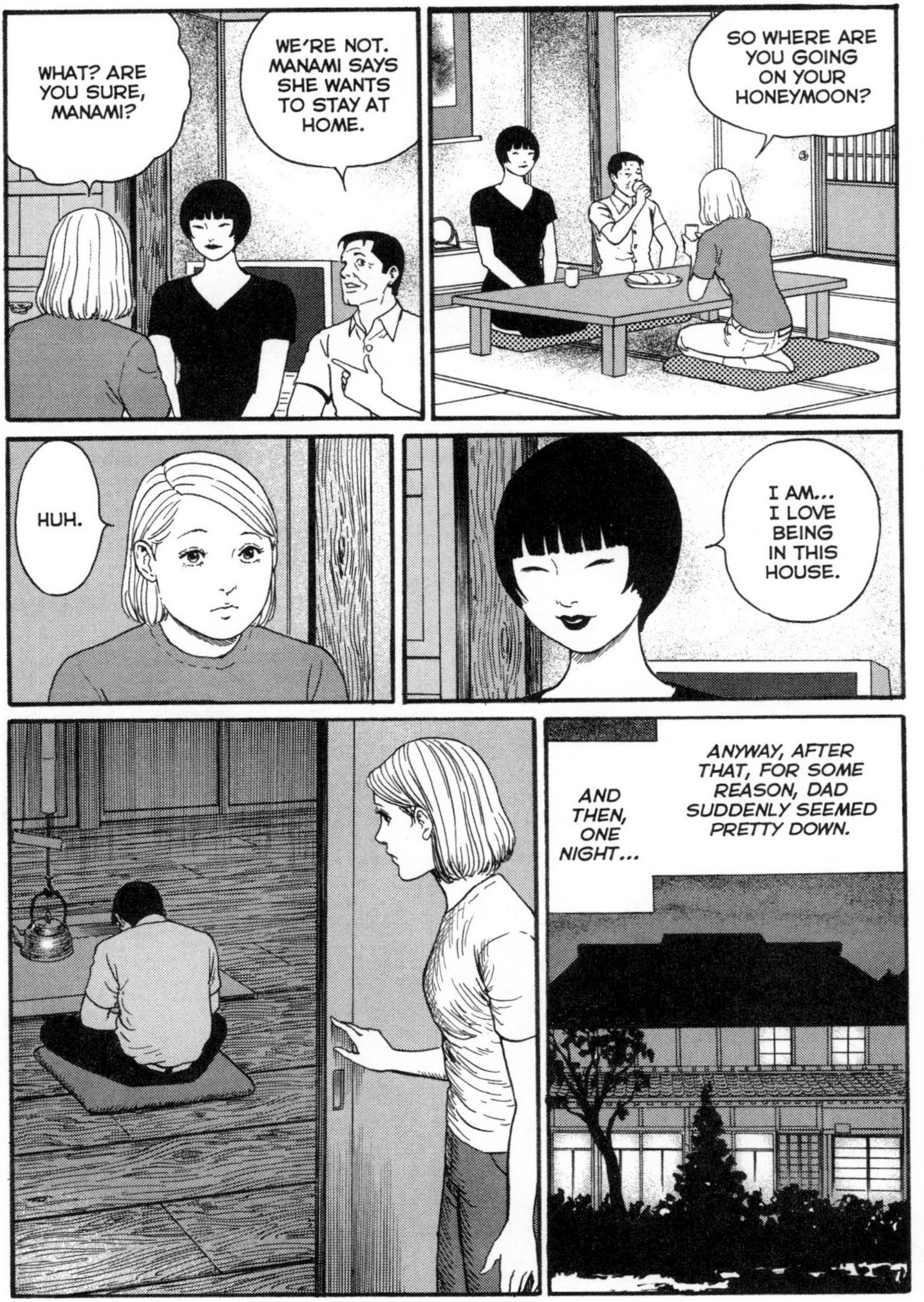
SO WHERE ARE YOU GOING ON YOUR HONEYMOON?
WE'RE NOT. MANAMI SAYS SHE WANTS TO STAY AT HOME.
WHAT? ARE YOU SURE, MANAMI?
I AM... I LOVE BEING IN THIS HOUSE.
HUH.
ANYWAY, AFTER THAT, FOR SOME REASON, DAD SUDDENLY SEEMED PRETTY DOWN.
AND THEN, ONE NIGHT...

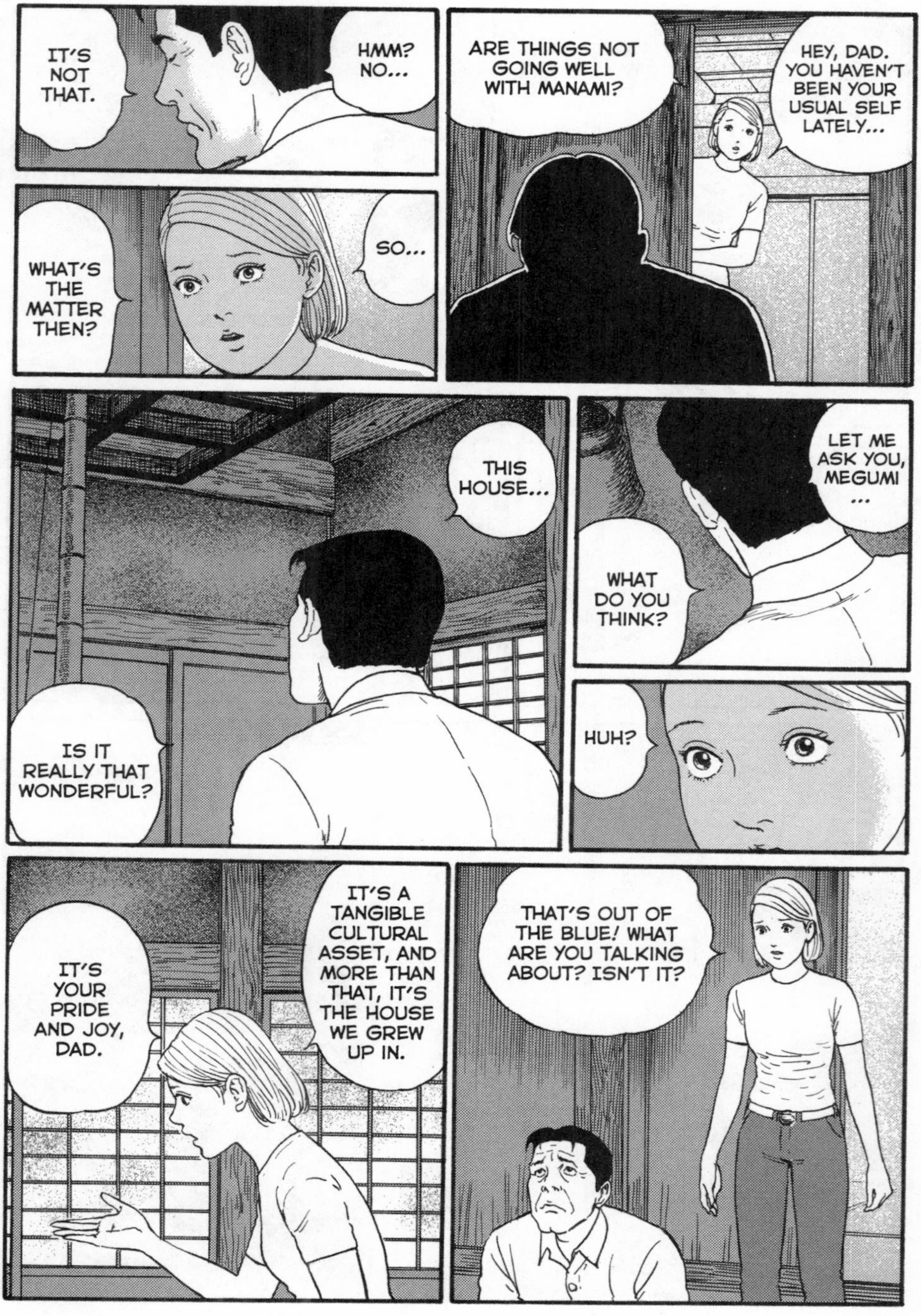
HEY, DAD. YOU HAVEN'T BEEN YOUR USUAL SELF LATELY...
ARE THINGS NOT GOING WELL WITH MANAMI?
HMM? NO...
IT'S NOT THAT.
SO...
WHAT'S THE MATTER THEN?
LET ME ASK YOU, MEGUMI ...
WHAT DO YOU THINK?
HUH?
THIS HOUSE...
IS IT REALLY THAT WONDERFUL?
THAT'S OUT OF THE BLUE! WHAT ARE YOU TALKING ABOUT? ISN'T IT?
IT'S A TANGIBLE CULTURAL ASSET, AND MORE THAN THAT, IT'S THE HOUSE WE GREW UP IN.
IT'S YOUR PRIDE AND JOY, DAD.

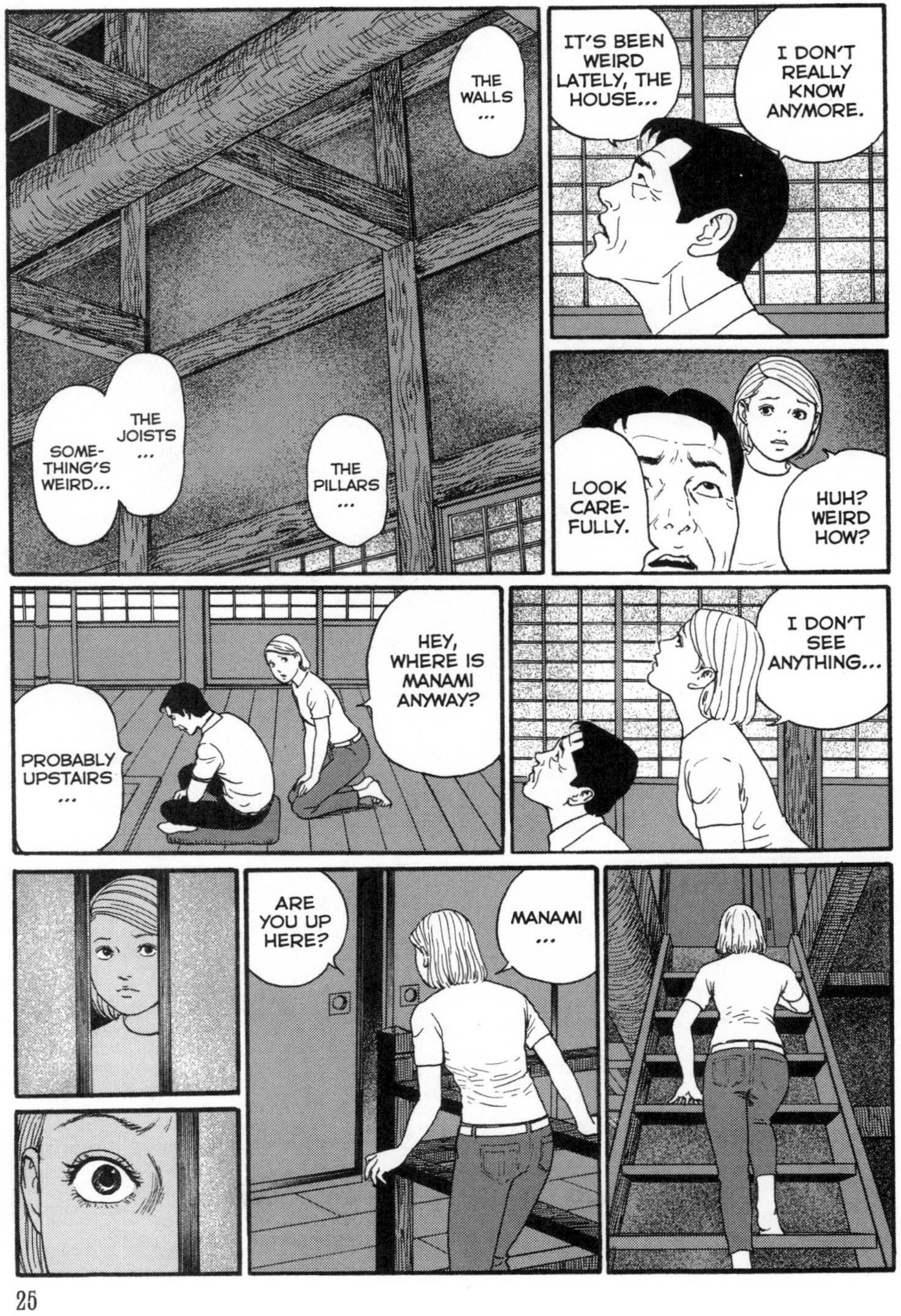
I DON'T REALLY KNOW ANYMORE.
IT'S BEEN WEIRD LATELY, THE HOUSE...
HUH? WEIRD HOW?
LOOK CAREFULLY.
THE WALLS ...
THE PILLARS ...
THE JOISTS ...
SOMETHING'S WEIRD...
I DON'T SEE ANYTHING...
HEY, WHERE IS MANAMI ANYWAY?
PROBABLY UPSTAIRS ...
MANAMI ...
ARE YOU UP HERE?

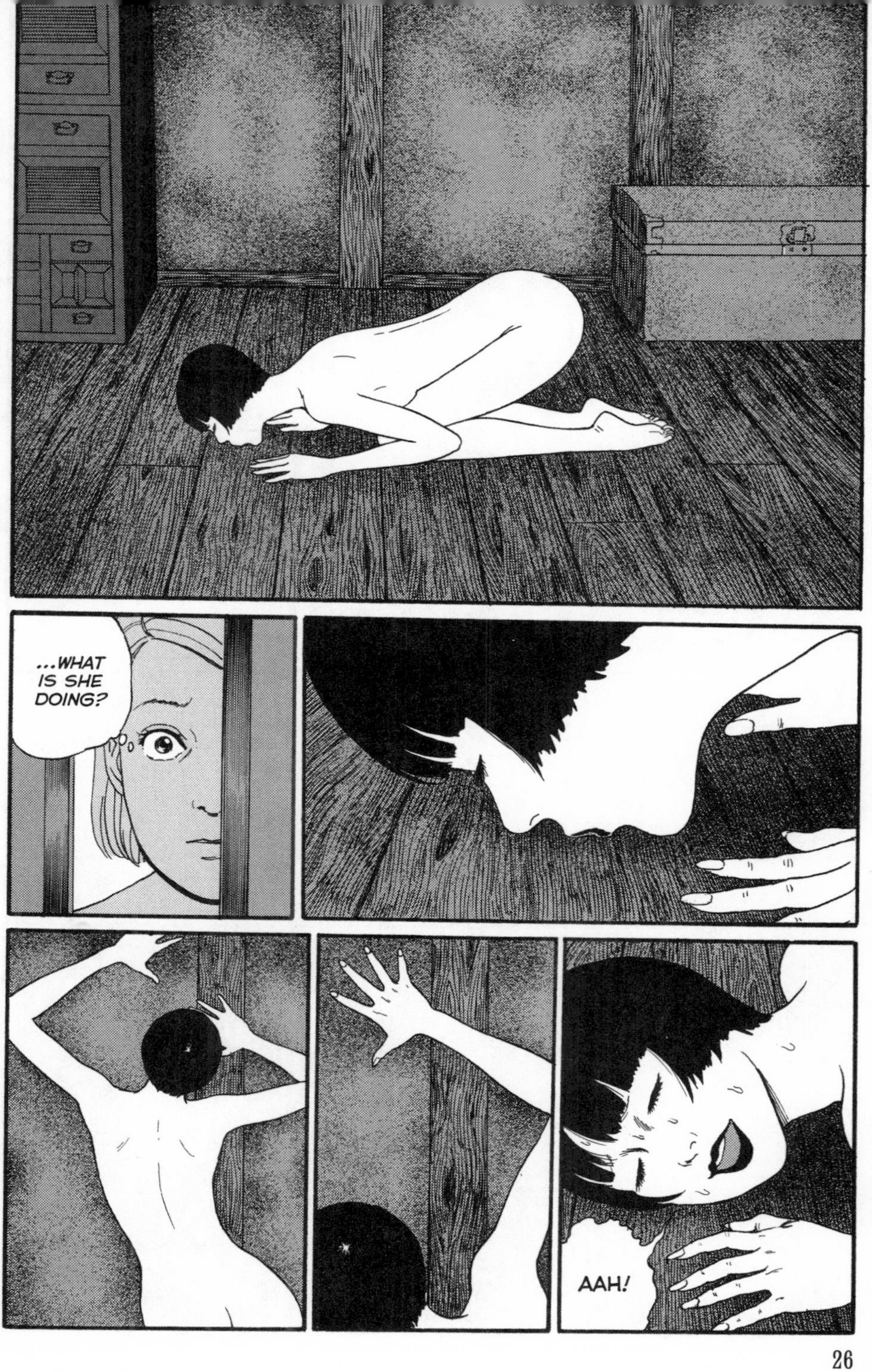
...WHAT IS SHE DOING?
AAH!

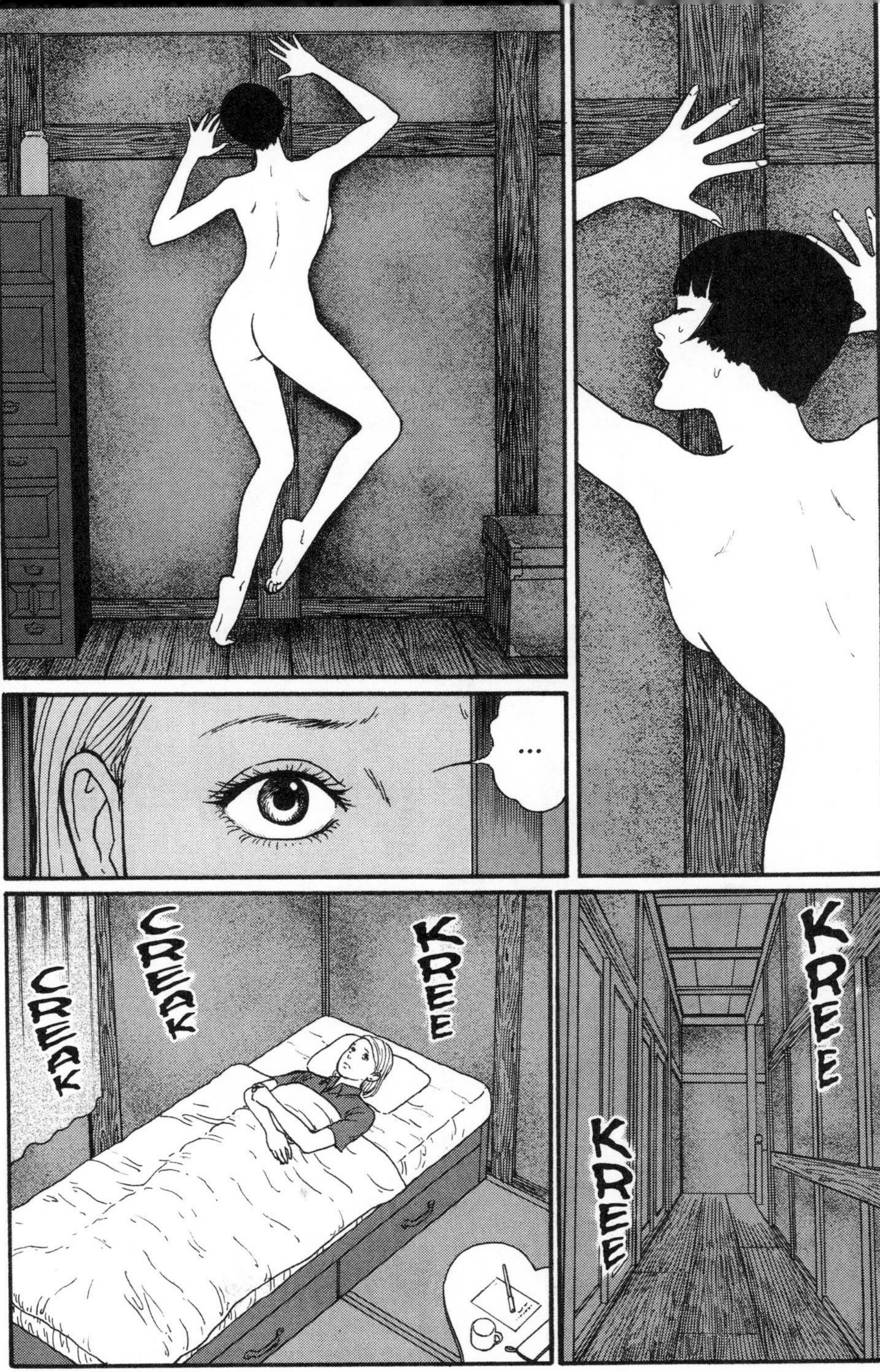
...
KREE
KREE
KREE
CREAK
CREAK

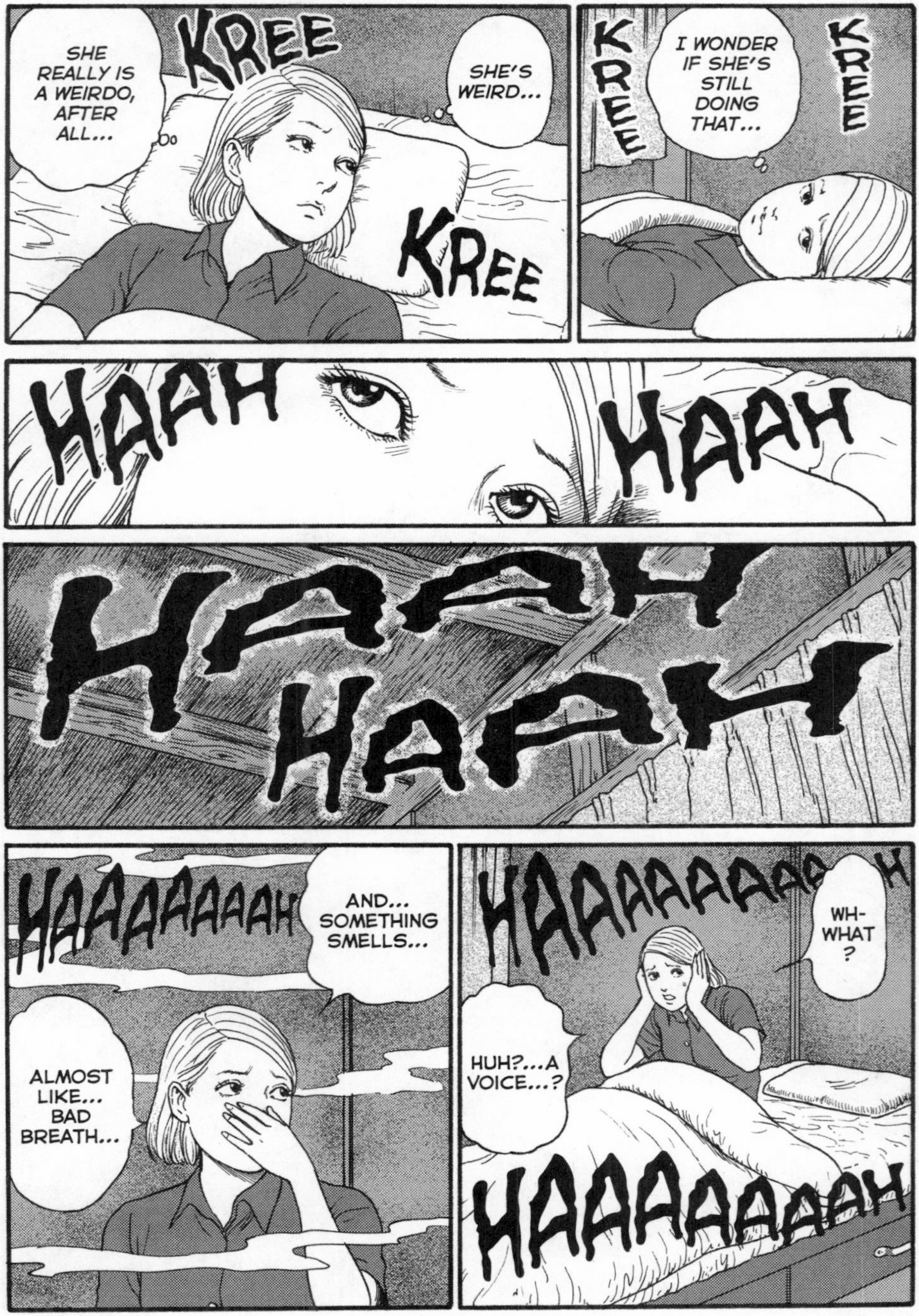
KREE
I WONDER IF SHE'S STILL DOING THAT...
KREE
SHE'S WEIRD...
KREE
SHE REALLY IS A WEIRDO, AFTER ALL...
KREE
HAAH
HAAH
HAAH
HAAH
HAAAAAAAAH
WH- WHAT?
HUH?...A VOICE...?
HAAAAAAAH
AND... SOMETHING SMELLS...
HAAAAAAAH
ALMOST LIKE... BAD BREATH...

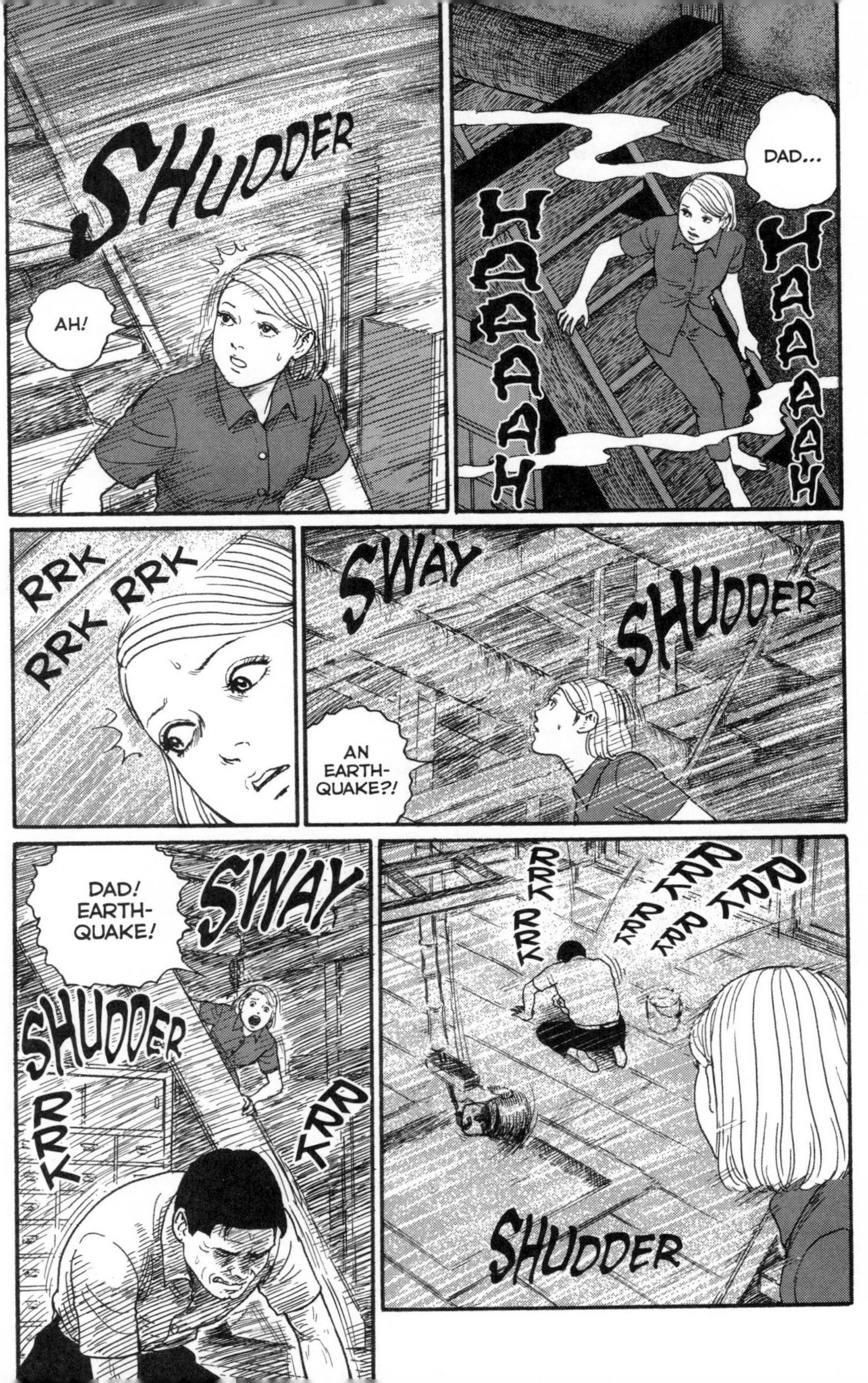
DAD...
HAAAAAH
HAAAAAH
SHUDDER
AH!
SWAY
SHUDDER
AN EARTH-QUAKE?!
RRK RRK RRK RRK
RRK RRK
SHUDDER
DAD! EARTH-QUAKE!
SWAY
SHUDDER
RRRK
TRRR

SWAY
DAD!
SHUDDER
MEGUMI! NOW IS NOT THE TIME!
WHO WOULD DO THIS?
DISGUSTING! JUST SICK!
RRK RRK
RRK
HUH?
DO WHAT?
RRK RRK
COME ON, DAD! DO THAT LATER! IT'S AN EARTH-QUAKE!
SHUDDER
SWAY
RRK RRK
IT'S SO STRANGE ...
I SCRUB AND SCRUB AND IT DOESN'T COME OFF.
THIS IS A REAL PROBLEM.
LOOK, MEGUMI!
WHAT IS WRONG?
AH!

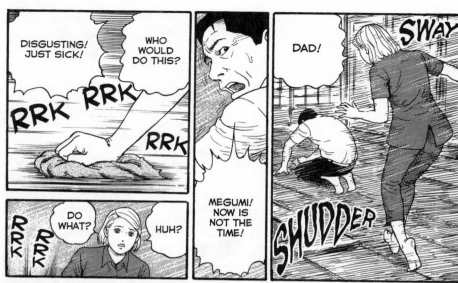

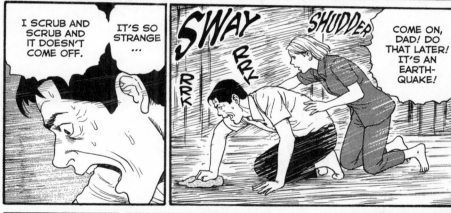

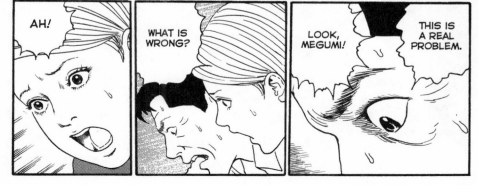

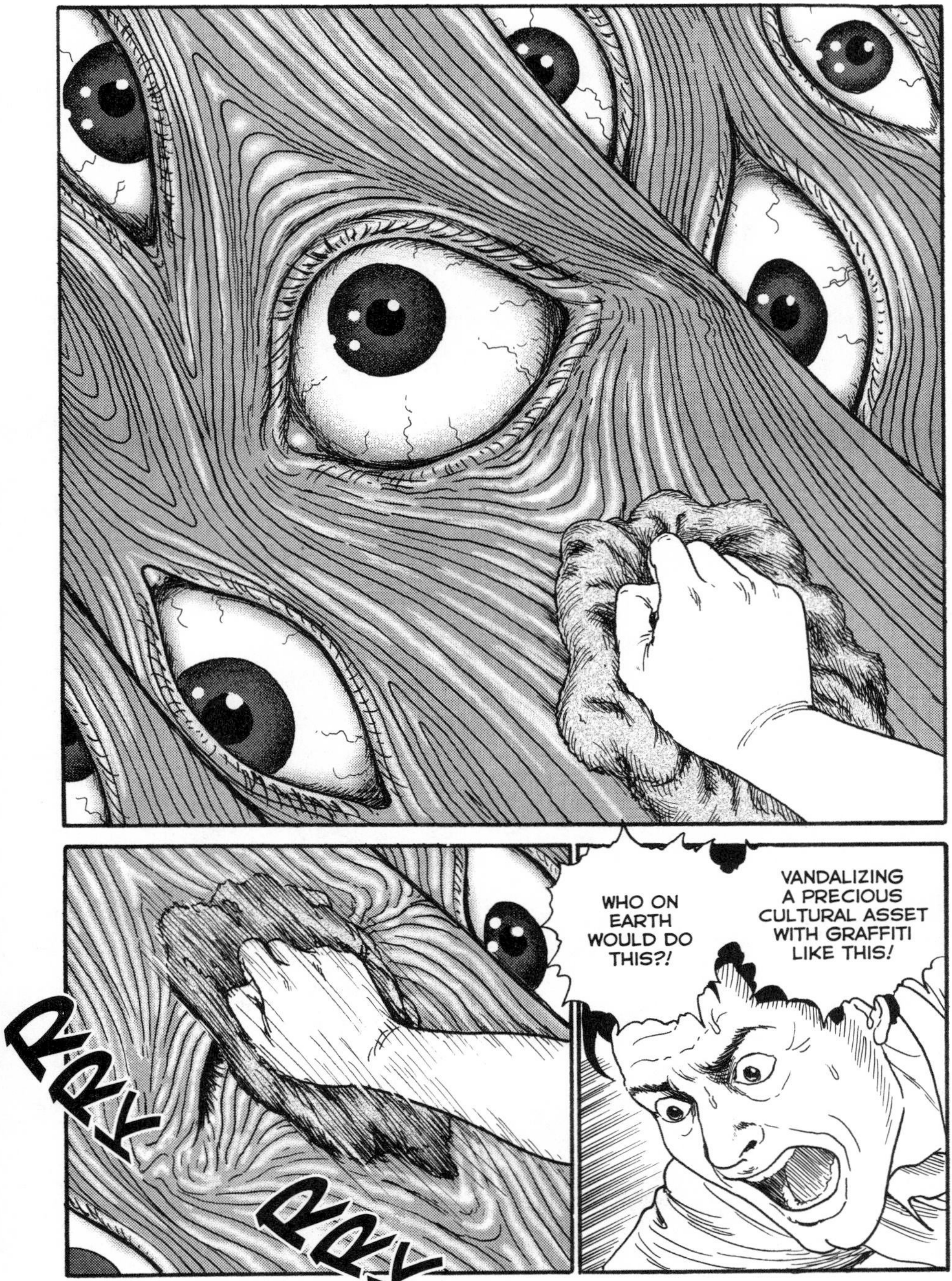
VANDALIZING A PRECIOUS CULTURAL ASSET WITH GRAFFITI LIKE THIS!
WHO ON EARTH WOULD DO THIS?!
RRK
RRK

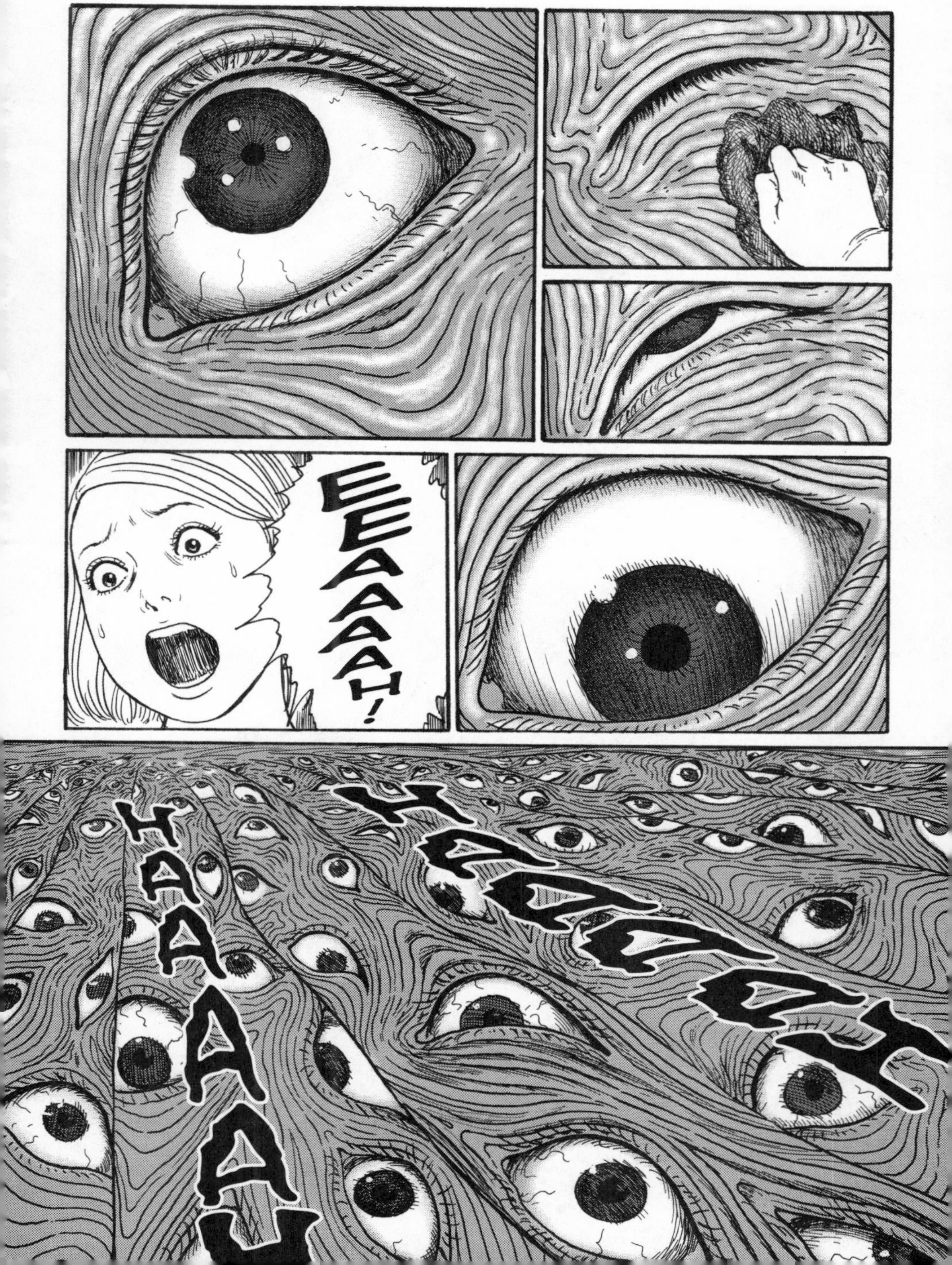
EEAAAAH!
HAAAA
HAAAA

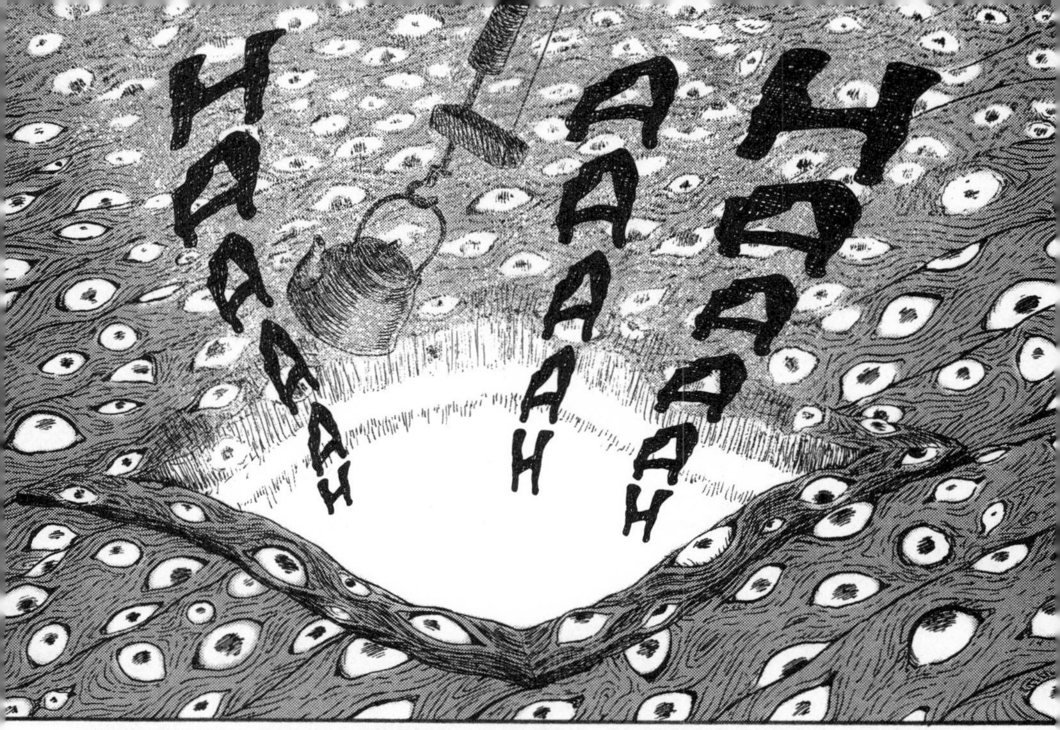
HAAAAAAH
HAAAAAAH
HAAAAAAH

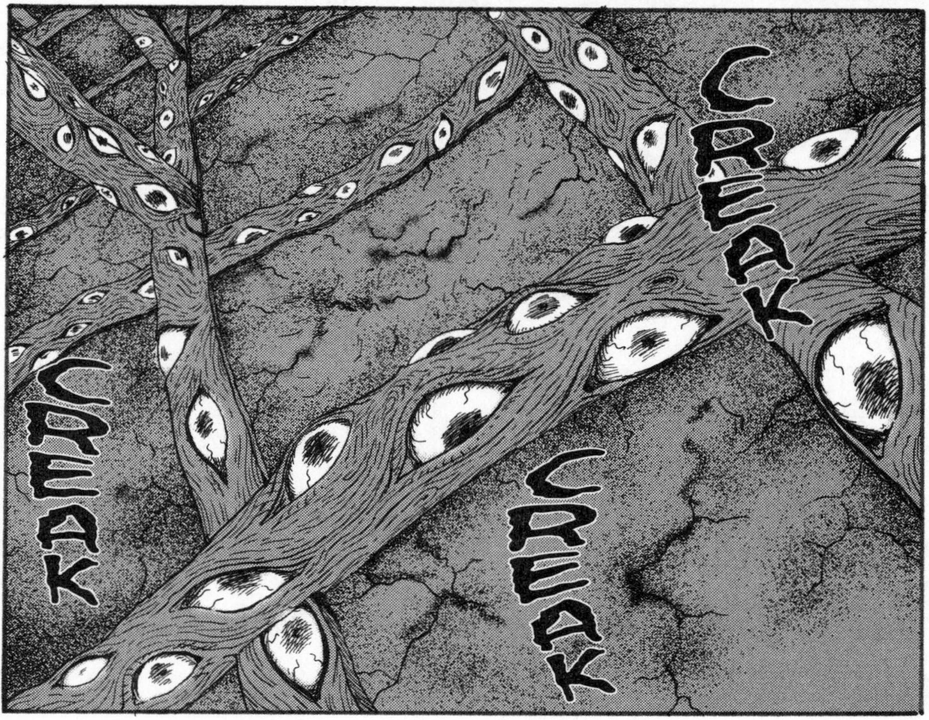
CREAK
CREAK
CREAK

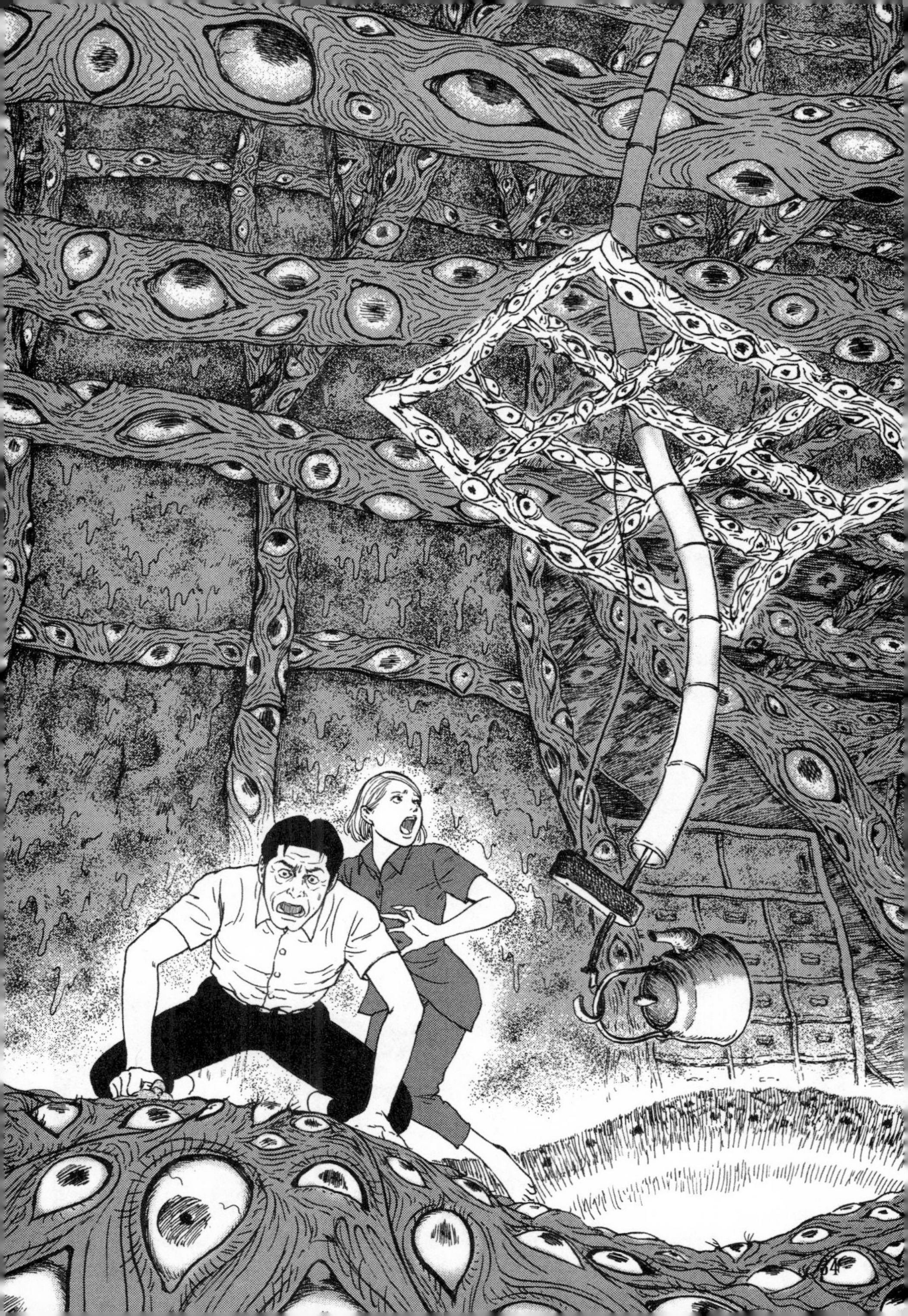

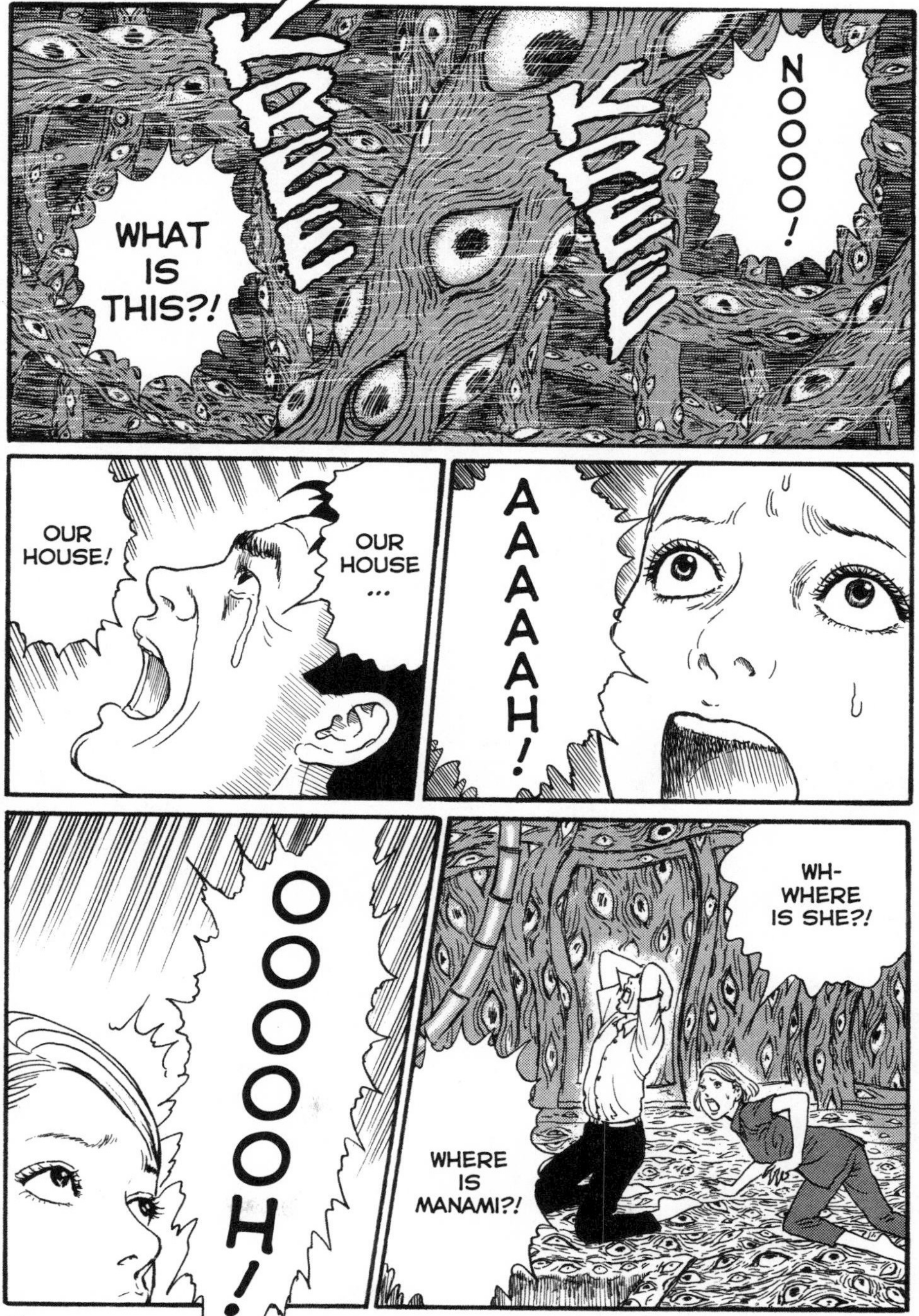
NOOOOO!
KREE
KREE
WHAT IS THIS?!
AAAAAH!
OUR HOUSE...
OUR HOUSE!
WH-WHERE IS SHE?!
WHERE IS MANAMI?!
OOOOOH!

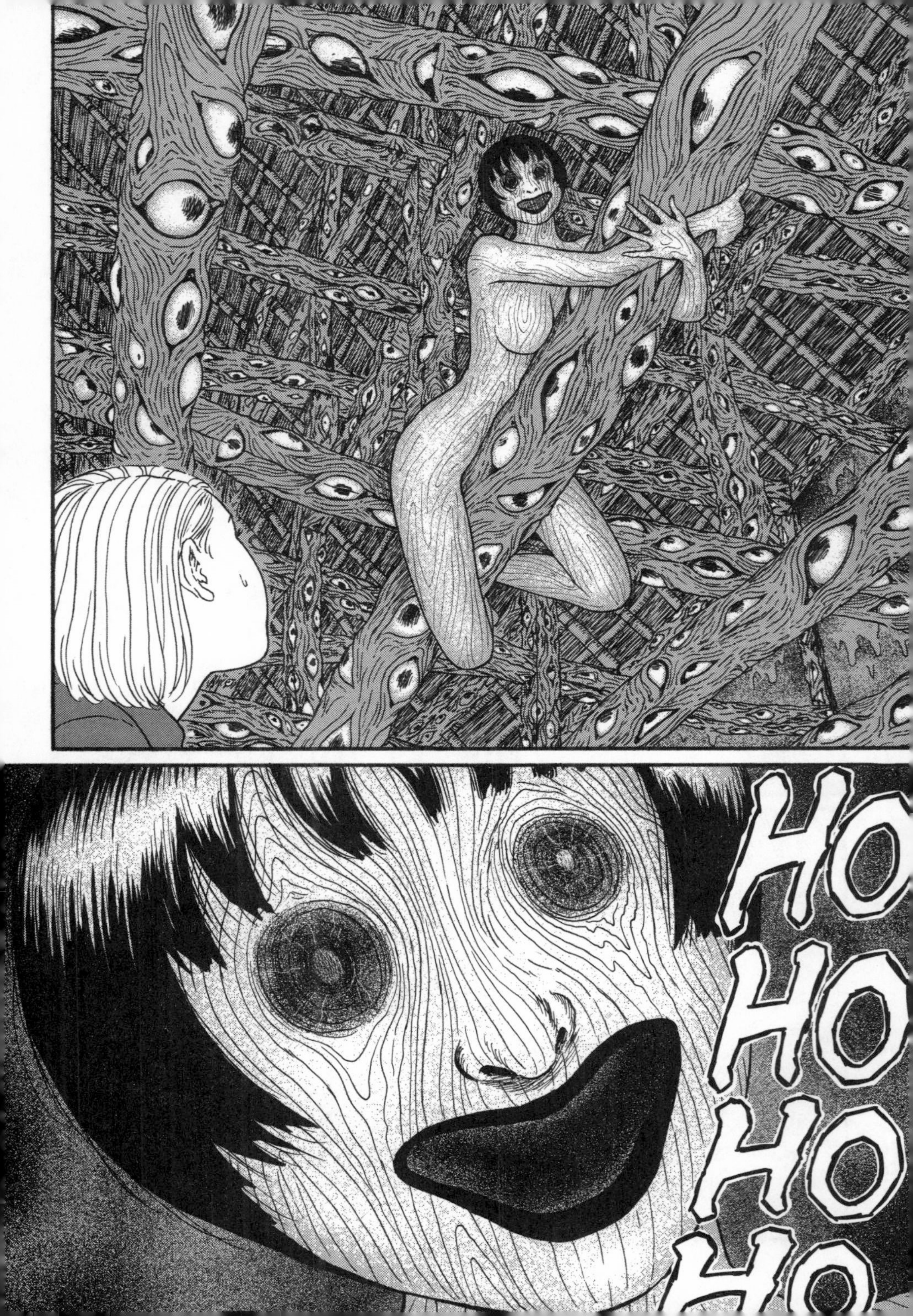
HO HO HO HO

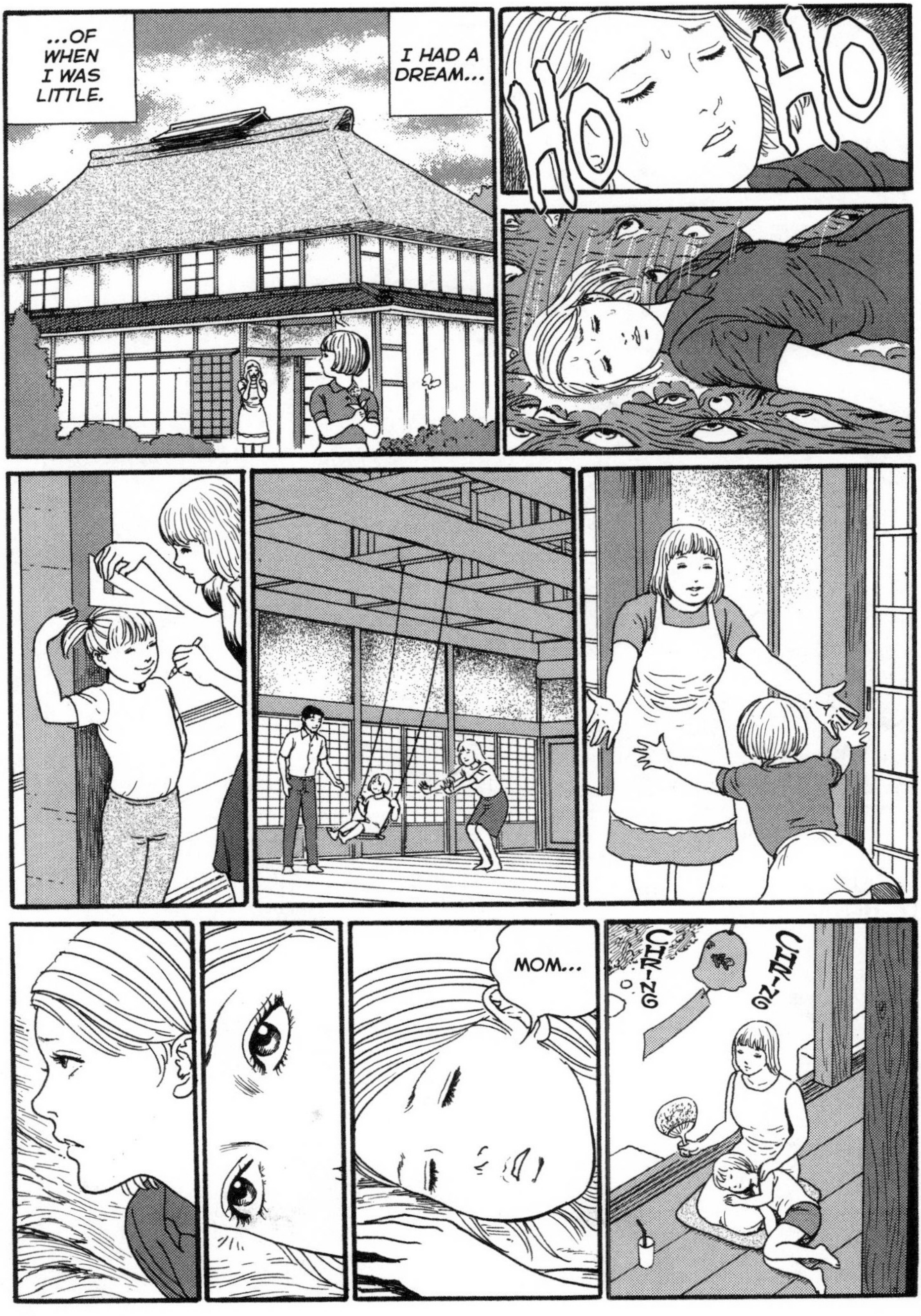
HO HO
I HAD A DREAM...
...OF WHEN I WAS LITTLE.
CHING
CHRING
MOM...

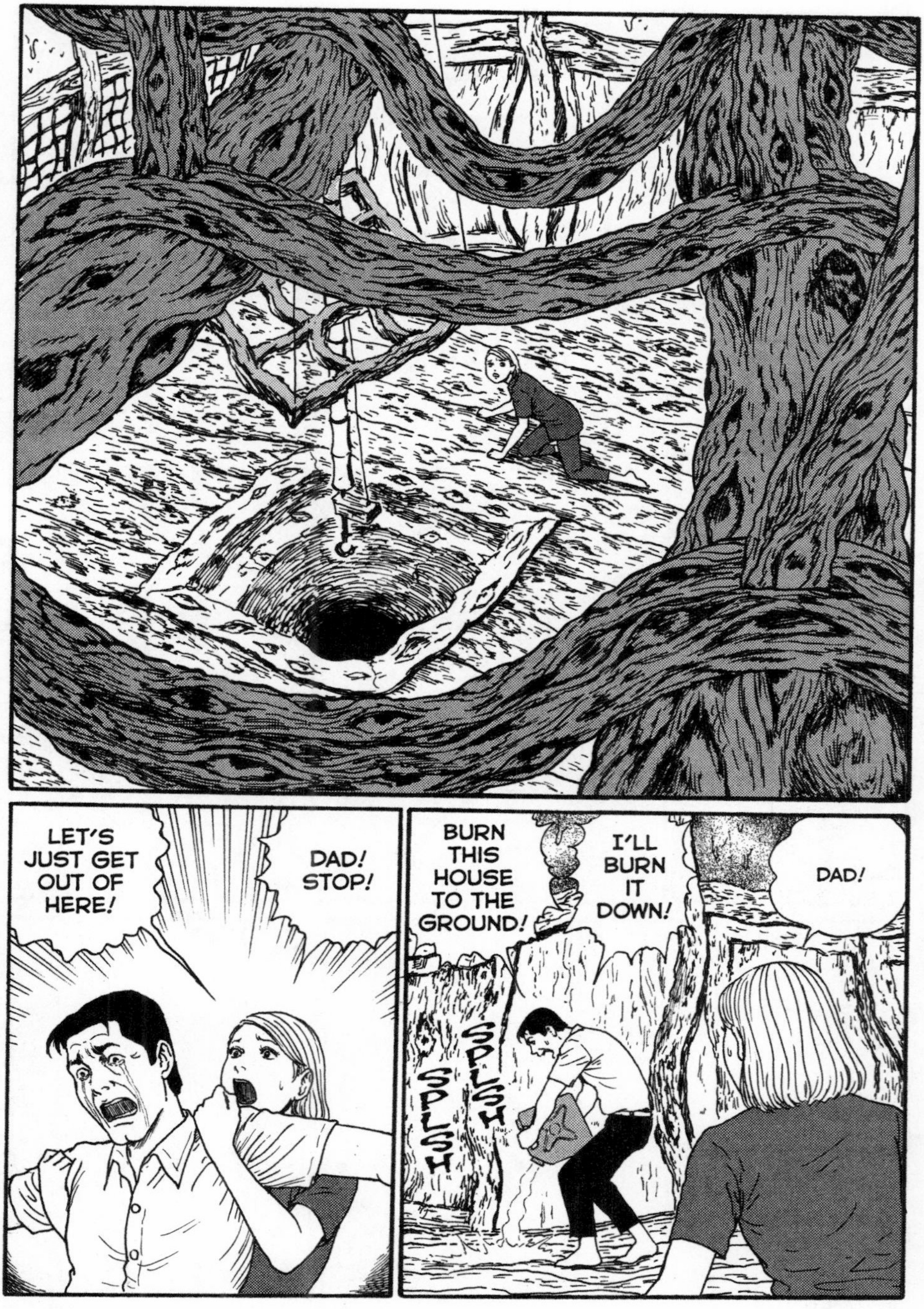
DAD!
I'LL BURN IT DOWN!
BURN THIS HOUSE TO THE GROUND!
SPLSH
SPLSH
DAD! STOP!
LET'S JUST GET OUT OF HERE!

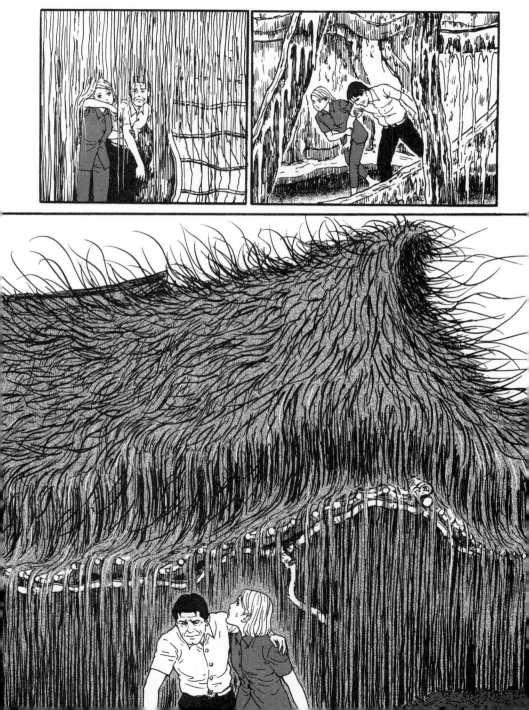

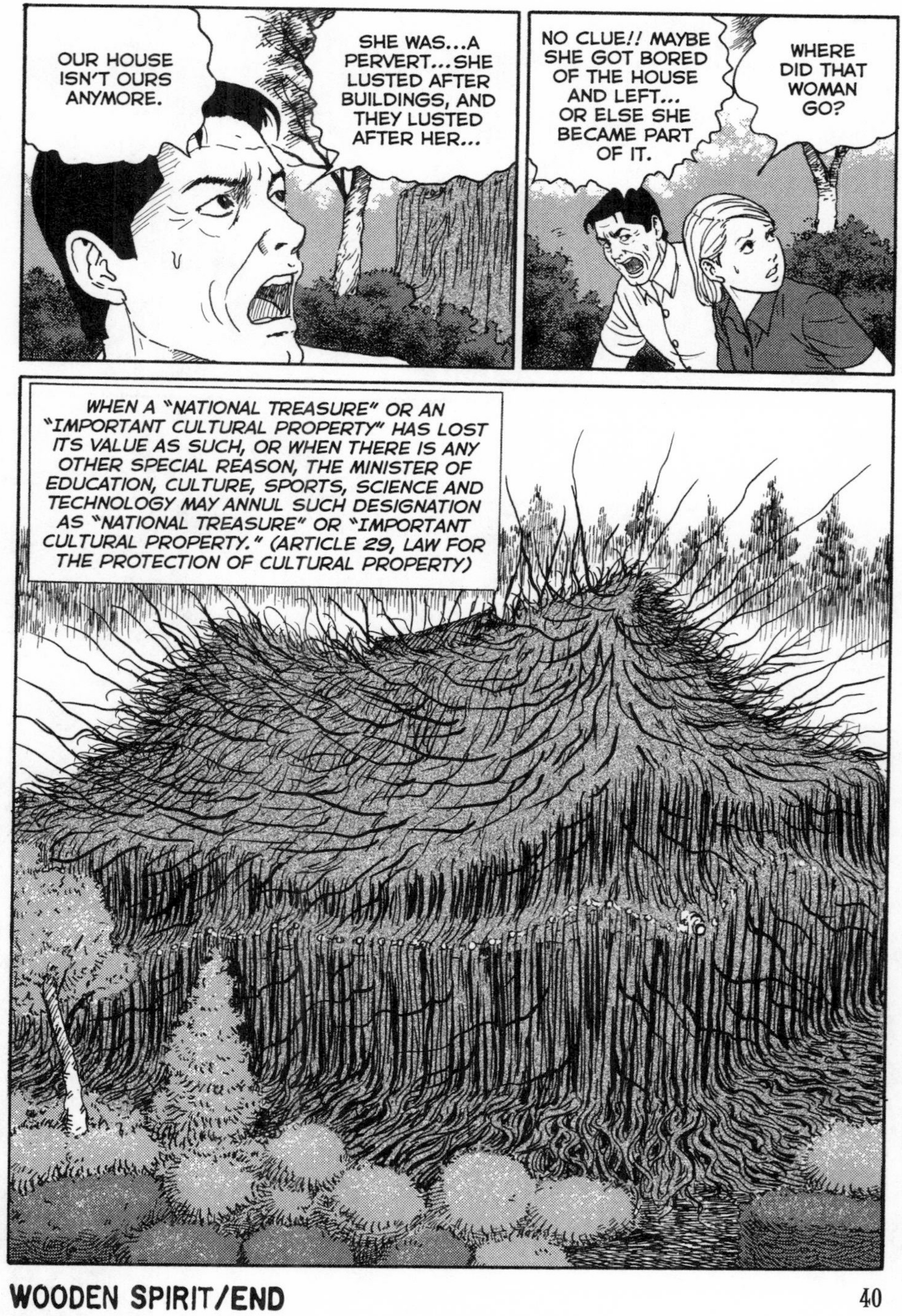
WHERE DID THAT WOMAN GO?
NO CLUE!! MAYBE SHE GOT BORED OF THE HOUSE AND LEFT... OR ELSE SHE BECAME PART OF IT.
SHE WAS...A PERVERT...SHE LUSTED AFTER BUILDINGS, AND THEY LUSTED AFTER HER...
OUR HOUSE ISN'T OURS ANYMORE.
WHEN A "NATIONAL TREASURE" OR AN "IMPORTANT CULTURAL PROPERTY" HAS LOST ITS VALUE AS SUCH, OR WHEN THERE IS ANY OTHER SPECIAL REASON, THE MINISTER OF EDUCATION, CULTURE, SPORTS, SCIENCE AND TECHNOLOGY MAY ANNUL SUCH DESIGNATION AS "NATIONAL TREASURE" OR "IMPORTANT CULTURAL PROPERTY." (ARTICLE 29, LAW FOR THE PROTECTION OF CULTURAL PROPERTY)

WOODEN SPIRIT/END

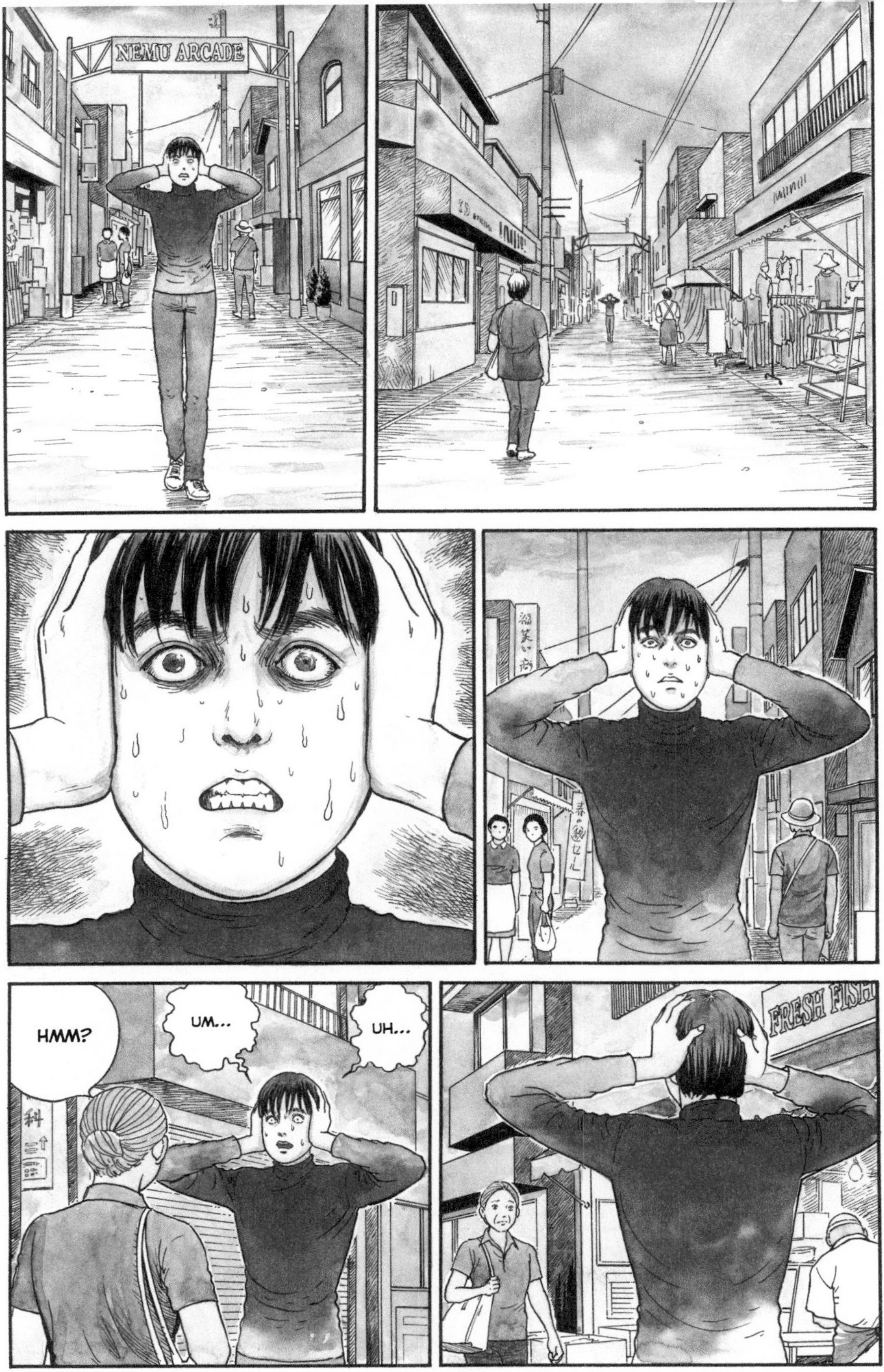
NEMU ARCADE
FRESH FIS
UH...
UM...
HMM?

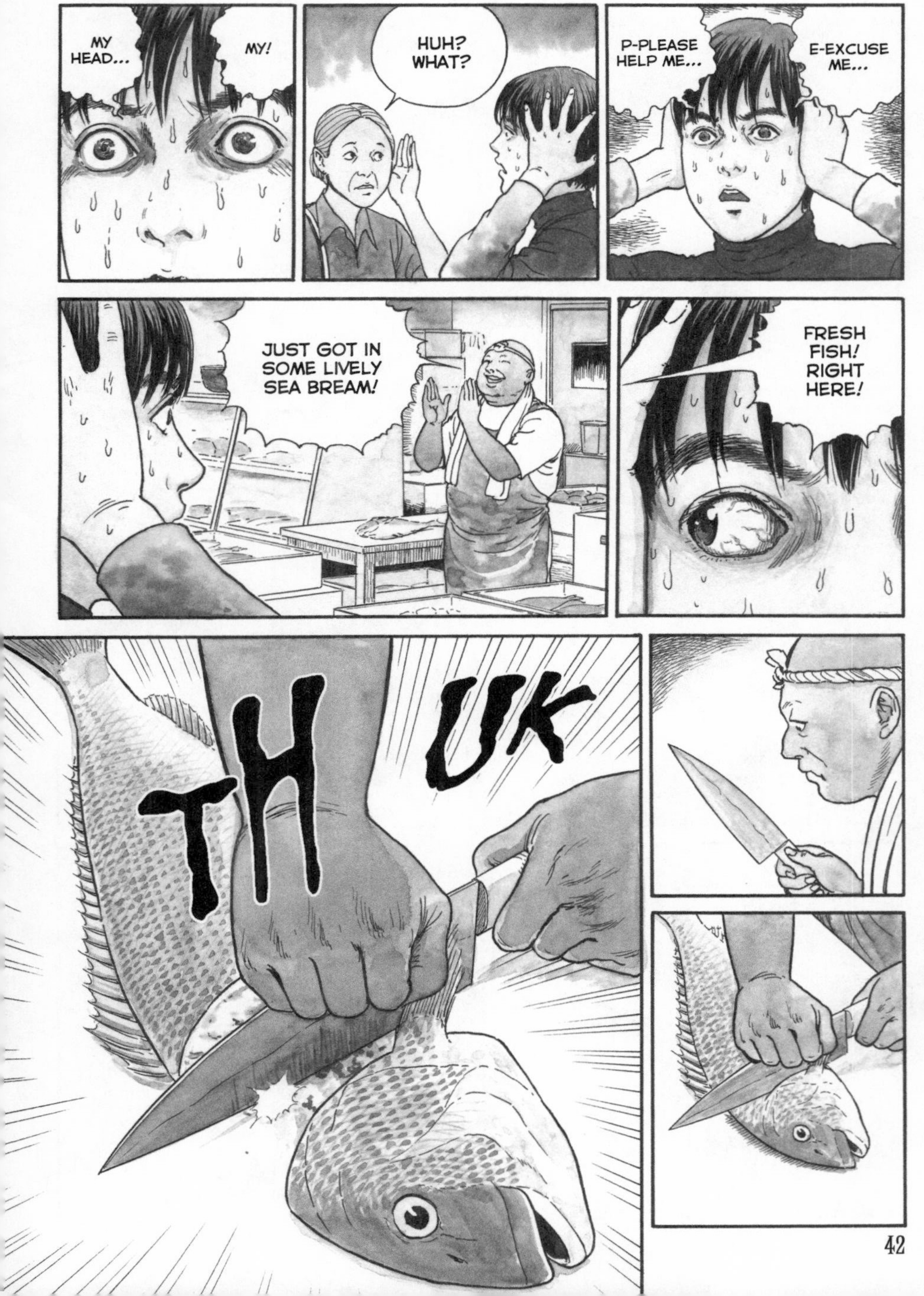
E-EXCUSE ME...
P-PLEASE HELP ME...
HUH? WHAT?
MY HEAD...
MY!
FRESH FISH! RIGHT HERE!
JUST GOT IN SOME LIVELY SEA BREAM!
THUK

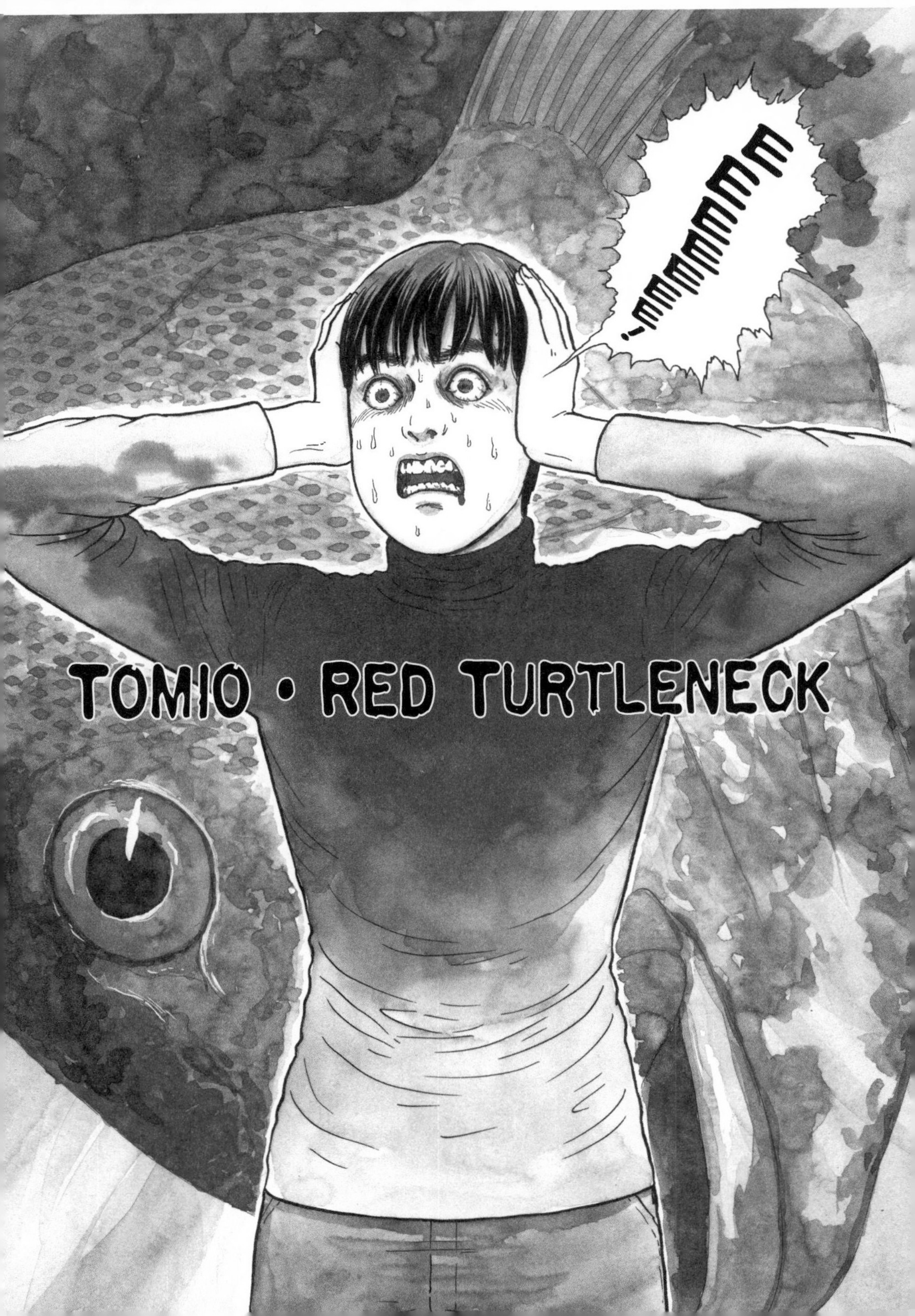
EEEEEEE!
TOMIO • RED TURTLENECK

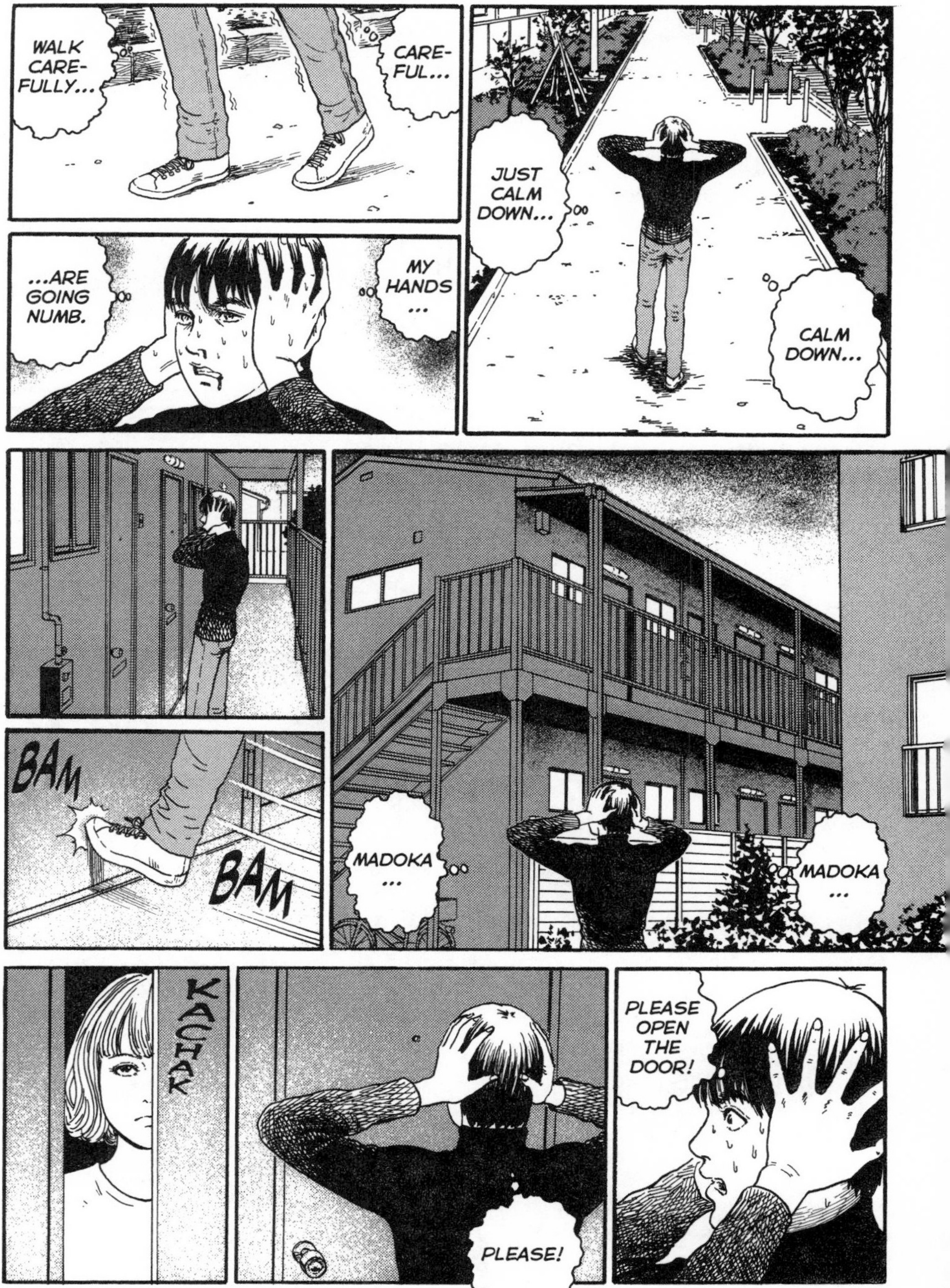
JUST CALM DOWN...
CALM DOWN...
CARE-FUL...
WALK CARE-FULLY...
MY HANDS ...
...ARE GOING NUMB.
MADOKA ...
MADOKA ...
BAM
BAM
PLEASE OPEN THE DOOR!
PLEASE!
KACHAK

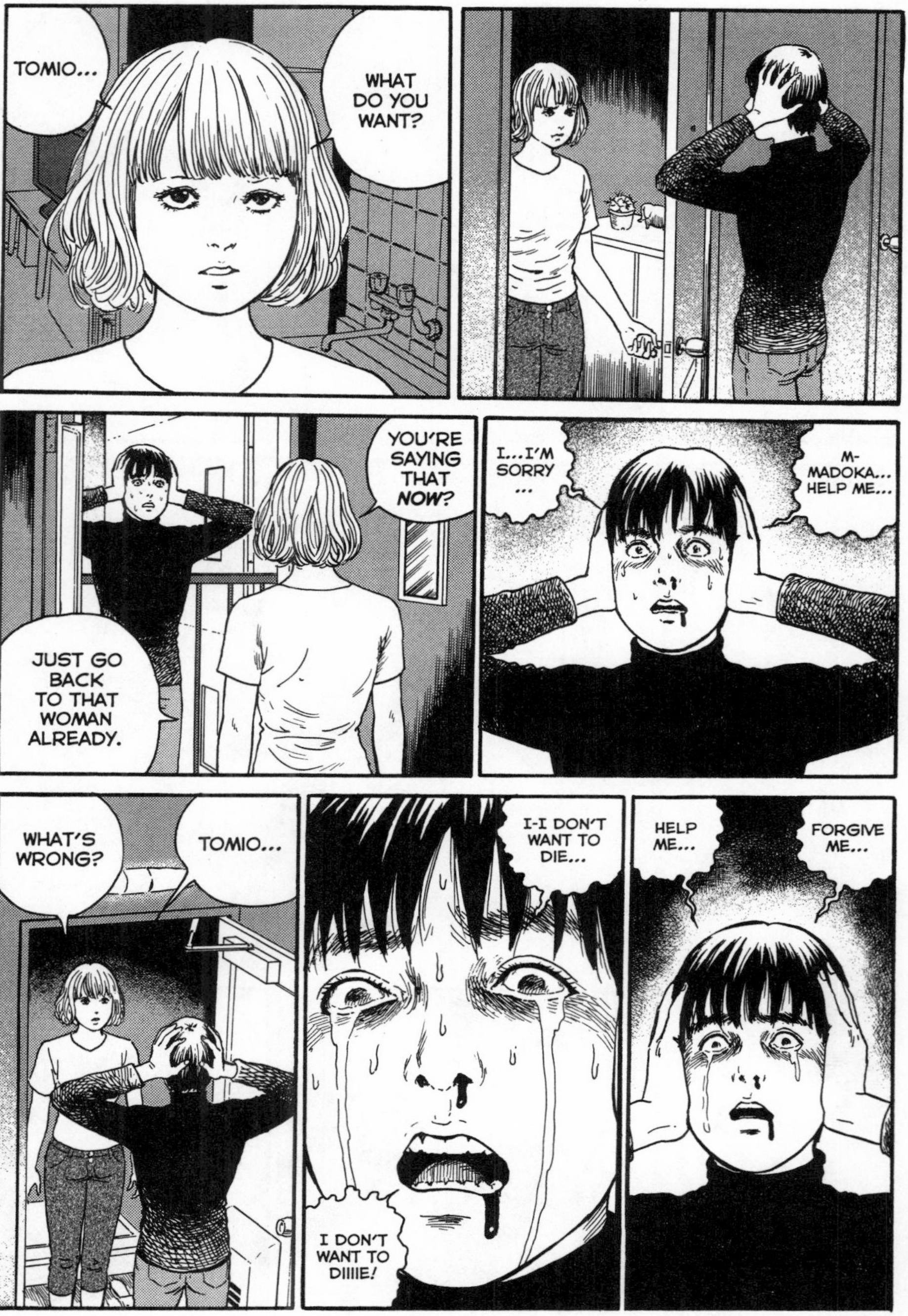
WHAT DO YOU WANT?
TOMIO...
M-MADOKA... HELP ME...
I...I'M SORRY ...
YOU'RE SAYING THAT *NOW*?
JUST GO BACK TO THAT WOMAN ALREADY.
FORGIVE ME...
HELP ME...
I-I DON'T WANT TO DIE...
I DON'T WANT TO DIIIIE!
TOMIO...
WHAT'S WRONG?

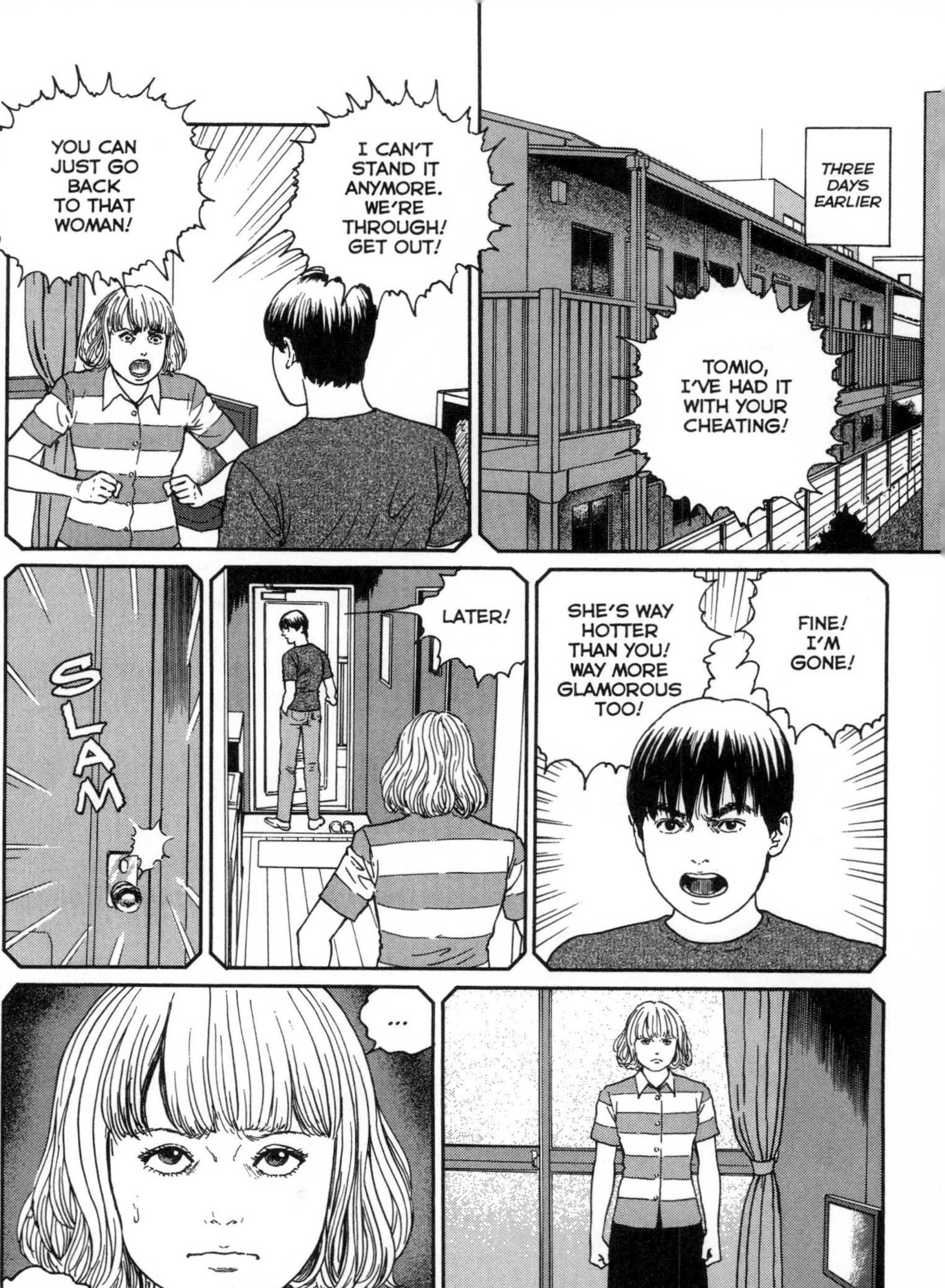
THREE DAYS EARLIER
TOMIO, I'VE HAD IT WITH YOUR CHEATING!
I CAN'T STAND IT ANYMORE. WE'RE THROUGH! GET OUT!
YOU CAN JUST GO BACK TO THAT WOMAN!
FINE! I'M GONE!
SHE'S WAY HOTTER THAN YOU! WAY MORE GLAMOROUS TOO!
LATER!
SLAM
...
THAT WOMAN...

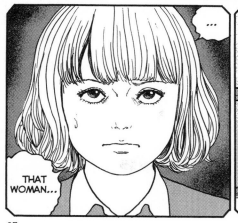

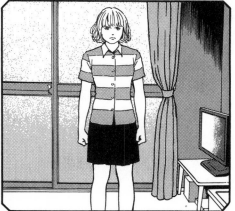

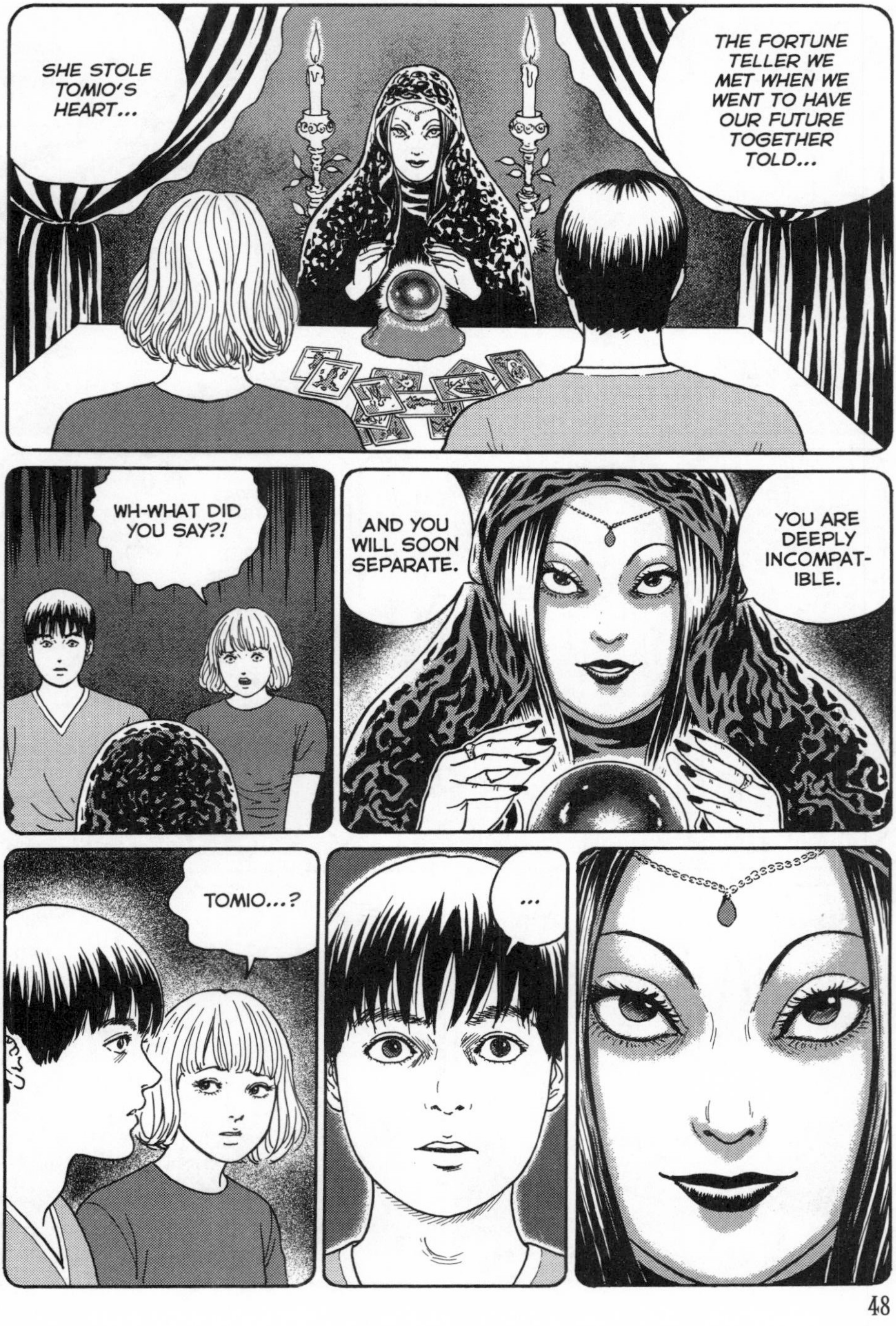
THE FORTUNE TELLER WE MET WHEN WE WENT TO HAVE OUR FUTURE TOGETHER TOLD...
SHE STOLE TOMIO'S HEART...
YOU ARE DEEPLY INCOMPAT-IBLE.
AND YOU WILL SOON SEPARATE.
WH-WHAT DID YOU SAY?!
...
TOMIO...?

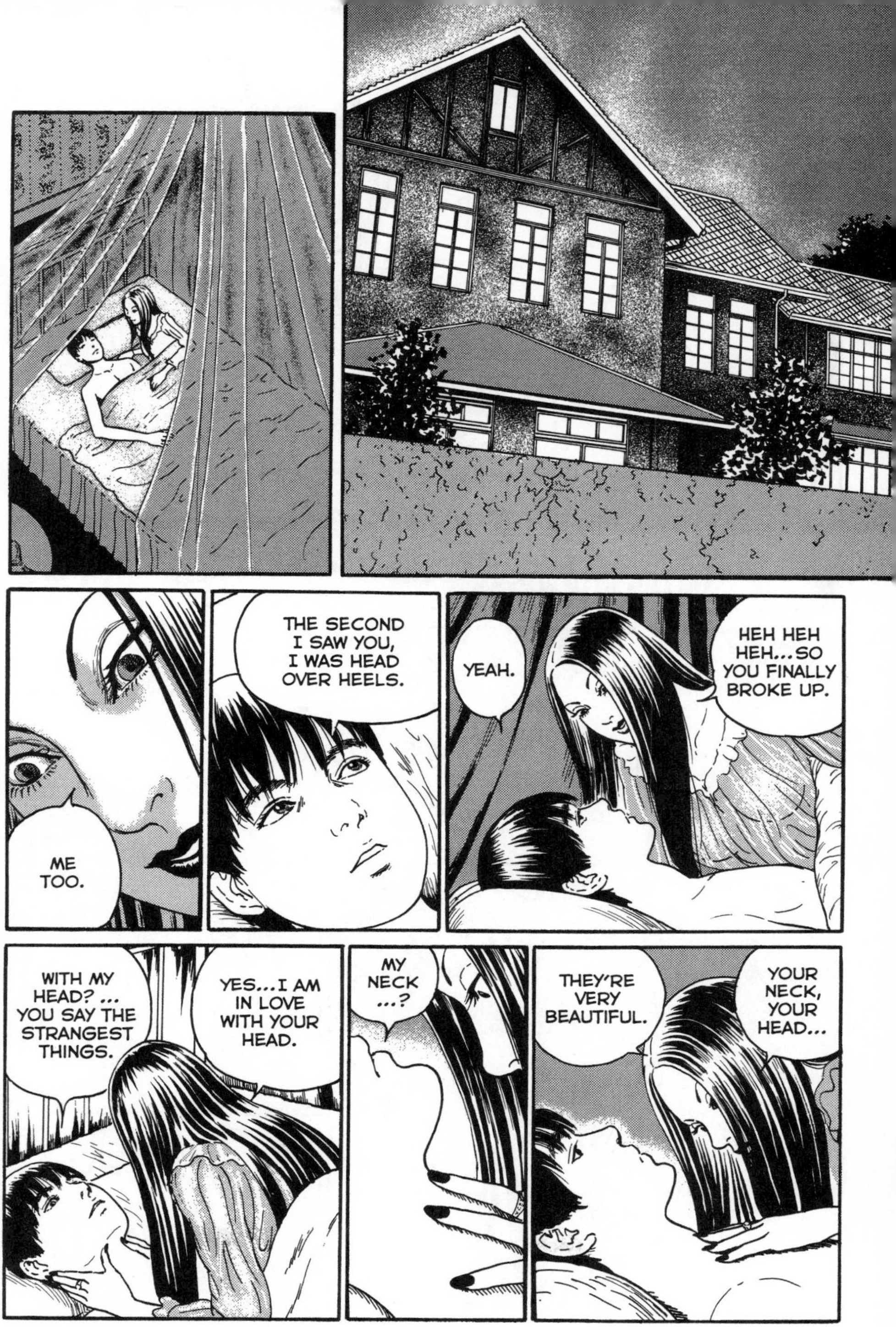
HEH HEH HEH...SO YOU FINALLY BROKE UP.
YEAH.
THE SECOND I SAW YOU, I WAS HEAD OVER HEELS.
ME TOO.
YOUR NECK, YOUR HEAD...
THEY'RE VERY BEAUTIFUL.
MY NECK ...?
YES...I AM IN LOVE WITH YOUR HEAD.
WITH MY HEAD? ... YOU SAY THE STRANGEST THINGS.

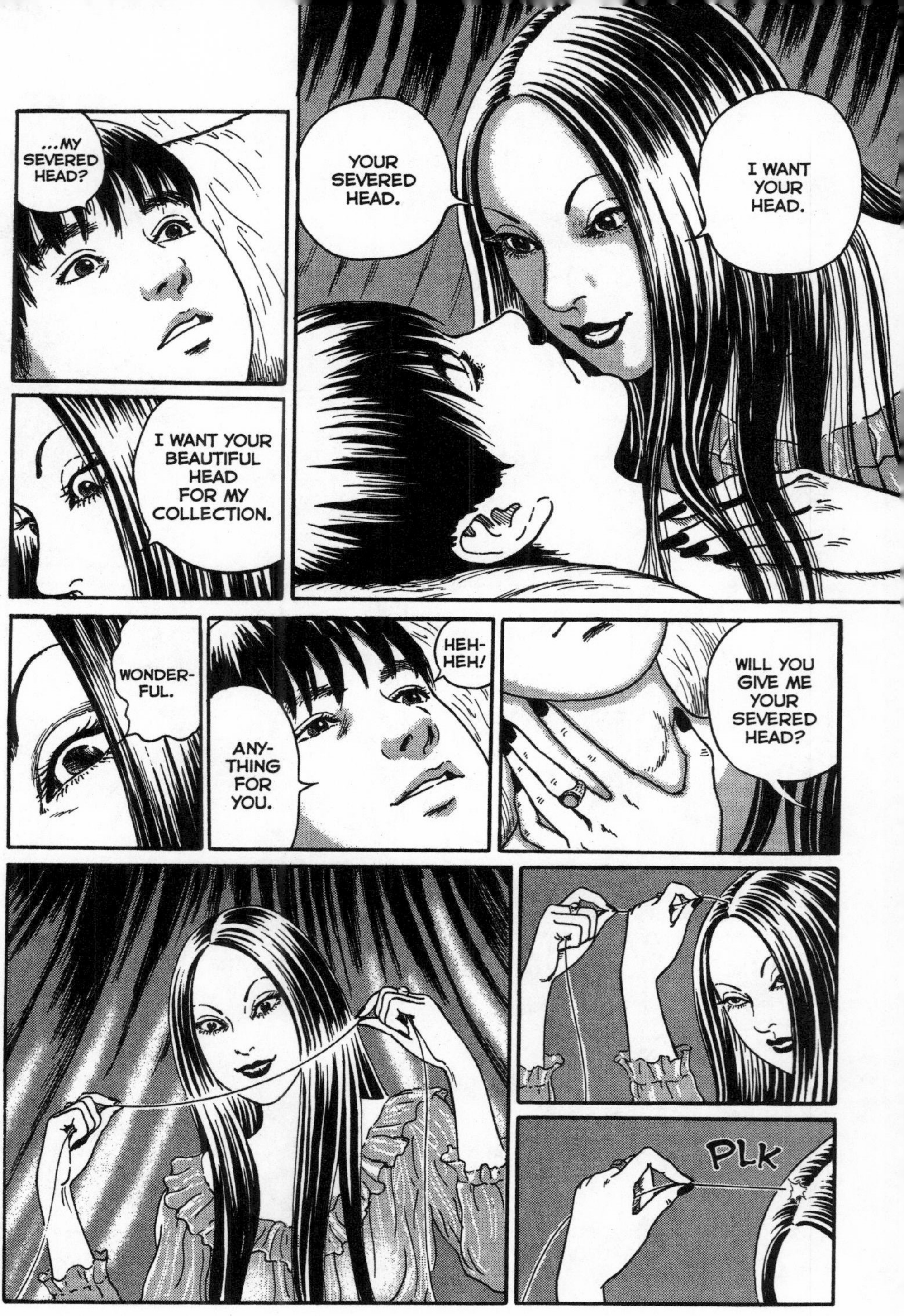
I WANT YOUR HEAD.
YOUR SEVERED HEAD.
...MY SEVERED HEAD?
I WANT YOUR BEAUTIFUL HEAD FOR MY COLLECTION.
WILL YOU GIVE ME YOUR SEVERED HEAD?
HEH-HEH!
ANY-THING FOR YOU.
WONDER-FUL.
PLK

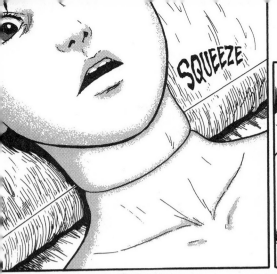

SQUEEZE

...WHAT
ARE YOU
DOING?

UNH!

SMACK

GRK GRK GRK GRK GRK

NGH
NGH...

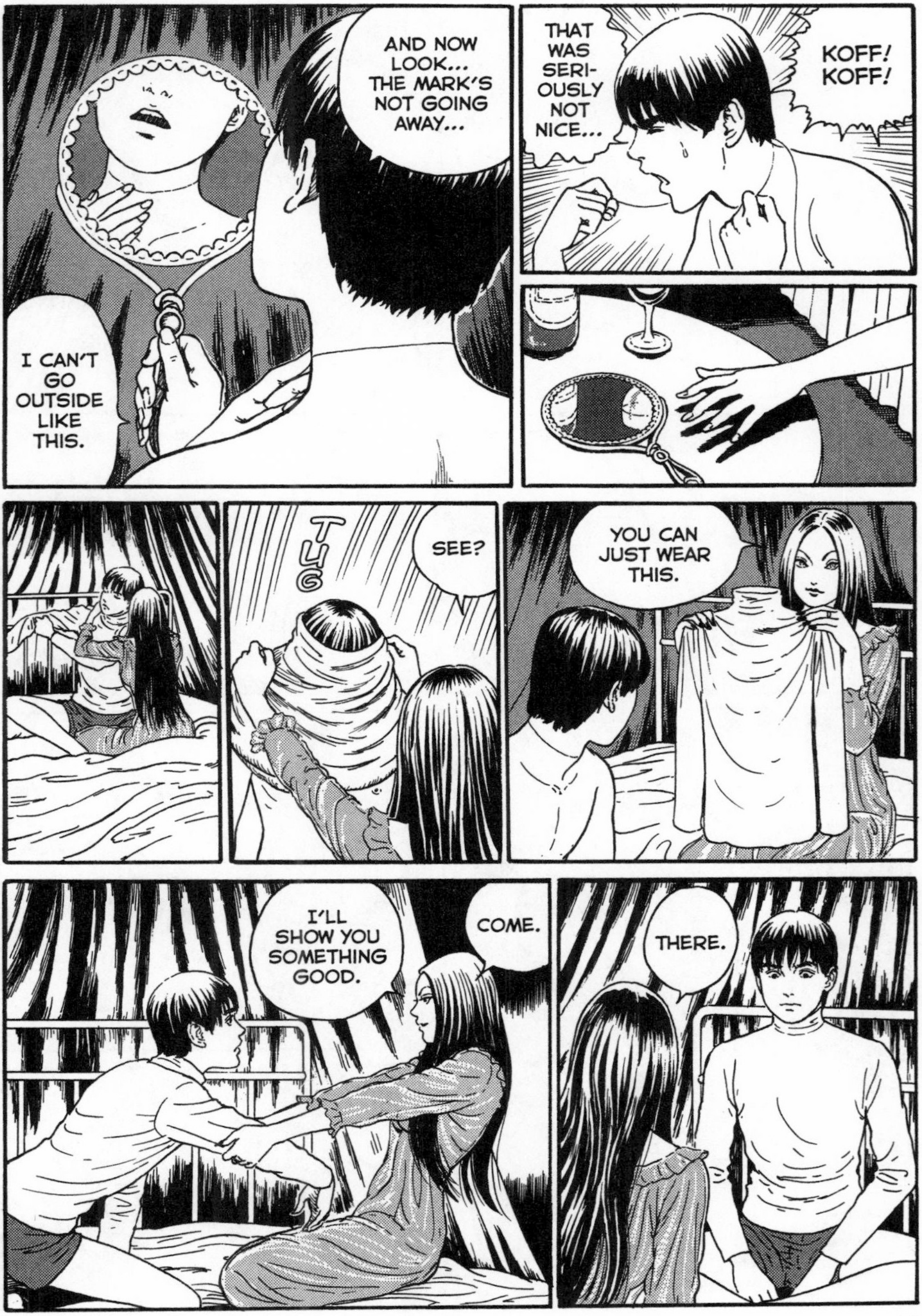
KOFF! KOFF!
THAT WAS SERIOUSLY NOT NICE...
AND NOW LOOK... THE MARK'S NOT GOING AWAY...
I CAN'T GO OUTSIDE LIKE THIS.
YOU CAN JUST WEAR THIS.
SEE?
TUG
THERE.
COME.
I'LL SHOW YOU SOMETHING GOOD.

THIS "SOMETHING GOOD"...

WHAT IS IT?

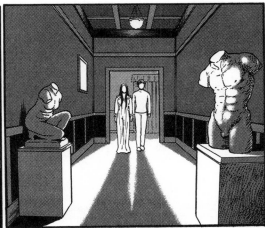

THAT.

HEH HEH HEH.

HMM?

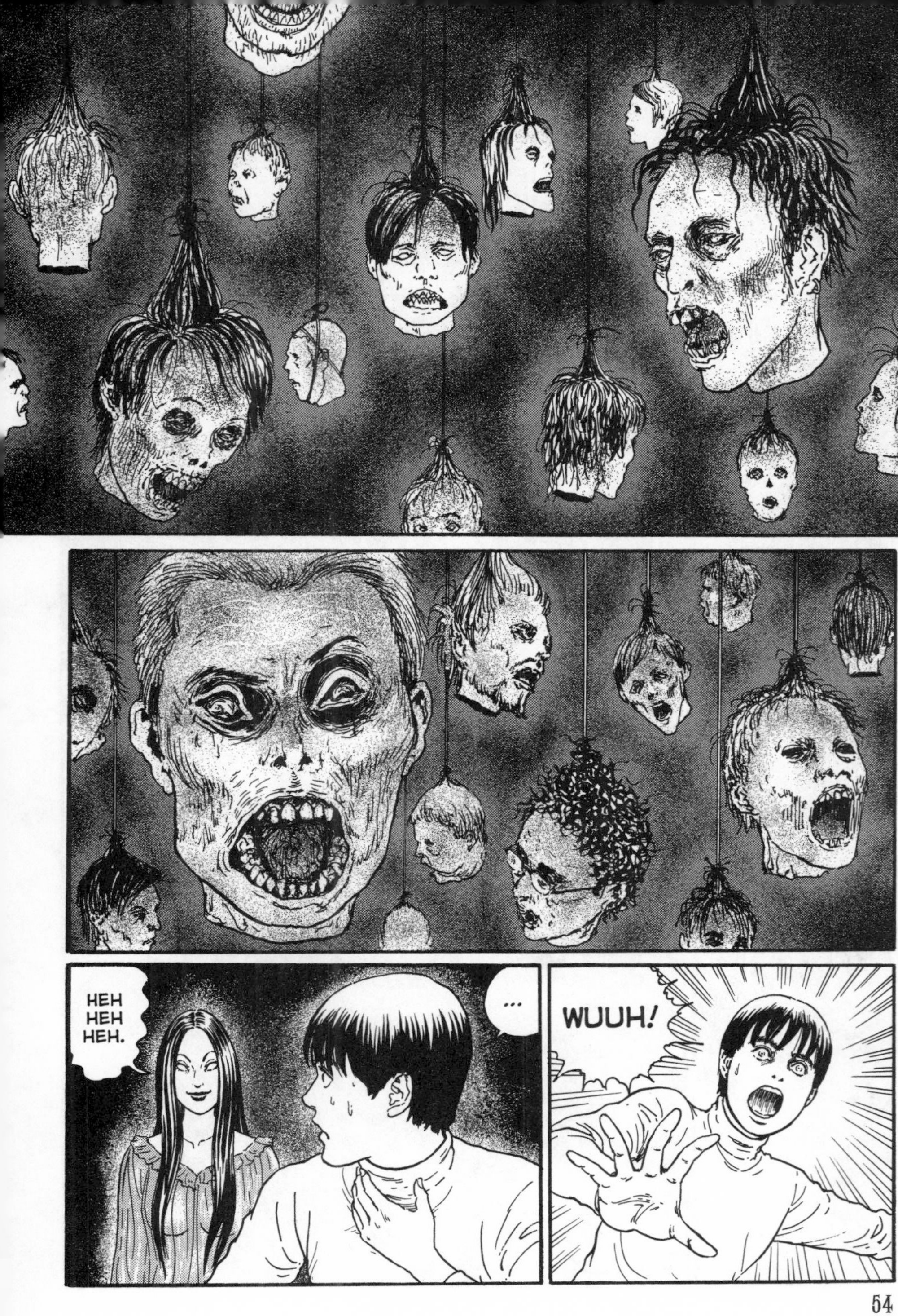
WUUH!
...
HEH HEH HEH.

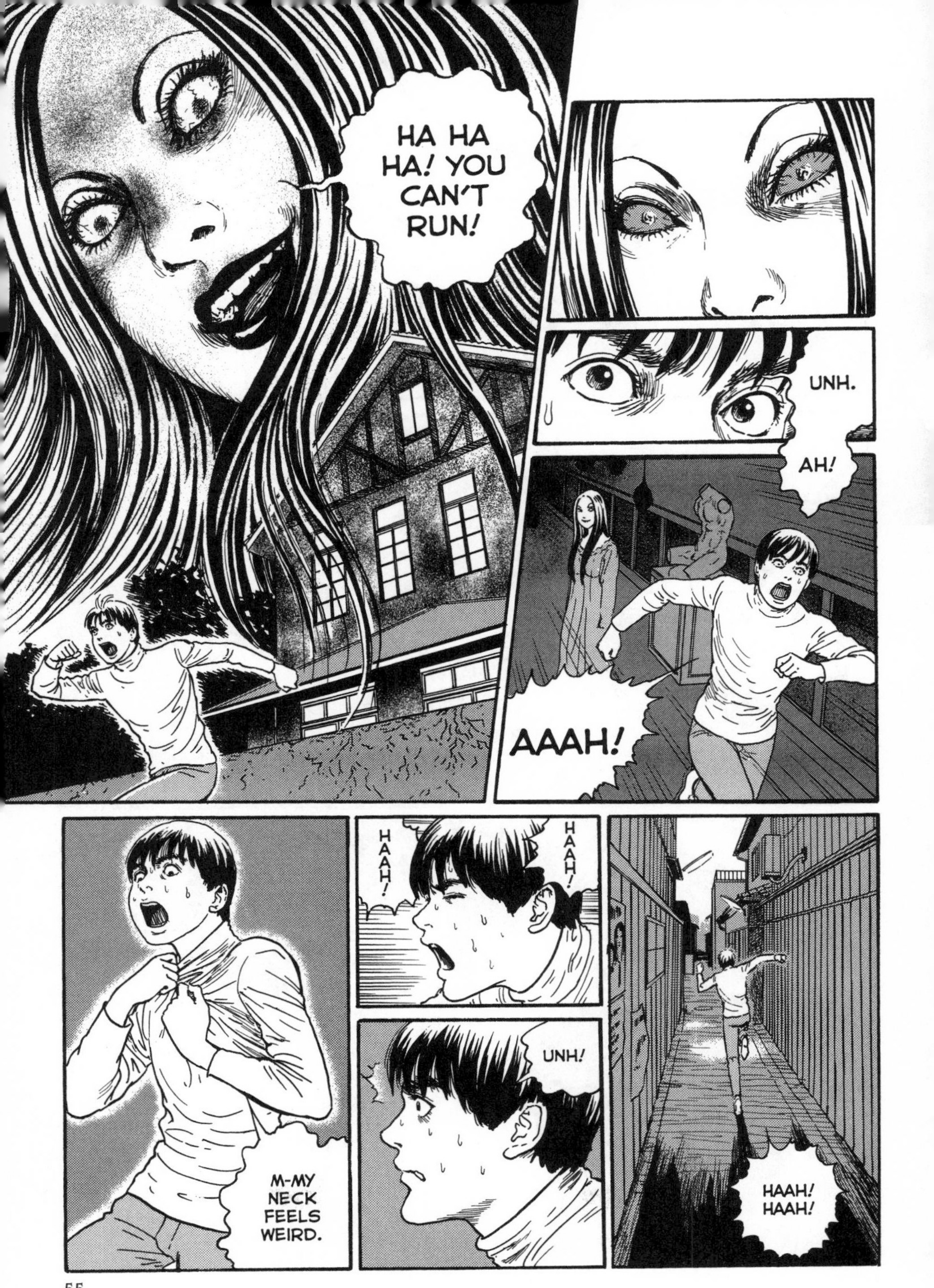
UNH.
AH!
AAAH!
HA HA HA! YOU CAN'T RUN!
HAAH! HAAH!
HAAH!
HAAH!
UNH!
M-MY NECK FEELS WEIRD.

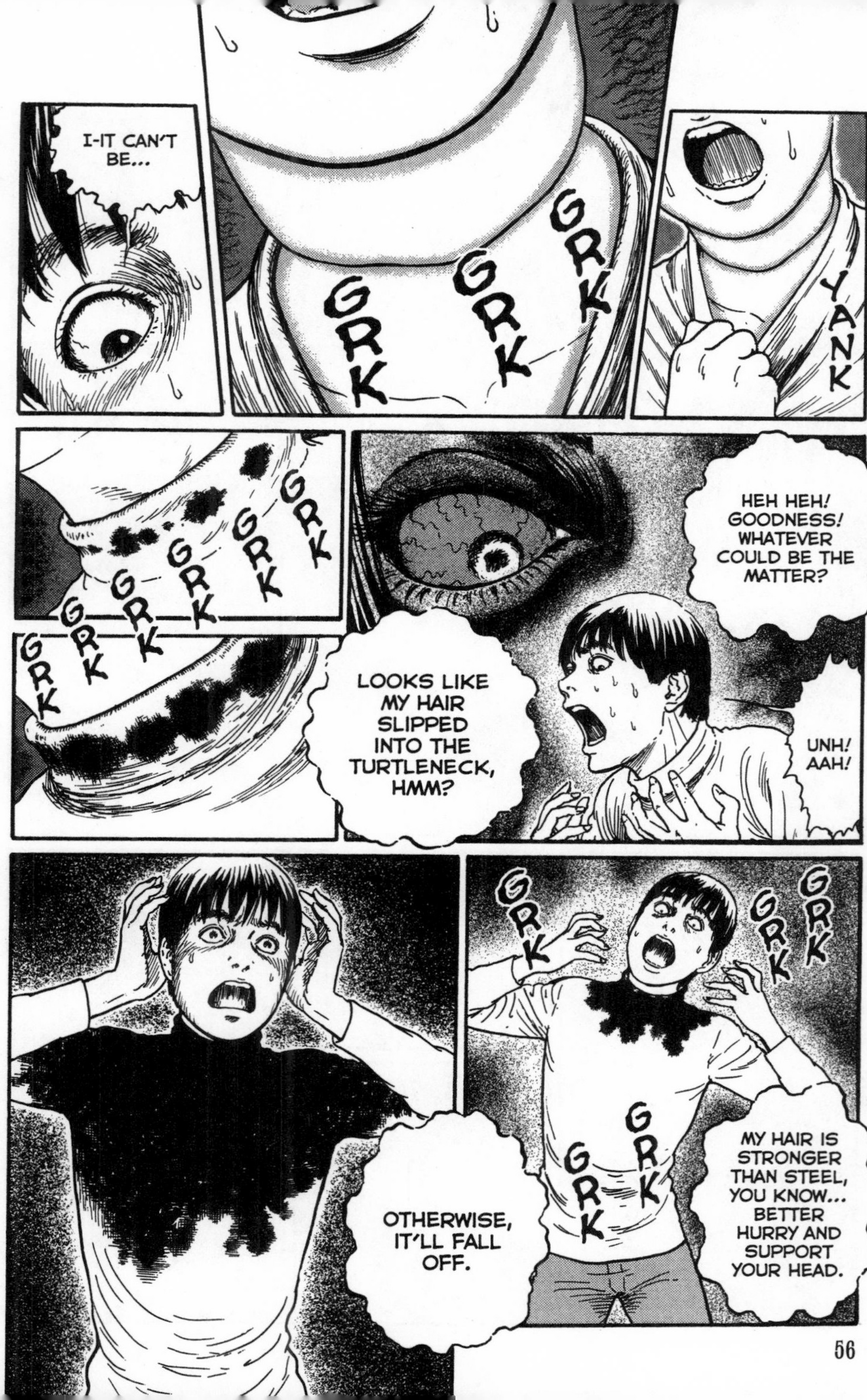
YANK
GRK GRK GRK
I-IT CAN'T BE...
HEH HEH! GOODNESS! WHATEVER COULD BE THE MATTER?
UNH! AAH!
LOOKS LIKE MY HAIR SLIPPED INTO THE TURTLENECK, HMM?
GRK GRK GRK GRK GRK
GRK GRK GRK
GRK GRK GRK
MY HAIR IS STRONGER THAN STEEL, YOU KNOW... BETTER HURRY AND SUPPORT YOUR HEAD.
GRK GRK
OTHERWISE, IT'LL FALL OFF.

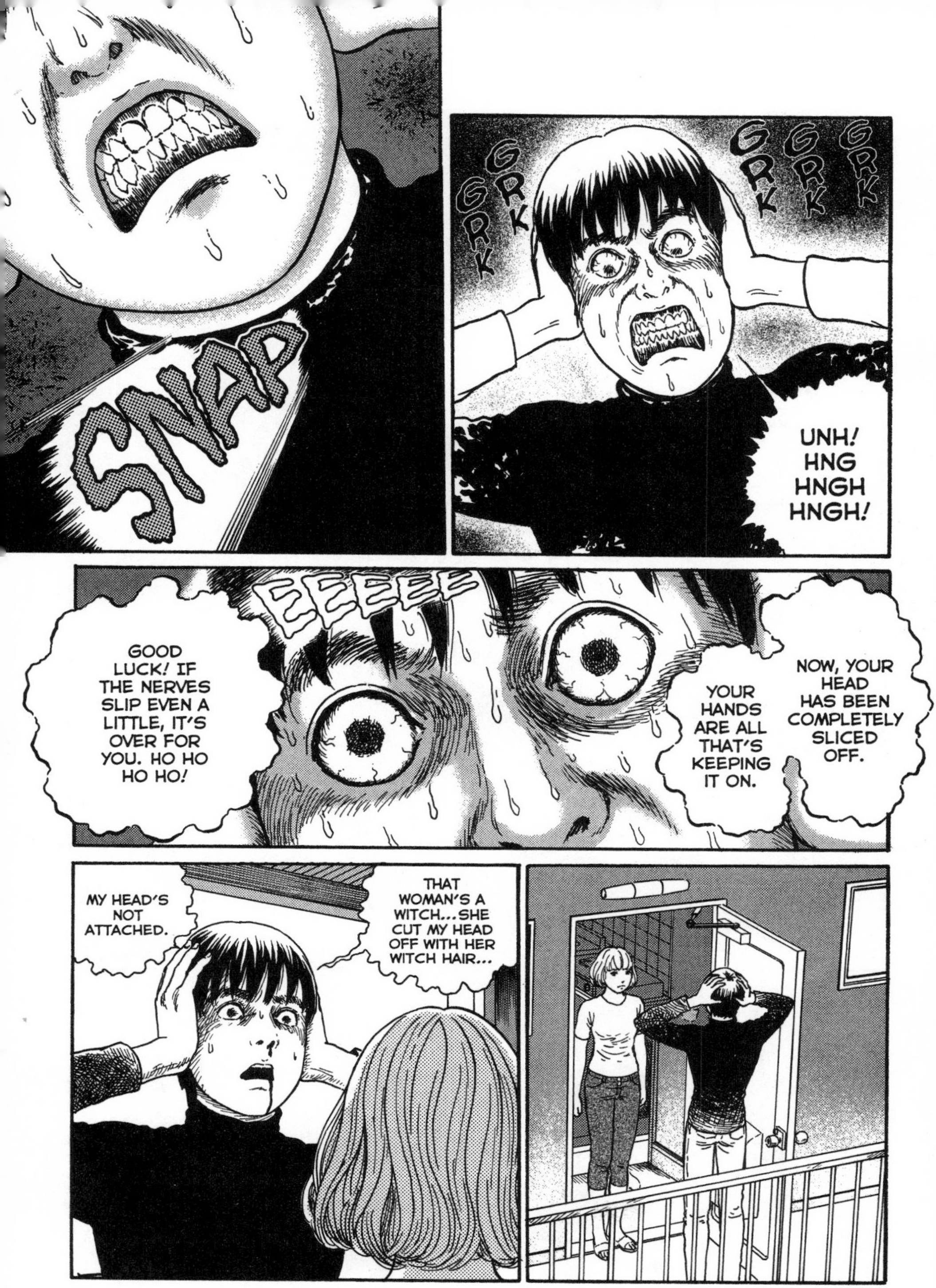
GRK GRK GRK GRK GRK
UNH! HNG HNGH HNGH!
SNAP
NOW, YOUR HEAD HAS BEEN COMPLETELY SLICED OFF.
YOUR HANDS ARE ALL THAT'S KEEPING IT ON.
EEEEE
GOOD LUCK! IF THE NERVES SLIP EVEN A LITTLE, IT'S OVER FOR YOU. HO HO HO HO!
THAT WOMAN'S A WITCH...SHE CUT MY HEAD OFF WITH HER WITCH HAIR...
MY HEAD'S NOT ATTACHED.

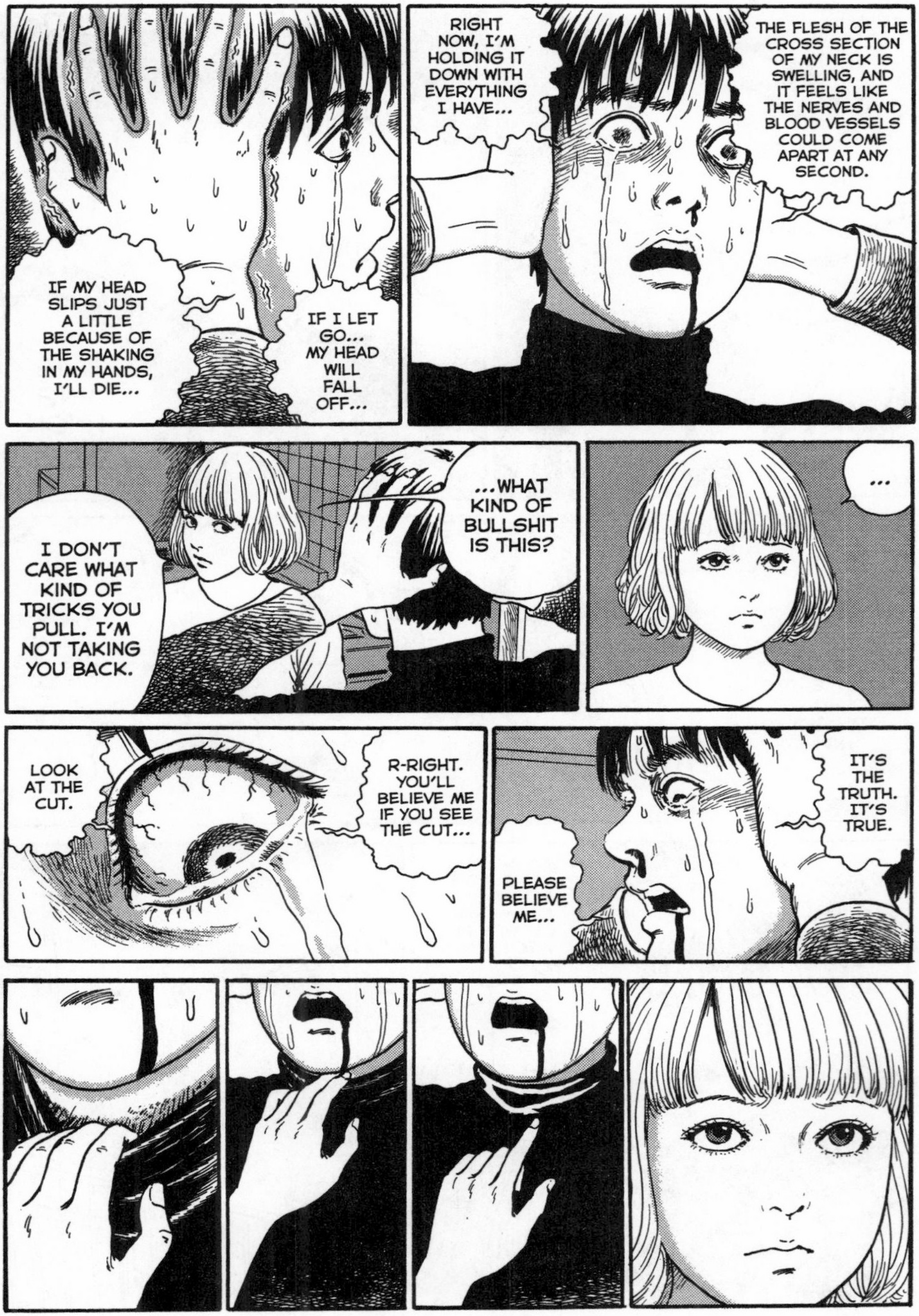
THE FLESH OF THE CROSS SECTION OF MY NECK IS SWELLING, AND IT FEELS LIKE THE NERVES AND BLOOD VESSELS COULD COME APART AT ANY SECOND.
RIGHT NOW, I'M HOLDING IT DOWN WITH EVERYTHING I HAVE...
IF I LET GO... MY HEAD WILL FALL OFF...
IF MY HEAD SLIPS JUST A LITTLE BECAUSE OF THE SHAKING IN MY HANDS, I'LL DIE...
...
...WHAT KIND OF BULLSHIT IS THIS?
I DON'T CARE WHAT KIND OF TRICKS YOU PULL. I'M NOT TAKING YOU BACK.
IT'S THE TRUTH. IT'S TRUE.
PLEASE BELIEVE ME...
R-RIGHT. YOU'LL BELIEVE ME IF YOU SEE THE CUT...
LOOK AT THE CUT.

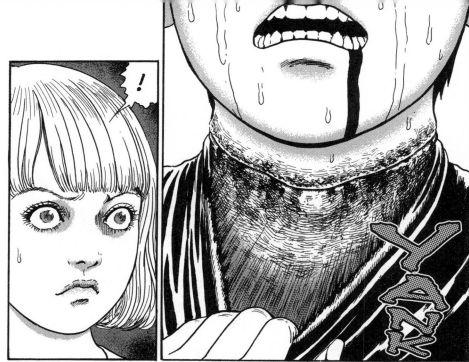

!

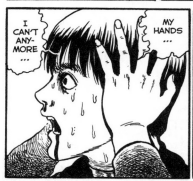

I CAN'T ANY- MORE ...

MY HANDS ...

DRIP

EEE!

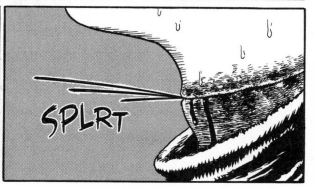

SPLRt

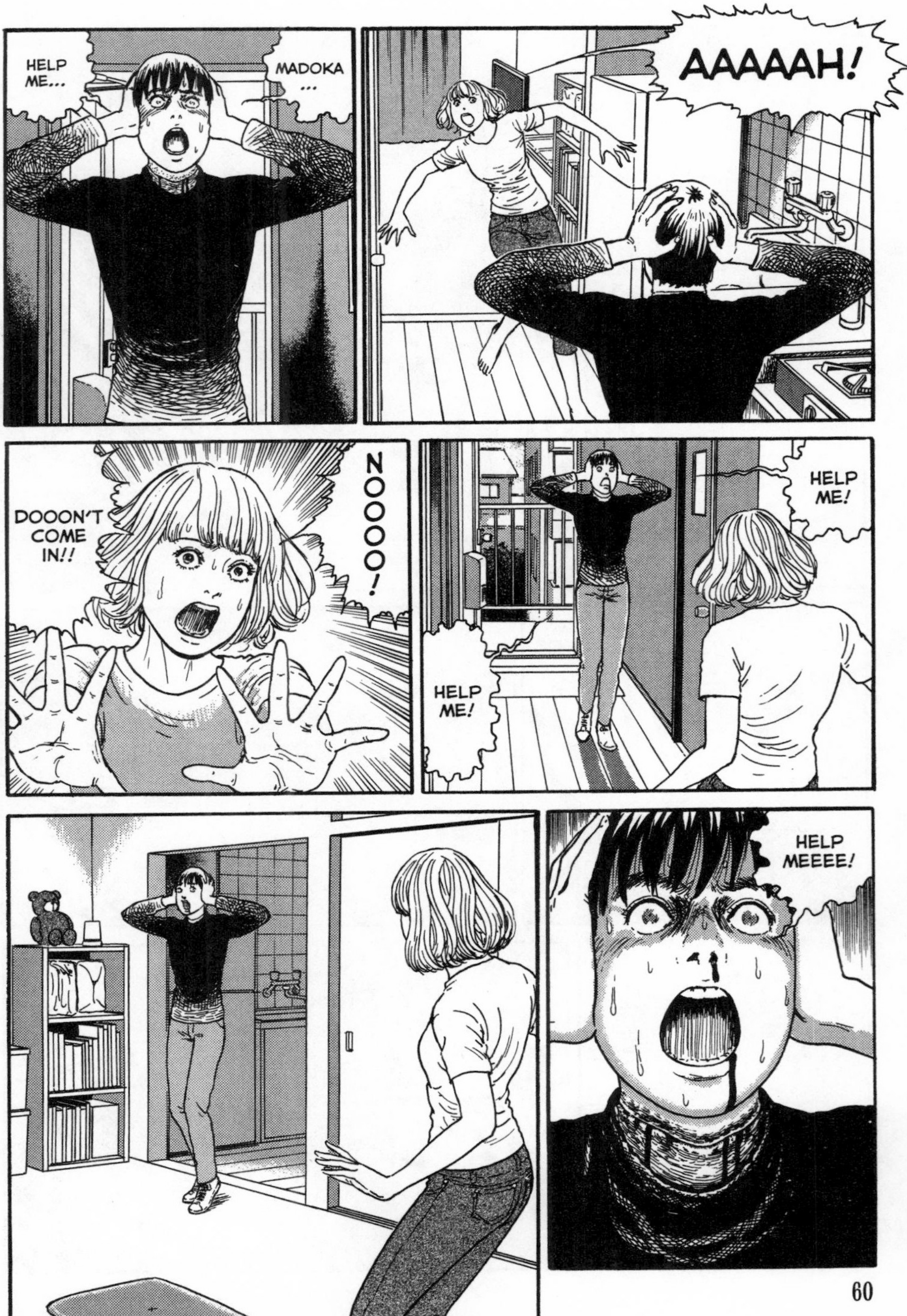
AAAAAH!
MADOKA ...
HELP ME...
HELP ME!
HELP ME!
NOOOOO!
DOOON'T COME IN!!
HELP MEEEE!

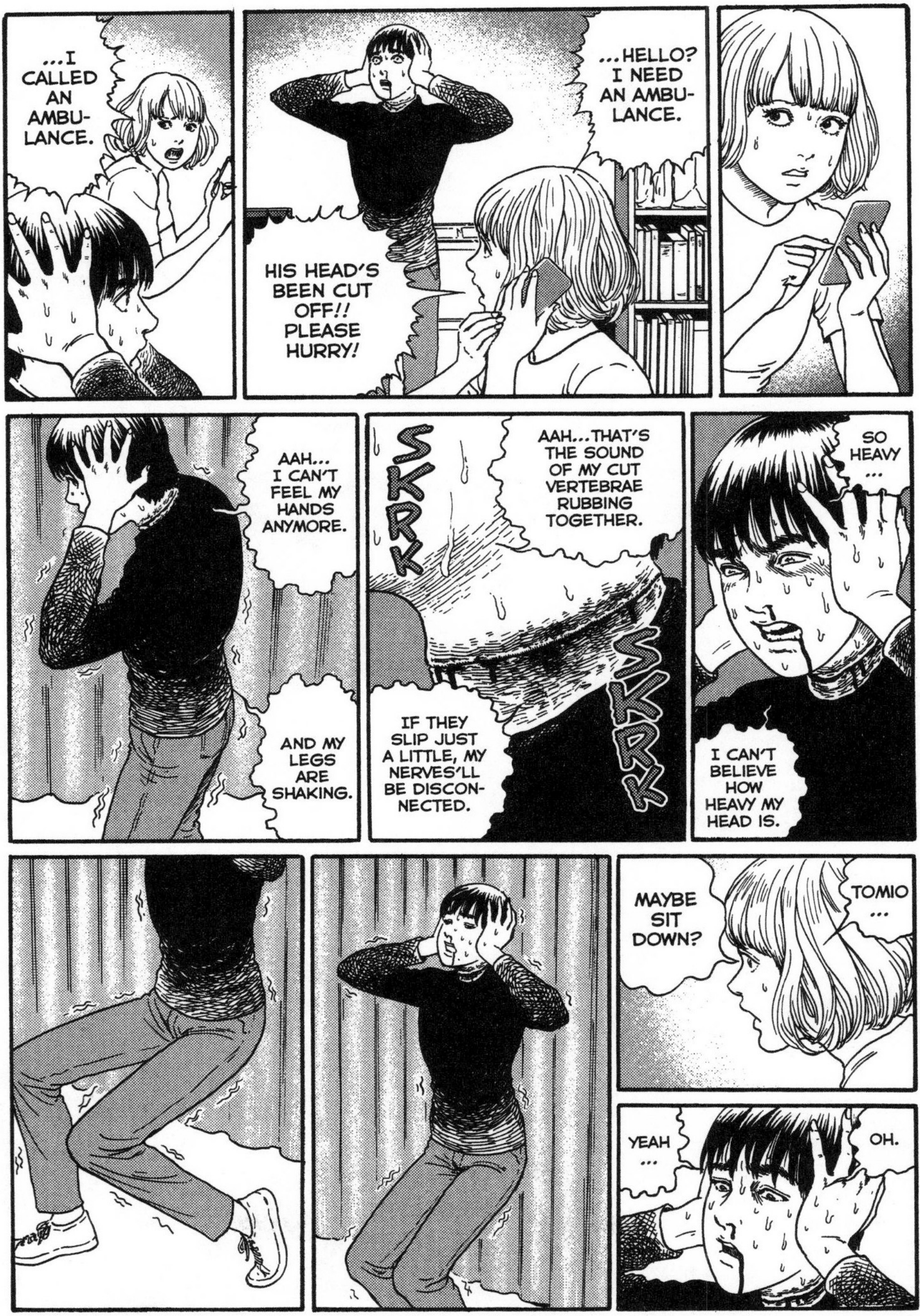
...HELLO? I NEED AN AMBU-LANCE.
HIS HEAD'S BEEN CUT OFF!! PLEASE HURRY!
...I CALLED AN AMBU-LANCE.
SO HEAVY ...
I CAN'T BELIEVE HOW HEAVY MY HEAD IS.
AAH...THAT'S THE SOUND OF MY CUT VERTEBRAE RUBBING TOGETHER.
SKRK
SKRK
IF THEY SLIP JUST A LITTLE, MY NERVES'LL BE DISCON-NECTED.
AAH... I CAN'T FEEL MY HANDS ANYMORE.
AND MY LEGS ARE SHAKING.
TOMIO ...
MAYBE SIT DOWN?
OH.
YEAH ...

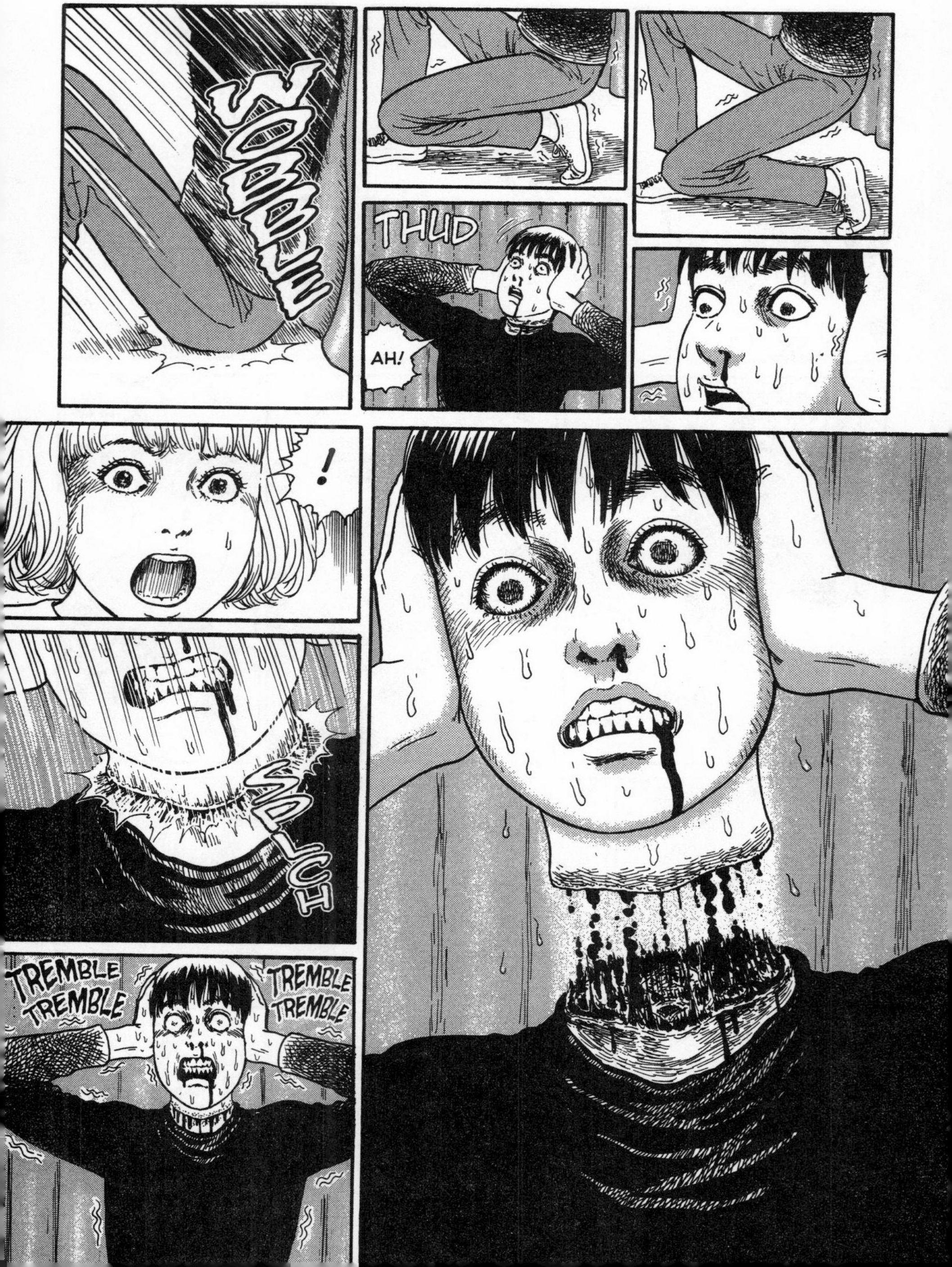
THUD
AH!
WOBBLE
!
SPLCH
TREMBLE TREMBLE
TREMBLE TREMBLE

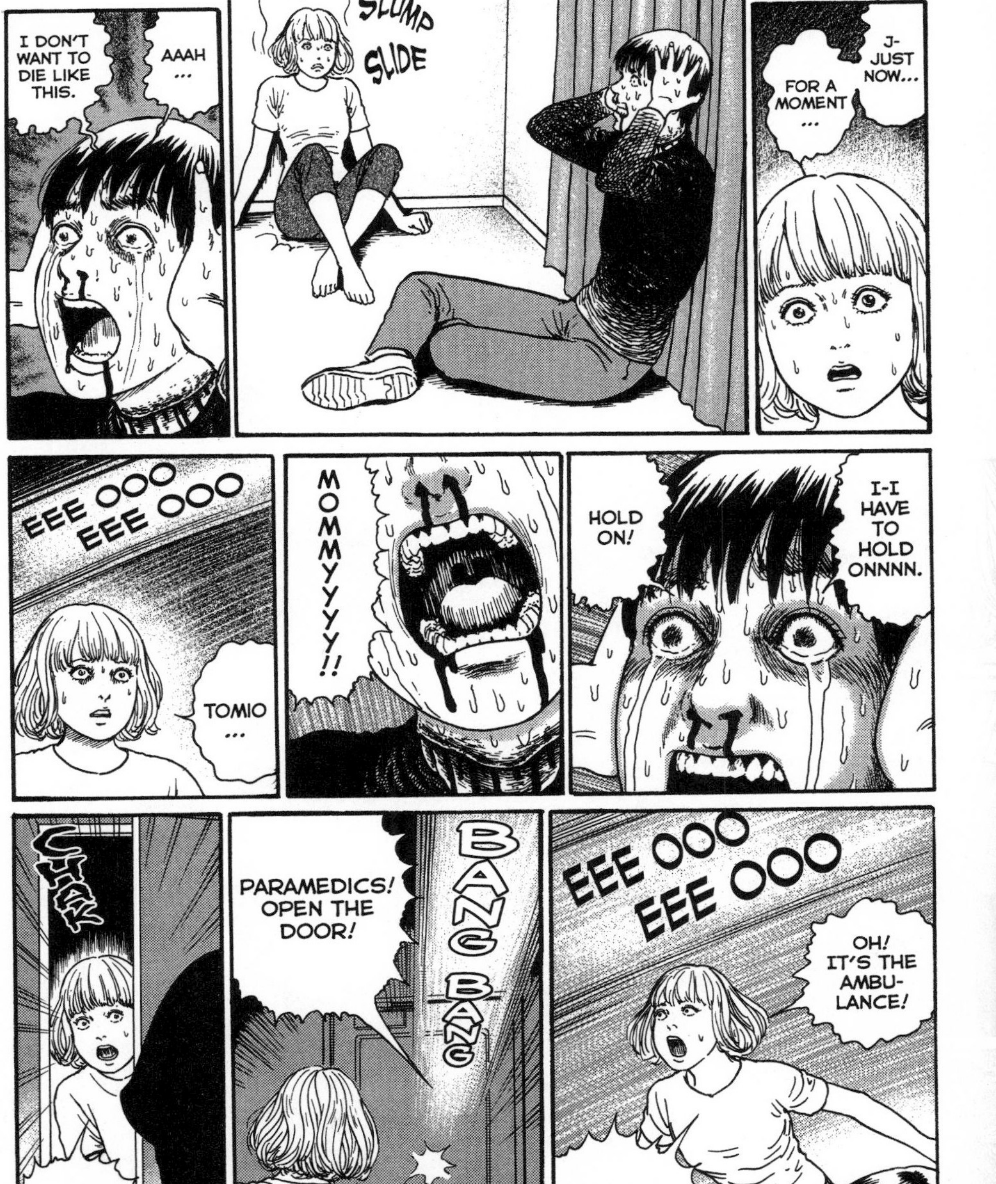
J-JUST NOW...
FOR A MOMENT...
SLUMP
SLIDE
AAAH...
I DON'T WANT TO DIE LIKE THIS.
I-I HAVE TO HOLD ONNNN.
HOLD ON!
MOMMYYYYY!!
EEE OOO EEE OOO
TOMIO...
EEE OOO EEE OOO
OH! IT'S THE AMBU-LANCE!
TOMIO... HANG ON A LITTLE LONGER!
BANG
BANG
PARAMEDICS! OPEN THE DOOR!
CHAK
YES! COME—

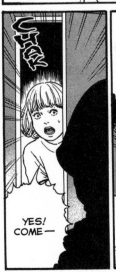

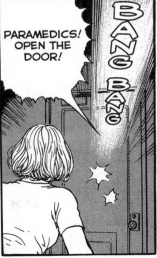

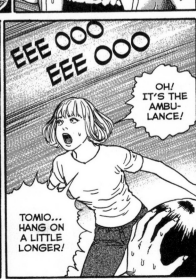

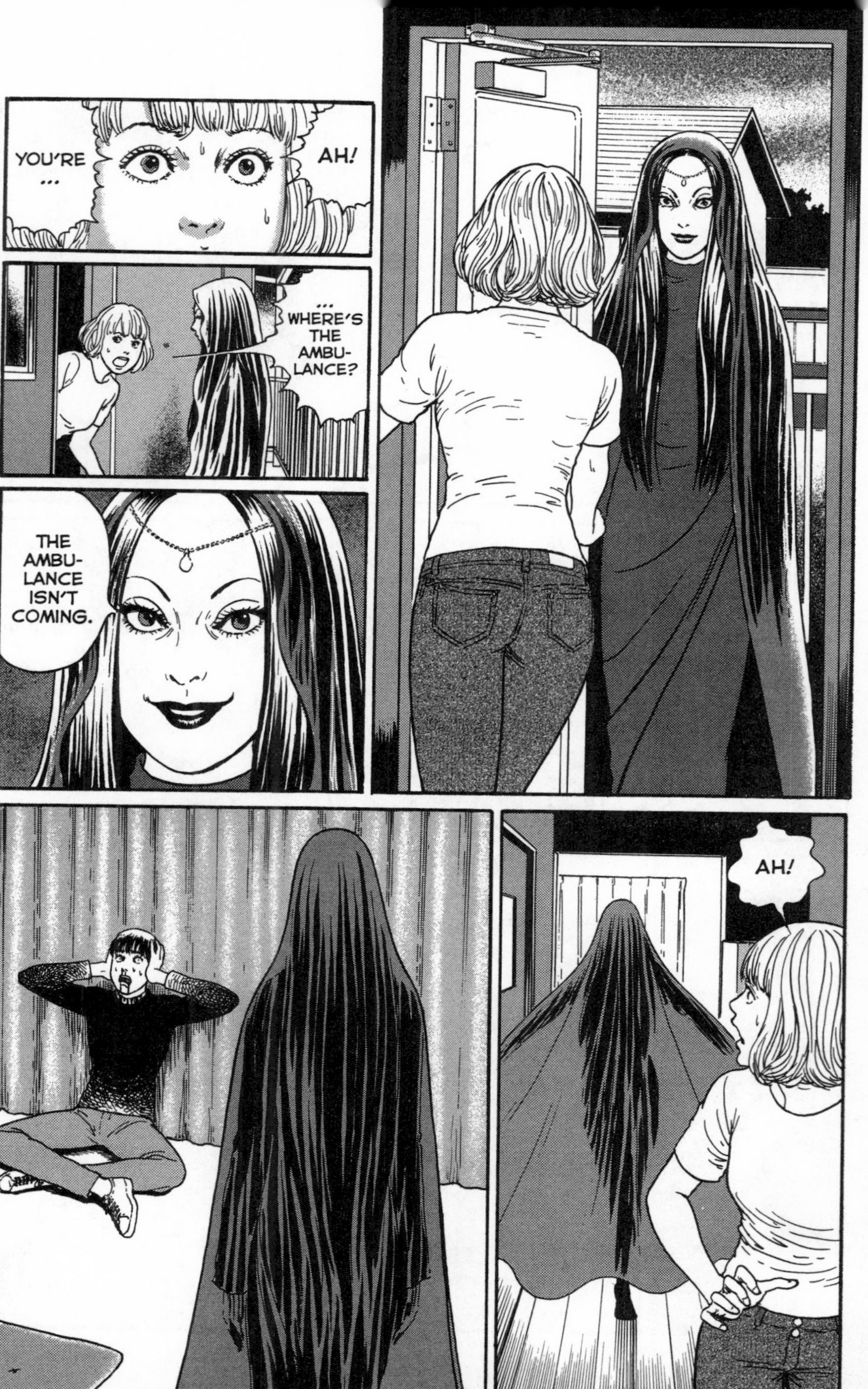
AH!
YOU'RE ...
... WHERE'S THE AMBU-LANCE?
THE AMBU-LANCE ISN'T COMING.
AH!

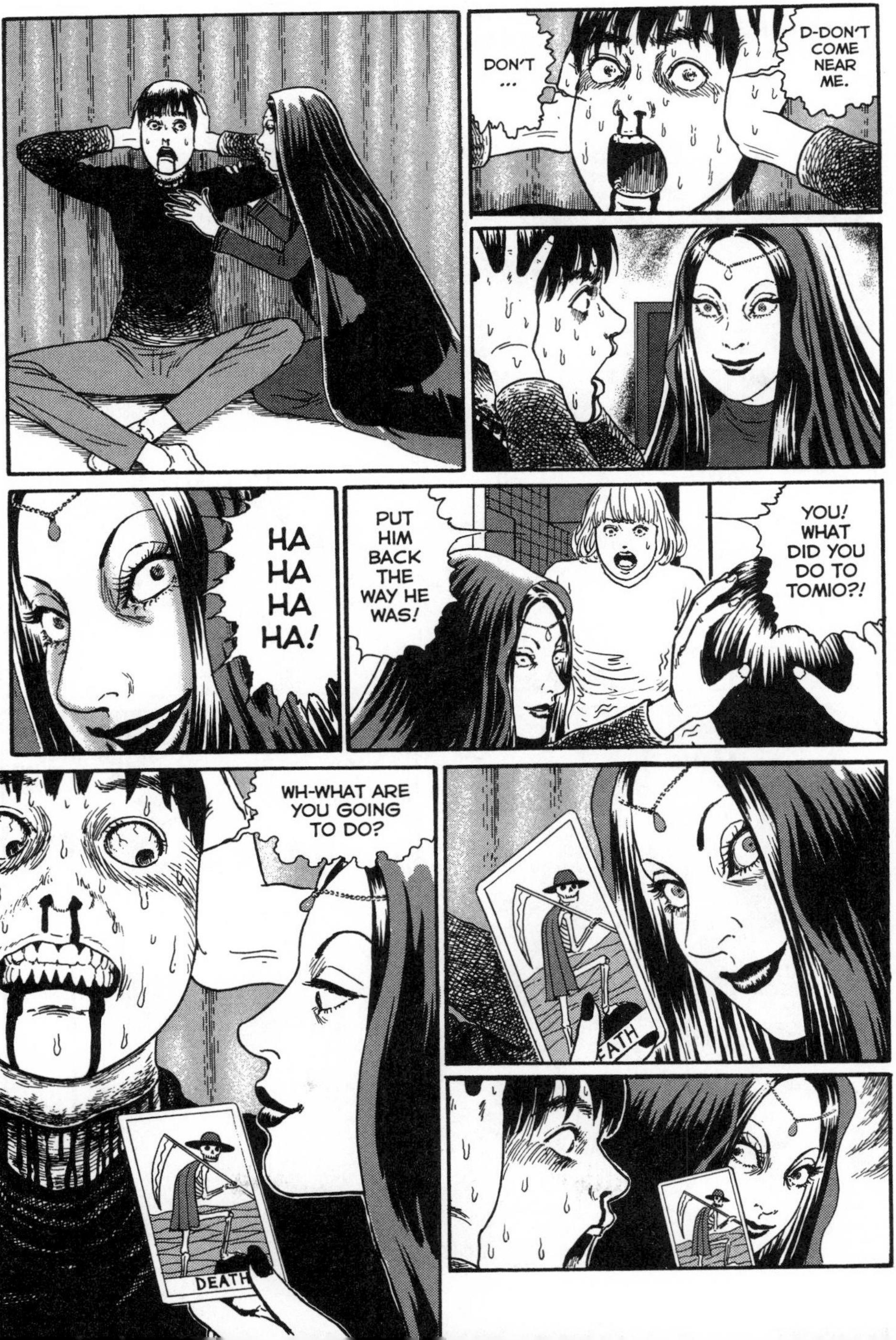
D-DON'T COME NEAR ME.
DON'T ...
YOU! WHAT DID YOU DO TO TOMIO?!
PUT HIM BACK THE WAY HE WAS!
HA HA HA HA!
WH-WHAT ARE YOU GOING TO DO?
DEATH

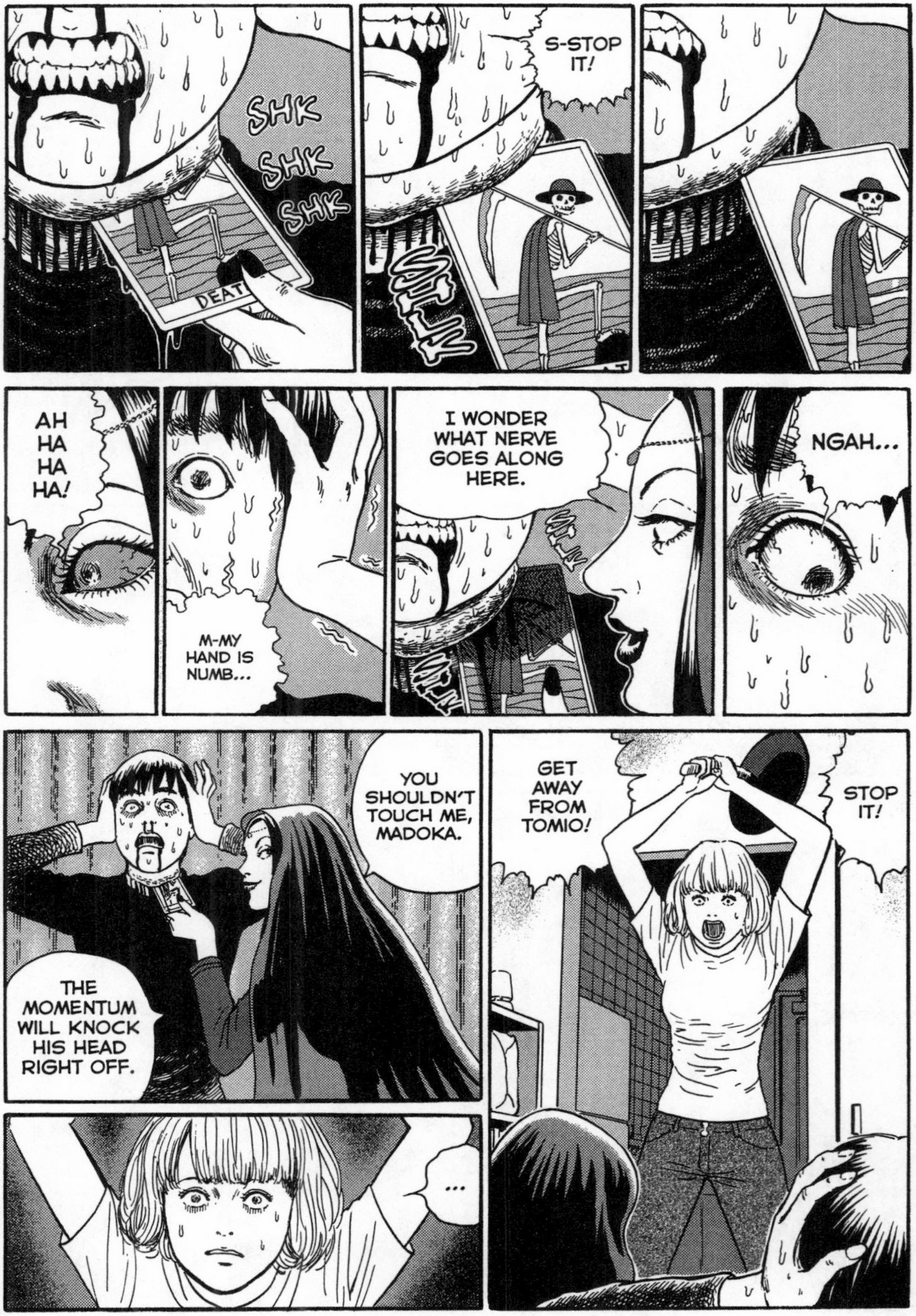
S-STOP IT!
SHK
SHK
SHK
DEAT
NGAH...
I WONDER WHAT NERVE GOES ALONG HERE.
M-MY HAND IS NUMB...
AH HA HA HA!
STOP IT!
GET AWAY FROM TOMIO!
YOU SHOULDN'T TOUCH ME, MADOKA.
THE MOMENTUM WILL KNOCK HIS HEAD RIGHT OFF.
...

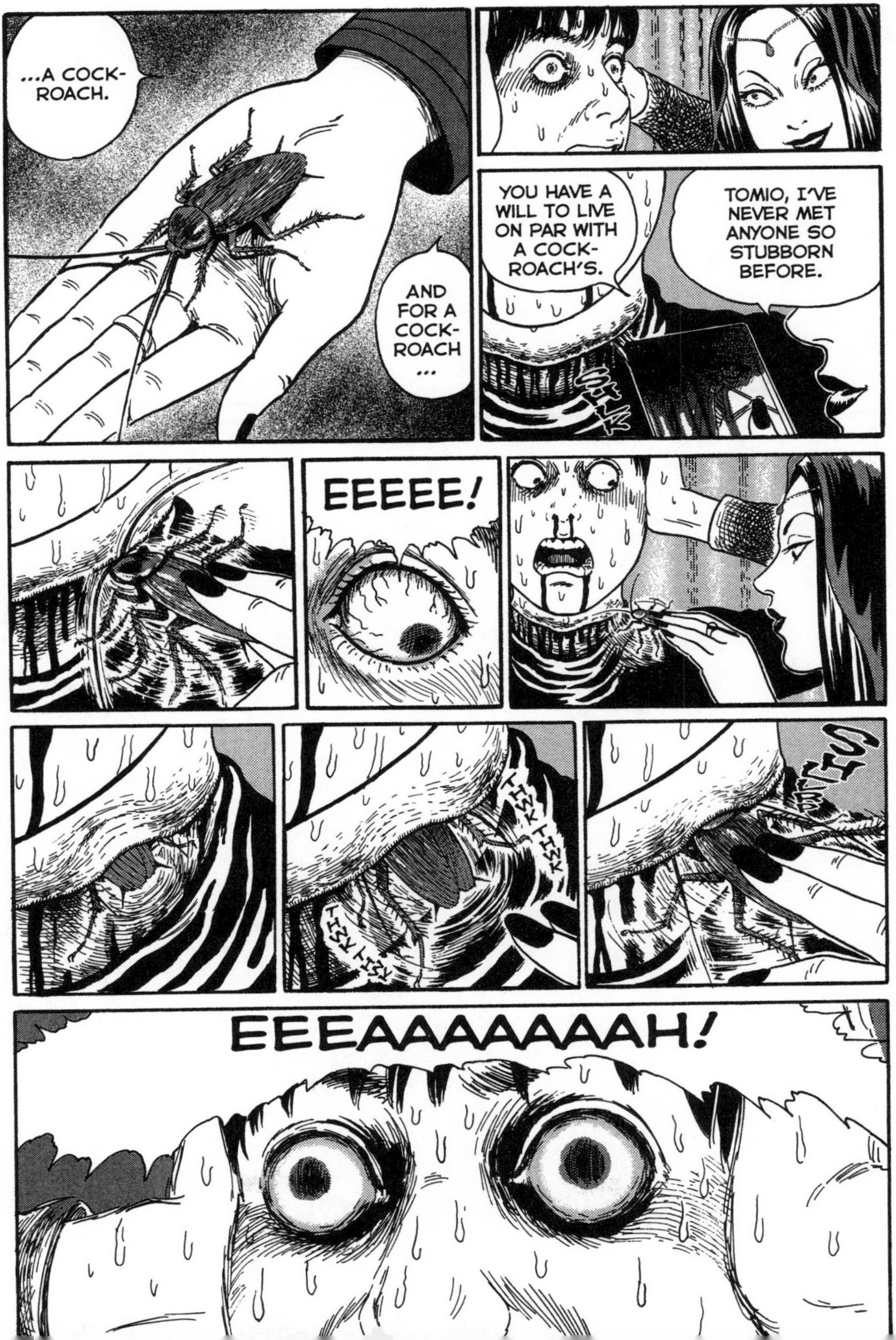
TOMIO, I'VE NEVER MET ANYONE SO STUBBORN BEFORE.
YOU HAVE A WILL TO LIVE ON PAR WITH A COCK-ROACH'S.
AND FOR A COCK-ROACH ...
...A COCK-ROACH.
EEEEE!
TISK TISK
TISK TISK
EEEAAAAAAAH!

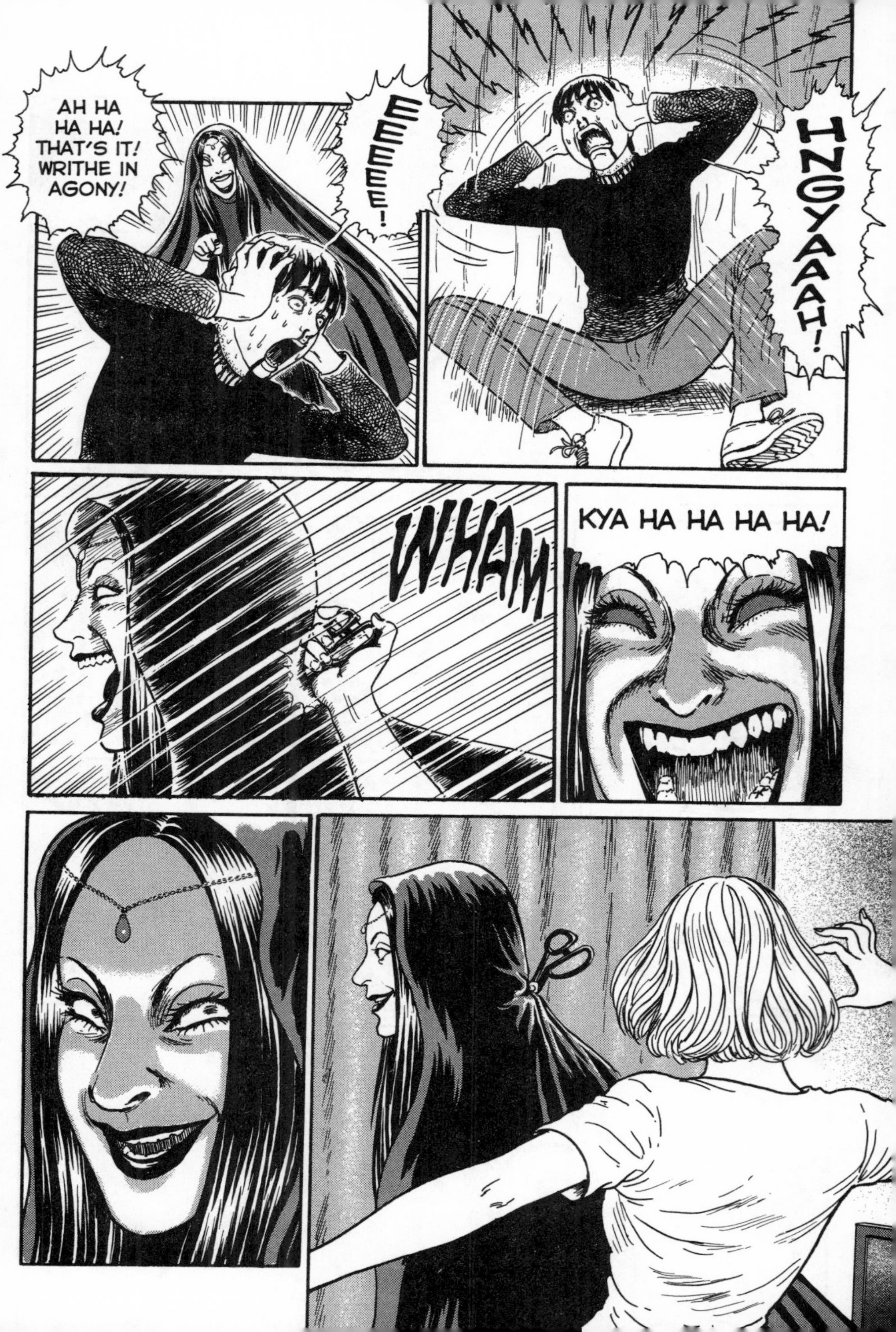
HNGYAAAH!
EEEEE!
AH HA HA HA! THAT'S IT! WRITHE IN AGONY!
KYA HA HA HA HA!
WHAM

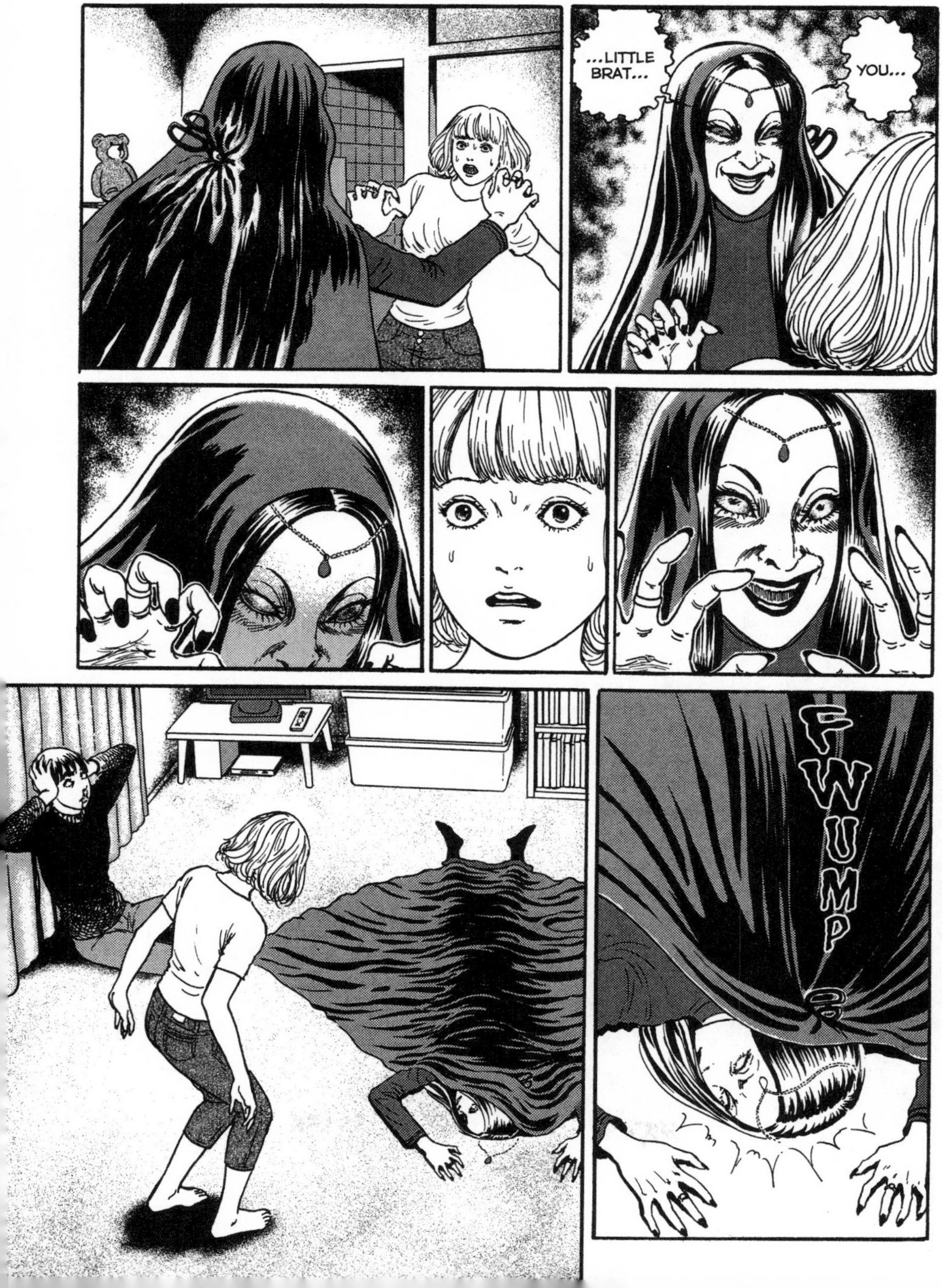
YOU...
...LITTLE BRAT...
FWUMP

IT'S OKAY... ...I SWALLOWED IT ALREADY...

TOMIO, WE HAVE TO HURRY AND GET THE COCKROACH OUT...

...IT'D BE GREAT IF THAT BROKE THE CURSE...

I-I KILLED HER...

Y-YOU DID.

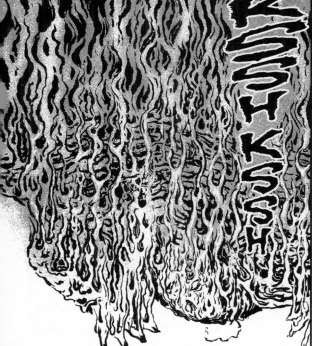

KSSH KSSH

KSSH KSSH

...

KSSH KSSH

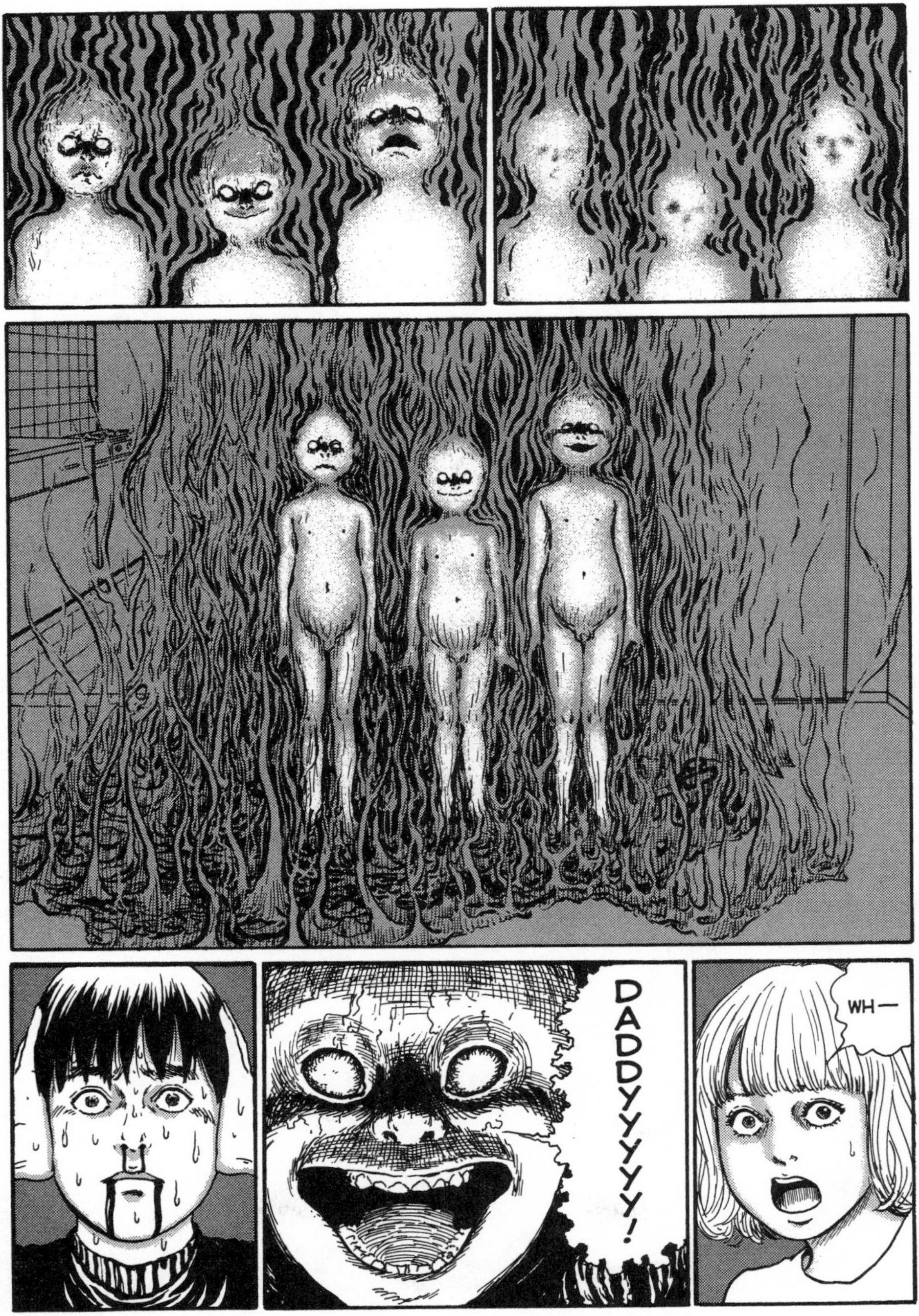
WH—
DADDYYYYYY!

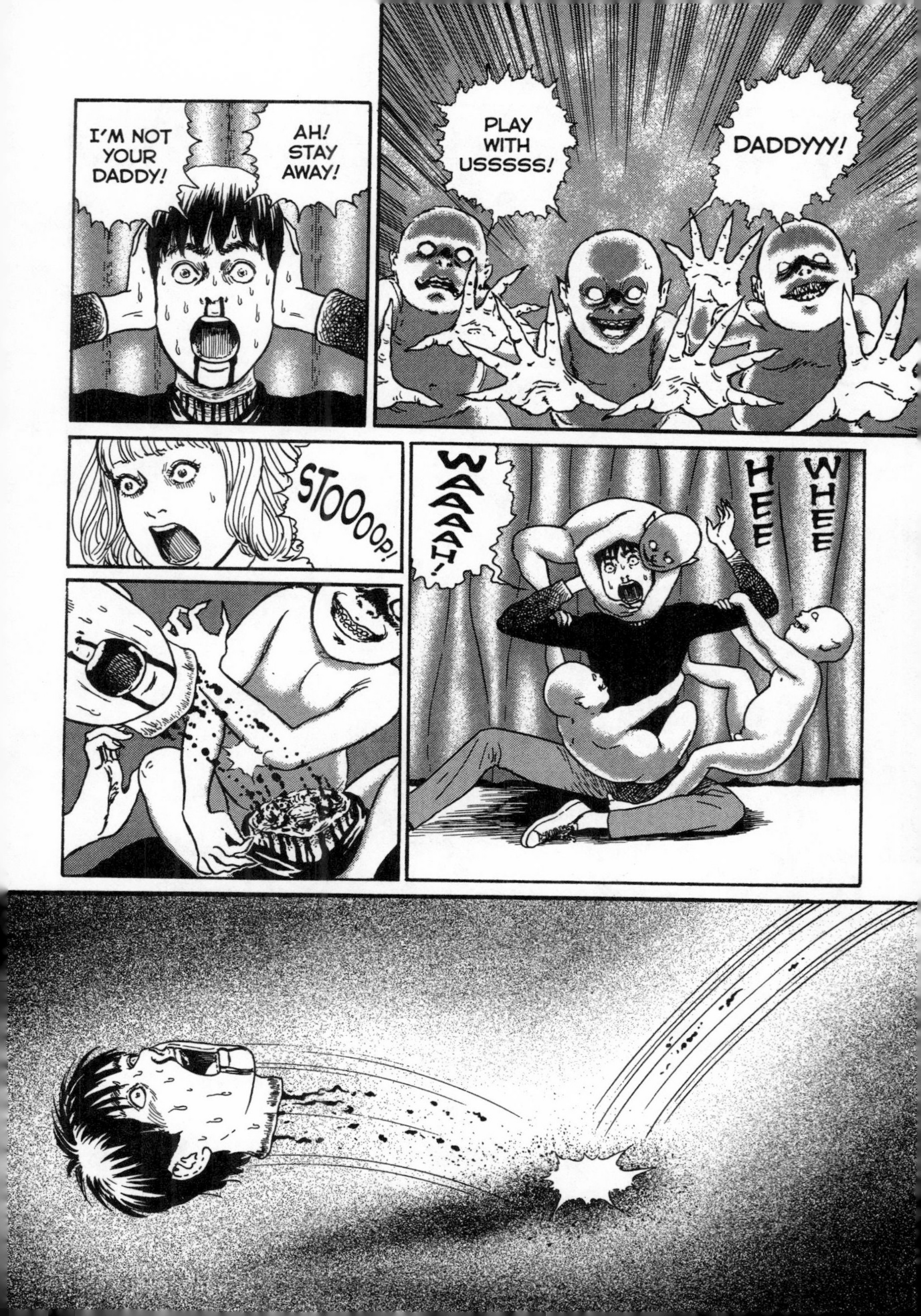
DADDYYY!
PLAY WITH USSSSS!
AH! STAY AWAY!
I'M NOT YOUR DADDY!
WHEE
HEE
WAAAAH!
STOOOOOP!

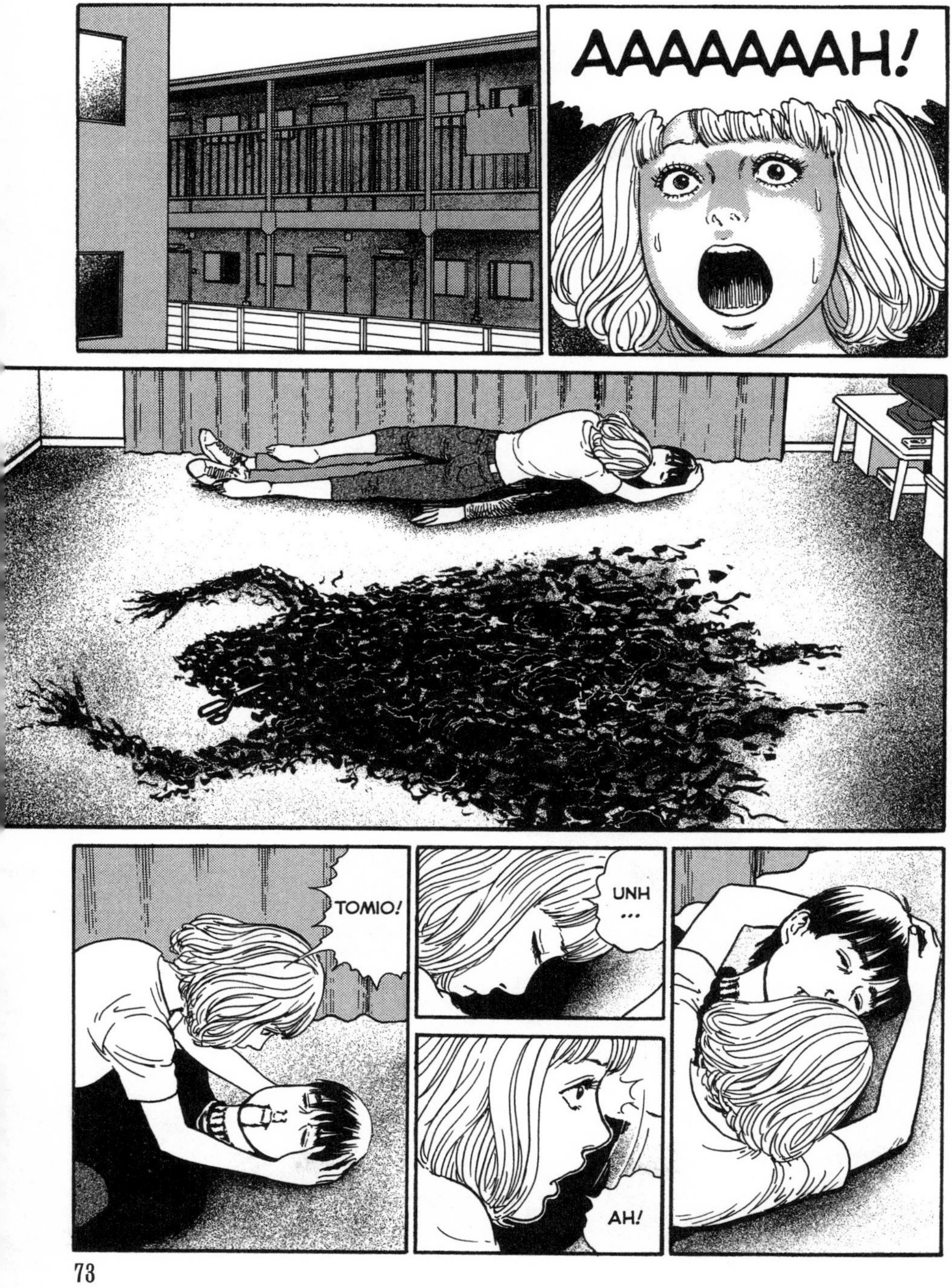
AAAAAAAH!
UNH ...
AH!
TOMIO!

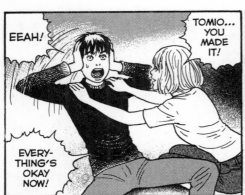

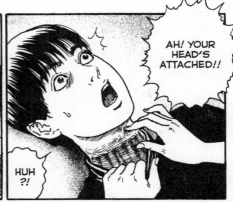

AH! YOUR HEAD'S ATTACHED!!
HUH ?!
TOMIO... YOU MADE IT!
EEAH!
EVERY-THING'S OKAY NOW!
MAYBE THE CHILDREN WERE JUST A HALLUCI-NATION ...
BUT THE WITCH DEFINITELY EXISTED AND REALLY DID CUT YOUR HEAD OFF...
AND YOU JUST KEPT DESPERATELY HOLDING ONTO IT, HUH, TOMIO...
REGARDLESS OF THE FACT THAT TOMIO'S HEAD IS ATTACHED...
...THE MEMORY OF THE TERROR KEEPS HIS HANDS IN PLACE EVEN NOW.

TOMIO • RED TURTLENECK/END

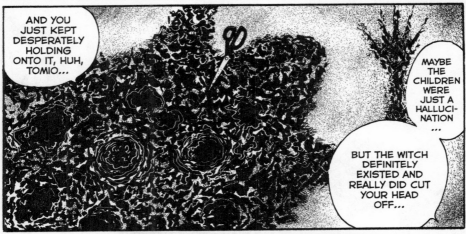

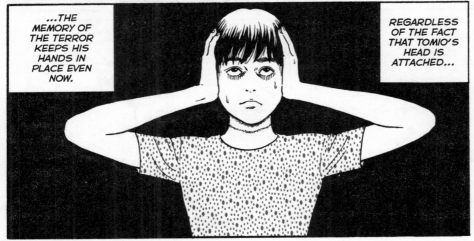

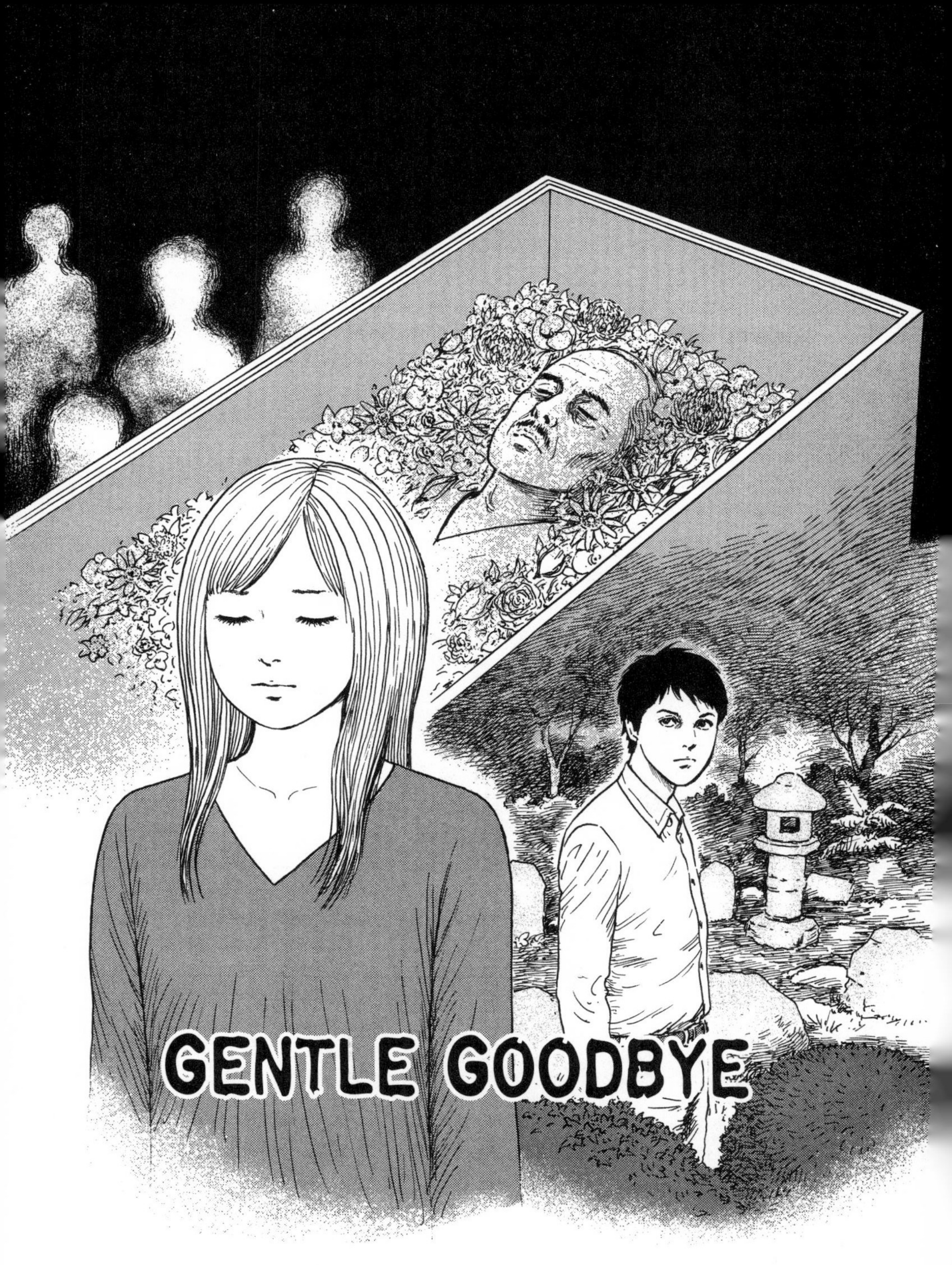
GENTLE GOODBYE

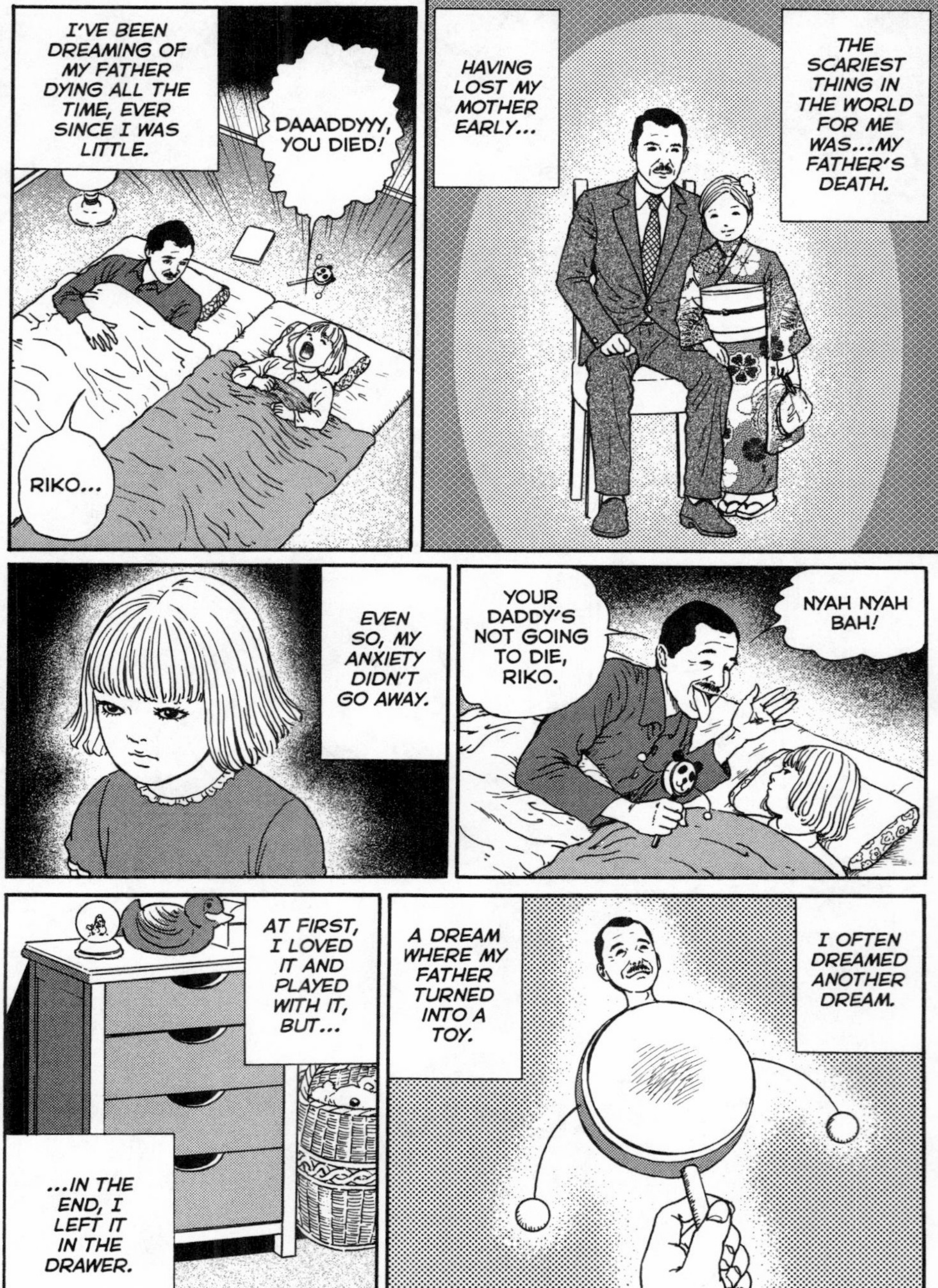
THE SCARIEST THING IN THE WORLD FOR ME WAS...MY FATHER'S DEATH.
HAVING LOST MY MOTHER EARLY...
I'VE BEEN DREAMING OF MY FATHER DYING ALL THE TIME, EVER SINCE I WAS LITTLE.
DAAADDYYY, YOU DIED!
RIKO...
YOUR DADDY'S NOT GOING TO DIE, RIKO.
NYAH NYAH BAH!
EVEN SO, MY ANXIETY DIDN'T GO AWAY.
I OFTEN DREAMED ANOTHER DREAM.
A DREAM WHERE MY FATHER TURNED INTO A TOY.
AT FIRST, I LOVED IT AND PLAYED WITH IT, BUT...
...IN THE END, I LEFT IT IN THE DRAWER.

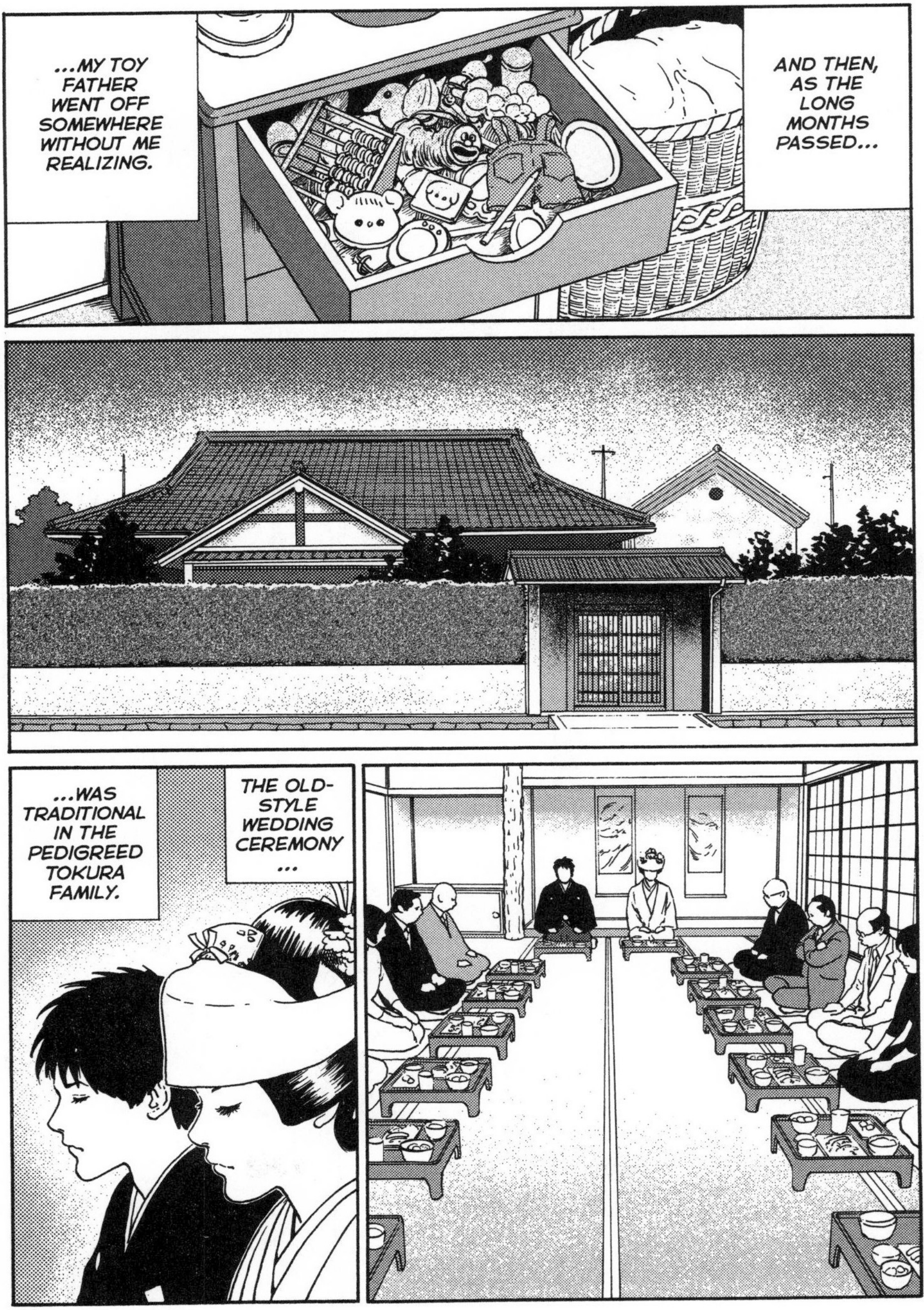
AND THEN, AS THE LONG MONTHS PASSED...
...MY TOY FATHER WENT OFF SOMEWHERE WITHOUT ME REALIZING.
THE OLD-STYLE WEDDING CEREMONY...
...WAS TRADITIONAL IN THE PEDIGREED TOKURA FAMILY.

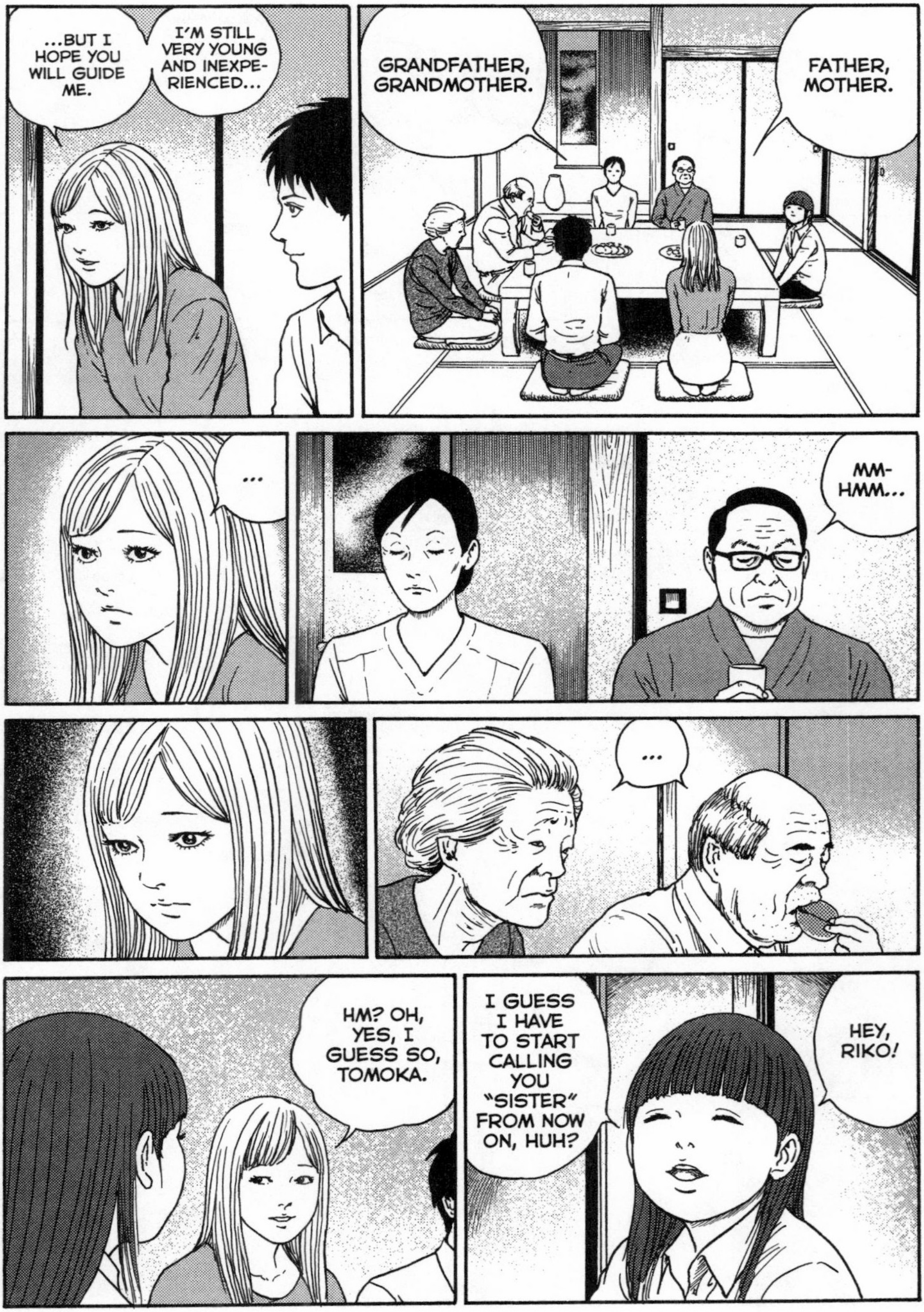
FATHER, MOTHER.
GRANDFATHER, GRANDMOTHER.
I'M STILL VERY YOUNG AND INEXPE-RIENCED...
...BUT I HOPE YOU WILL GUIDE ME.
MM-HMM...
...
...
HEY, RIKO!
I GUESS I HAVE TO START CALLING YOU "SISTER" FROM NOW ON, HUH?
HM? OH, YES, I GUESS SO, TOMOKA.

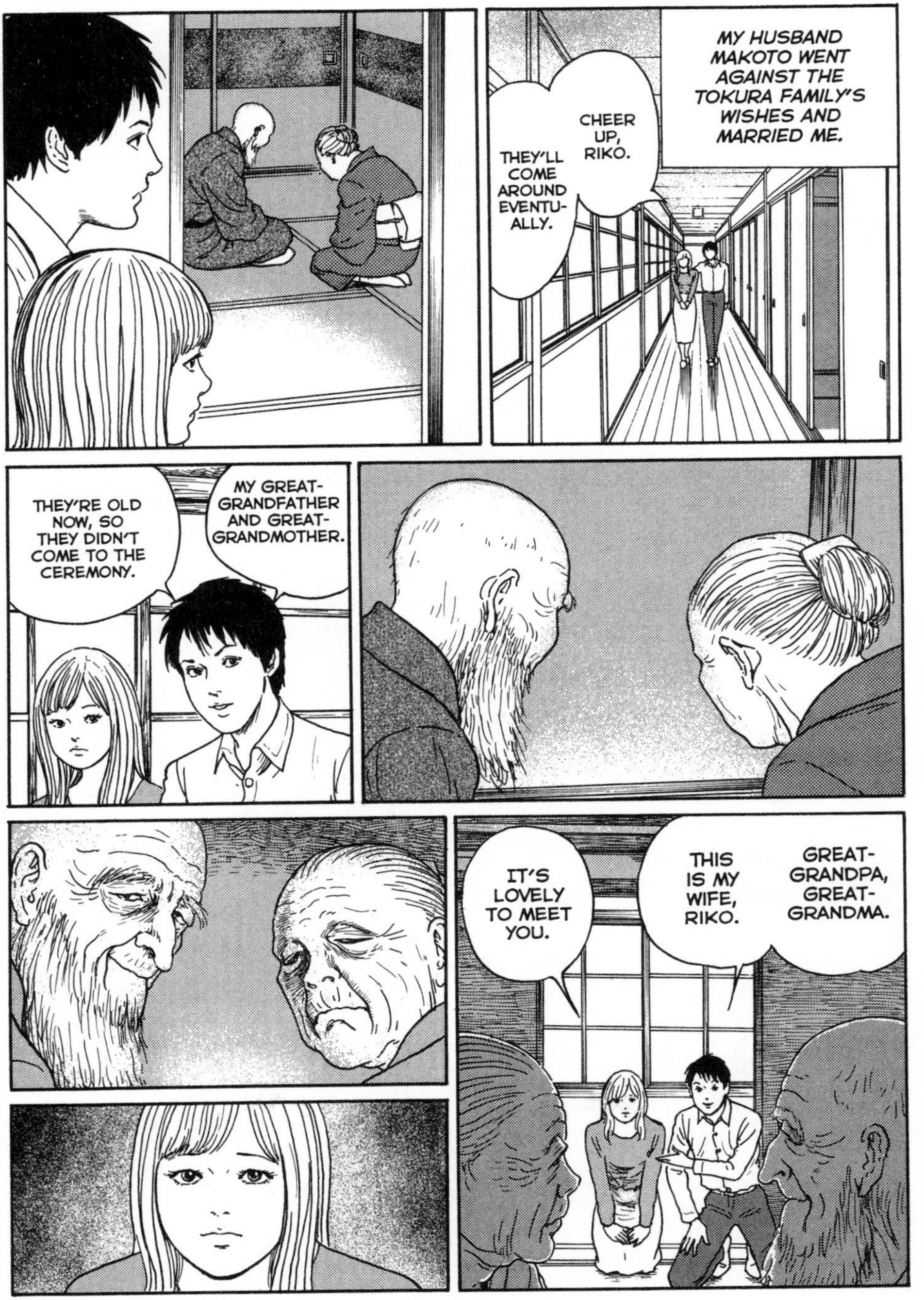
MY HUSBAND MAKOTO WENT AGAINST THE TOKURA FAMILY'S WISHES AND MARRIED ME.
CHEER UP, RIKO.
THEY'LL COME AROUND EVENTU-ALLY.
MY GREAT-GRANDFATHER AND GREAT-GRANDMOTHER.
THEY'RE OLD NOW, SO THEY DIDN'T COME TO THE CEREMONY.
GREAT-GRANDPA, GREAT-GRANDMA.
THIS IS MY WIFE, RIKO.
IT'S LOVELY TO MEET YOU.

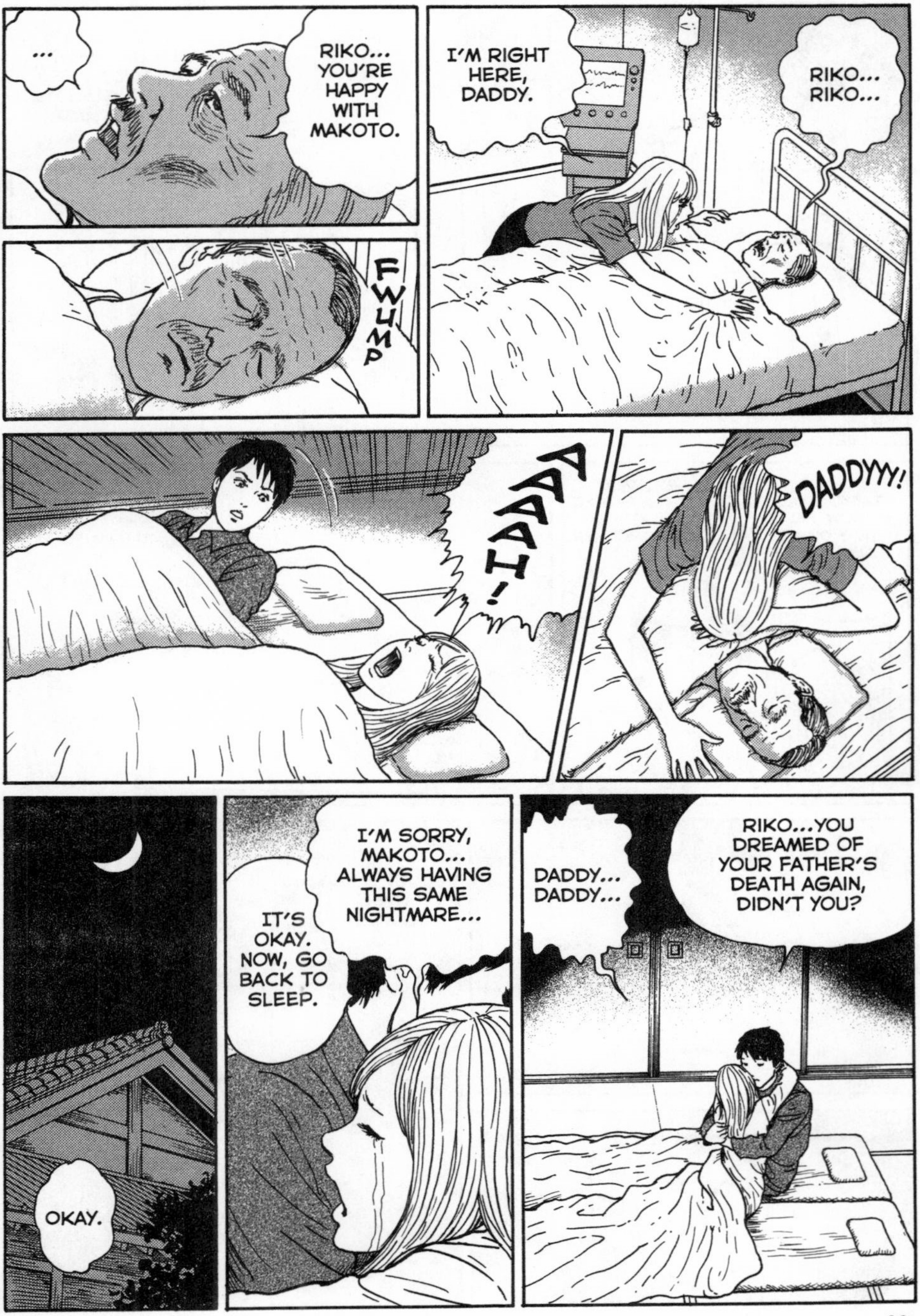
RIKO... RIKO...
I'M RIGHT HERE, DADDY.
RIKO... YOU'RE HAPPY WITH MAKOTO.
...
FWUMP
DADDYYY!
AAAAH!
RIKO...YOU DREAMED OF YOUR FATHER'S DEATH AGAIN, DIDN'T YOU?
DADDY... DADDY...
I'M SORRY, MAKOTO... ALWAYS HAVING THIS SAME NIGHTMARE...
IT'S OKAY. NOW, GO BACK TO SLEEP.
OKAY.

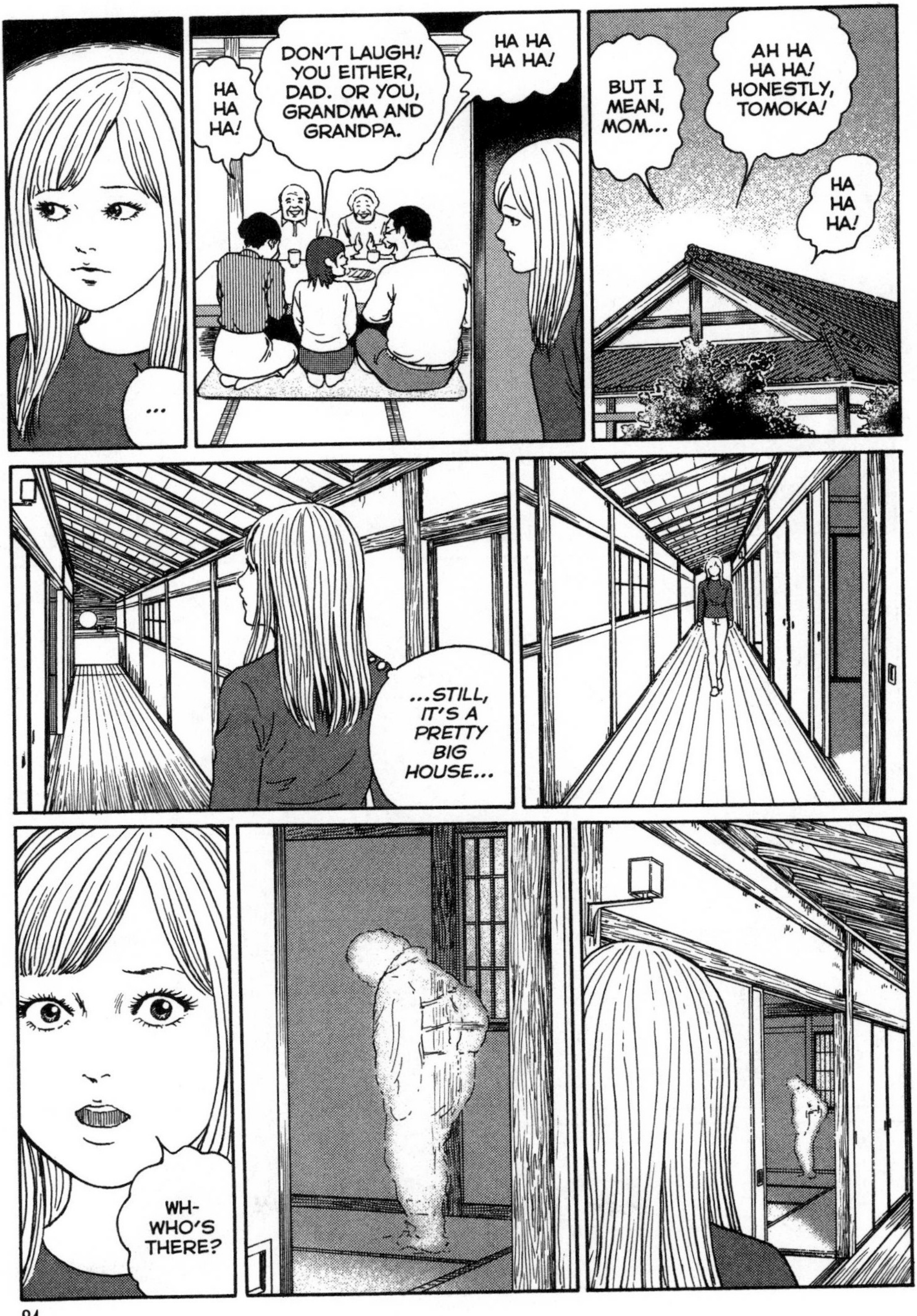
AH HA HA HA! HONESTLY, TOMOKA!
BUT I MEAN, MOM...
HA HA HA!
HA HA HA HA!
DON'T LAUGH! YOU EITHER, DAD. OR YOU, GRANDMA AND GRANDPA.
HA HA HA!
...
...STILL, IT'S A PRETTY BIG HOUSE...
WH- WHO'S THERE?

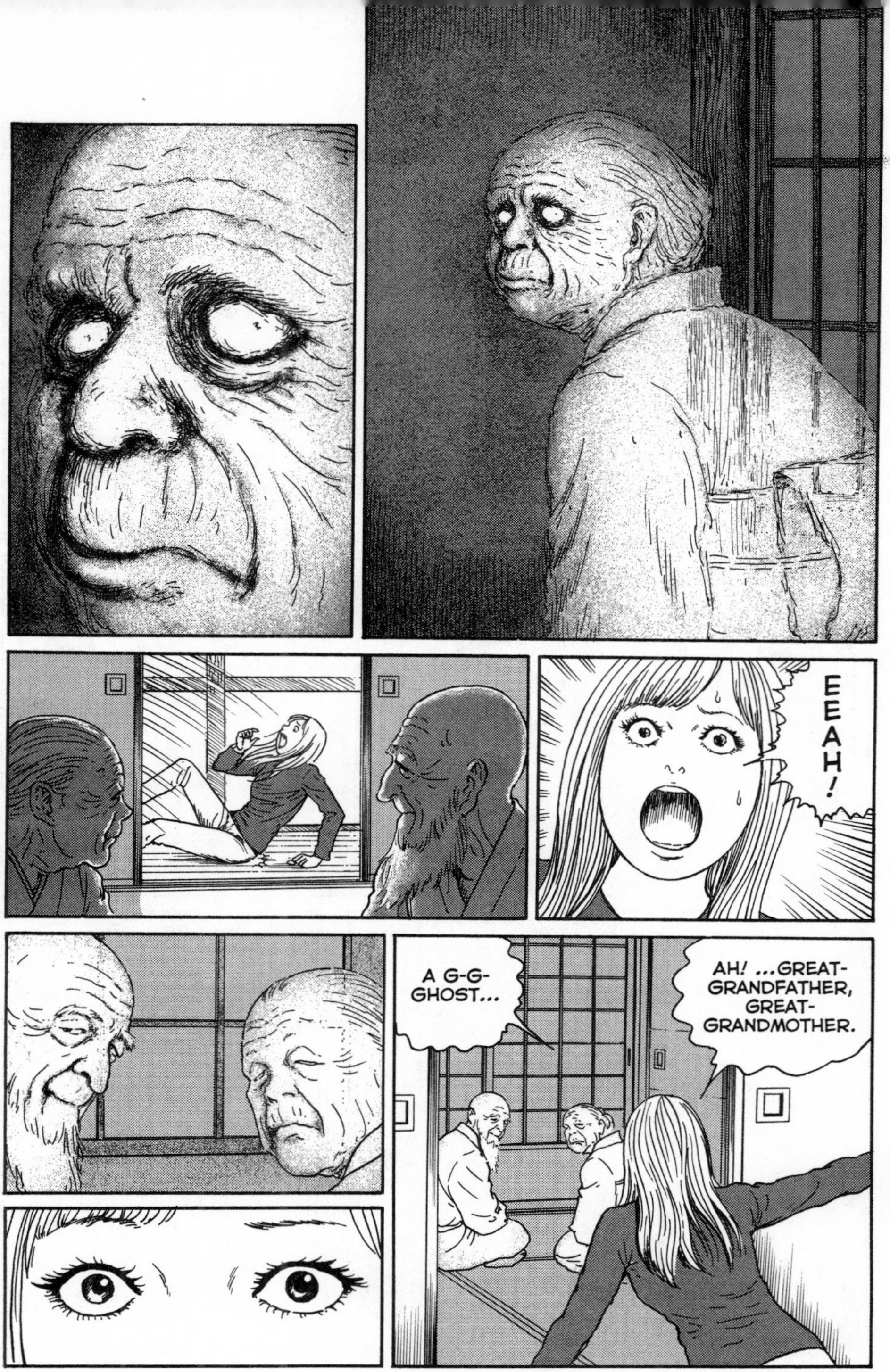
EEEAH!
AH! ...GREAT-GRANDFATHER, GREAT-GRANDMOTHER.
A G-G-GHOST...

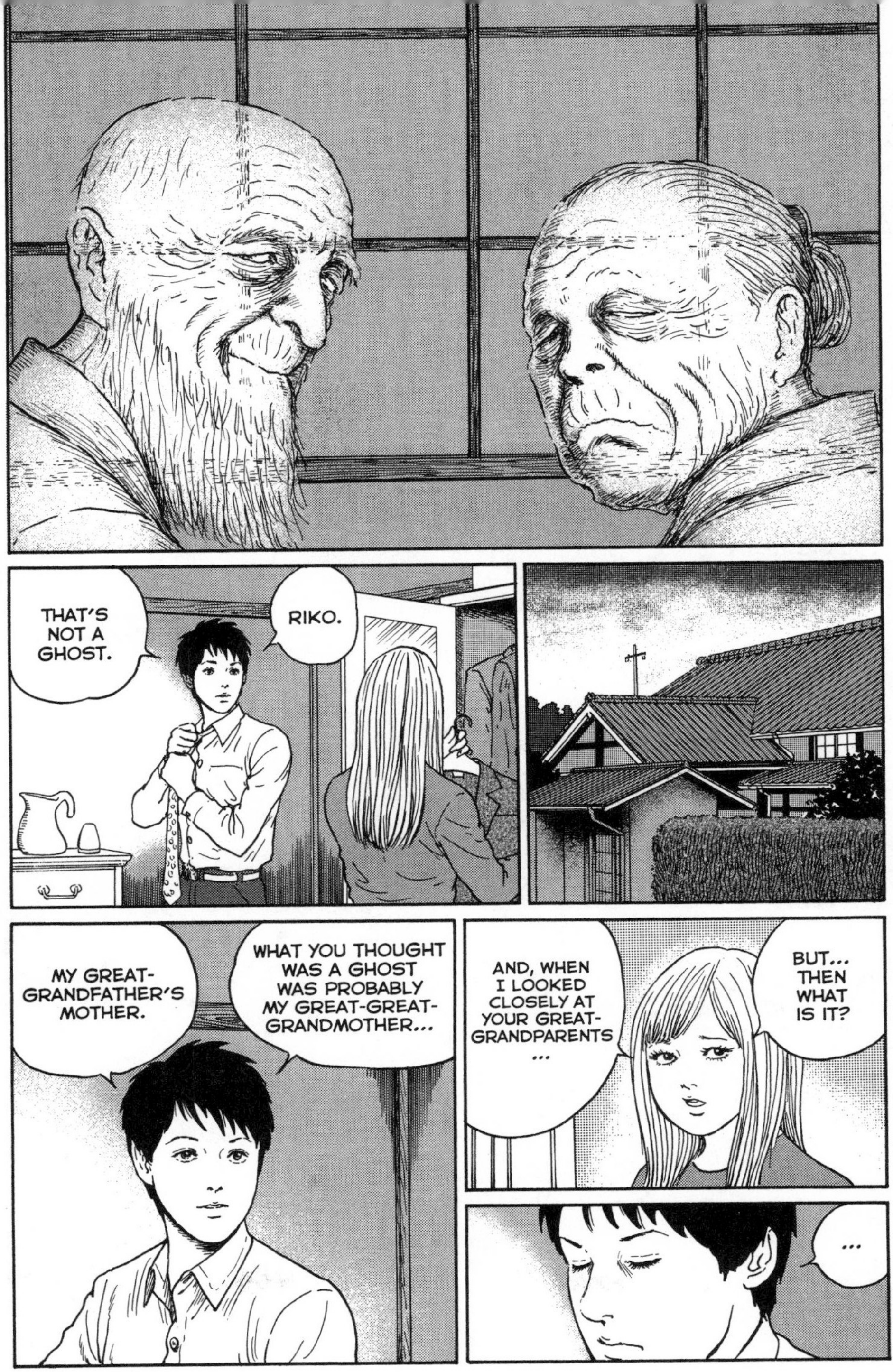
RIKO.
THAT'S NOT A GHOST.
BUT... THEN WHAT IS IT?
AND, WHEN I LOOKED CLOSELY AT YOUR GREAT-GRANDPARENTS ...
...
WHAT YOU THOUGHT WAS A GHOST WAS PROBABLY MY GREAT-GREAT-GRANDMOTHER...
MY GREAT-GRANDFATHER'S MOTHER.

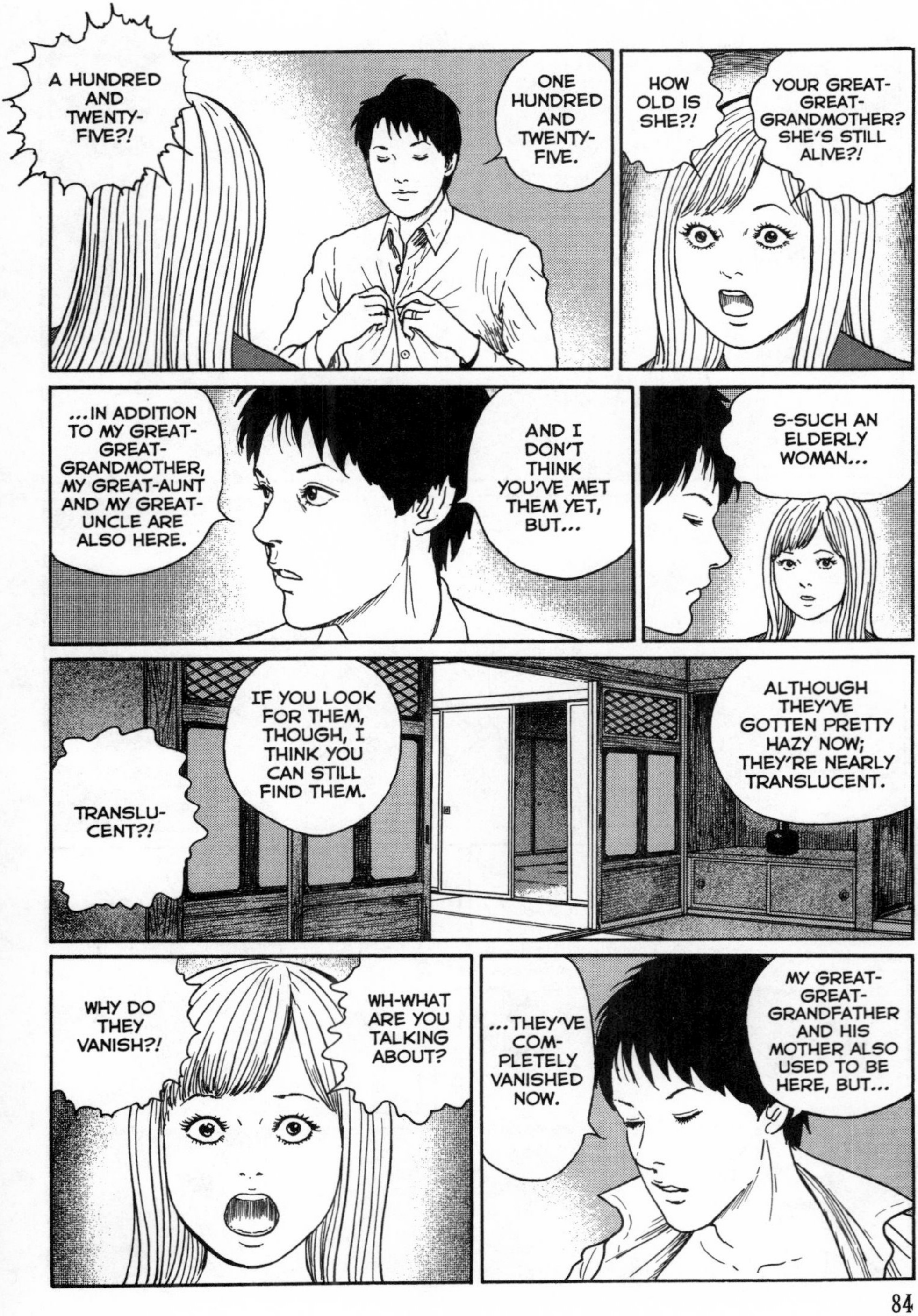
YOUR GREAT-GREAT-GRANDMOTHER? SHE'S STILL ALIVE?!
HOW OLD IS SHE?!
ONE HUNDRED AND TWENTY-FIVE.
A HUNDRED AND TWENTY-FIVE?!
S-SUCH AN ELDERLY WOMAN...
AND I DON'T THINK YOU'VE MET THEM YET, BUT...
...IN ADDITION TO MY GREAT-GREAT-GRANDMOTHER, MY GREAT-AUNT AND MY GREAT-UNCLE ARE ALSO HERE.
ALTHOUGH THEY'VE GOTTEN PRETTY HAZY NOW; THEY'RE NEARLY TRANSLUCENT.
IF YOU LOOK FOR THEM, THOUGH, I THINK YOU CAN STILL FIND THEM.
TRANSLU-CENT?!
MY GREAT-GREAT-GRANDFATHER AND HIS MOTHER ALSO USED TO BE HERE, BUT...
...THEY'VE COM-PLETELY VANISHED NOW.
WH-WHAT ARE YOU TALKING ABOUT?
WHY DO THEY VANISH?!

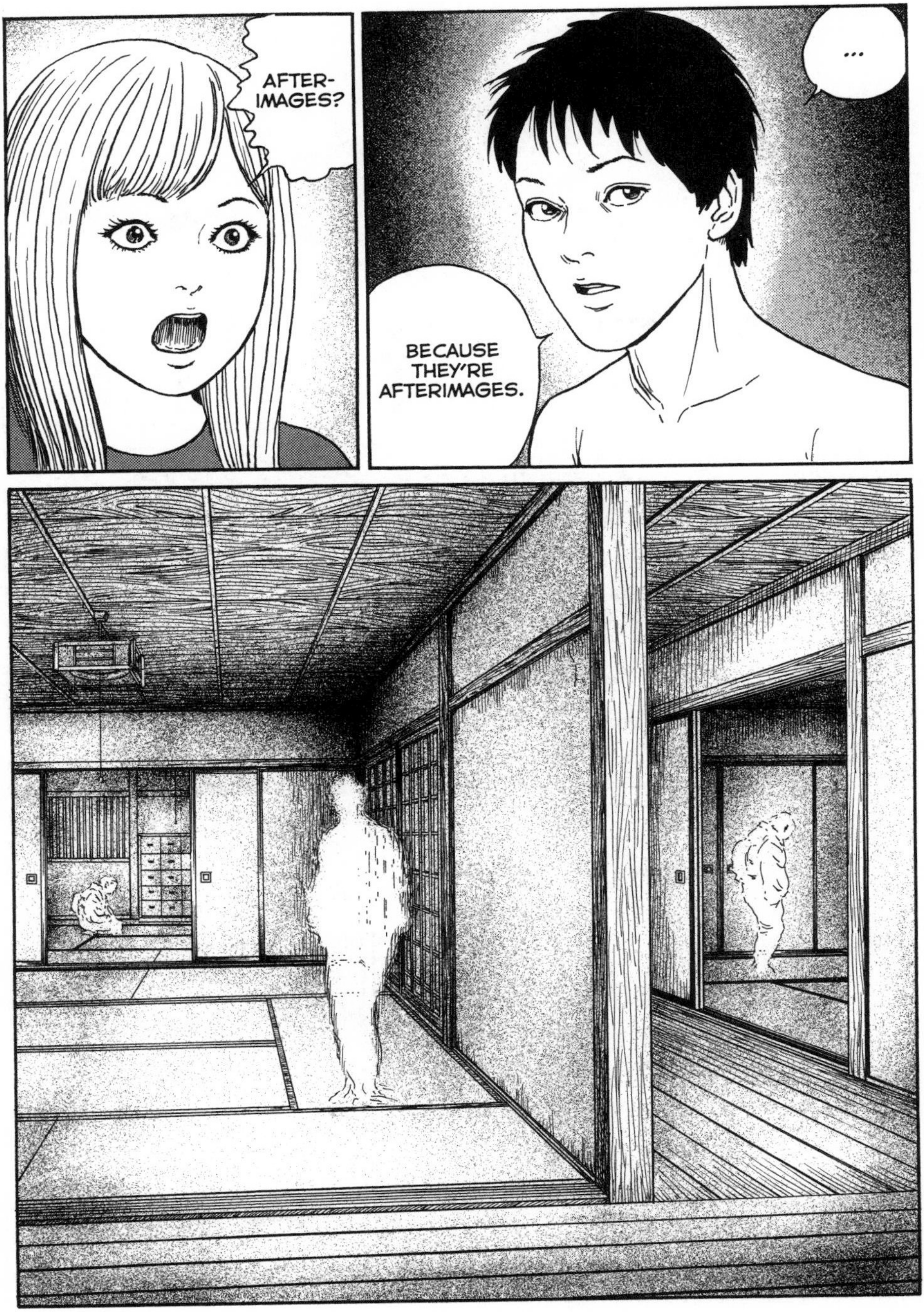
...
BECAUSE THEY'RE AFTERIMAGES.
AFTER-IMAGES?

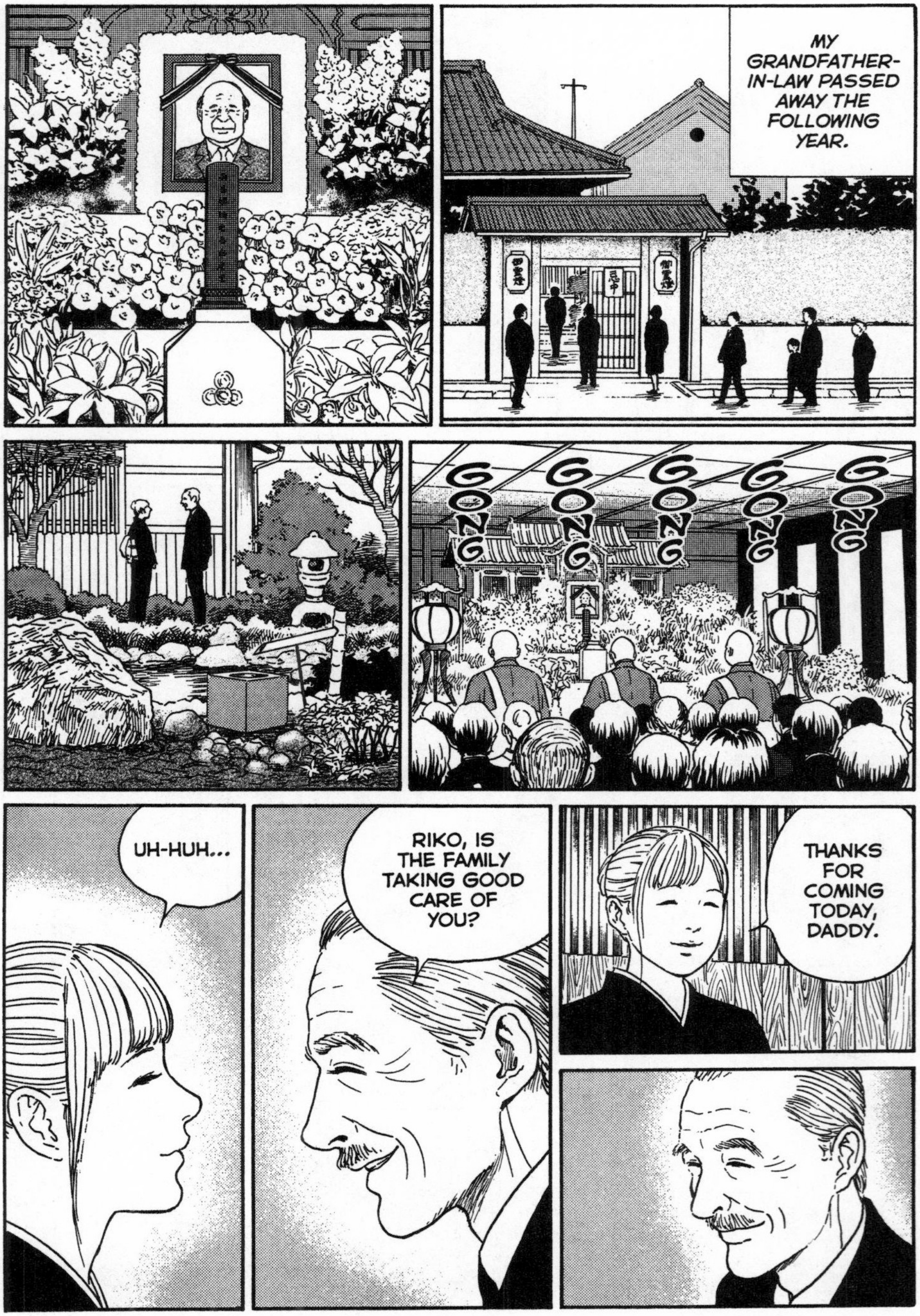
MY GRANDFATHER-IN-LAW PASSED AWAY THE FOLLOWING YEAR.
GONG
GONG
GONG
GONG
GONG
THANKS FOR COMING TODAY, DADDY.
RIKO, IS THE FAMILY TAKING GOOD CARE OF YOU?
UH-HUH...

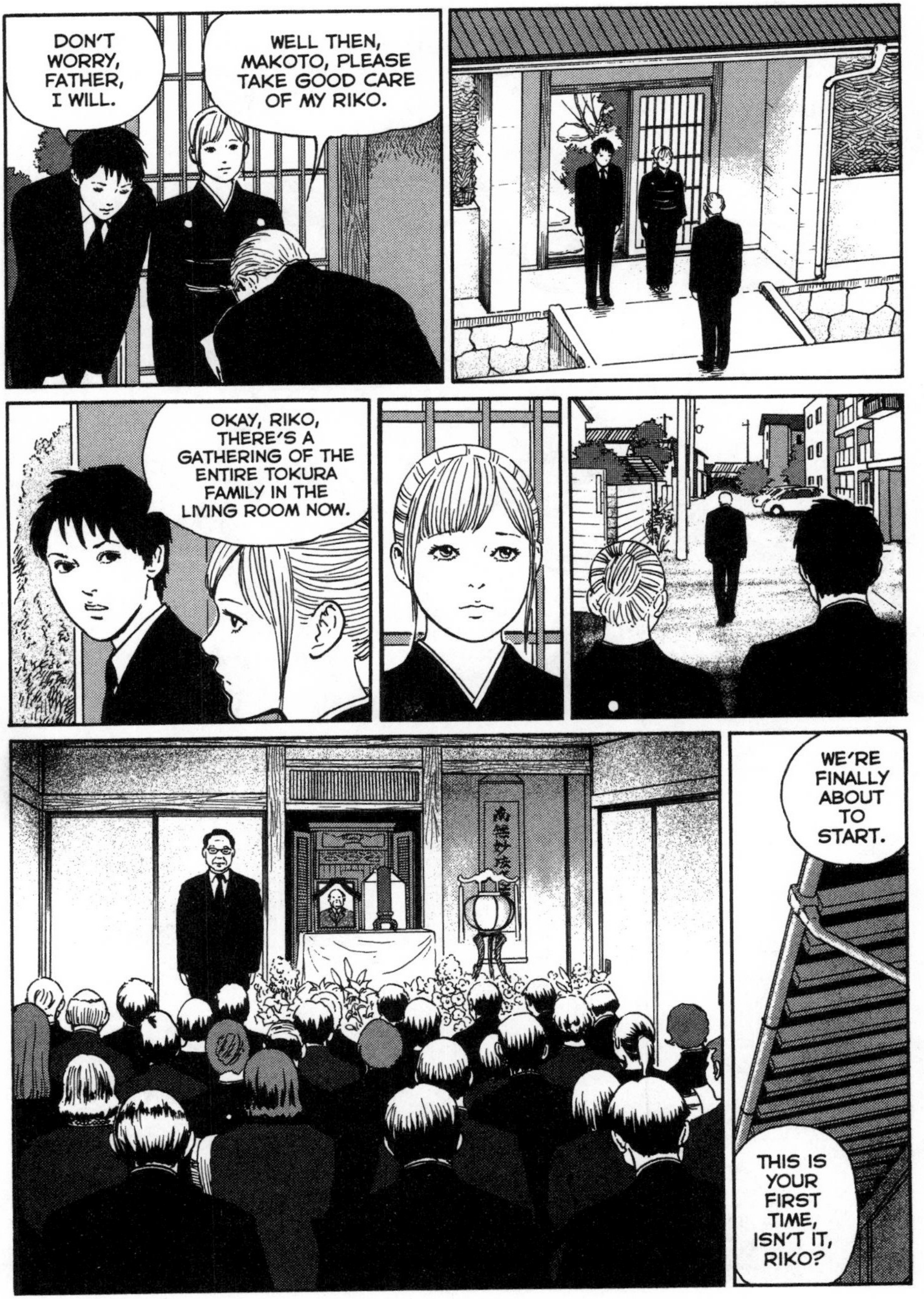
WELL THEN, MAKOTO, PLEASE TAKE GOOD CARE OF MY RIKO.
DON'T WORRY, FATHER, I WILL.
OKAY, RIKO, THERE'S A GATHERING OF THE ENTIRE TOKURA FAMILY IN THE LIVING ROOM NOW.
WE'RE FINALLY ABOUT TO START.
THIS IS YOUR FIRST TIME, ISN'T IT, RIKO?

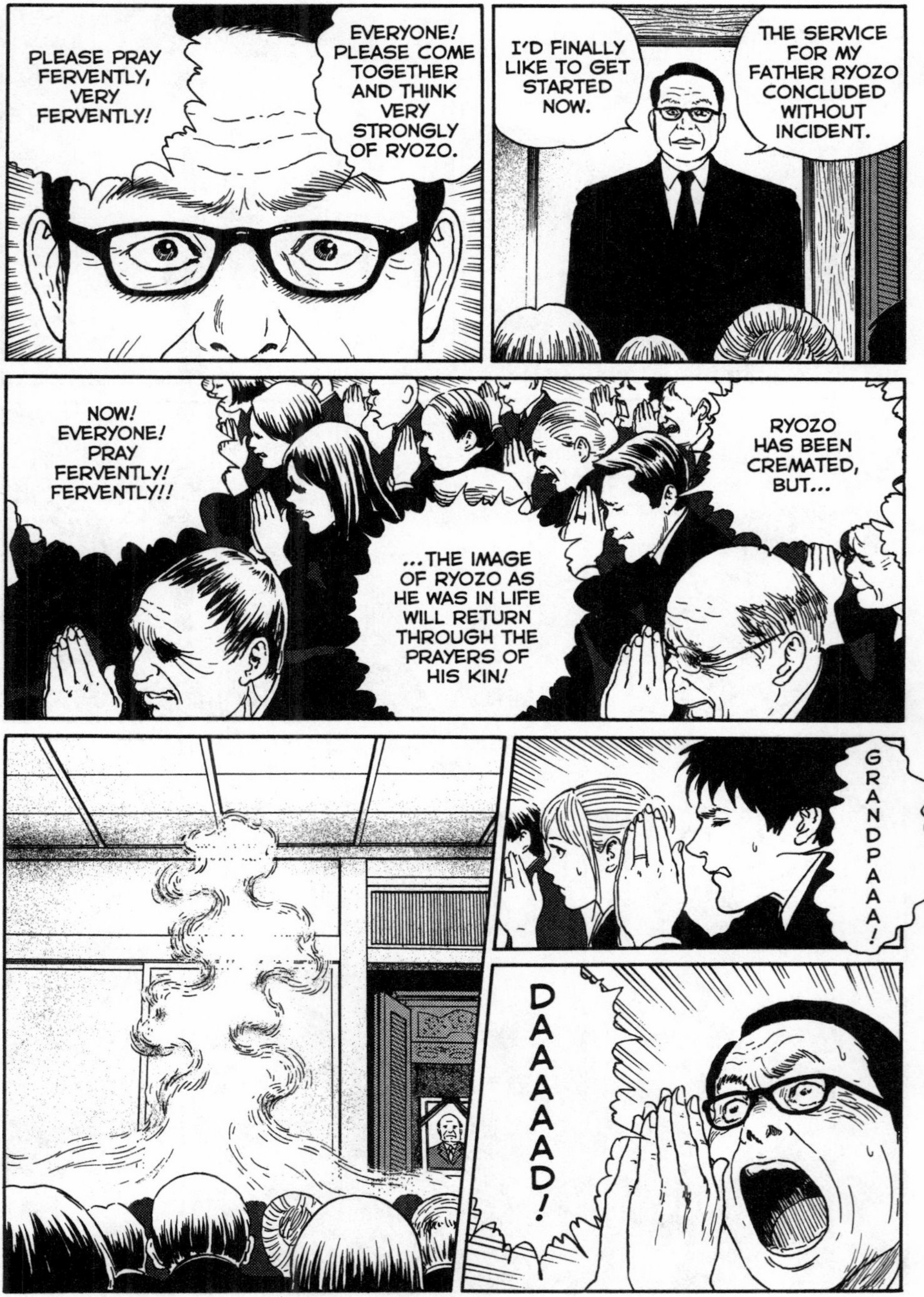
THE SERVICE FOR MY FATHER RYOZO CONCLUDED WITHOUT INCIDENT.
I'D FINALLY LIKE TO GET STARTED NOW.
EVERYONE! PLEASE COME TOGETHER AND THINK VERY STRONGLY OF RYOZO.
PLEASE PRAY FERVENTLY, VERY FERVENTLY!
RYOZO HAS BEEN CREMATED, BUT...
...THE IMAGE OF RYOZO AS HE WAS IN LIFE WILL RETURN THROUGH THE PRAYERS OF HIS KIN!
NOW! EVERYONE! PRAY FERVENTLY! FERVENTLY!!
GRANDPAAAA!
DAAAAAD!

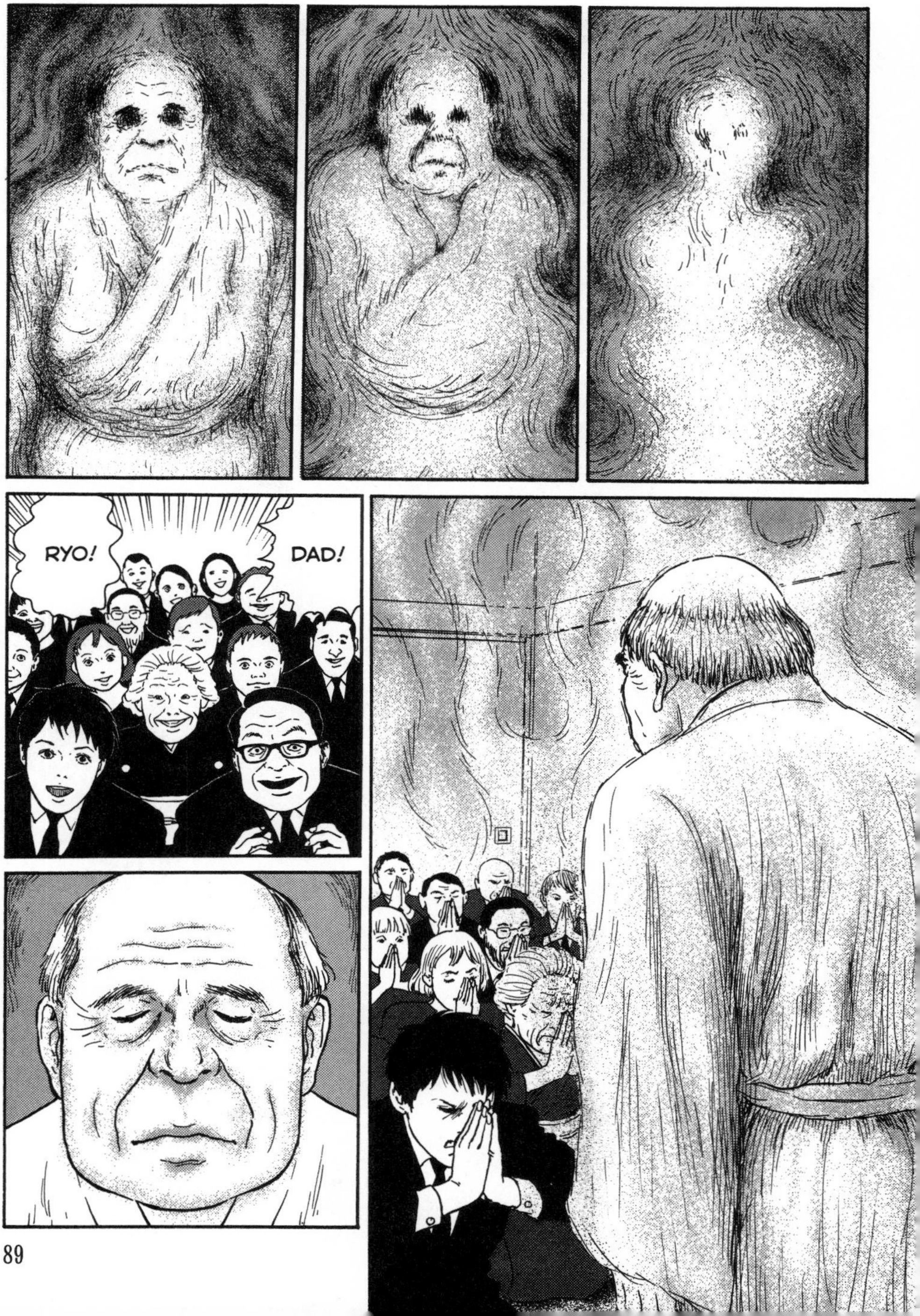
DAD!
RYO!

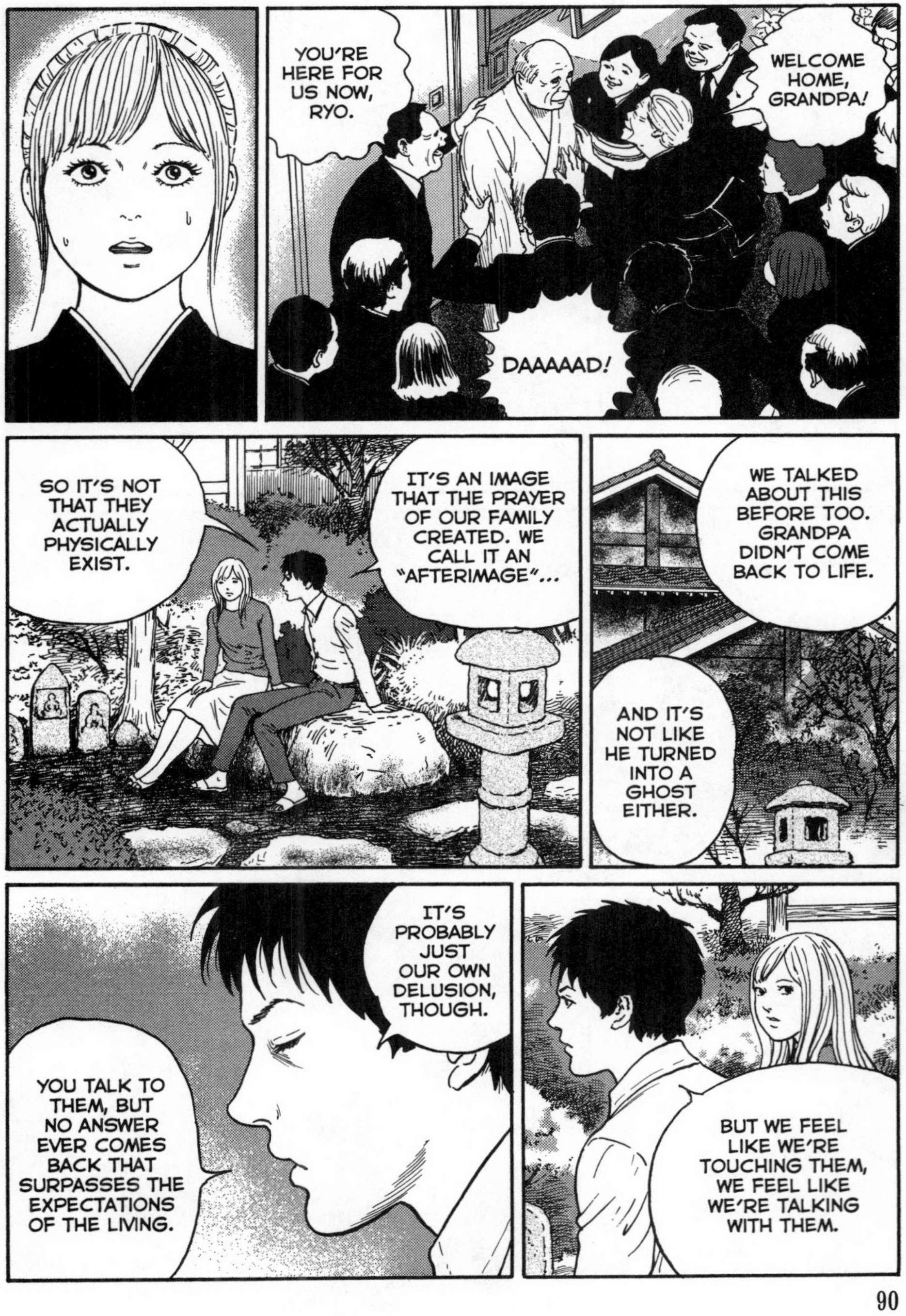
WELCOME HOME, GRANDPA!
YOU'RE HERE FOR US NOW, RYO.
DAAAAAD!
WE TALKED ABOUT THIS BEFORE TOO. GRANDPA DIDN'T COME BACK TO LIFE.
AND IT'S NOT LIKE HE TURNED INTO A GHOST EITHER.
IT'S AN IMAGE THAT THE PRAYER OF OUR FAMILY CREATED. WE CALL IT AN "AFTERIMAGE"...
SO IT'S NOT THAT THEY ACTUALLY PHYSICALLY EXIST.
BUT WE FEEL LIKE WE'RE TOUCHING THEM, WE FEEL LIKE WE'RE TALKING WITH THEM.
IT'S PROBABLY JUST OUR OWN DELUSION, THOUGH.
YOU TALK TO THEM, BUT NO ANSWER EVER COMES BACK THAT SURPASSES THE EXPECTATIONS OF THE LIVING.

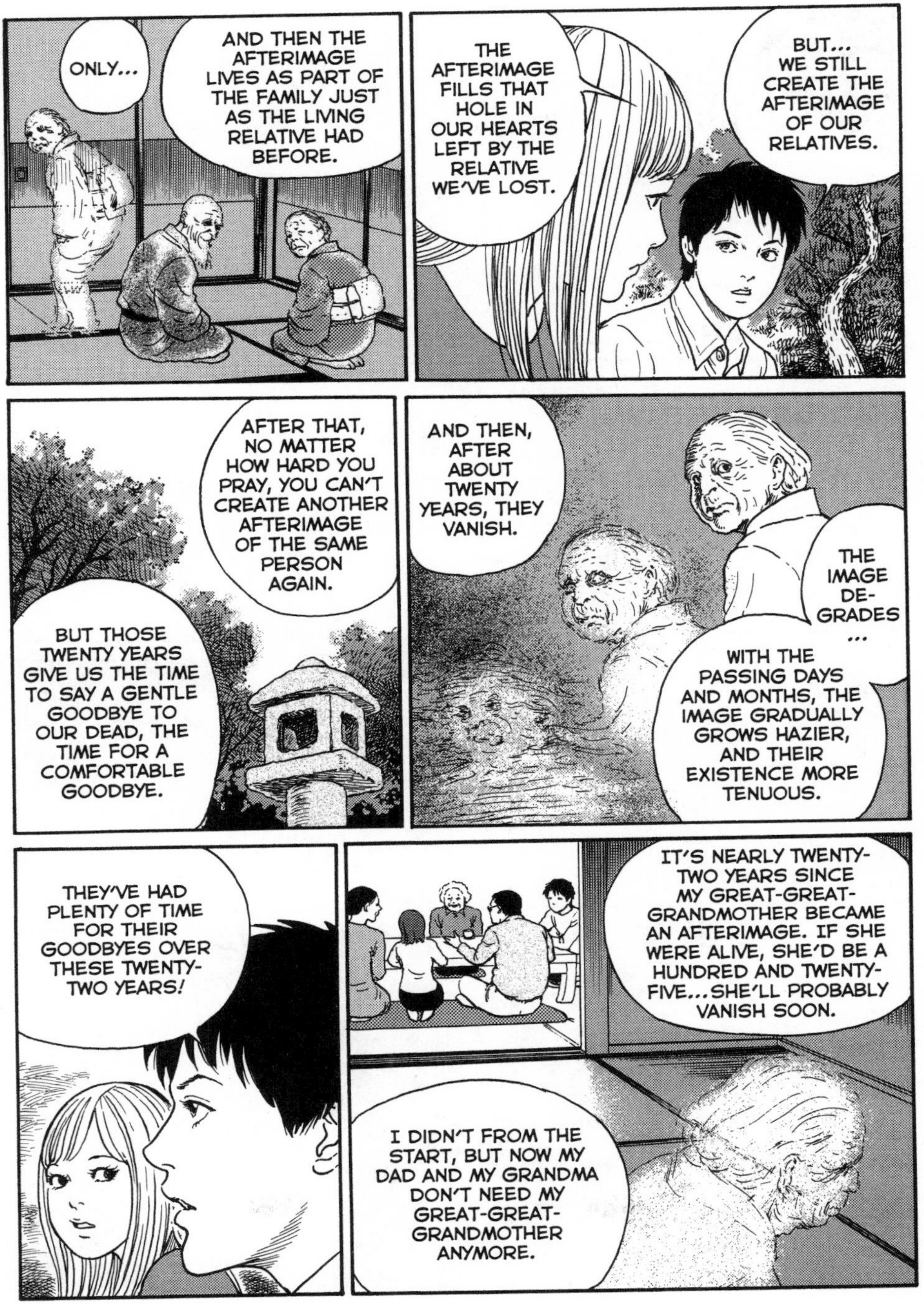
BUT... WE STILL CREATE THE AFTERIMAGE OF OUR RELATIVES.
THE AFTERIMAGE FILLS THAT HOLE IN OUR HEARTS LEFT BY THE RELATIVE WE'VE LOST.
AND THEN THE AFTERIMAGE LIVES AS PART OF THE FAMILY JUST AS THE LIVING RELATIVE HAD BEFORE.
ONLY...
AND THEN, AFTER ABOUT TWENTY YEARS, THEY VANISH.
THE IMAGE DE-GRADES...
WITH THE PASSING DAYS AND MONTHS, THE IMAGE GRADUALLY GROWS HAZIER, AND THEIR EXISTENCE MORE TENUOUS.
AFTER THAT, NO MATTER HOW HARD YOU PRAY, YOU CAN'T CREATE ANOTHER AFTERIMAGE OF THE SAME PERSON AGAIN.
BUT THOSE TWENTY YEARS GIVE US THE TIME TO SAY A GENTLE GOODBYE TO OUR DEAD, THE TIME FOR A COMFORTABLE GOODBYE.
IT'S NEARLY TWENTY-TWO YEARS SINCE MY GREAT-GREAT-GRANDMOTHER BECAME AN AFTERIMAGE. IF SHE WERE ALIVE, SHE'D BE A HUNDRED AND TWENTY-FIVE...SHE'LL PROBABLY VANISH SOON.
I DIDN'T FROM THE START, BUT NOW MY DAD AND MY GRANDMA DON'T NEED MY GREAT-GREAT-GRANDMOTHER ANYMORE.
THEY'VE HAD PLENTY OF TIME FOR THEIR GOODBYES OVER THESE TWENTY-TWO YEARS!

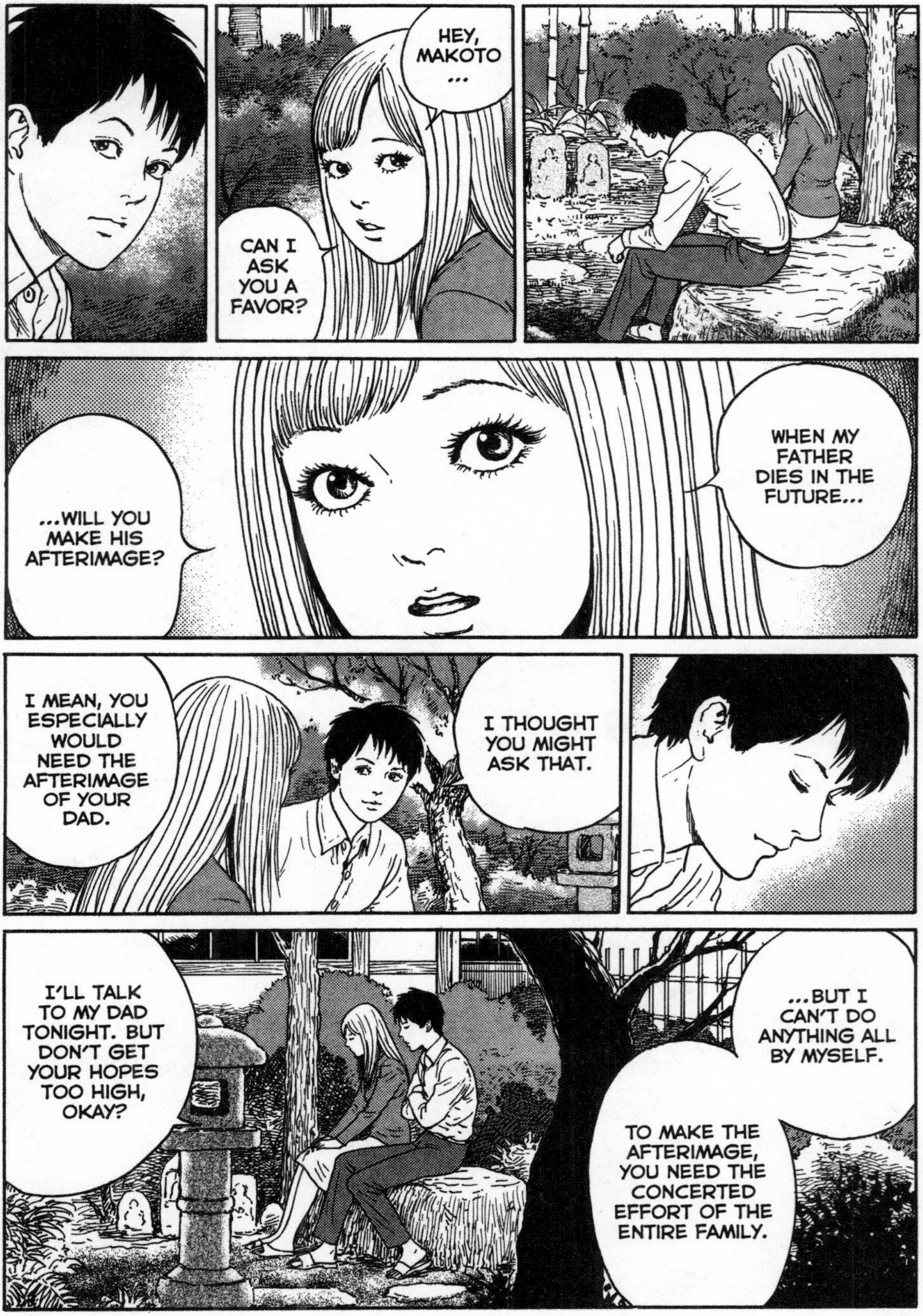
HEY, MAKOTO ...
CAN I ASK YOU A FAVOR?
WHEN MY FATHER DIES IN THE FUTURE...
...WILL YOU MAKE HIS AFTERIMAGE?
I THOUGHT YOU MIGHT ASK THAT.
I MEAN, YOU ESPECIALLY WOULD NEED THE AFTERIMAGE OF YOUR DAD.
...BUT I CAN'T DO ANYTHING ALL BY MYSELF.
TO MAKE THE AFTERIMAGE, YOU NEED THE CONCERTED EFFORT OF THE ENTIRE FAMILY.
I'LL TALK TO MY DAD TONIGHT. BUT DON'T GET YOUR HOPES TOO HIGH, OKAY?

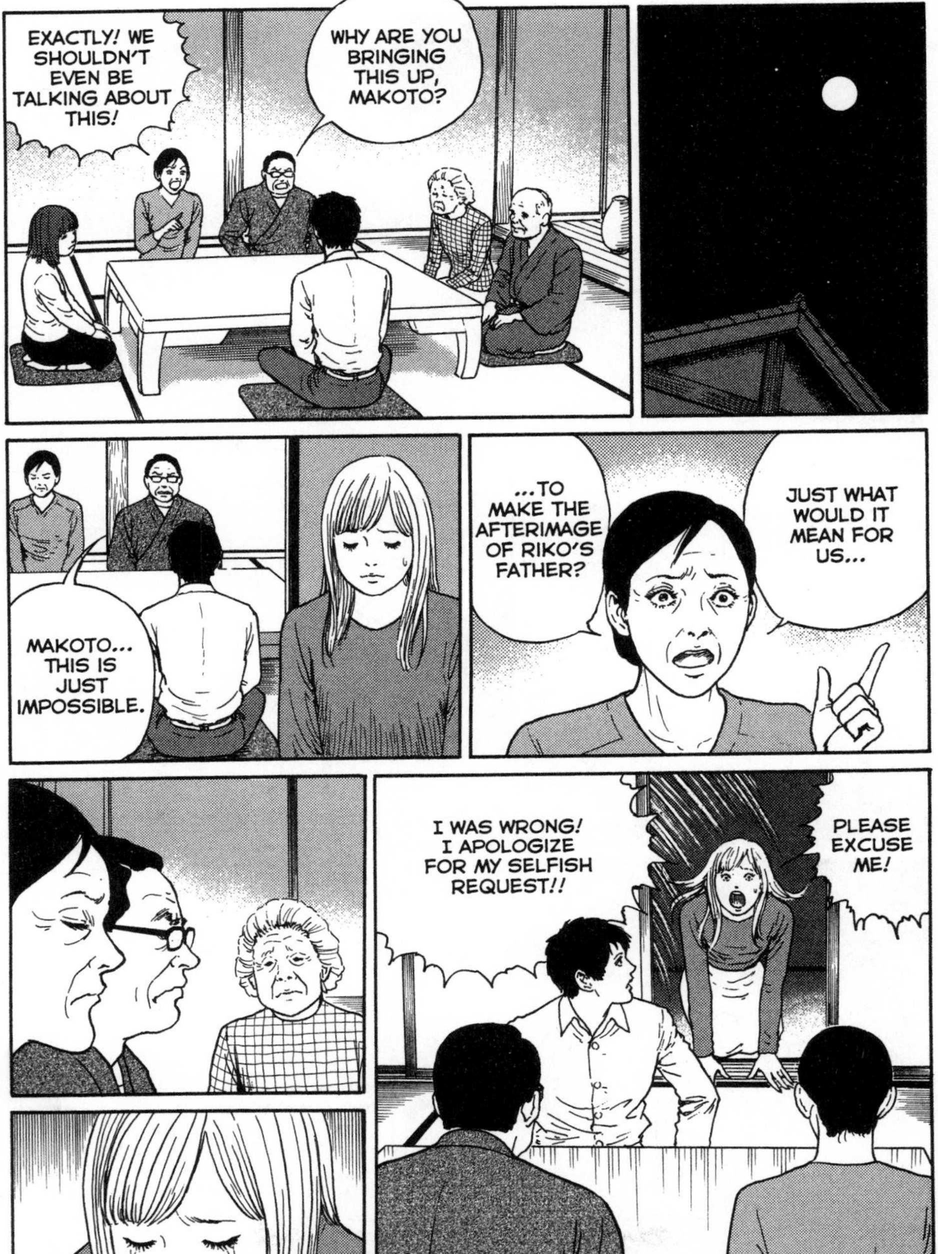
WHY ARE YOU BRINGING THIS UP, MAKOTO?
EXACTLY! WE SHOULDN'T EVEN BE TALKING ABOUT THIS!
JUST WHAT WOULD IT MEAN FOR US...
...TO MAKE THE AFTERIMAGE OF RIKO'S FATHER?
MAKOTO... THIS IS JUST IMPOSSIBLE.
PLEASE EXCUSE ME!
I WAS WRONG! I APOLOGIZE FOR MY SELFISH REQUEST!!

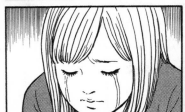

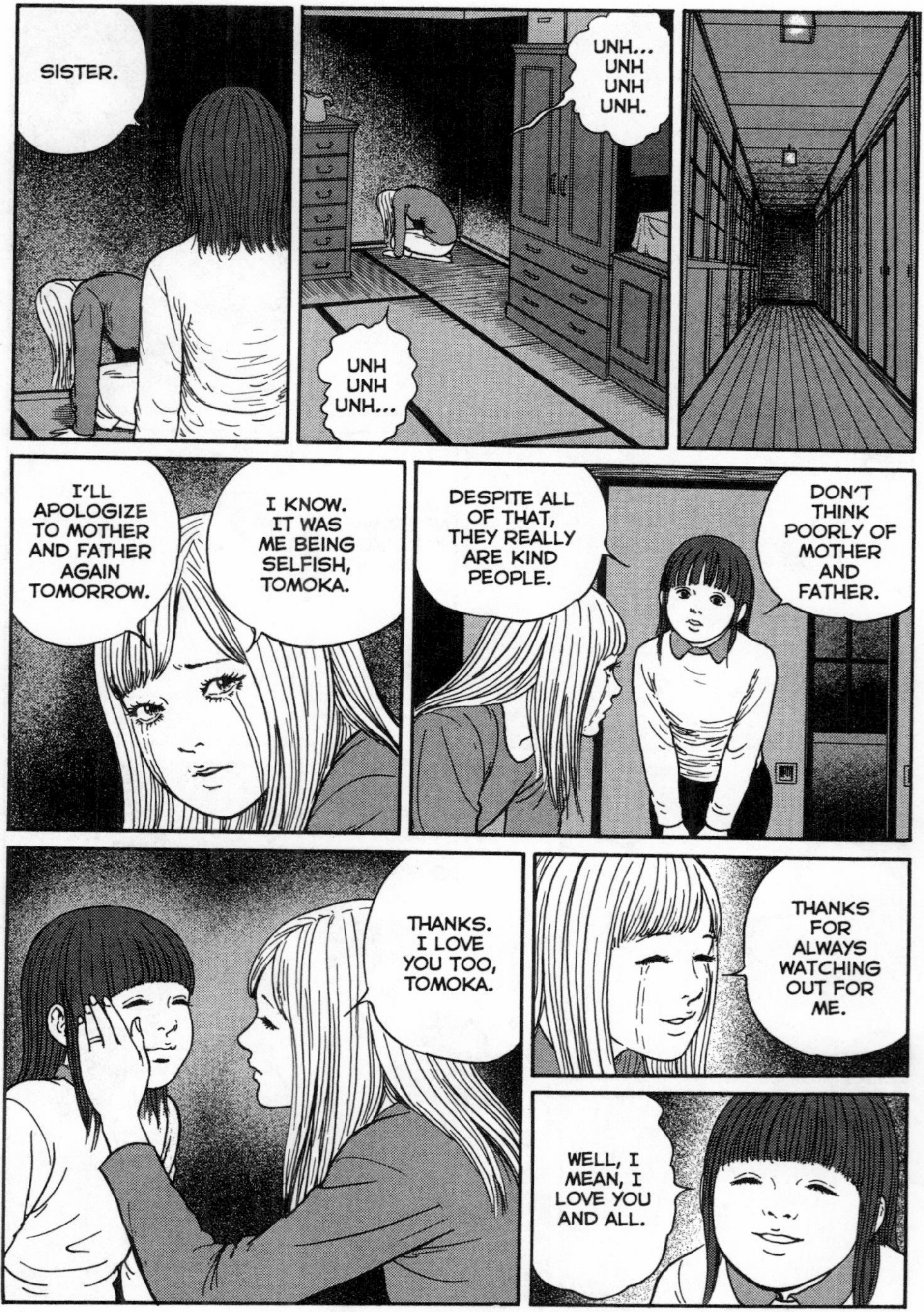
UNH... UNH UNH UNH.
UNH UNH UNH...
SISTER.
DON'T THINK POORLY OF MOTHER AND FATHER.
DESPITE ALL OF THAT, THEY REALLY ARE KIND PEOPLE.
I KNOW. IT WAS ME BEING SELFISH, TOMOKA.
I'LL APOLOGIZE TO MOTHER AND FATHER AGAIN TOMORROW.
THANKS FOR ALWAYS WATCHING OUT FOR ME.
WELL, I MEAN, I LOVE YOU AND ALL.
THANKS. I LOVE YOU TOO, TOMOKA.

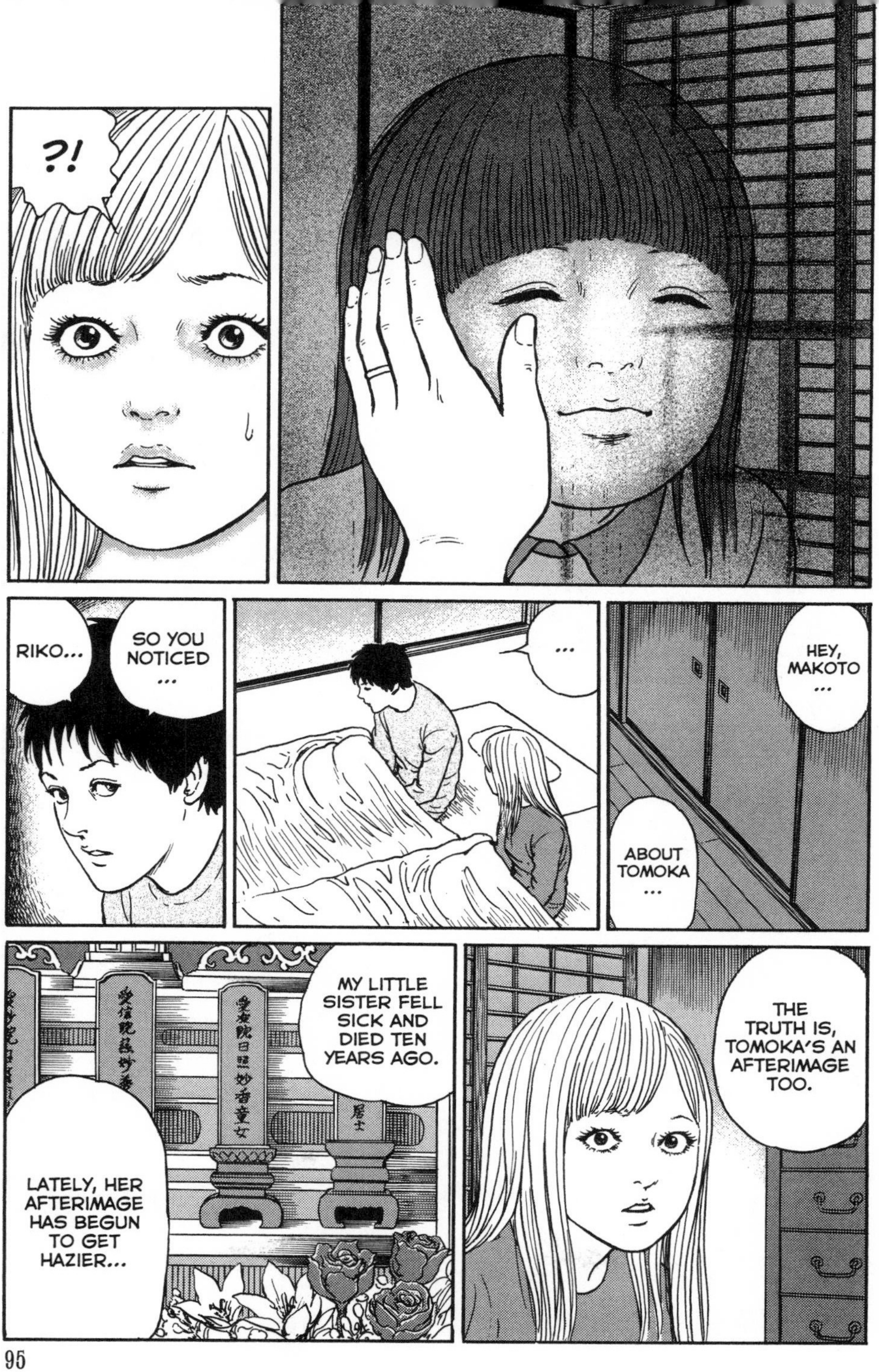
?!
HEY, MAKOTO ...
ABOUT TOMOKA ...
...
SO YOU NOTICED ...
RIKO...
THE TRUTH IS, TOMOKA'S AN AFTERIMAGE TOO.
MY LITTLE SISTER FELL SICK AND DIED TEN YEARS AGO.
LATELY, HER AFTERIMAGE HAS BEGUN TO GET HAZIER...

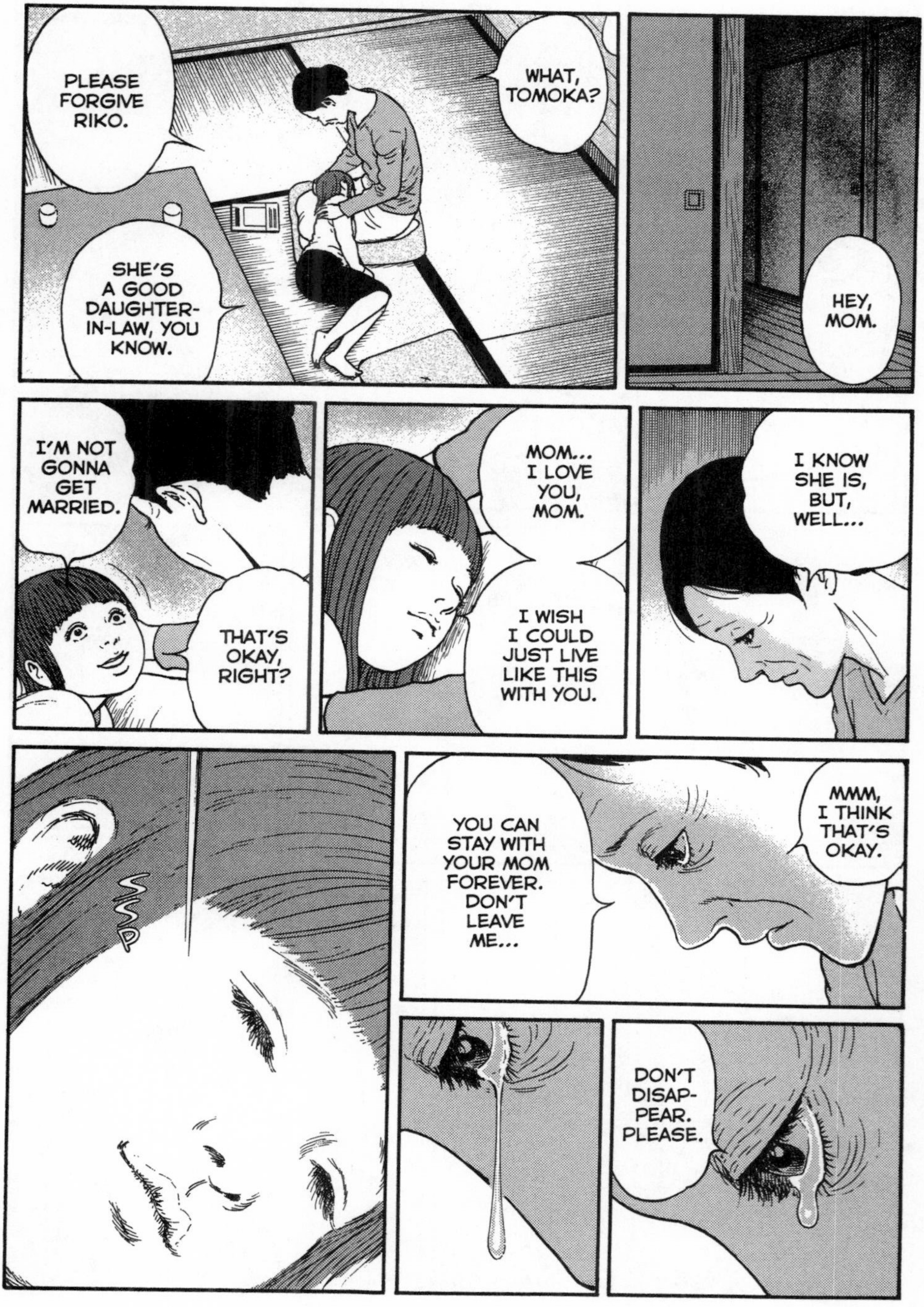
HEY, MOM.
WHAT, TOMOKA?
PLEASE FORGIVE RIKO.
SHE'S A GOOD DAUGHTER-IN-LAW, YOU KNOW.
I KNOW SHE IS, BUT, WELL...
MOM... I LOVE YOU, MOM.
I WISH I COULD JUST LIVE LIKE THIS WITH YOU.
I'M NOT GONNA GET MARRIED.
THAT'S OKAY, RIGHT?
MMM, I THINK THAT'S OKAY.
YOU CAN STAY WITH YOUR MOM FOREVER. DON'T LEAVE ME...
DON'T DISAPPEAR. PLEASE.
SSP

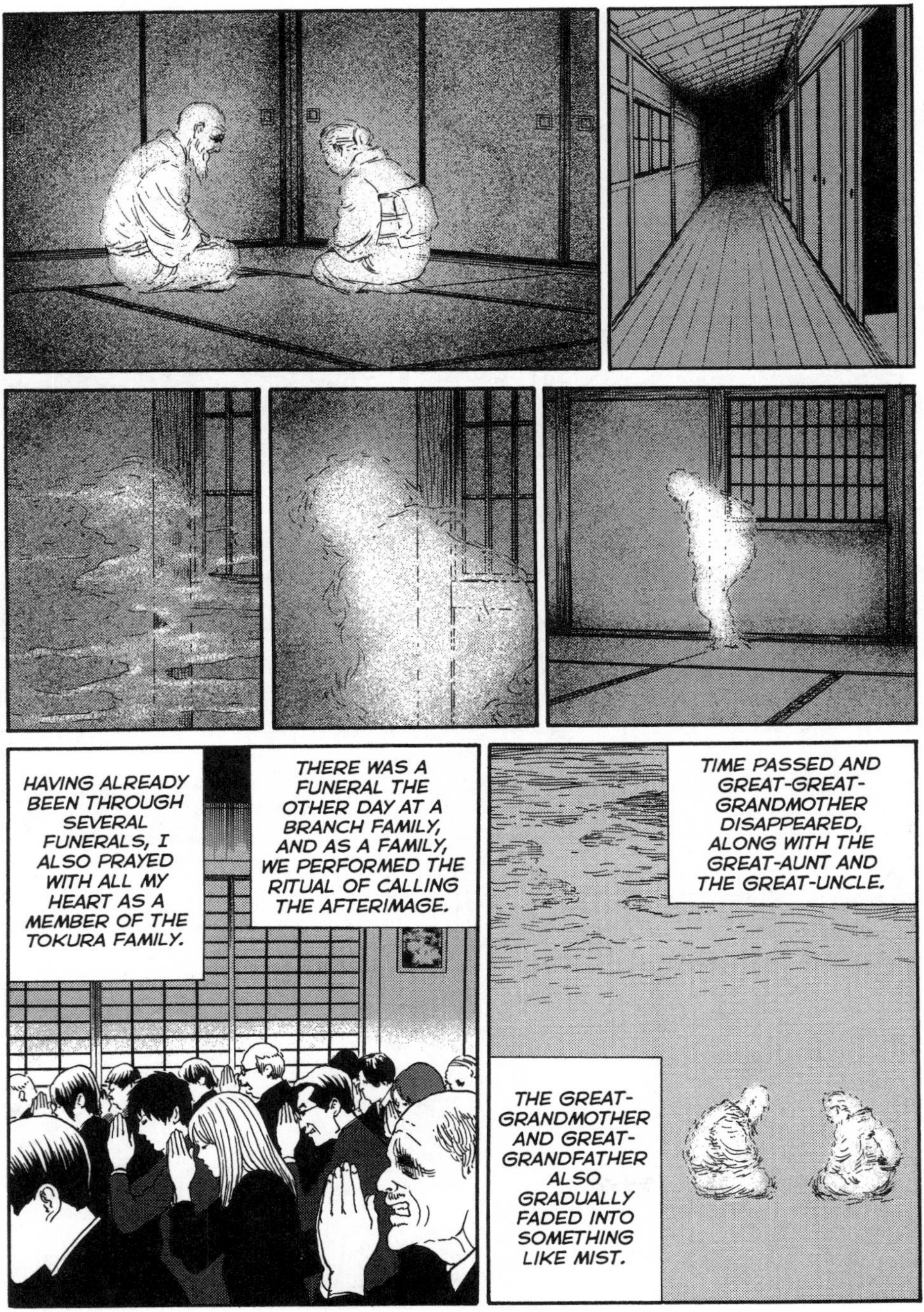
TIME PASSED AND GREAT-GREAT-GRANDMOTHER DISAPPEARED, ALONG WITH THE GREAT-AUNT AND THE GREAT-UNCLE.
THE GREAT-GRANDMOTHER AND GREAT-GRANDFATHER ALSO GRADUALLY FADED INTO SOMETHING LIKE MIST.
THERE WAS A FUNERAL THE OTHER DAY AT A BRANCH FAMILY, AND AS A FAMILY, WE PERFORMED THE RITUAL OF CALLING THE AFTERIMAGE.
HAVING ALREADY BEEN THROUGH SEVERAL FUNERALS, I ALSO PRAYED WITH ALL MY HEART AS A MEMBER OF THE TOKURA FAMILY.

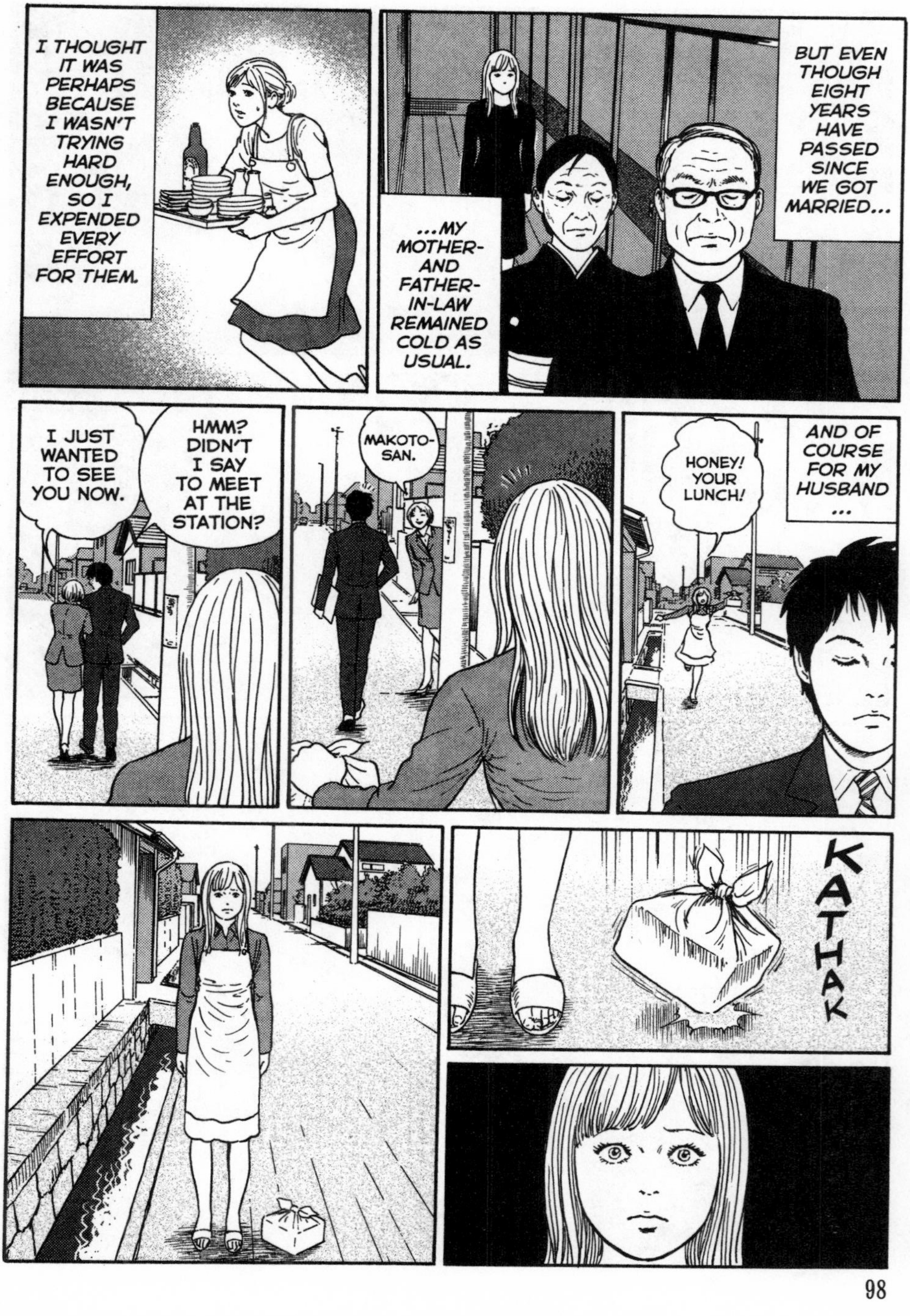
BUT EVEN THOUGH EIGHT YEARS HAVE PASSED SINCE WE GOT MARRIED...
...MY MOTHER- AND FATHER-IN-LAW REMAINED COLD AS USUAL.
I THOUGHT IT WAS PERHAPS BECAUSE I WASN'T TRYING HARD ENOUGH, SO I EXPENDED EVERY EFFORT FOR THEM.
AND OF COURSE FOR MY HUSBAND ...
HONEY! YOUR LUNCH!
MAKOTO-SAN.
HMM? DIDN'T I SAY TO MEET AT THE STATION?
I JUST WANTED TO SEE YOU NOW.
KATHAK

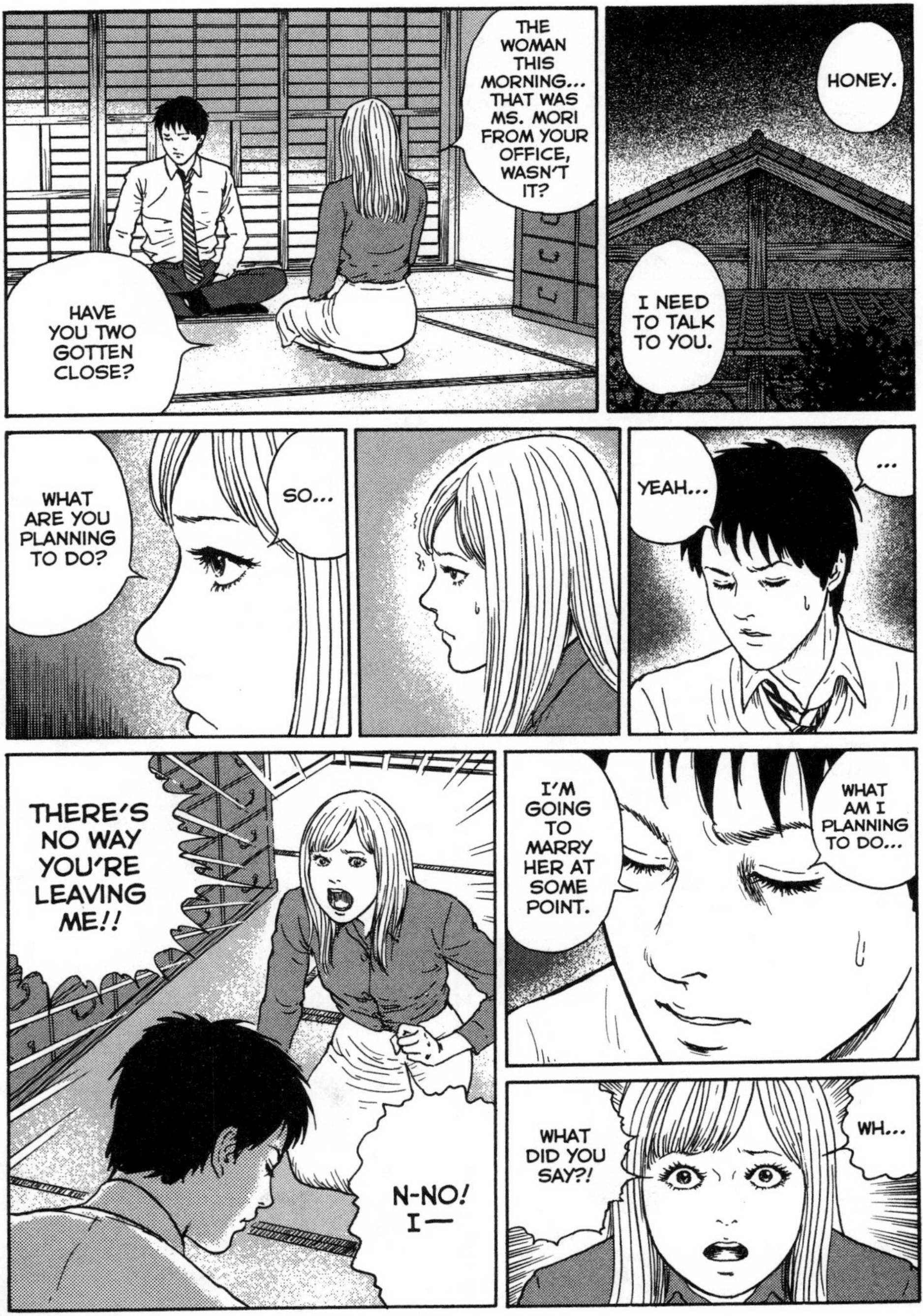
HONEY.
I NEED TO TALK TO YOU.
THE WOMAN THIS MORNING... THAT WAS MS. MORI FROM YOUR OFFICE, WASN'T IT?
HAVE YOU TWO GOTTEN CLOSE?
...
YEAH...
SO...
WHAT ARE YOU PLANNING TO DO?
WHAT AM I PLANNING TO DO...
I'M GOING TO MARRY HER AT SOME POINT.
WH...
WHAT DID YOU SAY?!
THERE'S NO WAY YOU'RE LEAVING ME!!
N-NO! I—

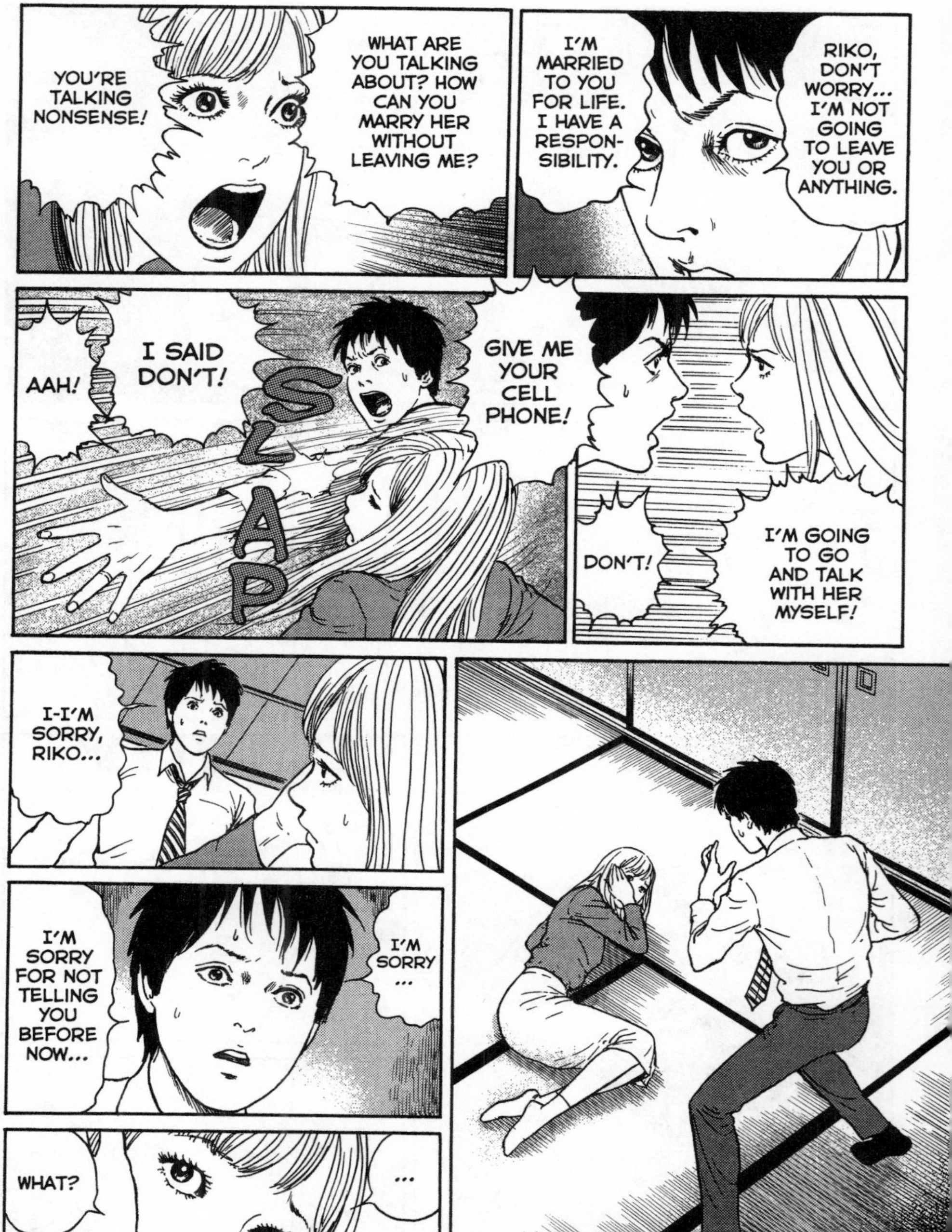
RIKO, DON'T WORRY... I'M NOT GOING TO LEAVE YOU OR ANYTHING.
I'M MARRIED TO YOU FOR LIFE. I HAVE A RESPONSIBILITY.
WHAT ARE YOU TALKING ABOUT? HOW CAN YOU MARRY HER WITHOUT LEAVING ME?
YOU'RE TALKING NONSENSE!
I'M GOING TO GO AND TALK WITH HER MYSELF!
GIVE ME YOUR CELL PHONE!
DON'T!
I SAID DON'T!
SLAP
AAH!
I-I'M SORRY, RIKO...
I'M SORRY...
I'M SORRY FOR NOT TELLING YOU BEFORE NOW...
...
WHAT?

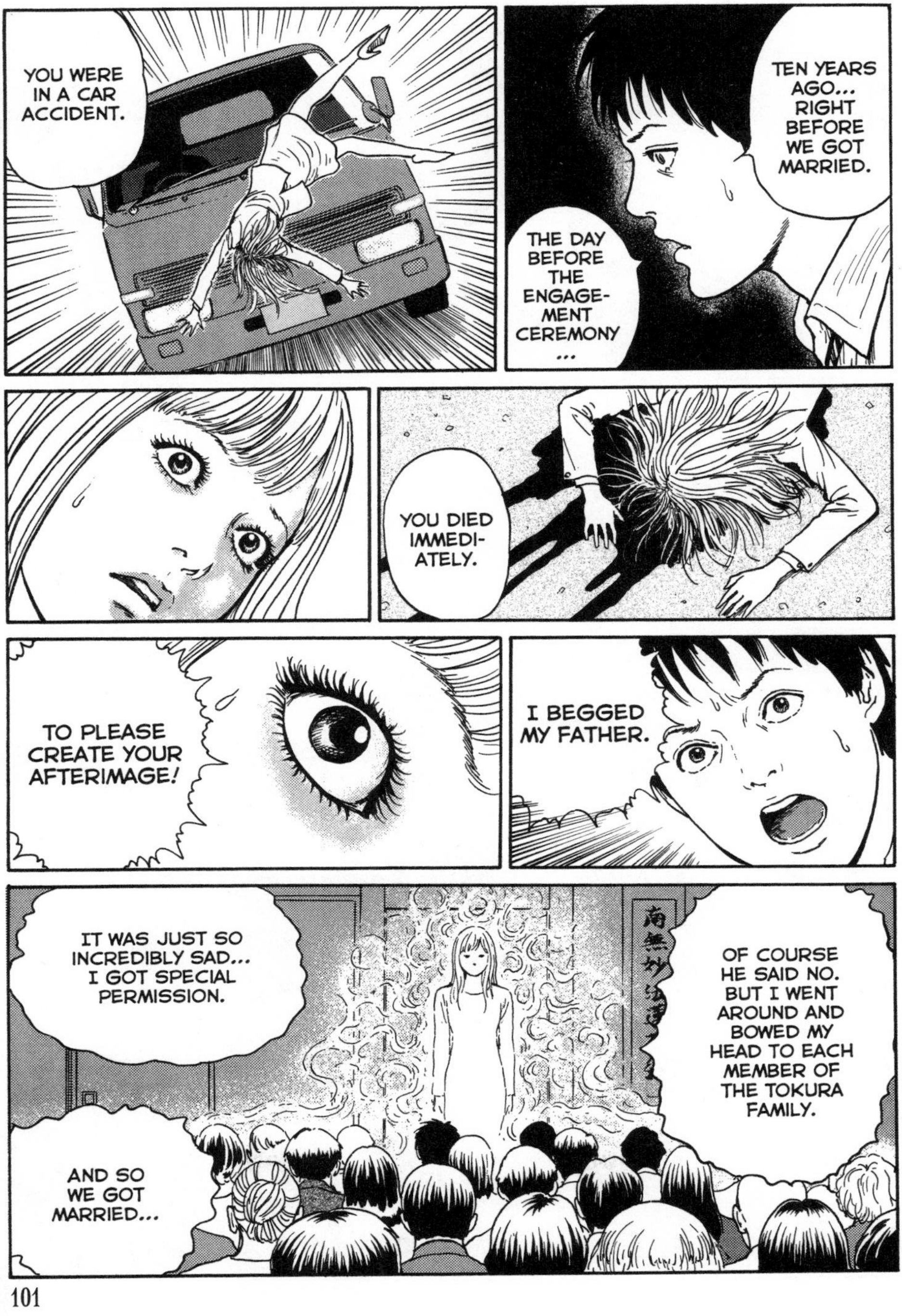
TEN YEARS AGO... RIGHT BEFORE WE GOT MARRIED.
THE DAY BEFORE THE ENGAGEMENT CEREMONY...
YOU WERE IN A CAR ACCIDENT.
YOU DIED IMMEDIATELY.
I BEGGED MY FATHER.
TO PLEASE CREATE YOUR AFTERIMAGE!
OF COURSE HE SAID NO. BUT I WENT AROUND AND BOWED MY HEAD TO EACH MEMBER OF THE TOKURA FAMILY.
IT WAS JUST SO INCREDIBLY SAD... I GOT SPECIAL PERMISSION.
AND SO WE GOT MARRIED...

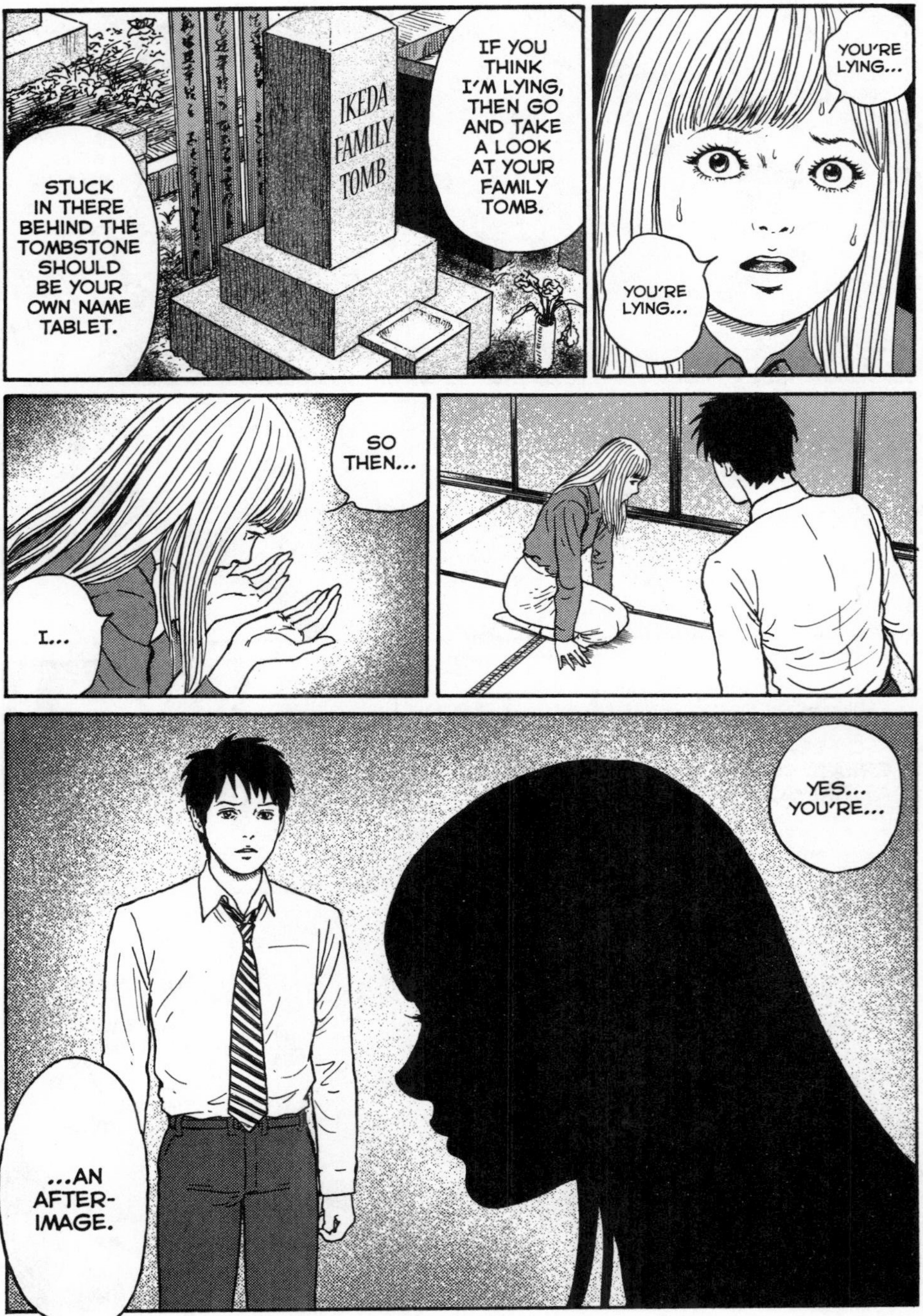
YOU'RE LYING...
YOU'RE LYING...
IF YOU THINK I'M LYING, THEN GO AND TAKE A LOOK AT YOUR FAMILY TOMB.
IKEDA FAMILY TOMB
STUCK IN THERE BEHIND THE TOMBSTONE SHOULD BE YOUR OWN NAME TABLET.
SO THEN...
I...
YES... YOU'RE...
...AN AFTER-IMAGE.

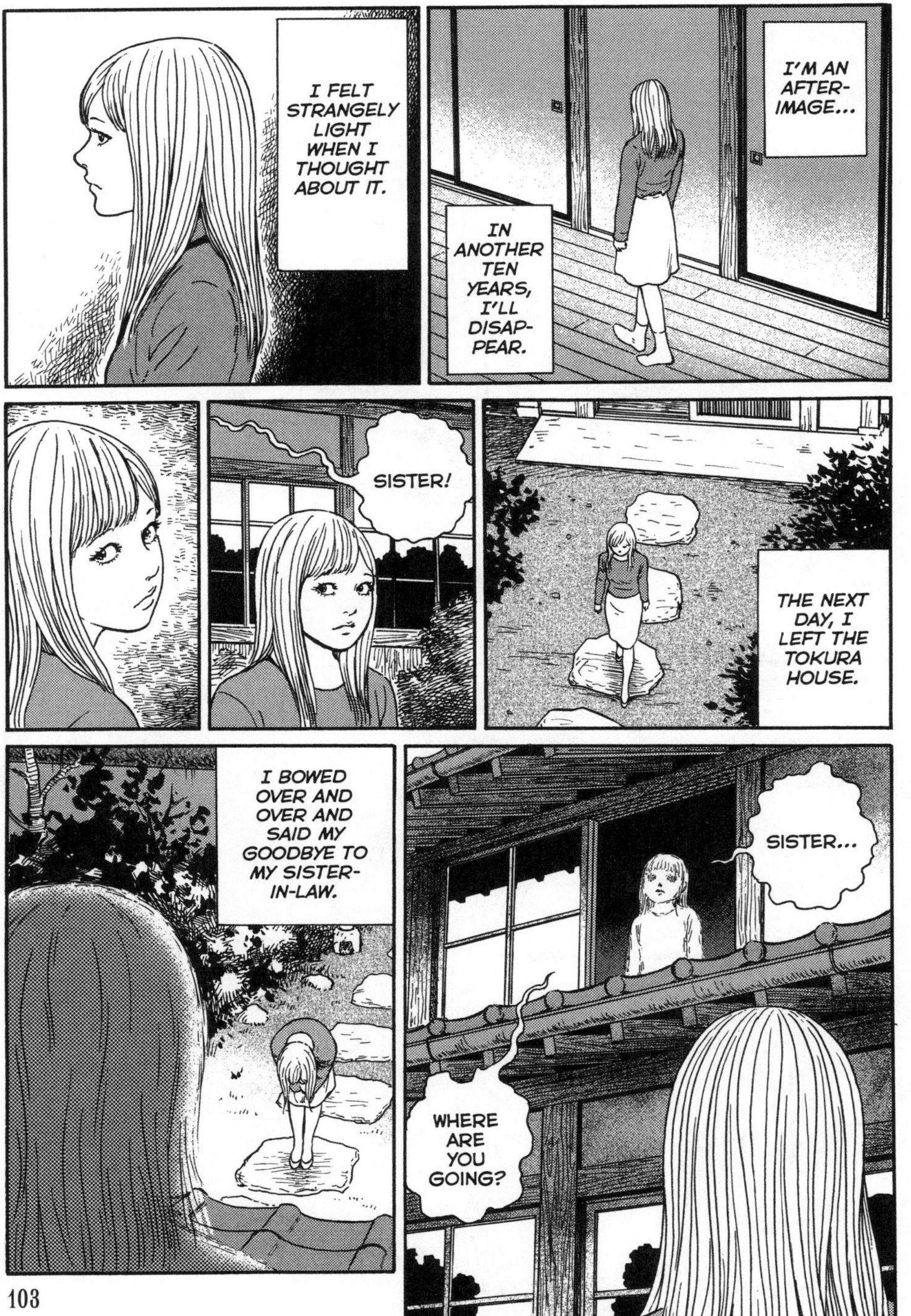
I'M AN AFTER-IMAGE...
IN ANOTHER TEN YEARS, I'LL DISAPPEAR.
I FELT STRANGELY LIGHT WHEN I THOUGHT ABOUT IT.
THE NEXT DAY, I LEFT THE TOKURA HOUSE.
SISTER!
SISTER...
WHERE ARE YOU GOING?
I BOWED OVER AND OVER AND SAID MY GOODBYE TO MY SISTER-IN-LAW.

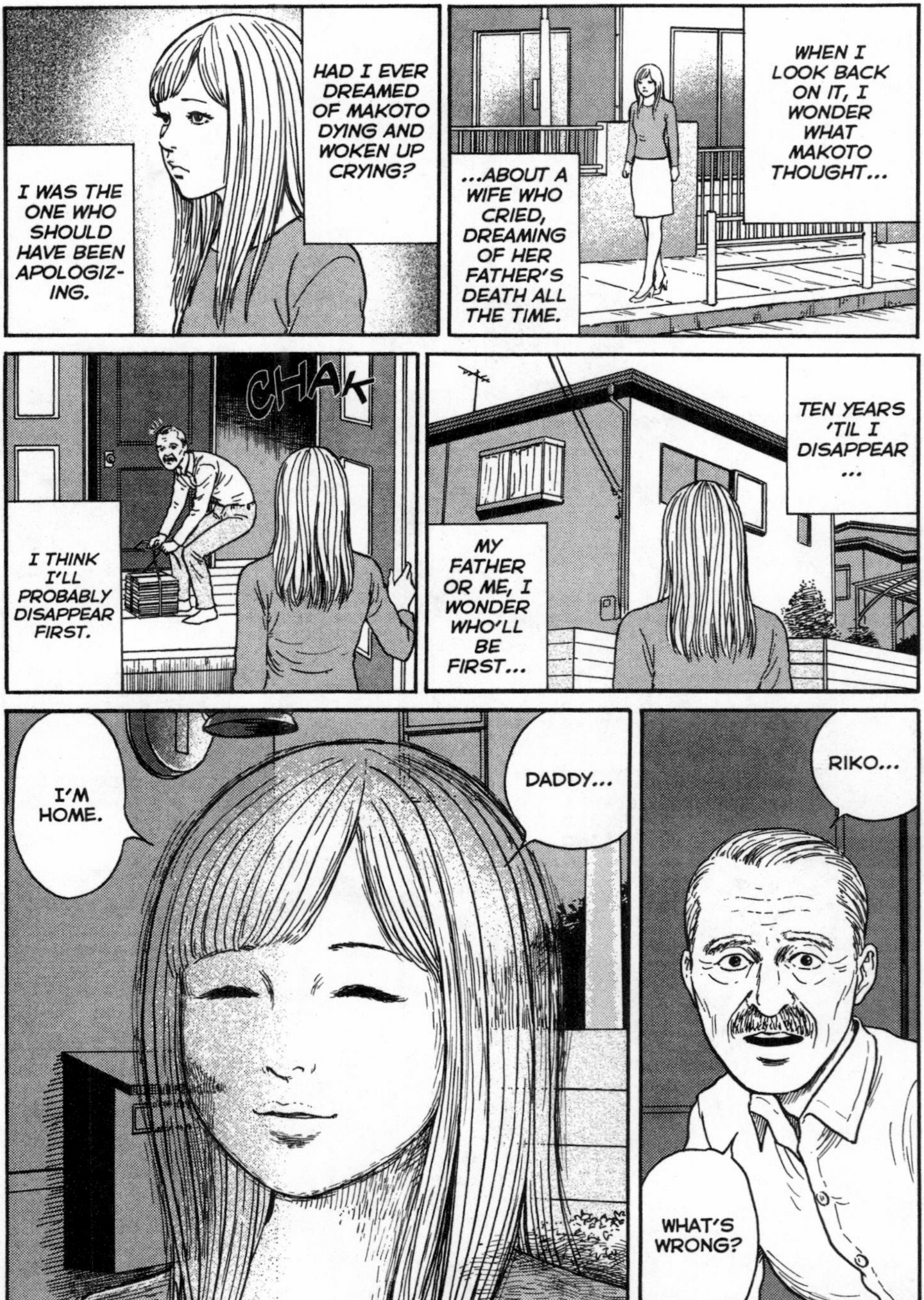
WHEN I LOOK BACK ON IT, I WONDER WHAT MAKOTO THOUGHT...
...ABOUT A WIFE WHO CRIED, DREAMING OF HER FATHER'S DEATH ALL THE TIME.
HAD I EVER DREAMED OF MAKOTO DYING AND WOKEN UP CRYING?
I WAS THE ONE WHO SHOULD HAVE BEEN APOLOGIZING.
TEN YEARS 'TIL I DISAPPEAR...
MY FATHER OR ME, I WONDER WHO'LL BE FIRST...
CHAK
I THINK I'LL PROBABLY DISAPPEAR FIRST.
RIKO...
WHAT'S WRONG?
DADDY...
I'M HOME.

GENTLE GOODBYE/END

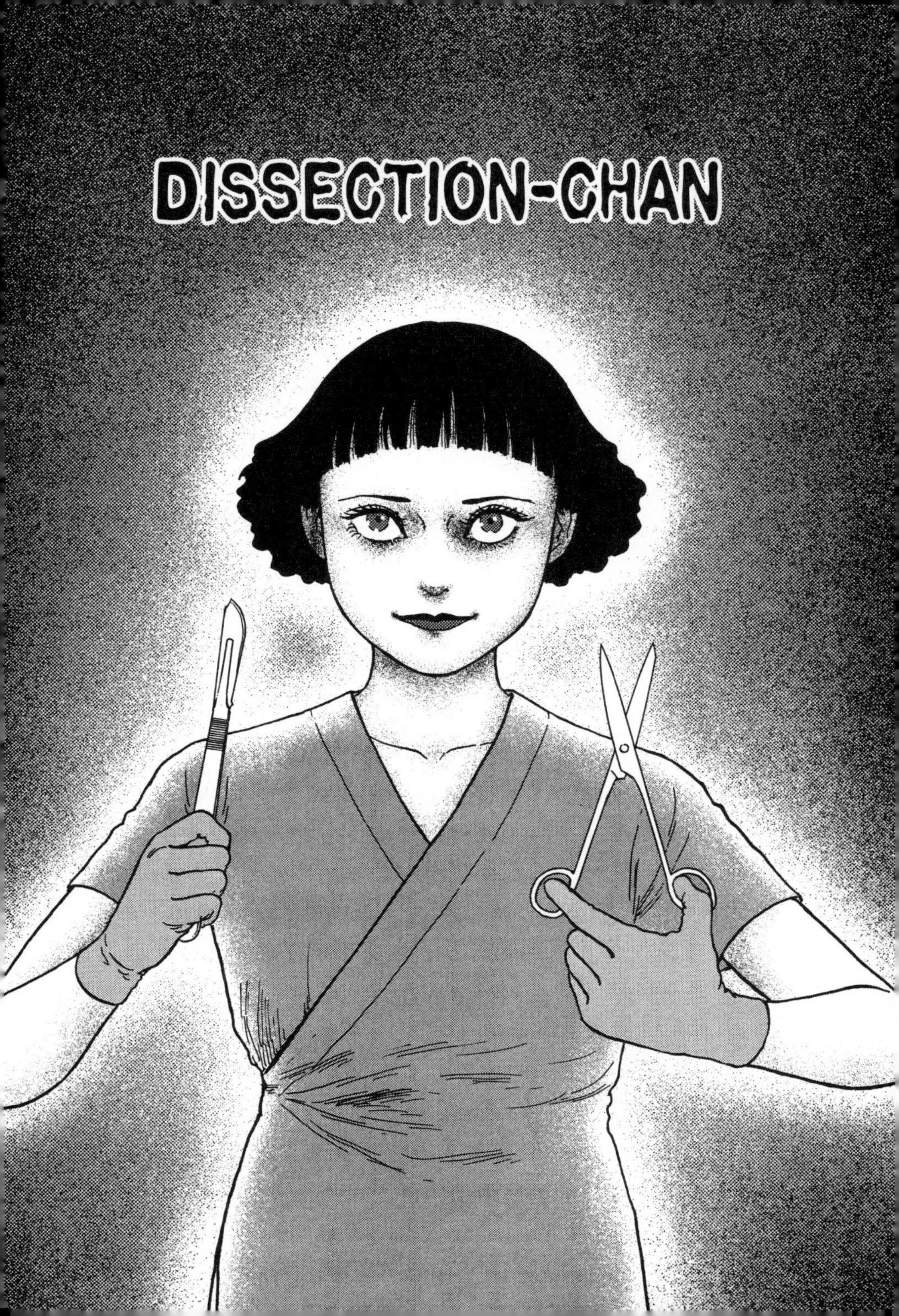
DISSECTION-CHAN

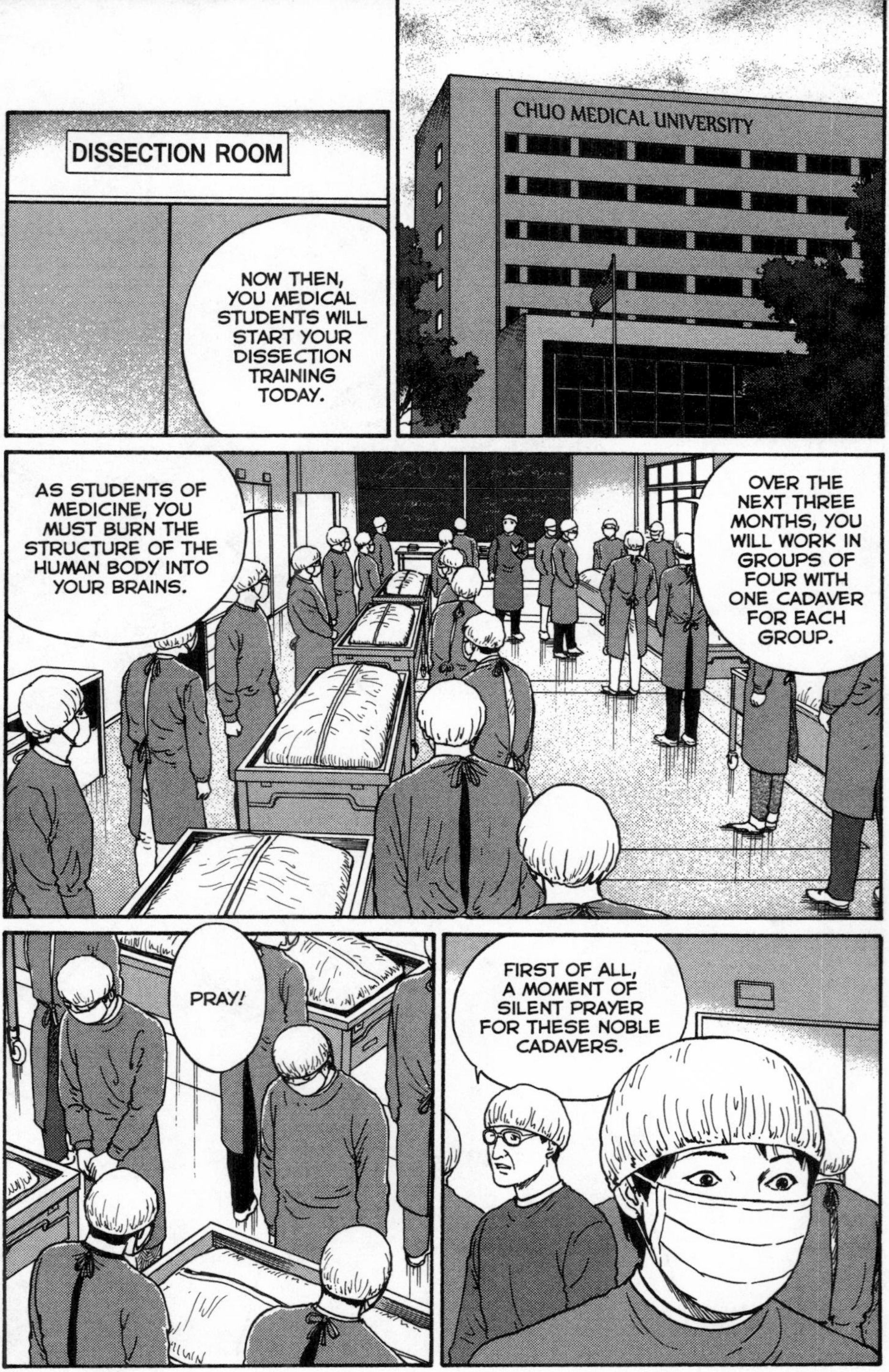
CHUO MEDICAL UNIVERSITY
DISSECTION ROOM
NOW THEN, YOU MEDICAL STUDENTS WILL START YOUR DISSECTION TRAINING TODAY.
OVER THE NEXT THREE MONTHS, YOU WILL WORK IN GROUPS OF FOUR WITH ONE CADAVER FOR EACH GROUP.
AS STUDENTS OF MEDICINE, YOU MUST BURN THE STRUCTURE OF THE HUMAN BODY INTO YOUR BRAINS.
FIRST OF ALL, A MOMENT OF SILENT PRAYER FOR THESE NOBLE CADAVERS.
PRAY!

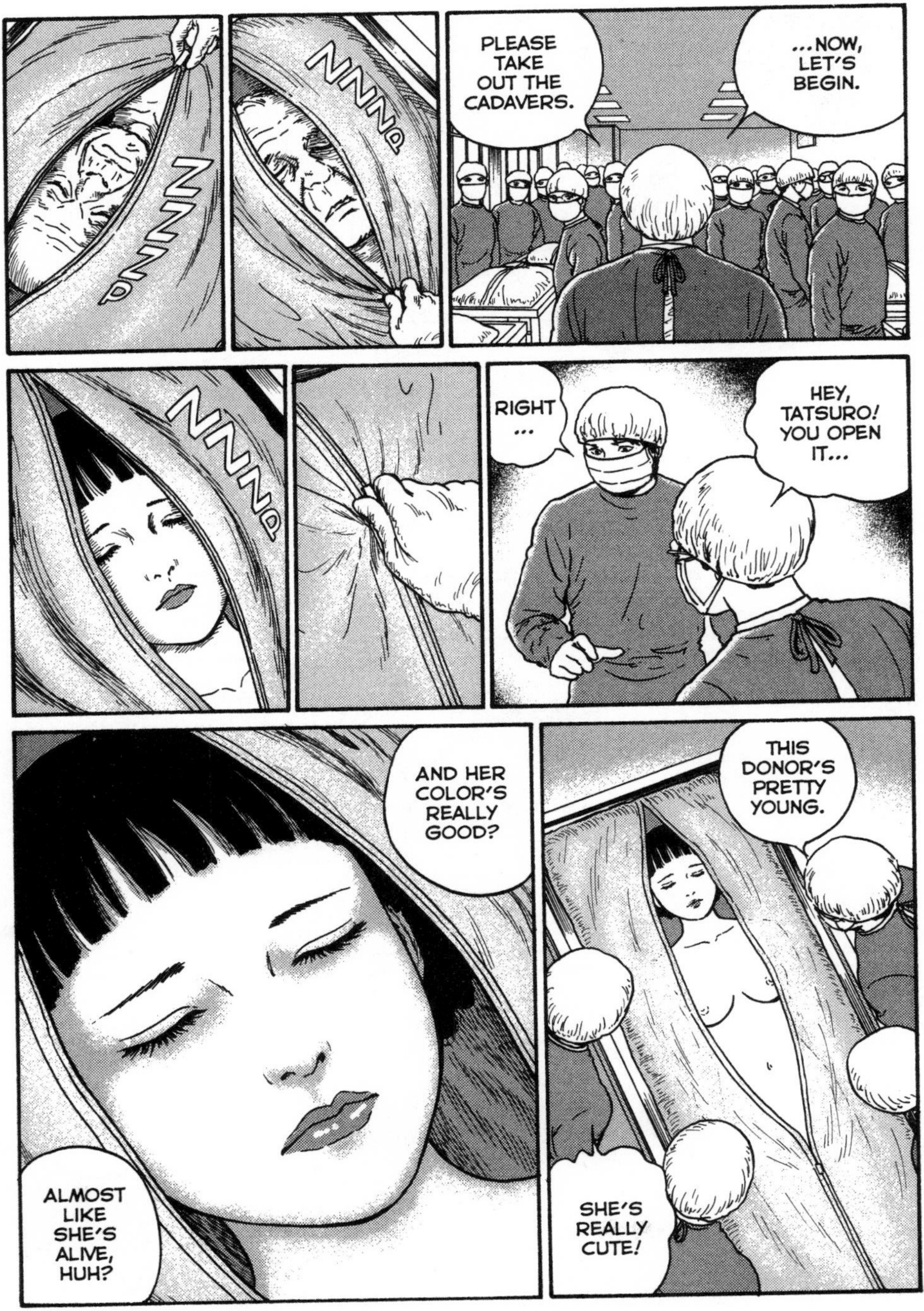
...NOW, LET'S BEGIN.
PLEASE TAKE OUT THE CADAVERS.
HEY, TATSURO! YOU OPEN IT...
RIGHT ...
THIS DONOR'S PRETTY YOUNG.
SHE'S REALLY CUTE!
AND HER COLOR'S REALLY GOOD?
ALMOST LIKE SHE'S ALIVE, HUH?

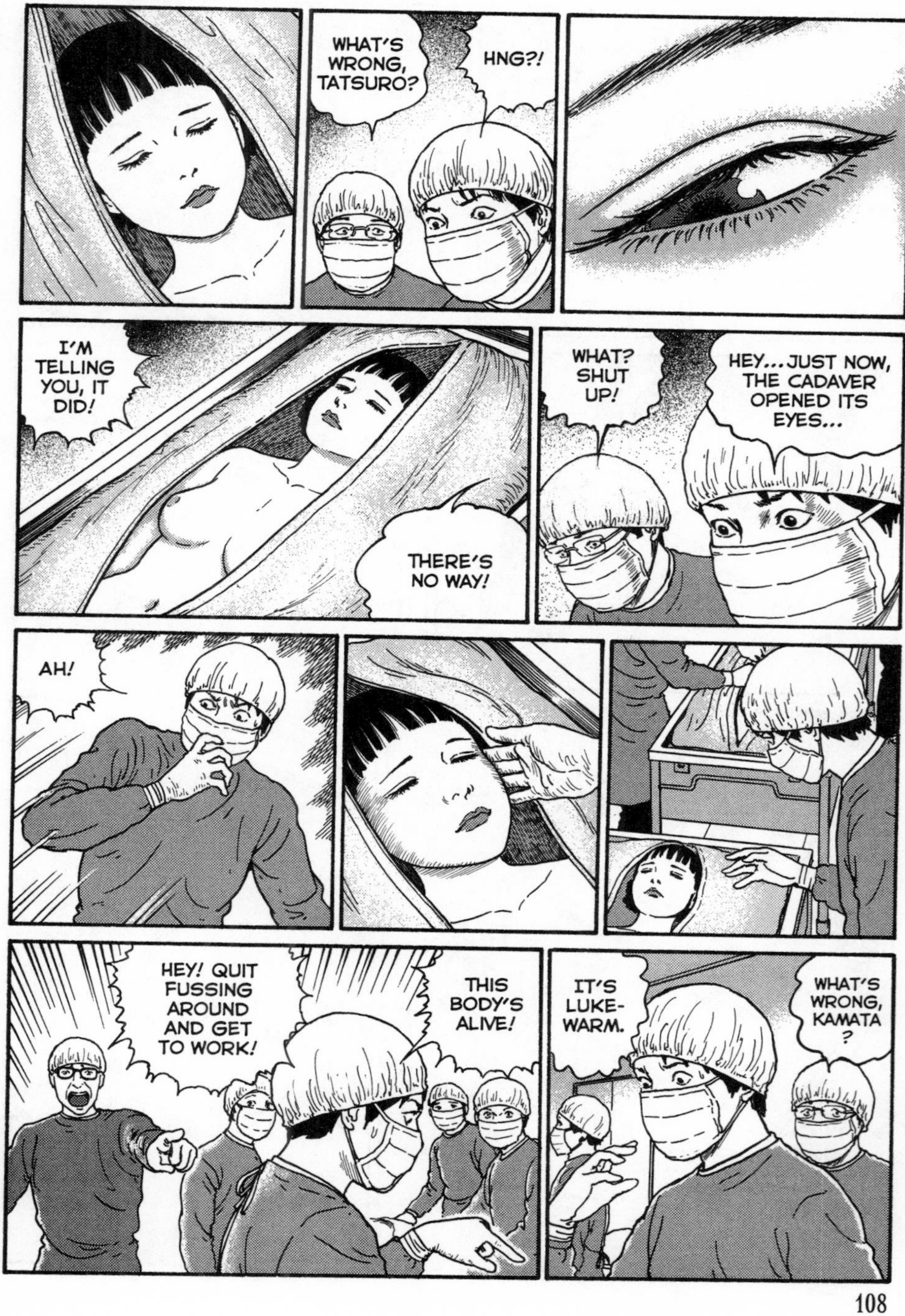
HNG?!
WHAT'S WRONG, TATSURO?
HEY... JUST NOW, THE CADAVER OPENED ITS EYES...
WHAT? SHUT UP!
THERE'S NO WAY!
I'M TELLING YOU, IT DID!
AH!
WHAT'S WRONG, KAMATA ?
IT'S LUKE-WARM.
THIS BODY'S ALIVE!
HEY! QUIT FUSSING AROUND AND GET TO WORK!

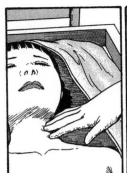

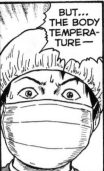

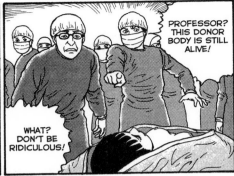

PROFESSOR? THIS DONOR BODY IS STILL ALIVE!
WHAT? DON'T BE RIDICULOUS!
BUT... THE BODY TEMPERA-TURE—
HMM...
...IT IS WARM. AND THE ELASTICITY OF THIS SKIN...
IT'S NOT LIKE THAT OF A CADAVER PRESERVED IN FORMALIN.
GRIN
HM?!
IT DEFINITELY SMILED JUST NOW!
THIS ONE'S ALIVE!
HEY, YOU! OPEN YOUR EYES!
HEY!

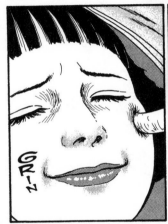

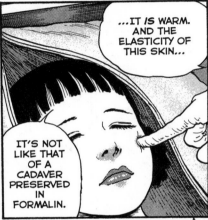

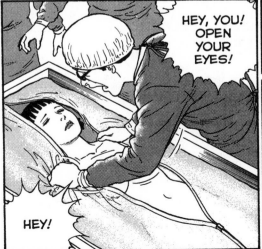

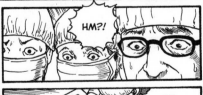

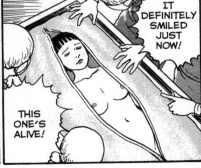

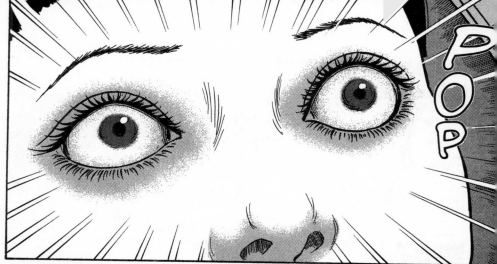

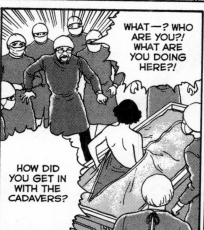

POP
LEAP
HOW DID YOU FIGURE IT OUT?
WHAT—? WHO ARE YOU?! WHAT ARE YOU DOING HERE?!
HOW DID YOU GET IN WITH THE CADAVERS?
WELL, THIS IS WHERE YOU COME TO BE DISSECTED, RIGHT?
I WANT TO BE DISSECTED!
WH—
WHAT?!

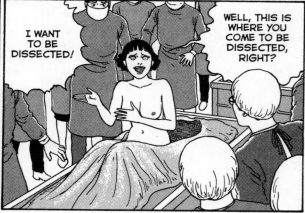

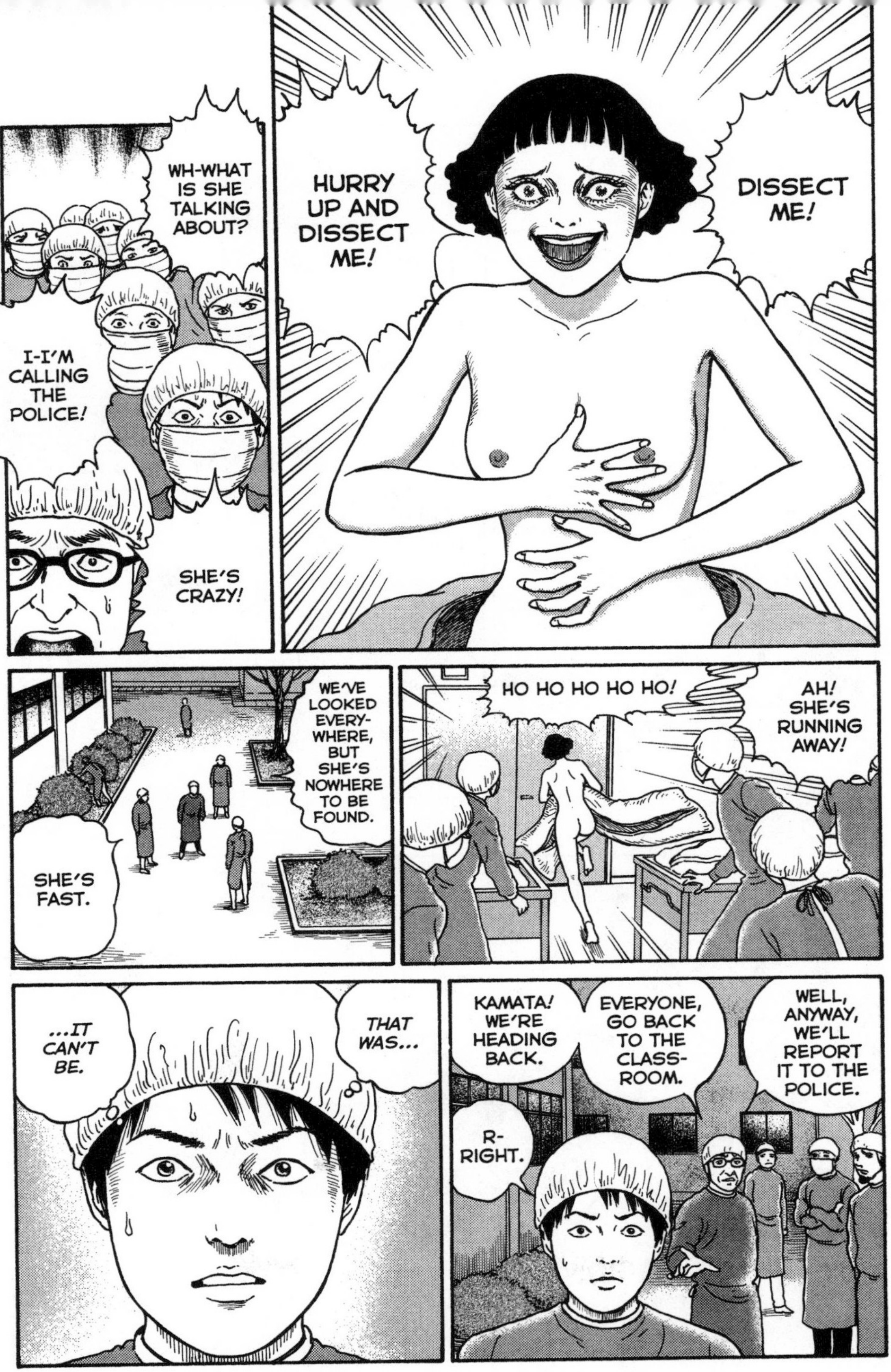
DISSECT ME!
HURRY UP AND DISSECT ME!
WH-WHAT IS SHE TALKING ABOUT?
I-I'M CALLING THE POLICE!
SHE'S CRAZY!
AH! SHE'S RUNNING AWAY!
HO HO HO HO HO!
WE'VE LOOKED EVERY-WHERE, BUT SHE'S NOWHERE TO BE FOUND.
SHE'S FAST.
WELL, ANYWAY, WE'LL REPORT IT TO THE POLICE.
EVERYONE, GO BACK TO THE CLASS-ROOM.
KAMATA! WE'RE HEADING BACK.
R-RIGHT.
THAT WAS...
...IT CAN'T BE.

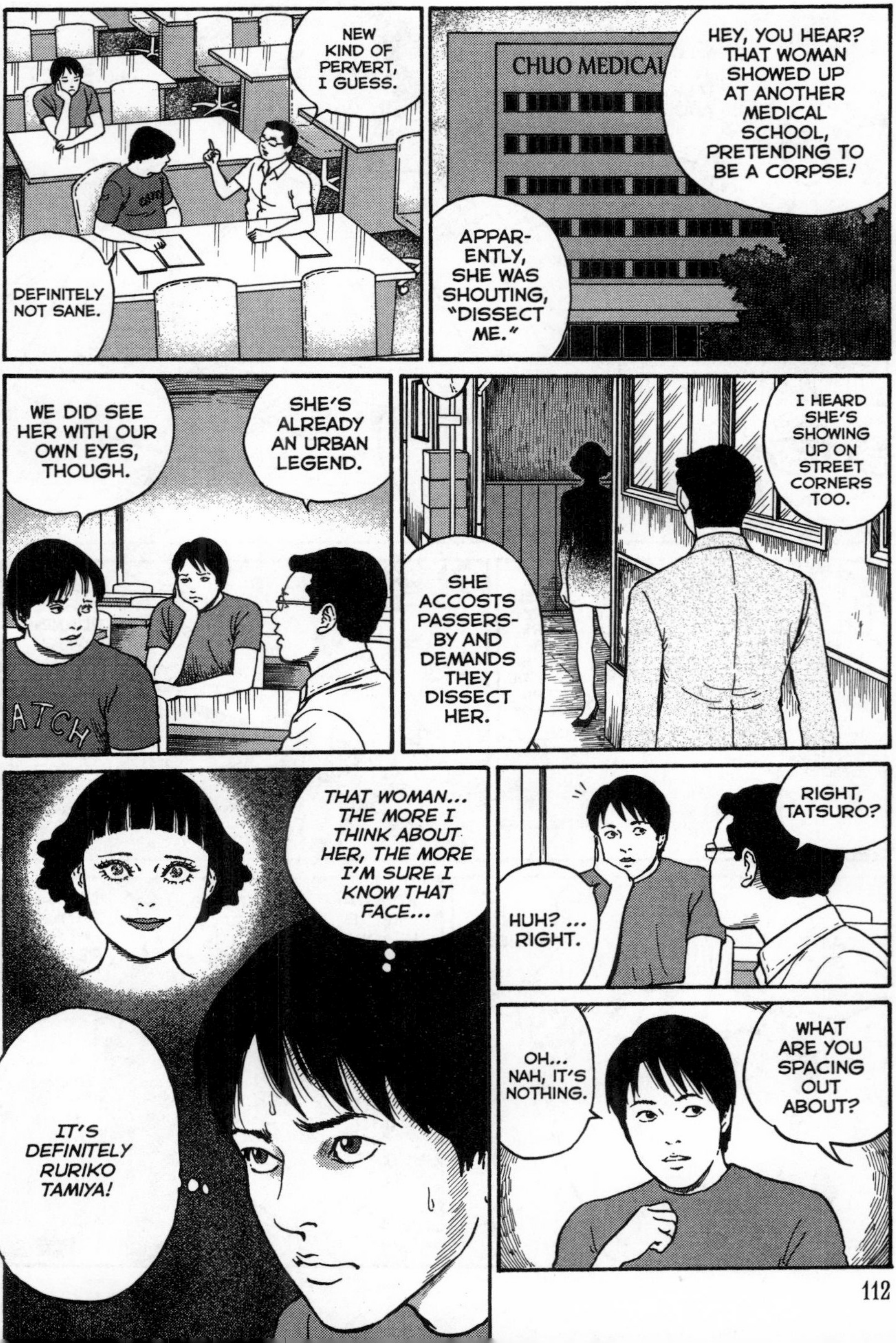
CHUO MEDICAL
HEY, YOU HEAR? THAT WOMAN SHOWED UP AT ANOTHER MEDICAL SCHOOL, PRETENDING TO BE A CORPSE!
APPARENTLY, SHE WAS SHOUTING, "DISSECT ME."
NEW KIND OF PERVERT, I GUESS.
DEFINITELY NOT SANE.
I HEARD SHE'S SHOWING UP ON STREET CORNERS TOO.
SHE ACCOSTS PASSERSBY AND DEMANDS THEY DISSECT HER.
SHE'S ALREADY AN URBAN LEGEND.
WE DID SEE HER WITH OUR OWN EYES, THOUGH.
RIGHT, TATSURO?
HUH? ... RIGHT.
WHAT ARE YOU SPACING OUT ABOUT?
OH... NAH, IT'S NOTHING.
THAT WOMAN... THE MORE I THINK ABOUT HER, THE MORE I'M SURE I KNOW THAT FACE...
IT'S DEFINITELY RURIKO TAMIYA!

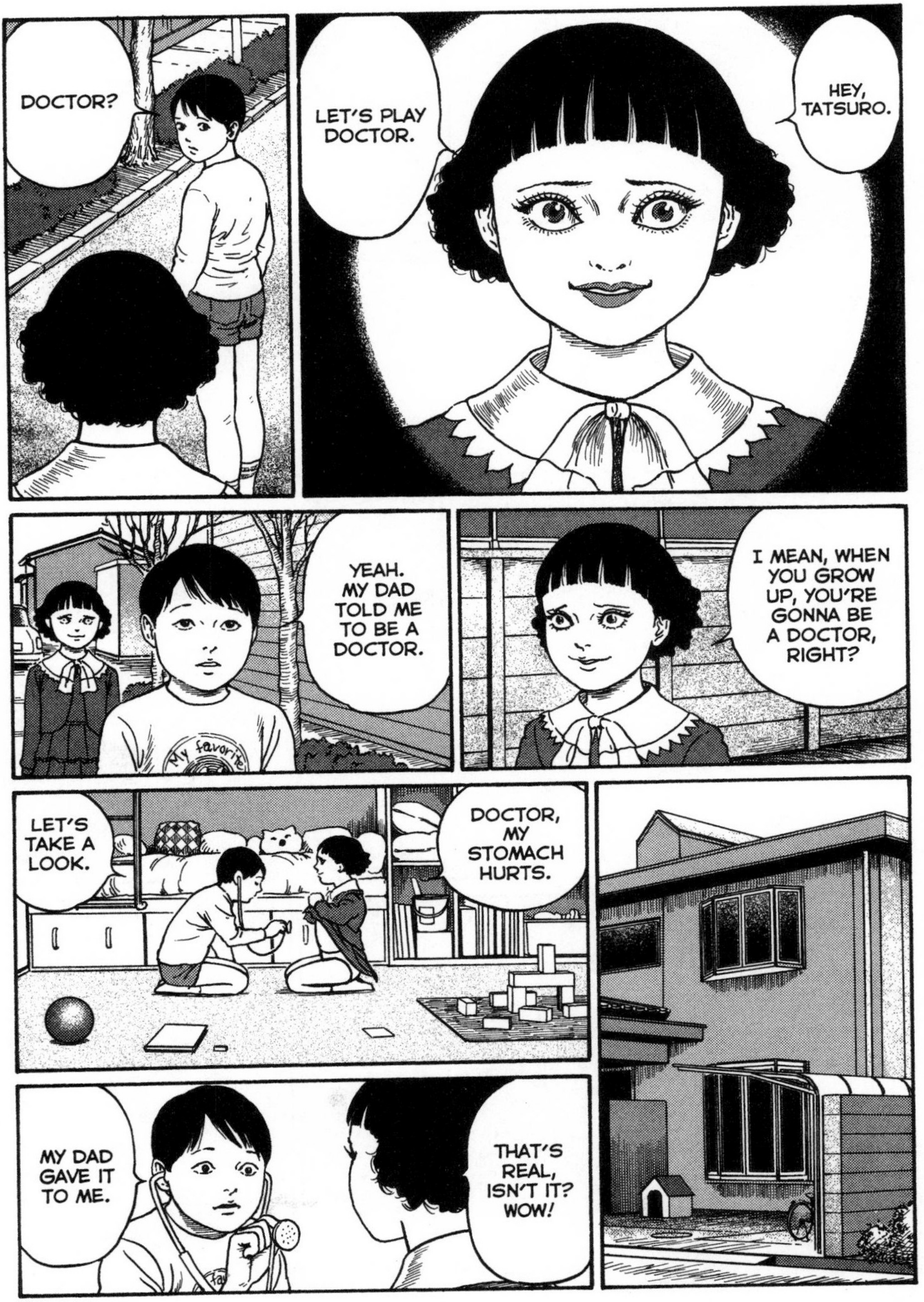
HEY, TATSURO.
LET'S PLAY DOCTOR.
DOCTOR?
I MEAN, WHEN YOU GROW UP, YOU'RE GONNA BE A DOCTOR, RIGHT?
YEAH. MY DAD TOLD ME TO BE A DOCTOR.
My favorite
DOCTOR, MY STOMACH HURTS.
LET'S TAKE A LOOK.
THAT'S REAL, ISN'T IT? WOW!
MY DAD GAVE IT TO ME.

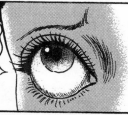

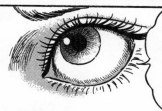

SO DID YOU GET A SCALPEL TOO?
HE'S NOT GONNA GIVE ME A SCALPEL.
HEY, BRING ONE NEXT TIME.
WHAT? I CAN'T.
YOU CAN JUST GET ONE FROM YOUR DAD'S CLINIC.
IF YOU SNEAK IT OUT, HE'LL NEVER KNOW.
KAMATA SURGICAL CLINIC
WHAT'S THIS? TATSURO?
YOUR FATHER IS SEEING A PATIENT RIGHT NOW. DID YOU NEED SOMETHING?
UH-UH. JUST STOPPED BY.
I'M ON MY WAY HOME ALREADY.
YOU ARE? WELL, BE CAREFUL.

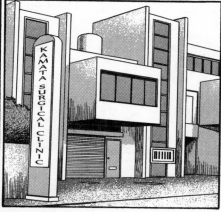

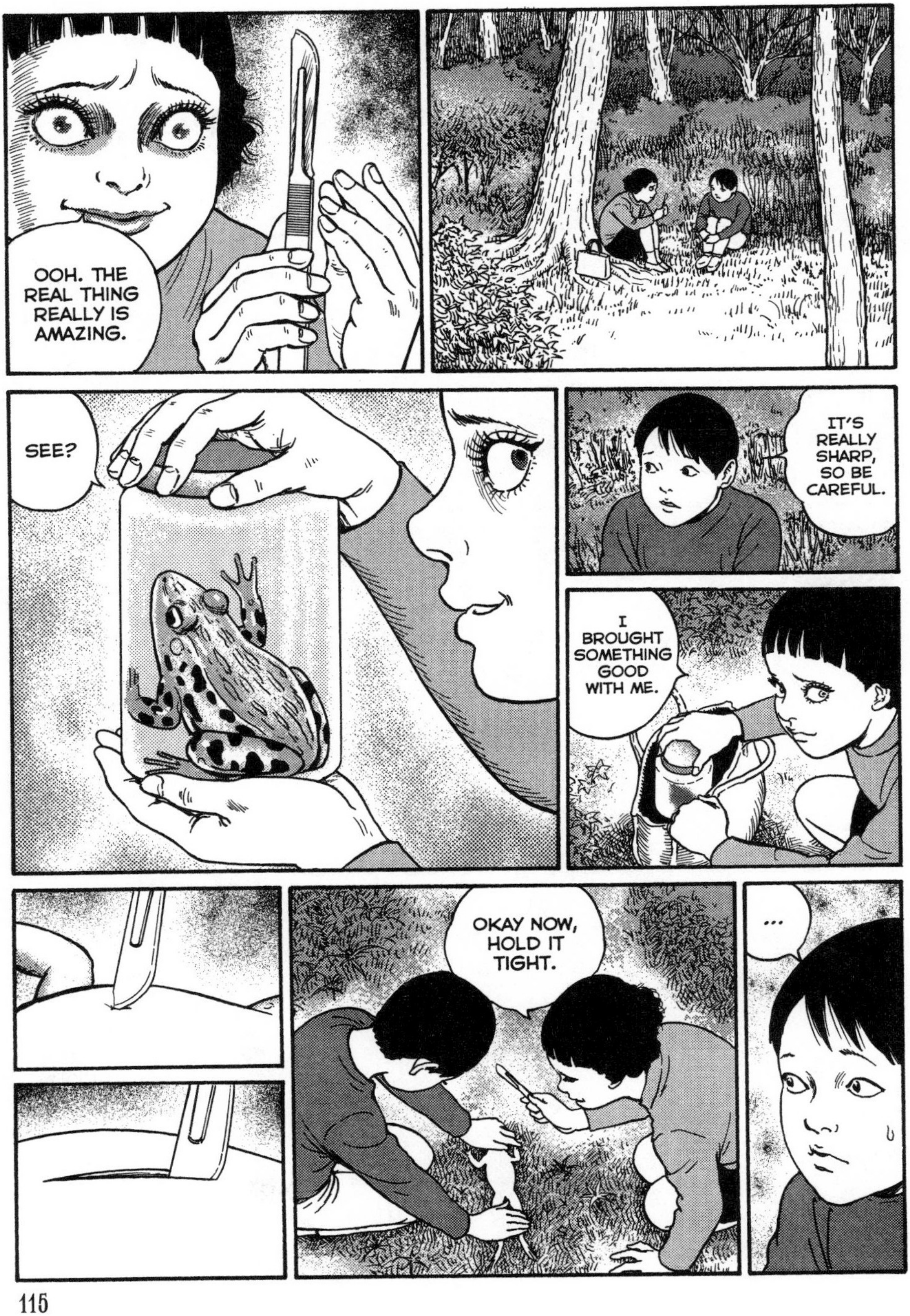
OOH. THE REAL THING REALLY IS AMAZING.
IT'S REALLY SHARP, SO BE CAREFUL.
I BROUGHT SOMETHING GOOD WITH ME.
SEE?
...
OKAY NOW, HOLD IT TIGHT.

WHOA!
GROSS!
BYON
SPROING
SPROING
AAAW.
HEY, TATSURO. CAN I HAVE THIS SCALPEL?
TO MAKE UP FOR LETTING THE FROG GET AWAY.
...BUT I HAVE TO PUT IT BACK.
NO WAY!
IF YOU DON'T LET ME HAVE IT, I'LL TELL YOUR DAD YOU STOLE IT.

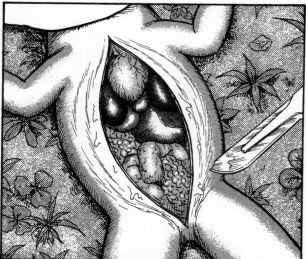

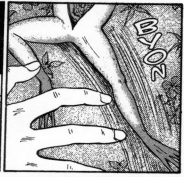

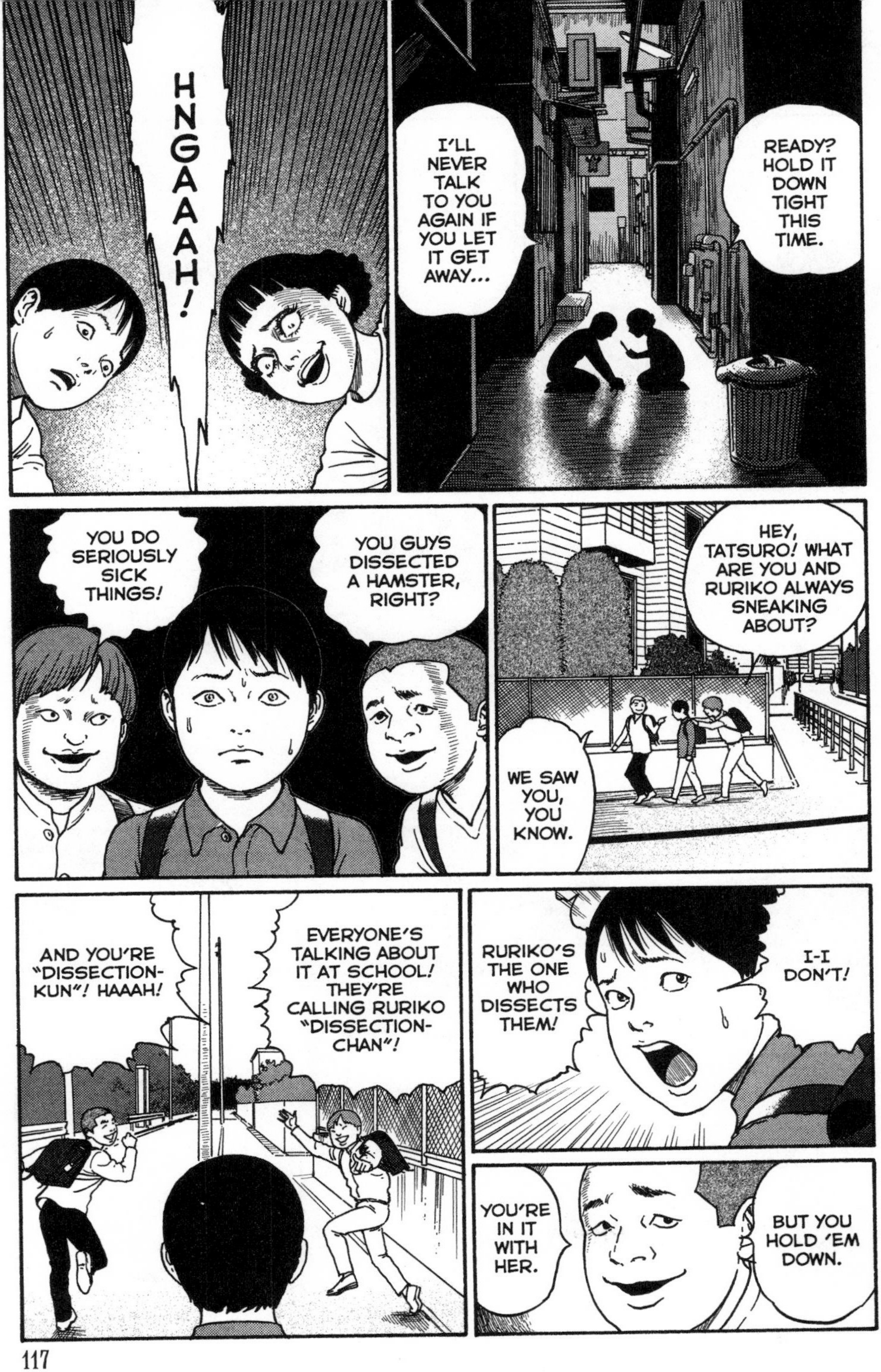
READY? HOLD IT DOWN TIGHT THIS TIME.
I'LL NEVER TALK TO YOU AGAIN IF YOU LET IT GET AWAY...
HNGAAAAH!
HEY, TATSURO! WHAT ARE YOU AND RURIKO ALWAYS SNEAKING ABOUT?
WE SAW YOU, YOU KNOW.
YOU GUYS DISSECTED A HAMSTER, RIGHT?
YOU DO SERIOUSLY SICK THINGS!
I-I DON'T!
RURIKO'S THE ONE WHO DISSECTS THEM!
BUT YOU HOLD 'EM DOWN.
YOU'RE IN IT WITH HER.
EVERYONE'S TALKING ABOUT IT AT SCHOOL! THEY'RE CALLING RURIKO "DISSECTION-CHAN"!
AND YOU'RE "DISSECTION-KUN"! HAAAH!

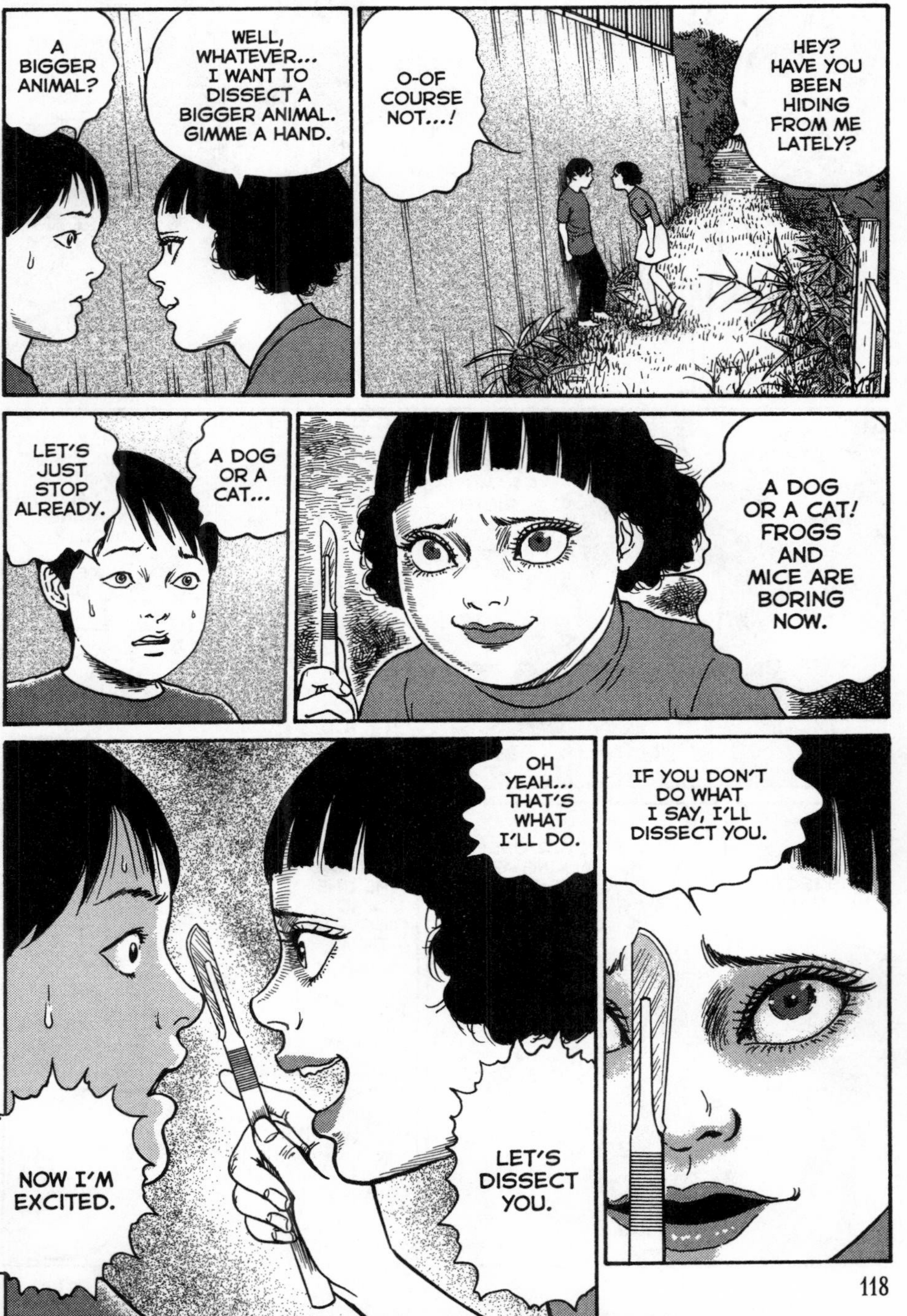
HEY? HAVE YOU BEEN HIDING FROM ME LATELY?
O-OF COURSE NOT...!
WELL, WHATEVER... I WANT TO DISSECT A BIGGER ANIMAL. GIMME A HAND.
A BIGGER ANIMAL?
A DOG OR A CAT! FROGS AND MICE ARE BORING NOW.
A DOG OR A CAT...
LET'S JUST STOP ALREADY.
IF YOU DON'T DO WHAT I SAY, I'LL DISSECT YOU.
OH YEAH... THAT'S WHAT I'LL DO.
LET'S DISSECT YOU.
NOW I'M EXCITED.

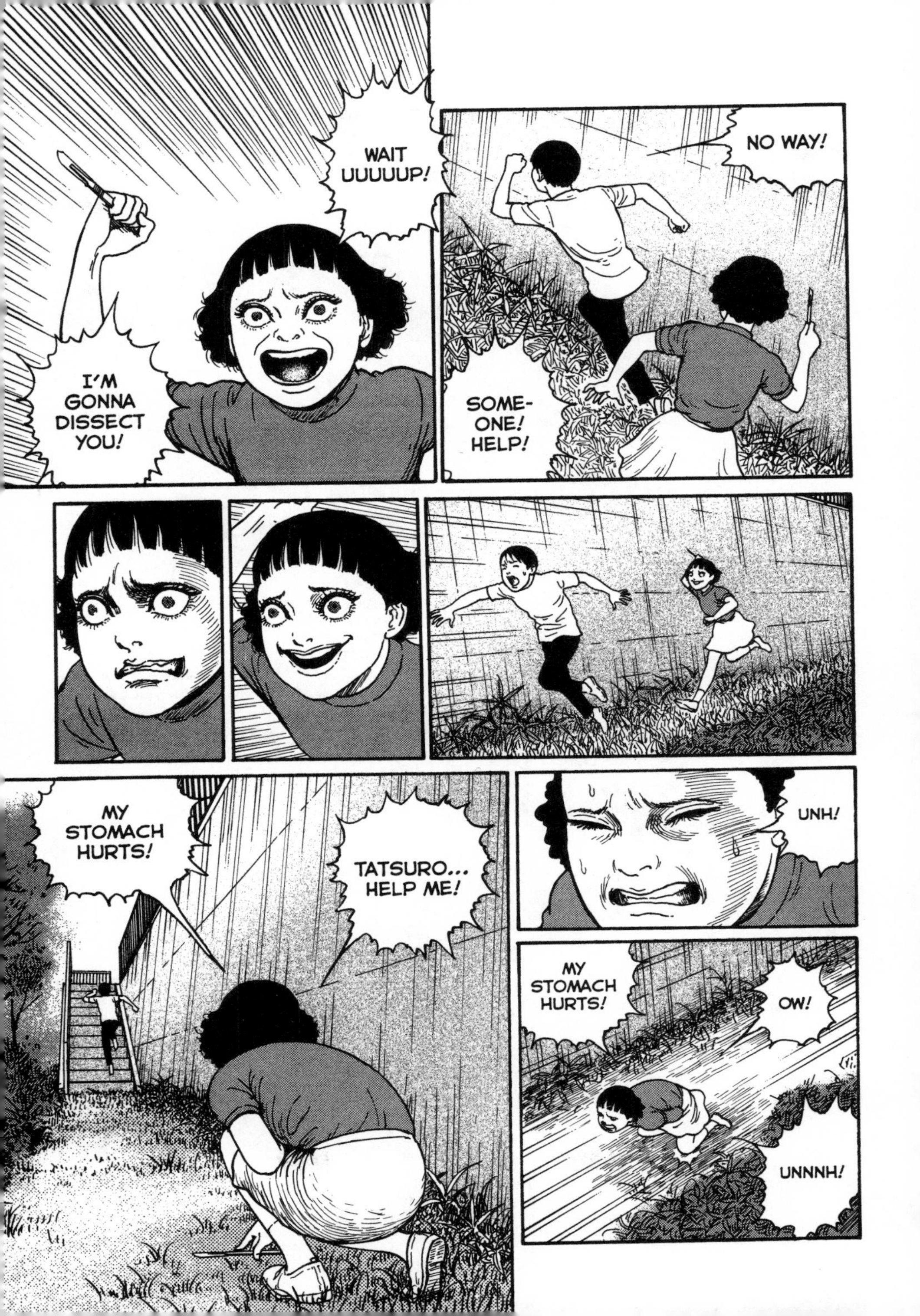
NO WAY!
SOME-ONE! HELP!
WAIT UUUUUP!
I'M GONNA DISSECT YOU!
UNH!
MY STOMACH HURTS!
OW!
UNNNH!
MY STOMACH HURTS!
TATSURO... HELP ME!

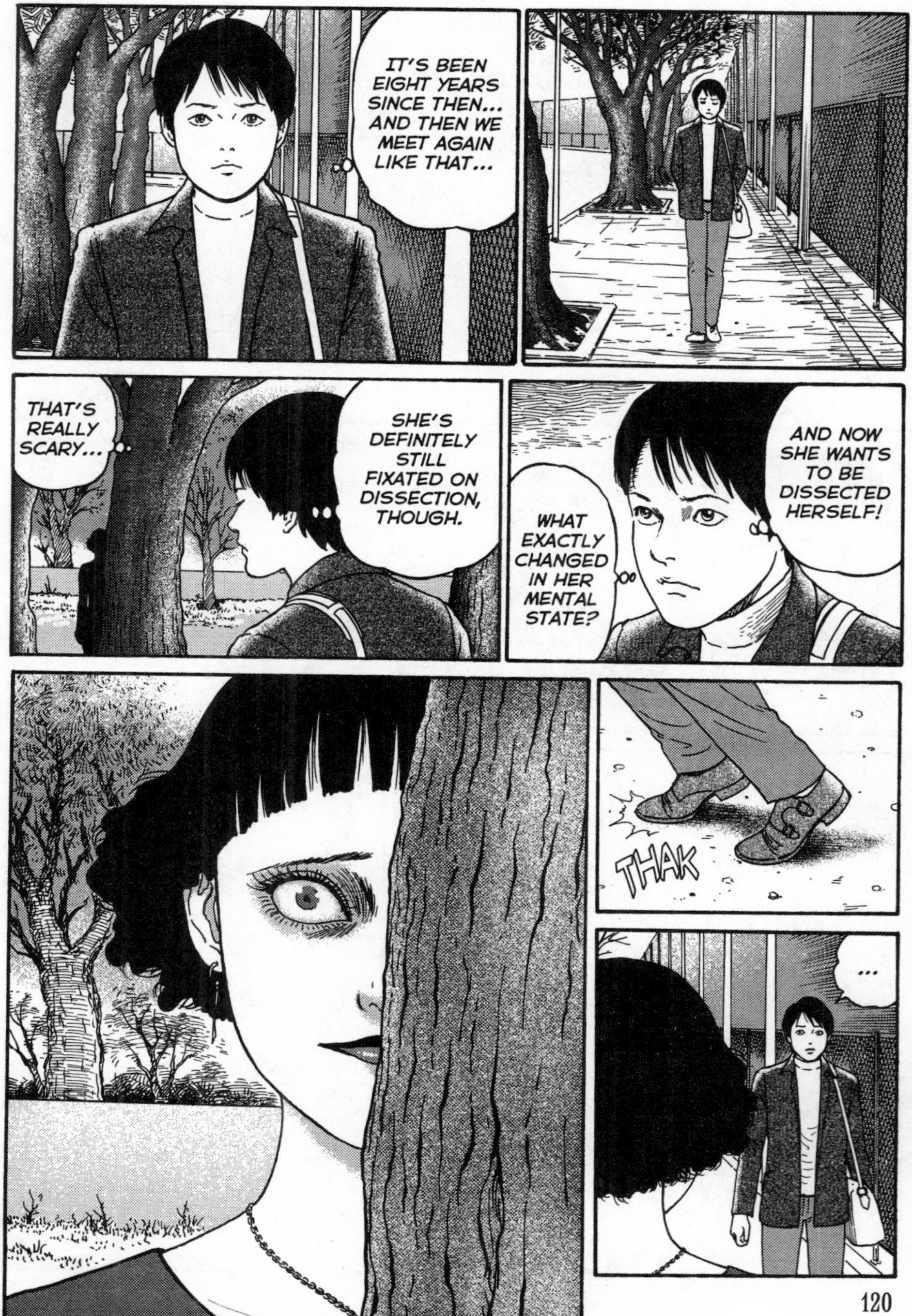
IT'S BEEN EIGHT YEARS SINCE THEN... AND THEN WE MEET AGAIN LIKE THAT...
AND NOW SHE WANTS TO BE DISSECTED HERSELF!
WHAT EXACTLY CHANGED IN HER MENTAL STATE?
SHE'S DEFINITELY STILL FIXATED ON DISSECTION, THOUGH.
THAT'S REALLY SCARY...
THAK
...

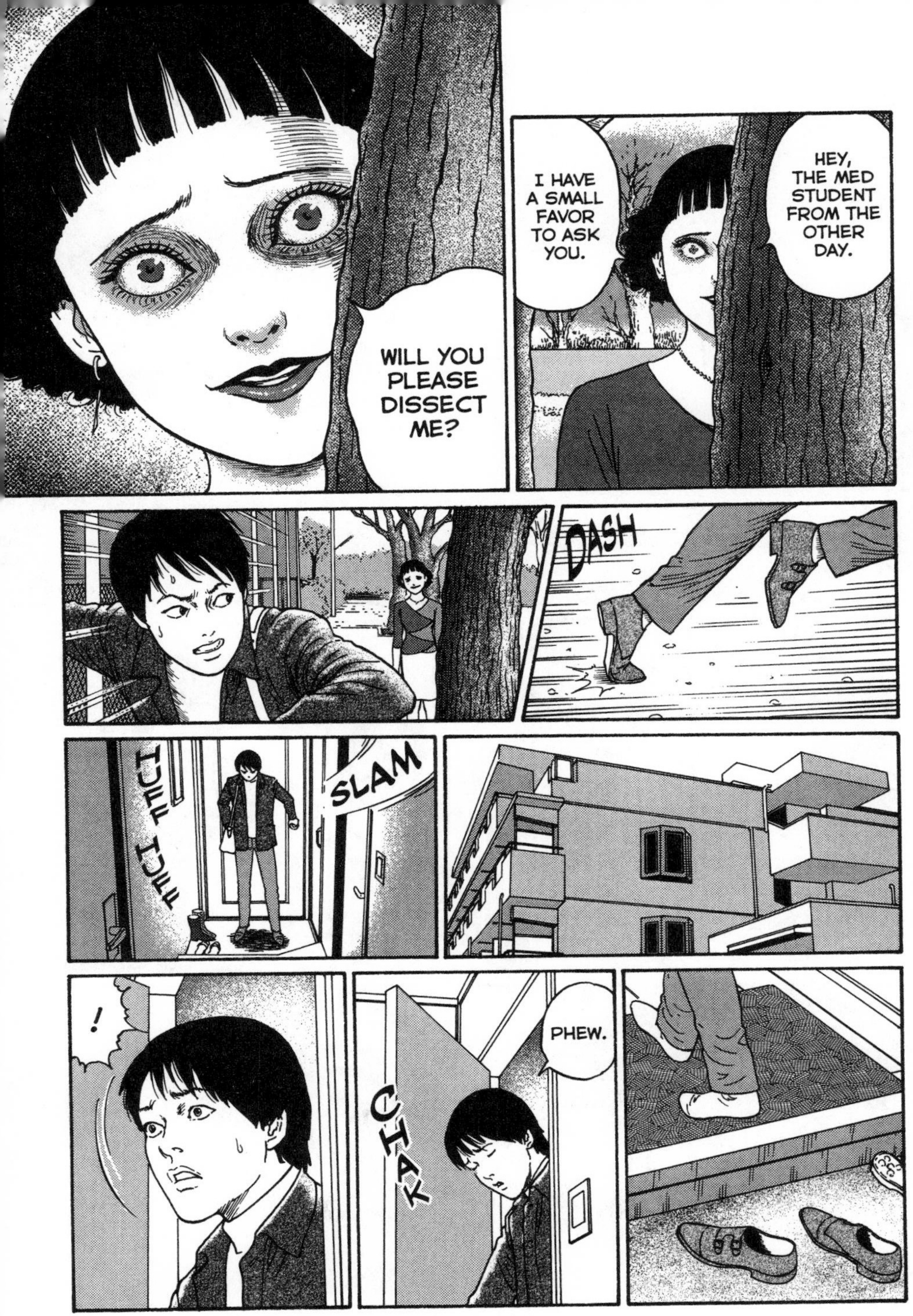
HEY, THE MED STUDENT FROM THE OTHER DAY.
I HAVE A SMALL FAVOR TO ASK YOU.
WILL YOU PLEASE DISSECT ME?
DASH
SLAM
HUFF HUFF
PHEW.
CHAK
!

FWK

HOW DID YOU GET IN HERE?!

HU—

BAM

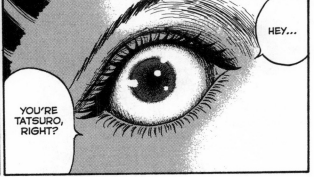

HEY...

YOU'RE TATSURO, RIGHT?

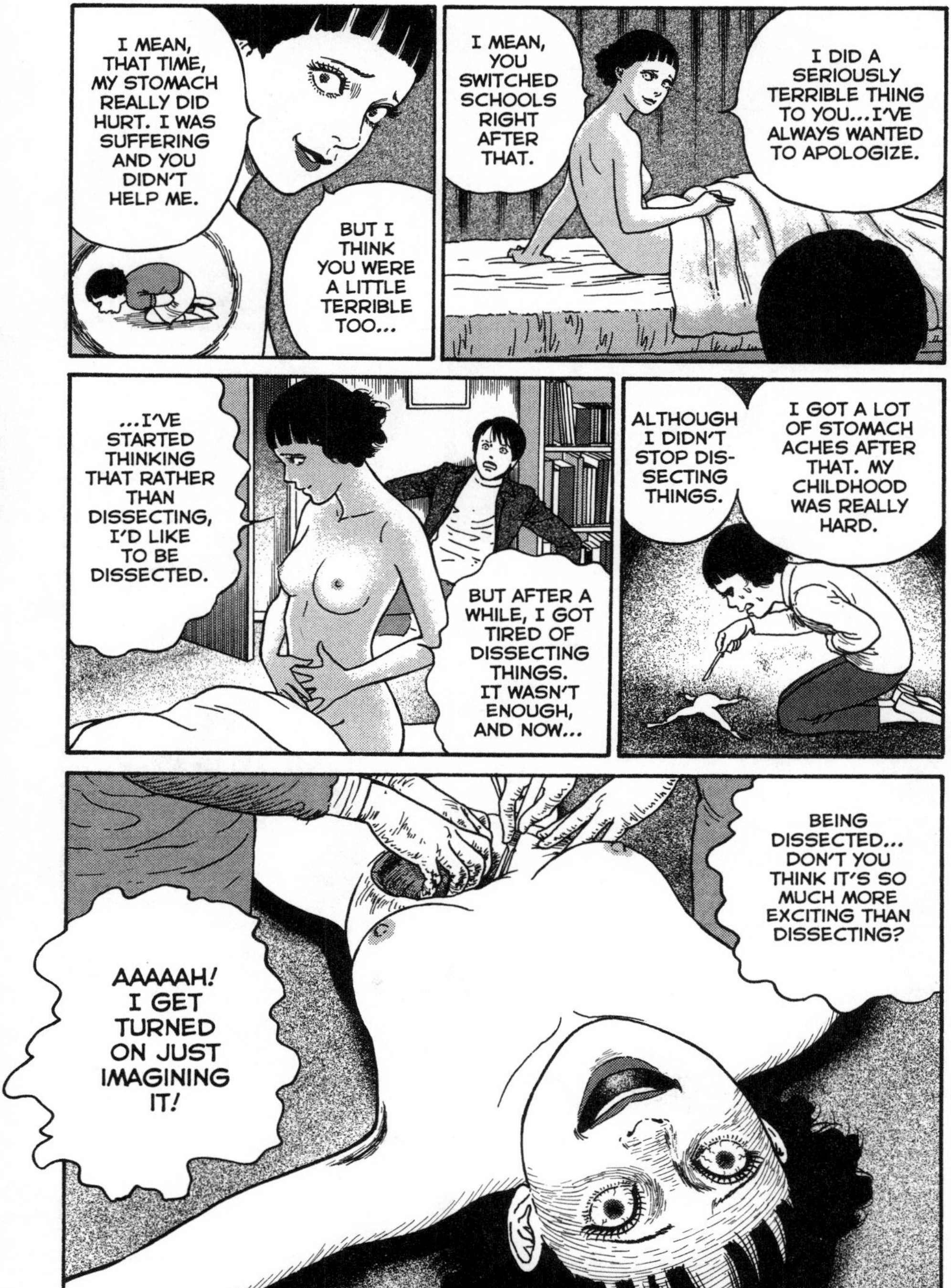
I DID A SERIOUSLY TERRIBLE THING TO YOU...I'VE ALWAYS WANTED TO APOLOGIZE.
I MEAN, YOU SWITCHED SCHOOLS RIGHT AFTER THAT.
I MEAN, THAT TIME, MY STOMACH REALLY DID HURT. I WAS SUFFERING AND YOU DIDN'T HELP ME.
BUT I THINK YOU WERE A LITTLE TERRIBLE TOO...
I GOT A LOT OF STOMACH ACHES AFTER THAT. MY CHILDHOOD WAS REALLY HARD.
ALTHOUGH I DIDN'T STOP DIS-SECTING THINGS.
BUT AFTER A WHILE, I GOT TIRED OF DISSECTING THINGS. IT WASN'T ENOUGH, AND NOW...
...I'VE STARTED THINKING THAT RATHER THAN DISSECTING, I'D LIKE TO BE DISSECTED.
BEING DISSECTED... DON'T YOU THINK IT'S SO MUCH MORE EXCITING THAN DISSECTING?
AAAAAH! I GET TURNED ON JUST IMAGINING IT!

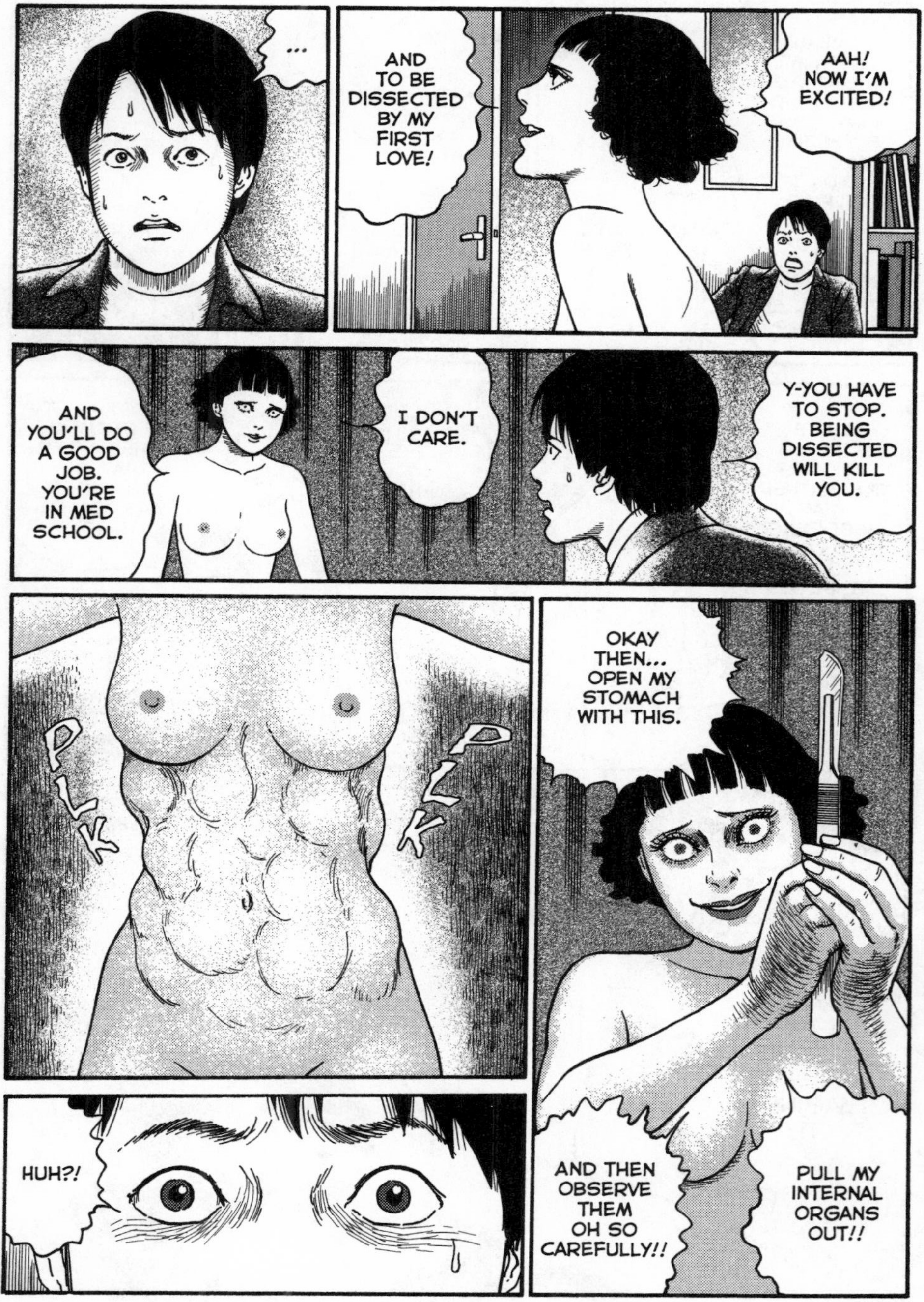
AAH! NOW I'M EXCITED!
AND TO BE DISSECTED BY MY FIRST LOVE!
...
Y-YOU HAVE TO STOP. BEING DISSECTED WILL KILL YOU.
I DON'T CARE.
AND YOU'LL DO A GOOD JOB. YOU'RE IN MED SCHOOL.
OKAY THEN... OPEN MY STOMACH WITH THIS.
PULL MY INTERNAL ORGANS OUT!!
AND THEN OBSERVE THEM OH SO CAREFULLY!!
PLK
PLK
HUH?!

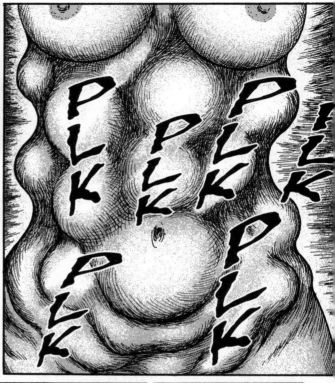

AAAH!

HURRY AND DISSECT MEEEEE!

AAAAH!

I'M JUST DREAMING!

IT'S A DREAM...

DASH

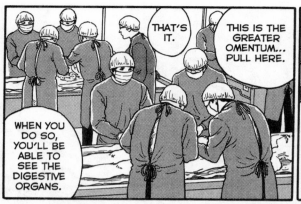

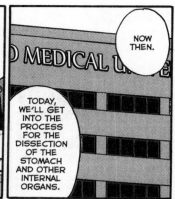

NOW THEN.
TODAY, WE'LL GET INTO THE PROCESS FOR THE DISSECTION OF THE STOMACH AND OTHER INTERNAL ORGANS.
THIS IS THE GREATER OMENTUM... PULL HERE.
THAT'S IT.
WHEN YOU DO SO, YOU'LL BE ABLE TO SEE THE DIGESTIVE ORGANS.
HEY, TATSURO?
HM?
I WAS ON THIS DATING SITE YESTERDAY, RIGHT?
AND I SAW A PRETTY STRANGE POST.
STRANGE HOW?
IT SAID, "I'M LOOKING FOR A SPECIAL SOMEONE TO DISSECT ME!"
IT HAS TO BE THAT WOMAN, RIGHT?
WHAT DID YOU SAY...?!
STAGGER
WHAT'S WRONG, KAMATA?
IF YOU'RE NOT FEELING WELL, GO LIE DOWN.

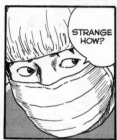

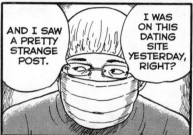

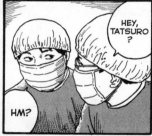

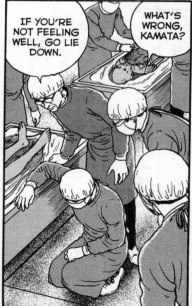

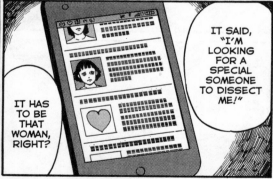

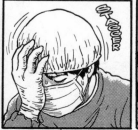

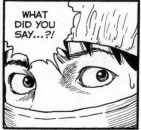

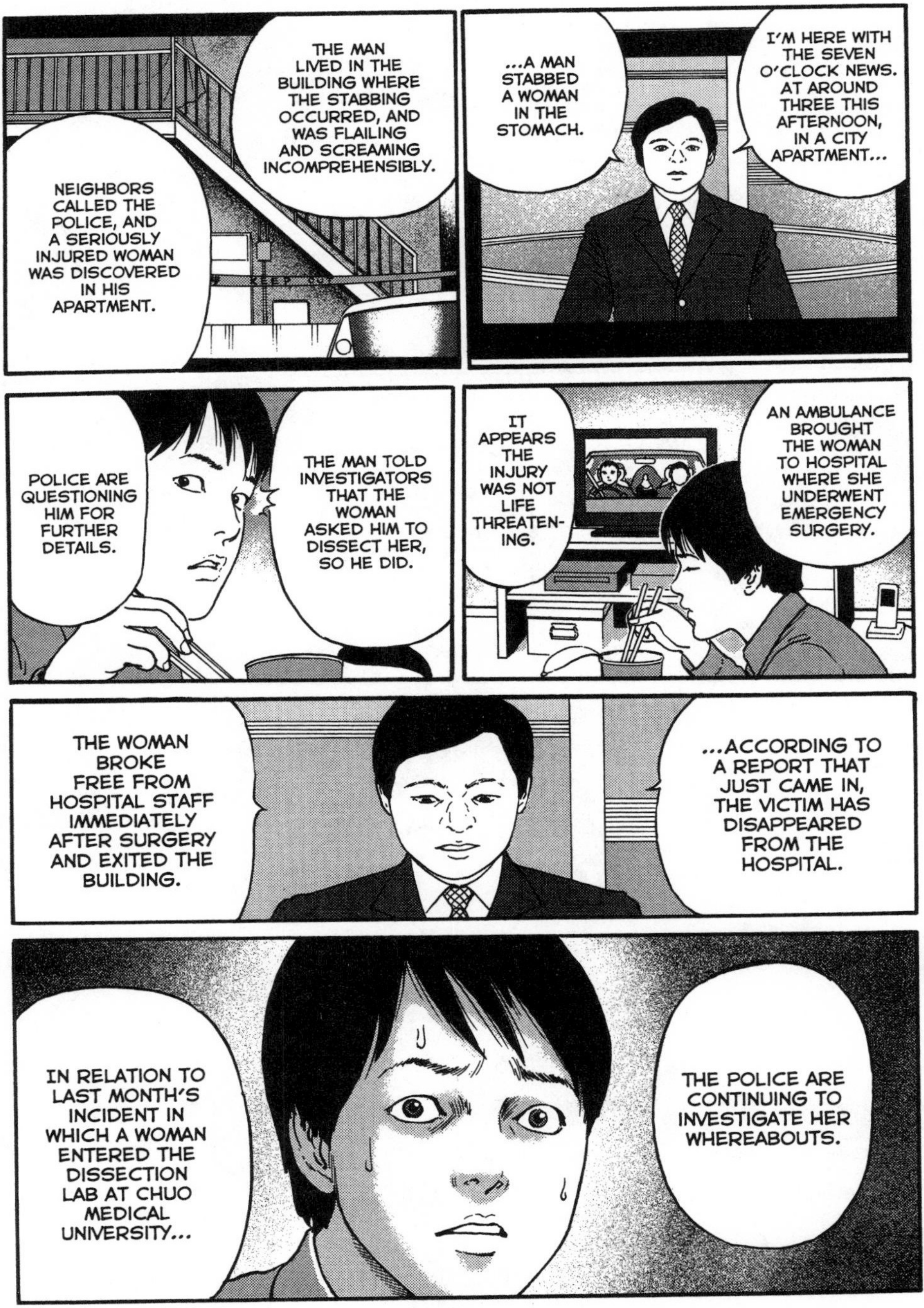
I'M HERE WITH THE SEVEN O'CLOCK NEWS. AT AROUND THREE THIS AFTERNOON, IN A CITY APARTMENT...
...A MAN STABBED A WOMAN IN THE STOMACH.
THE MAN LIVED IN THE BUILDING WHERE THE STABBING OCCURRED, AND WAS FLAILING AND SCREAMING INCOMPREHENSIBLY.
NEIGHBORS CALLED THE POLICE, AND A SERIOUSLY INJURED WOMAN WAS DISCOVERED IN HIS APARTMENT.
AN AMBULANCE BROUGHT THE WOMAN TO HOSPITAL WHERE SHE UNDERWENT EMERGENCY SURGERY.
IT APPEARS THE INJURY WAS NOT LIFE THREATEN-ING.
THE MAN TOLD INVESTIGATORS THAT THE WOMAN ASKED HIM TO DISSECT HER, SO HE DID.
POLICE ARE QUESTIONING HIM FOR FURTHER DETAILS.
...ACCORDING TO A REPORT THAT JUST CAME IN, THE VICTIM HAS DISAPPEARED FROM THE HOSPITAL.
THE WOMAN BROKE FREE FROM HOSPITAL STAFF IMMEDIATELY AFTER SURGERY AND EXITED THE BUILDING.
THE POLICE ARE CONTINUING TO INVESTIGATE HER WHEREABOUTS.
IN RELATION TO LAST MONTH'S INCIDENT IN WHICH A WOMAN ENTERED THE DISSECTION LAB AT CHUO MEDICAL UNIVERSITY...

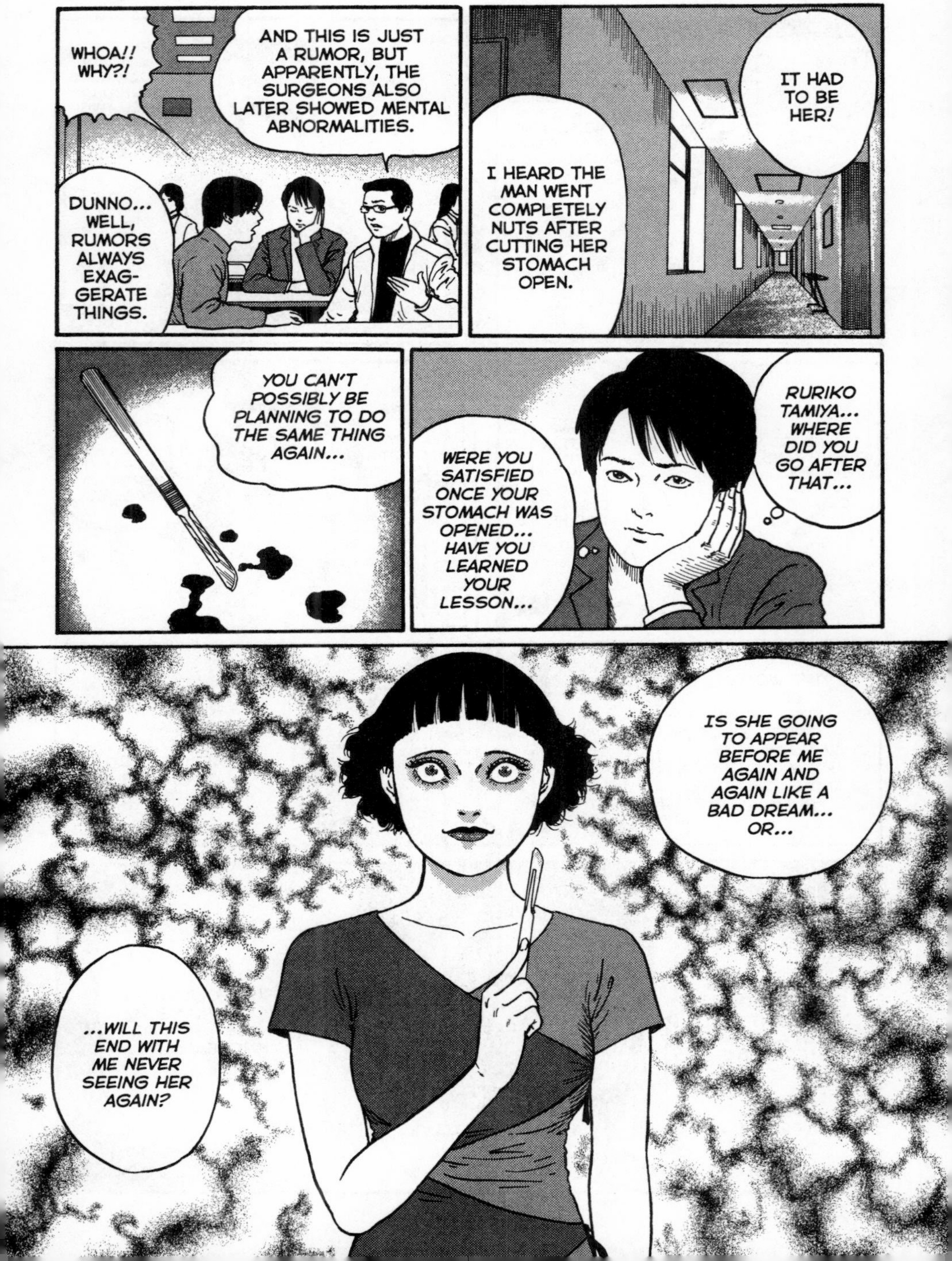
IT HAD TO BE HER!
I HEARD THE MAN WENT COMPLETELY NUTS AFTER CUTTING HER STOMACH OPEN.
AND THIS IS JUST A RUMOR, BUT APPARENTLY, THE SURGEONS ALSO LATER SHOWED MENTAL ABNORMALITIES.
WHOA!! WHY?!
DUNNO... WELL, RUMORS ALWAYS EXAG-GERATE THINGS.
RURIKO TAMIYA... WHERE DID YOU GO AFTER THAT...
WERE YOU SATISFIED ONCE YOUR STOMACH WAS OPENED... HAVE YOU LEARNED YOUR LESSON...
YOU CAN'T POSSIBLY BE PLANNING TO DO THE SAME THING AGAIN...
IS SHE GOING TO APPEAR BEFORE ME AGAIN AND AGAIN LIKE A BAD DREAM... OR...
...WILL THIS END WITH ME NEVER SEEING HER AGAIN?

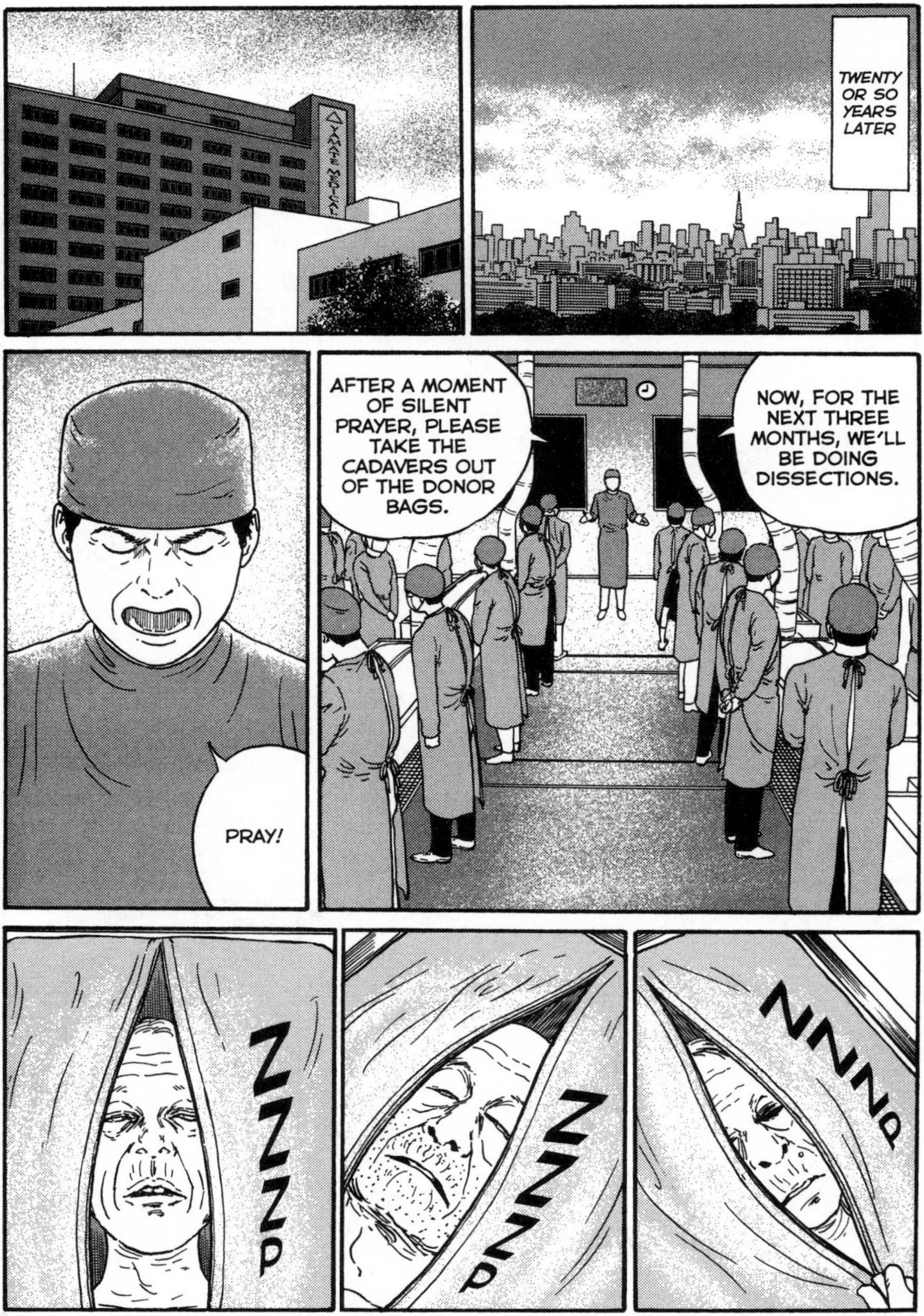
TWENTY OR SO YEARS LATER
YAMATE MEDICAL
NOW, FOR THE NEXT THREE MONTHS, WE'LL BE DOING DISSECTIONS.
AFTER A MOMENT OF SILENT PRAYER, PLEASE TAKE THE CADAVERS OUT OF THE DONOR BAGS.
PRAY!
ZZZP
ZZZZP
ZZZZP

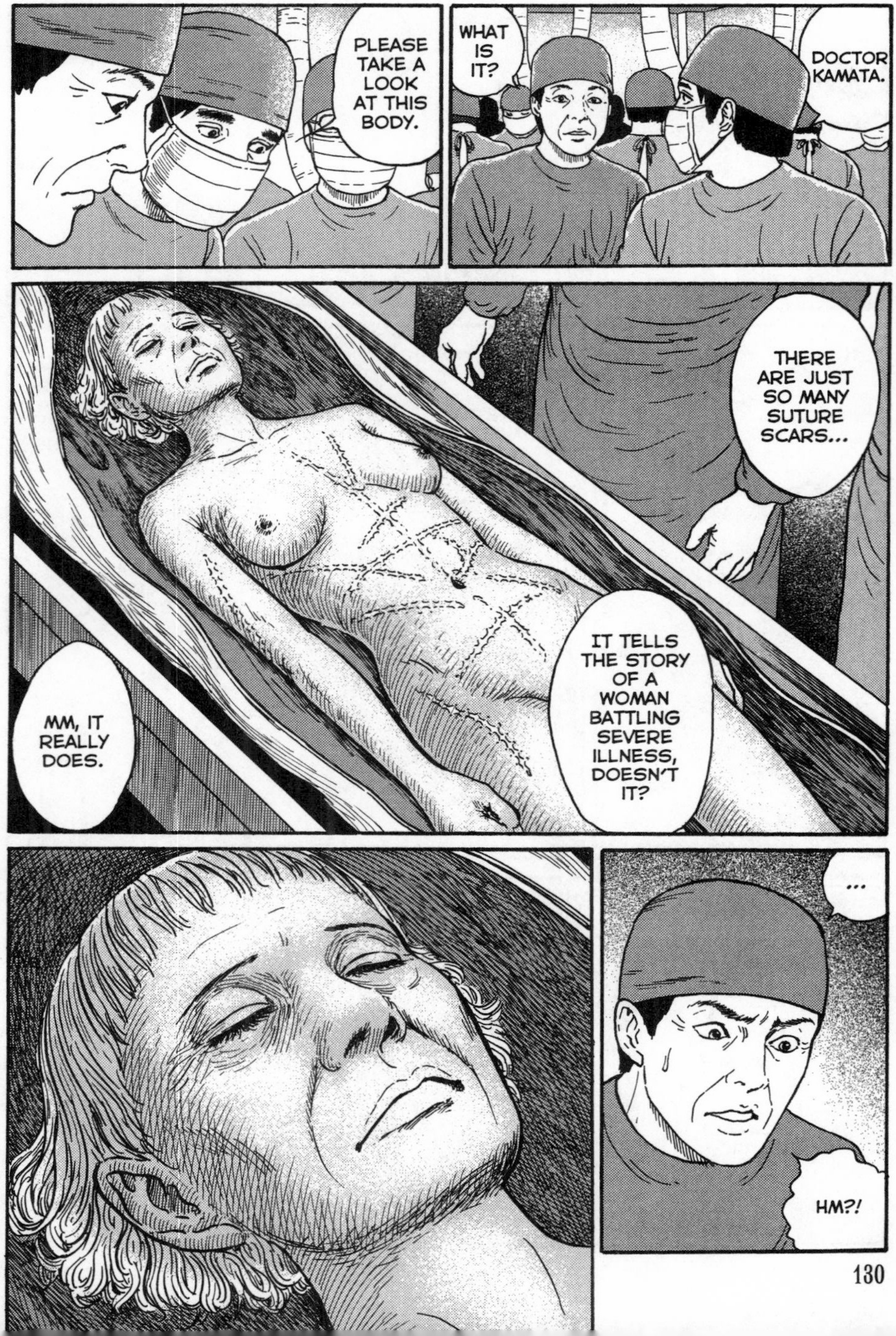
DOCTOR KAMATA.
WHAT IS IT?
PLEASE TAKE A LOOK AT THIS BODY.
THERE ARE JUST SO MANY SUTURE SCARS...
IT TELLS THE STORY OF A WOMAN BATTLING SEVERE ILLNESS, DOESN'T IT?
MM, IT REALLY DOES.
...
HM?!

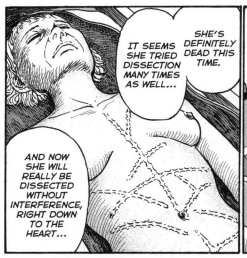

TH- THIS IS...
...RURIKO TAMIYA?
SHE'S DEFINITELY DEAD THIS TIME.
IT SEEMS SHE TRIED DISSECTION MANY TIMES AS WELL...
AND NOW SHE WILL REALLY BE DISSECTED WITHOUT INTERFERENCE, RIGHT DOWN TO THE HEART...
ALL RIGHT. TODAY, WE'LL BE GETTING INTO DISSECTION OF THE INTERNAL ORGANS.
PLEASE PAY CLOSE ATTENTION TO THE MUSCLES OF THE STOMACH WALL AS YOU PROCEED WITH THE DISSECTION.
YAMATE MEDICAL UNIVERSIT
AH! DOCTOR KAMATA!
WHAT? WHAT'S WRONG?
P- PLEASE TAKE A LOOK AT THIS!
AH!!

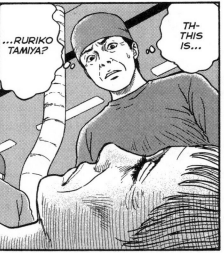

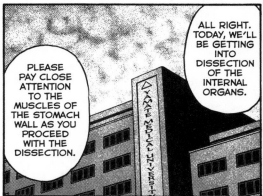

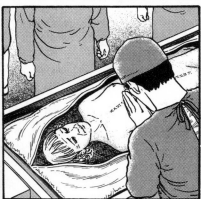

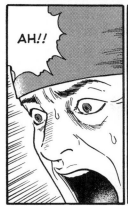

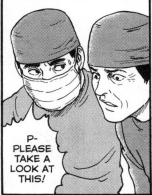

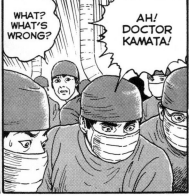

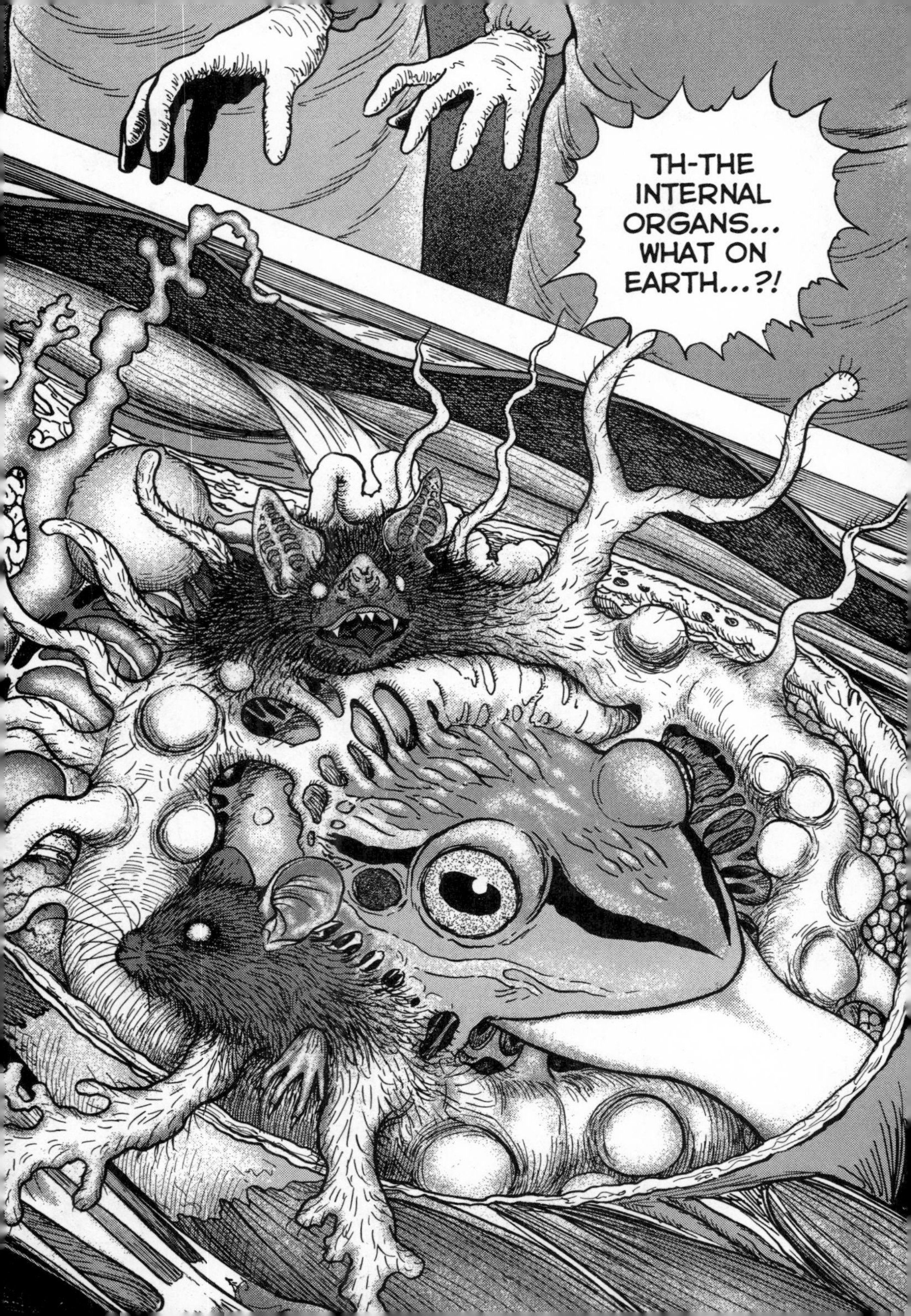
TH-THE INTERNAL ORGANS... WHAT ON EARTH...?!

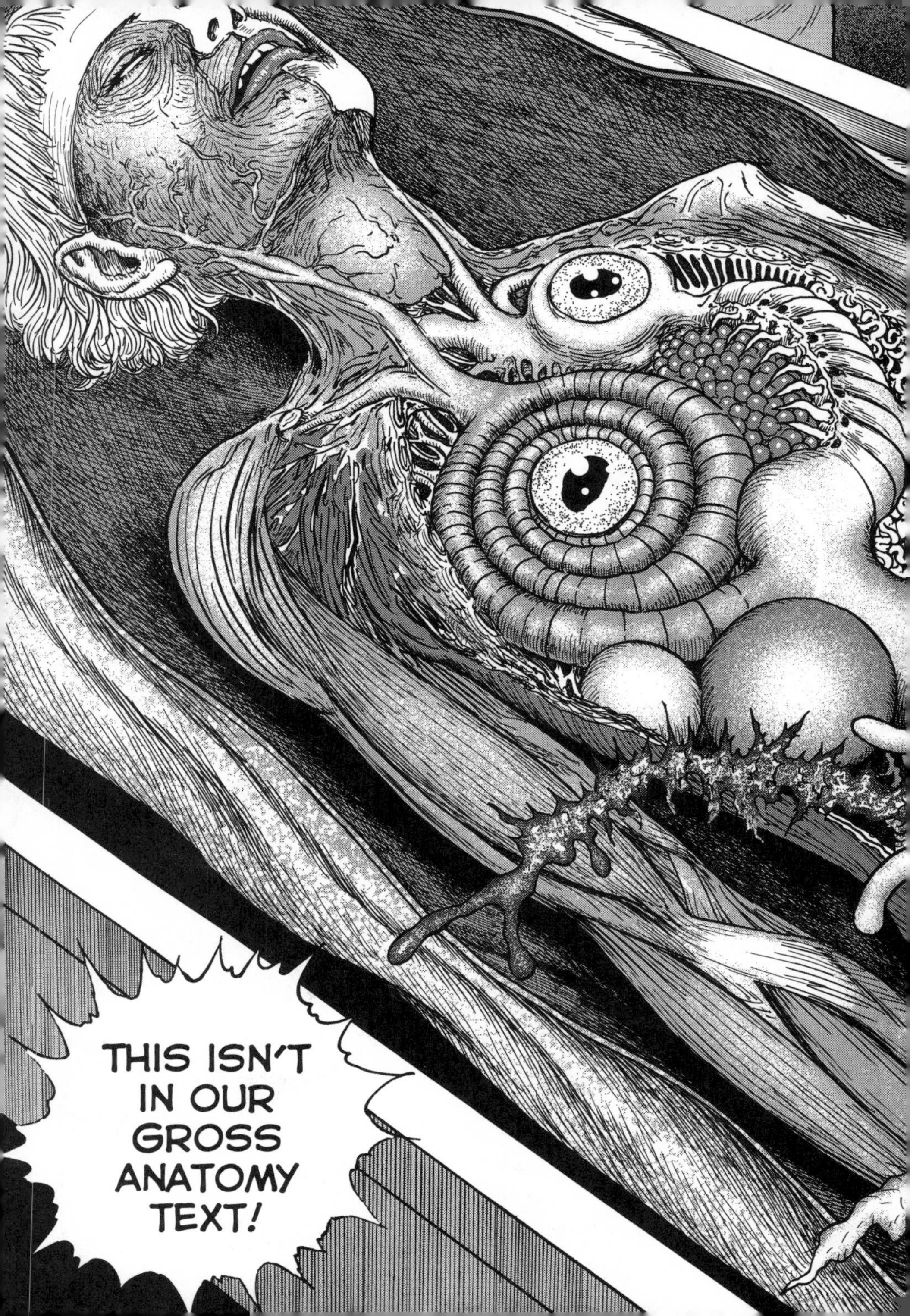
THIS ISN'T IN OUR GROSS ANATOMY TEXT!

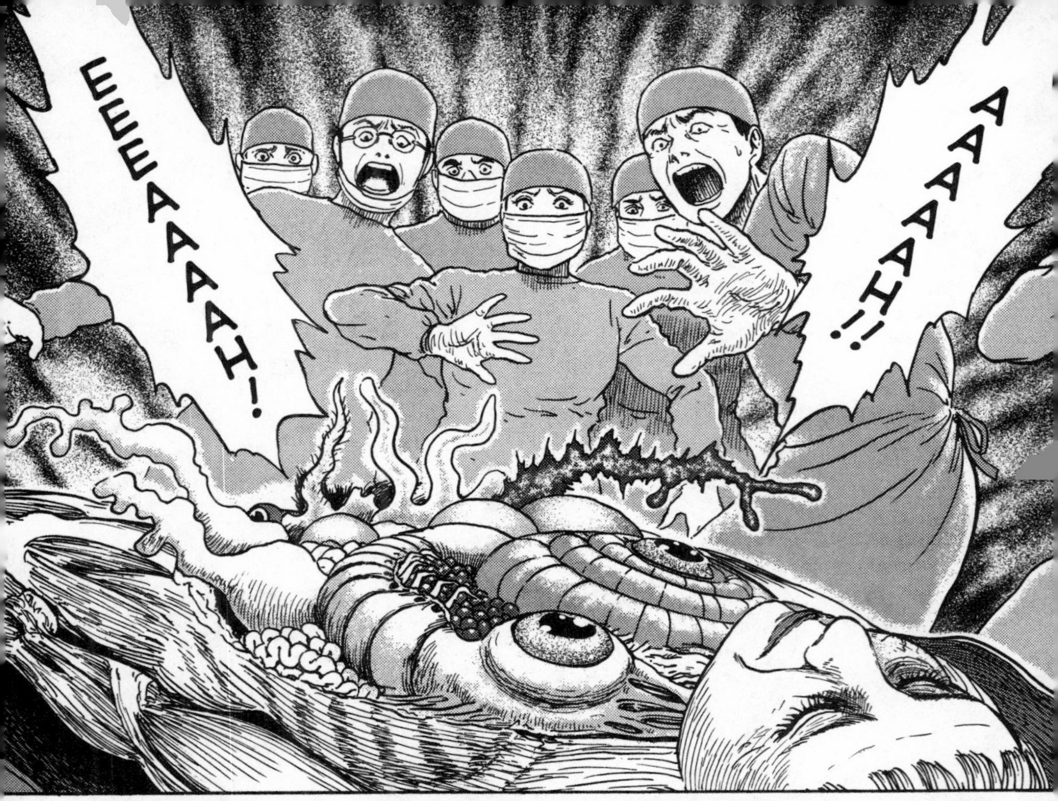
AAAAAAH!!
EEEAAAAH!

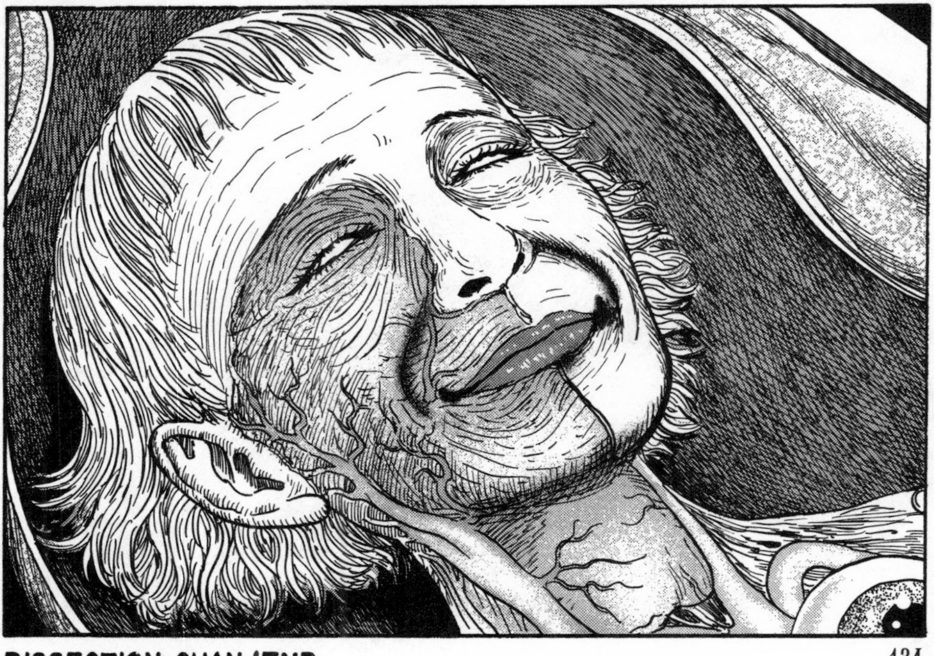

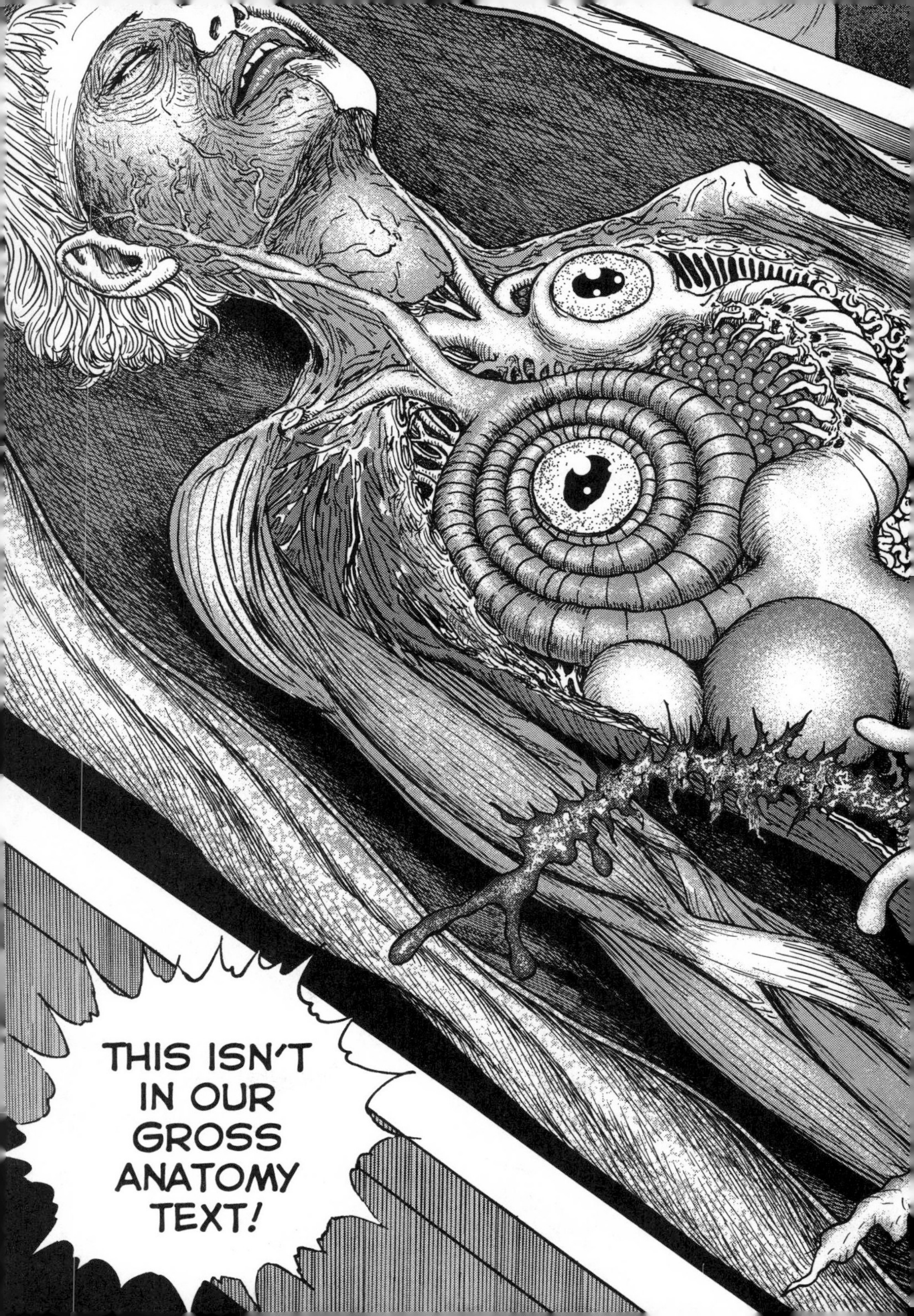
THIS ISN'T IN OUR GROSS ANATOMY TEXT!

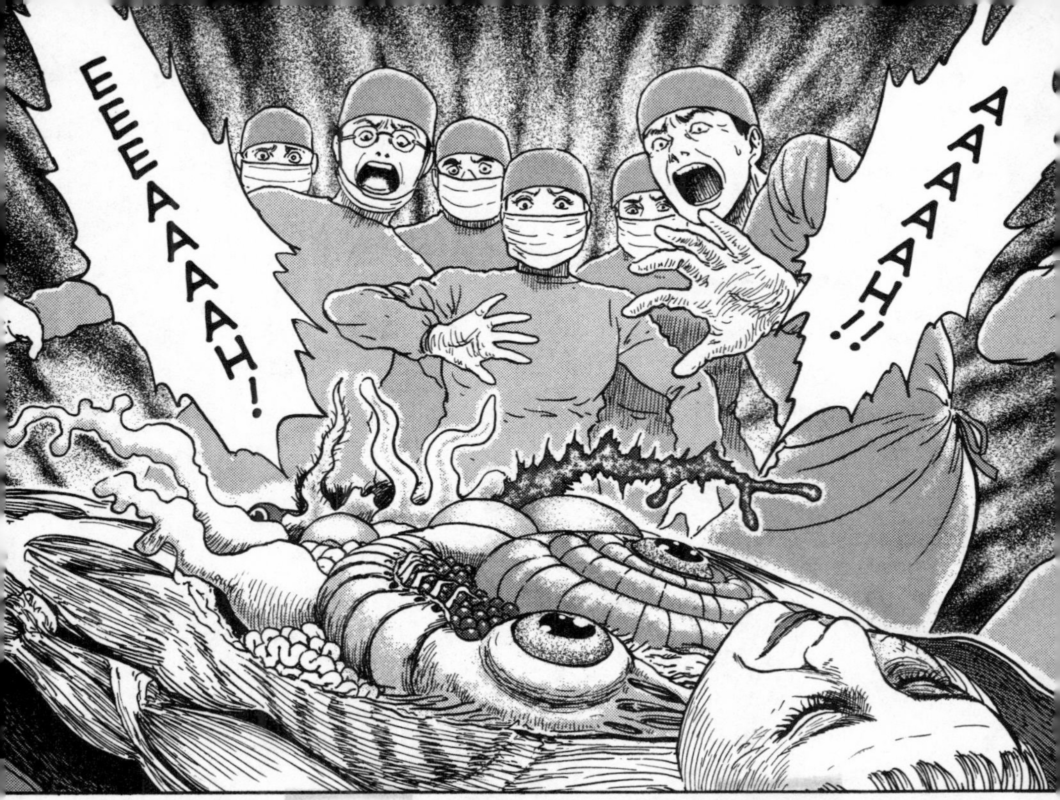
AAAAAH!!
EEEEAAAAH!

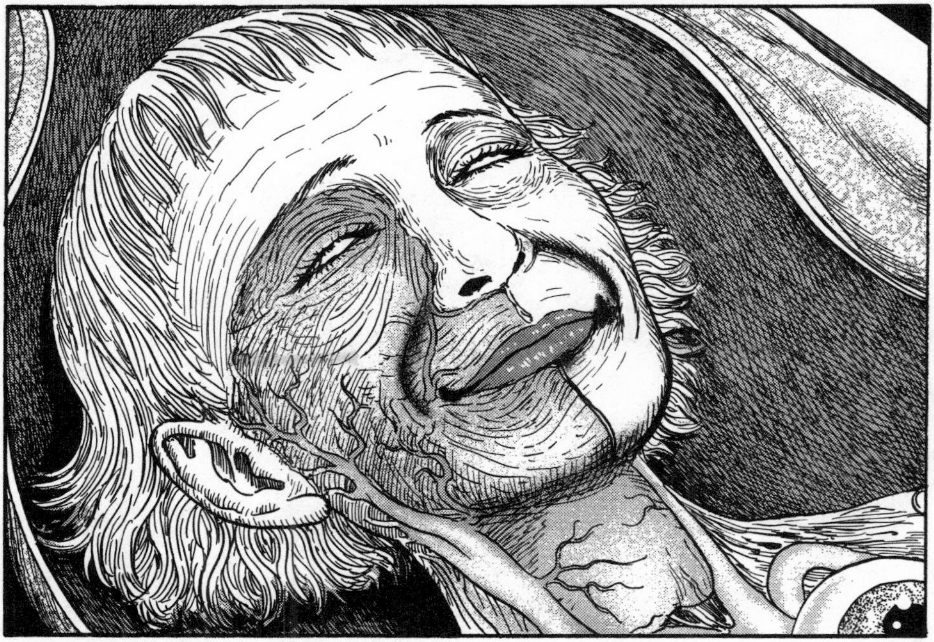

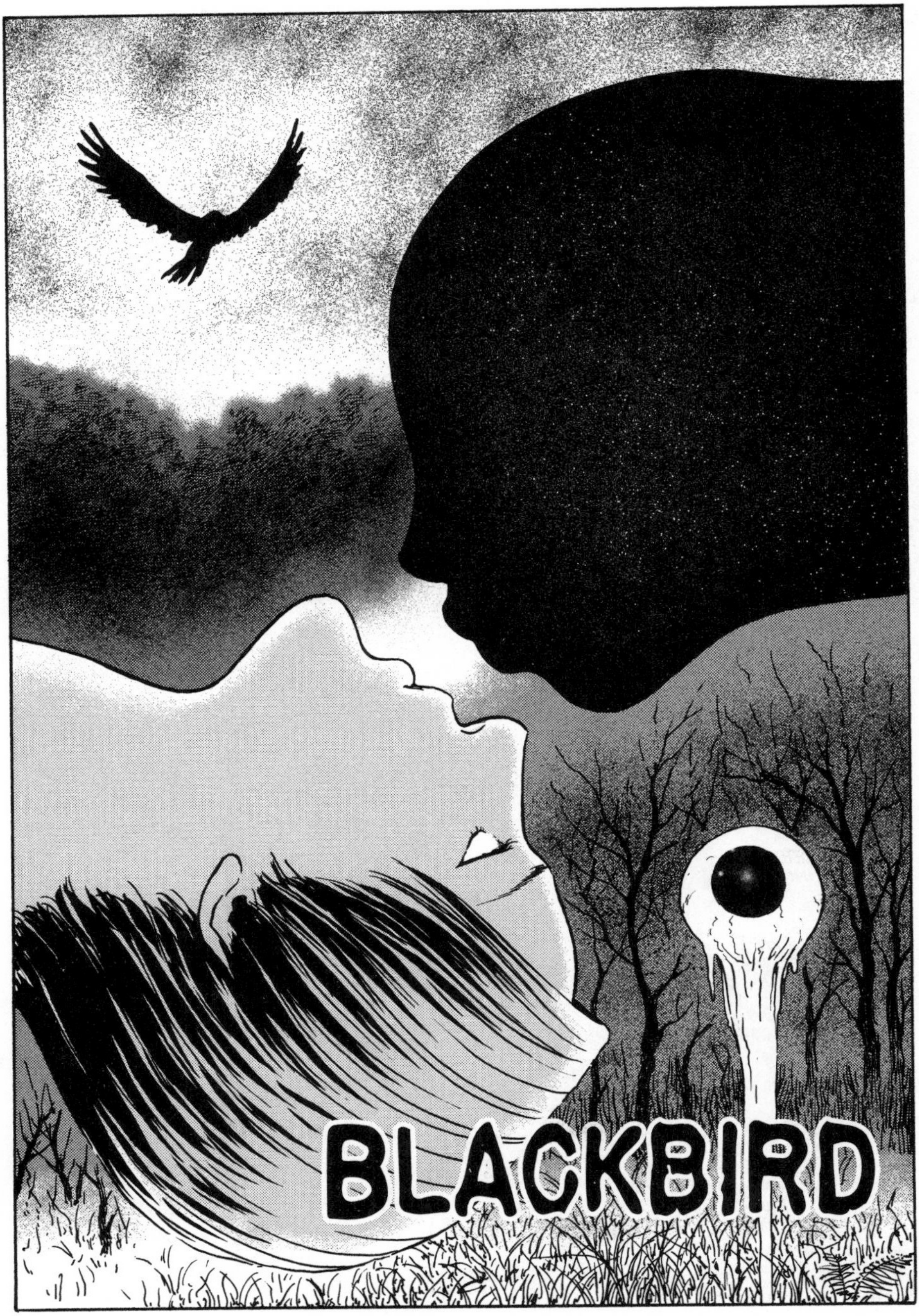
BLACKBIRD

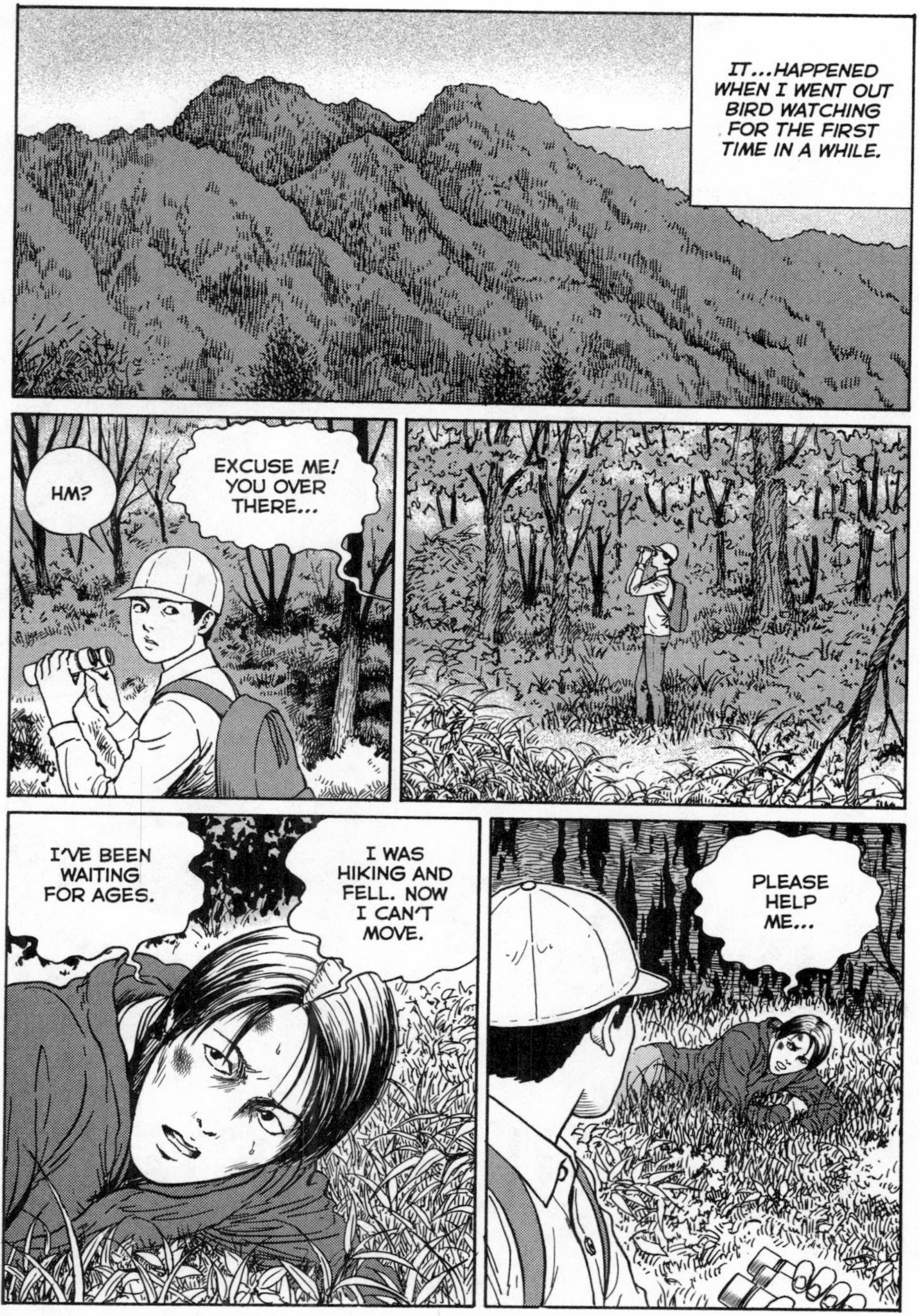
IT...HAPPENED WHEN I WENT OUT BIRD WATCHING FOR THE FIRST TIME IN A WHILE.
EXCUSE ME! YOU OVER THERE...
HM?
PLEASE HELP ME...
I WAS HIKING AND FELL. NOW I CAN'T MOVE.
I'VE BEEN WAITING FOR AGES.

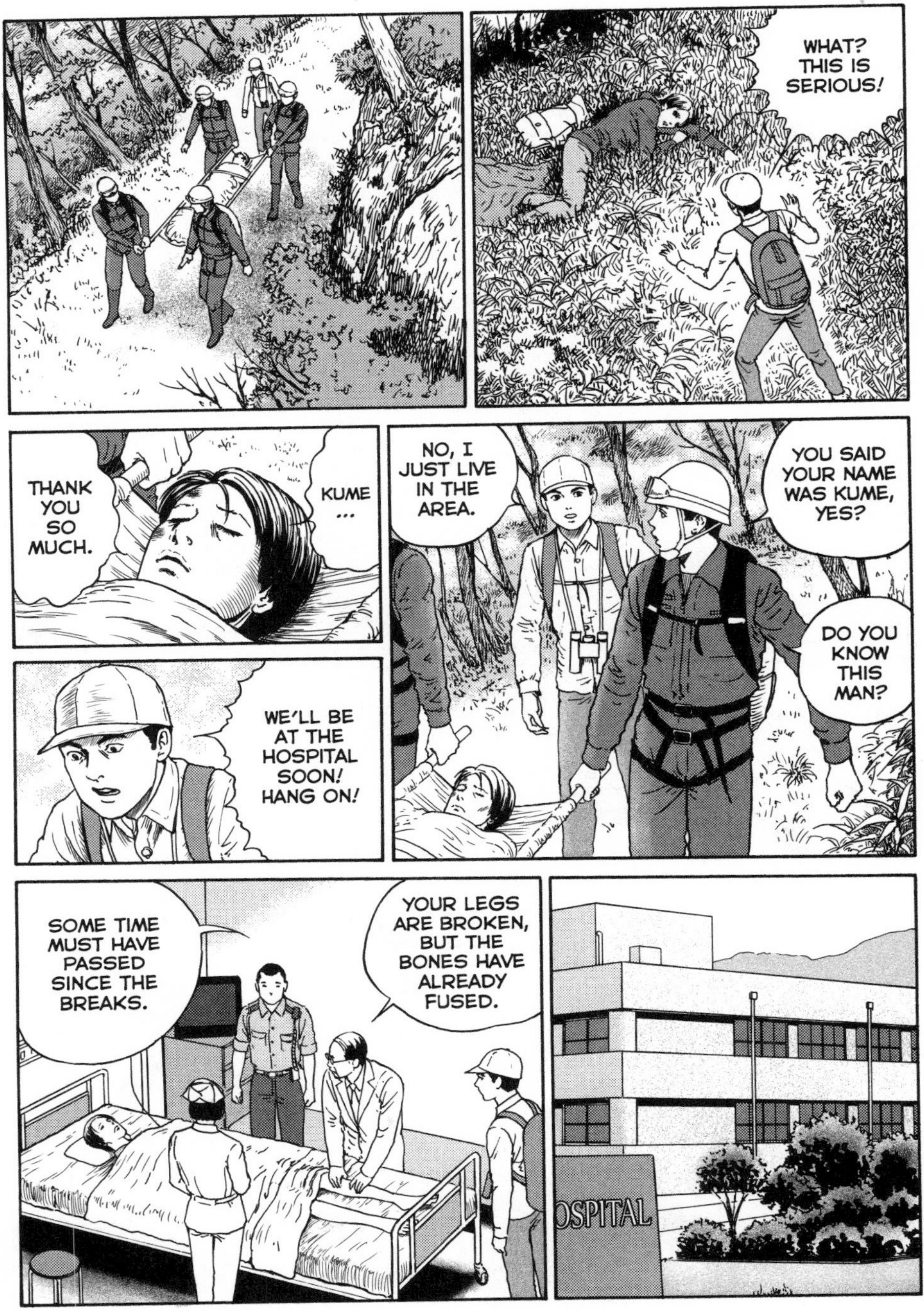
WHAT? THIS IS SERIOUS!
YOU SAID YOUR NAME WAS KUME, YES?
DO YOU KNOW THIS MAN?
NO, I JUST LIVE IN THE AREA.
KUME...
THANK YOU SO MUCH.
WE'LL BE AT THE HOSPITAL SOON! HANG ON!
OSPITAL
YOUR LEGS ARE BROKEN, BUT THE BONES HAVE ALREADY FUSED.
SOME TIME MUST HAVE PASSED SINCE THE BREAKS.

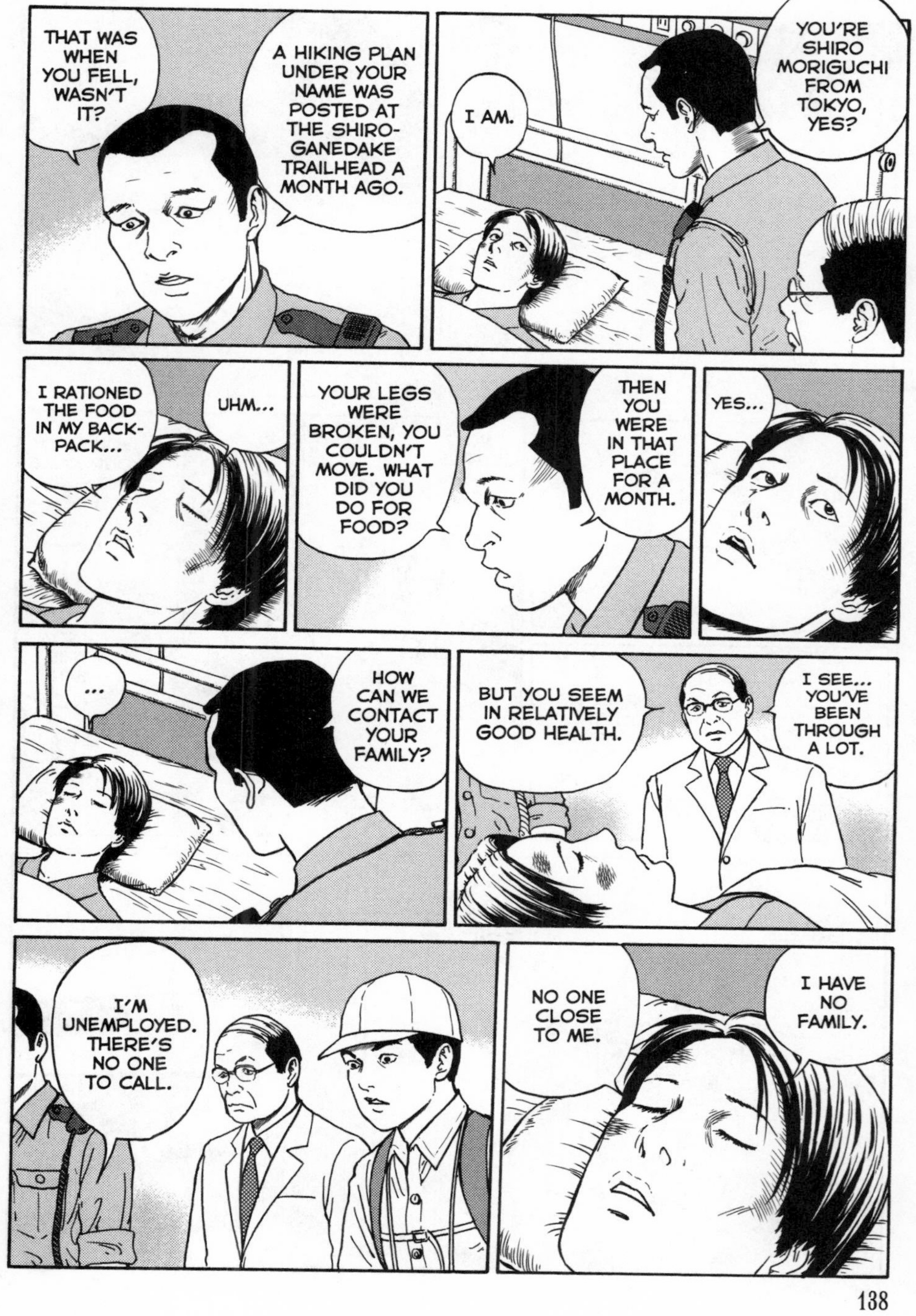
YOU'RE SHIRO MORIGUCHI FROM TOKYO, YES?
I AM.
A HIKING PLAN UNDER YOUR NAME WAS POSTED AT THE SHIRO-GANEDAKE TRAILHEAD A MONTH AGO.
THAT WAS WHEN YOU FELL, WASN'T IT?
YES...
THEN YOU WERE IN THAT PLACE FOR A MONTH.
YOUR LEGS WERE BROKEN, YOU COULDN'T MOVE. WHAT DID YOU DO FOR FOOD?
UHM...
I RATIONED THE FOOD IN MY BACK-PACK...
I SEE... YOU'VE BEEN THROUGH A LOT.
BUT YOU SEEM IN RELATIVELY GOOD HEALTH.
HOW CAN WE CONTACT YOUR FAMILY?
...
I HAVE NO FAMILY.
NO ONE CLOSE TO ME.
I'M UNEMPLOYED. THERE'S NO ONE TO CALL.

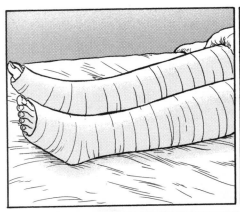

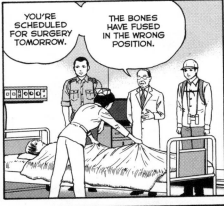

THE BONES HAVE FUSED IN THE WRONG POSITION.
YOU'RE SCHEDULED FOR SURGERY TOMORROW.
MORIGUCHI, YOU WERE ON THE NEWS.
EVERYONE'S TALKING ABOUT HOW YOU SURVIVED A MONTH ON THE FOOD IN YOUR BACKPACK.
HM?
YOU DON'T LOOK GOOD. WHAT'S WRONG?
KUME...
I HAVE A FAVOR TO ASK YOU.
HM?
WHAT IS IT?

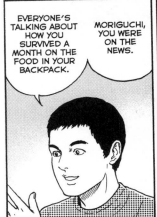

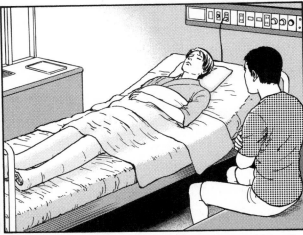

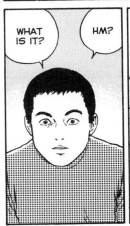

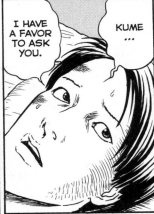

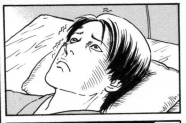

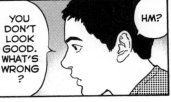

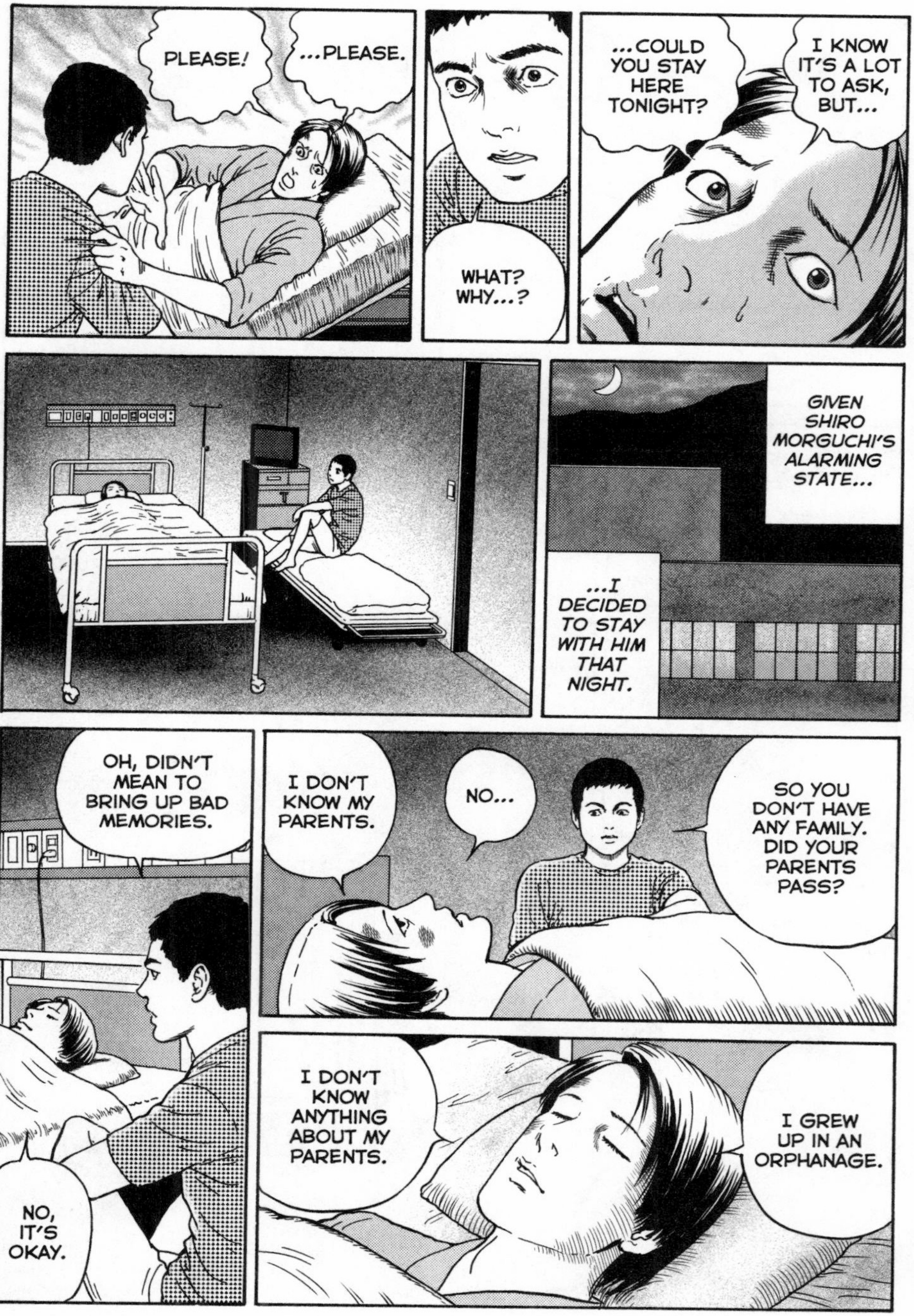
I KNOW IT'S A LOT TO ASK, BUT...
...COULD YOU STAY HERE TONIGHT?
WHAT? WHY...?
...PLEASE.
PLEASE!
GIVEN SHIRO MORGUCHI'S ALARMING STATE...
...I DECIDED TO STAY WITH HIM THAT NIGHT.
SO YOU DON'T HAVE ANY FAMILY. DID YOUR PARENTS PASS?
NO...
I DON'T KNOW MY PARENTS.
I GREW UP IN AN ORPHANAGE.
I DON'T KNOW ANYTHING ABOUT MY PARENTS.
OH, DIDN'T MEAN TO BRING UP BAD MEMORIES.
NO, IT'S OKAY.

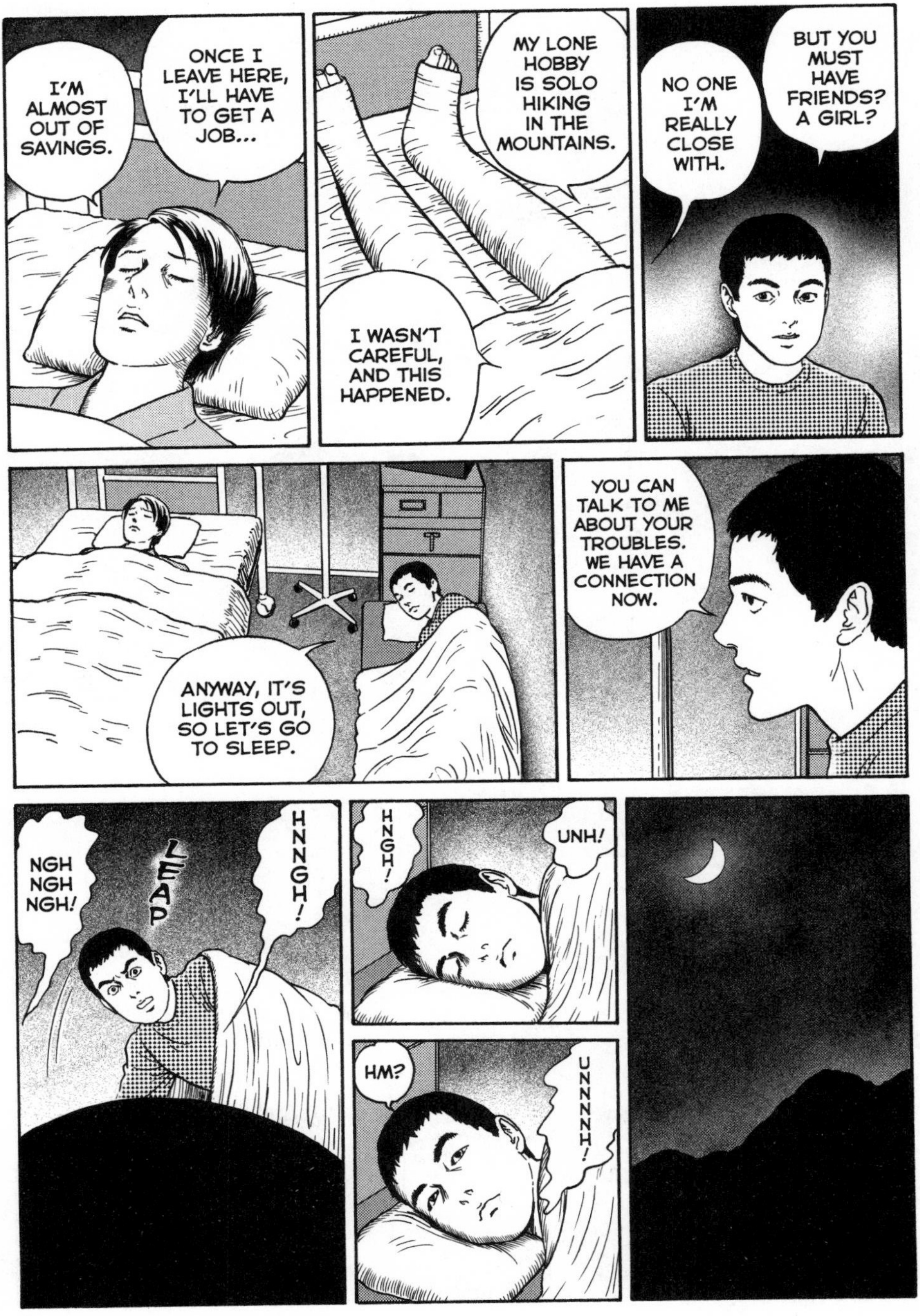
BUT YOU MUST HAVE FRIENDS? A GIRL?
NO ONE I'M REALLY CLOSE WITH.
MY LONE HOBBY IS SOLO HIKING IN THE MOUNTAINS.
I WASN'T CAREFUL, AND THIS HAPPENED.
ONCE I LEAVE HERE, I'LL HAVE TO GET A JOB...
I'M ALMOST OUT OF SAVINGS.
YOU CAN TALK TO ME ABOUT YOUR TROUBLES. WE HAVE A CONNECTION NOW.
ANYWAY, IT'S LIGHTS OUT, SO LET'S GO TO SLEEP.
UNH!
HNGH!
UNNNNH!
HM?
HNNGH!
LEAP
NGH NGH NGH!

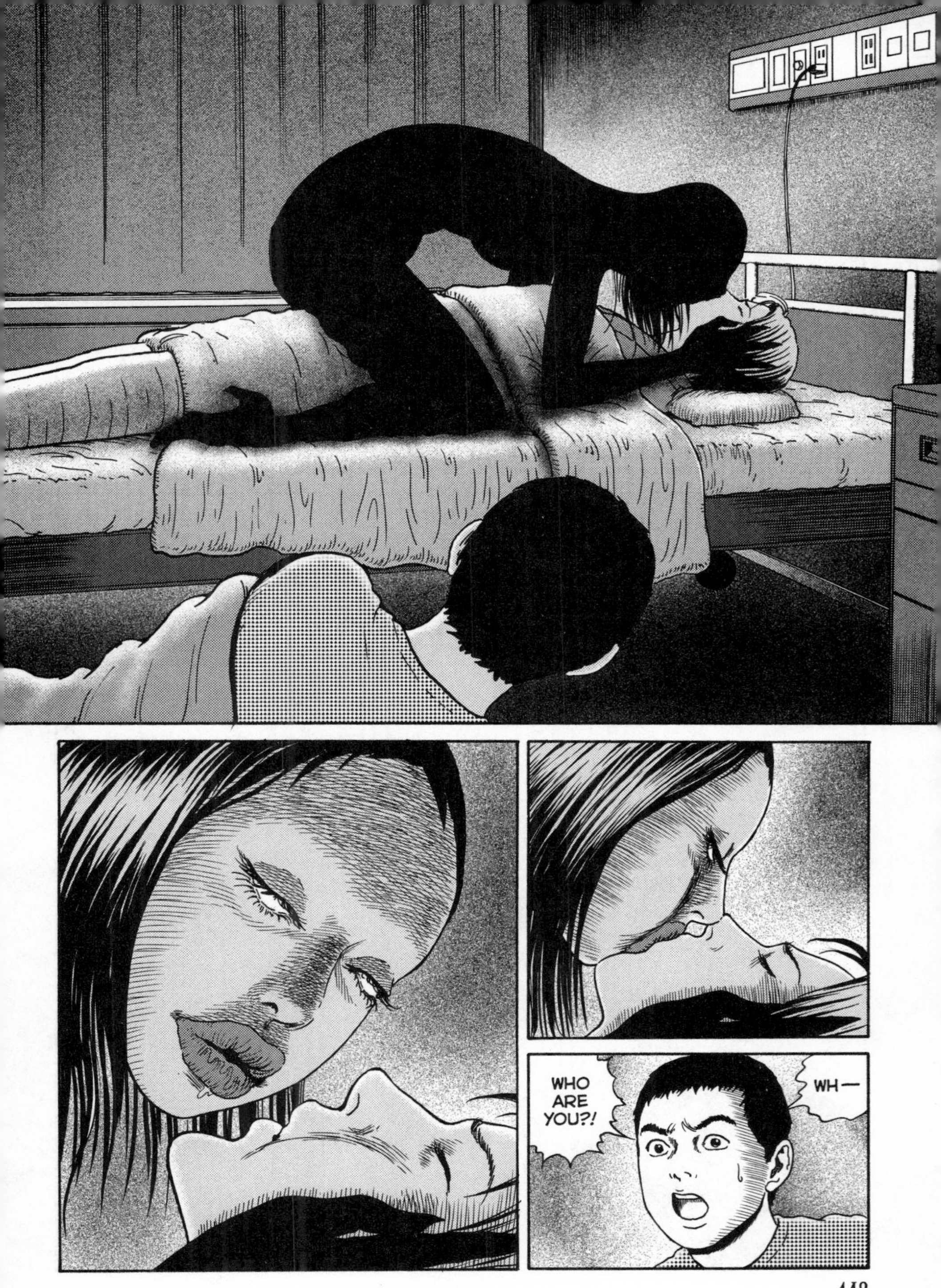
WH—
WHO ARE YOU?!

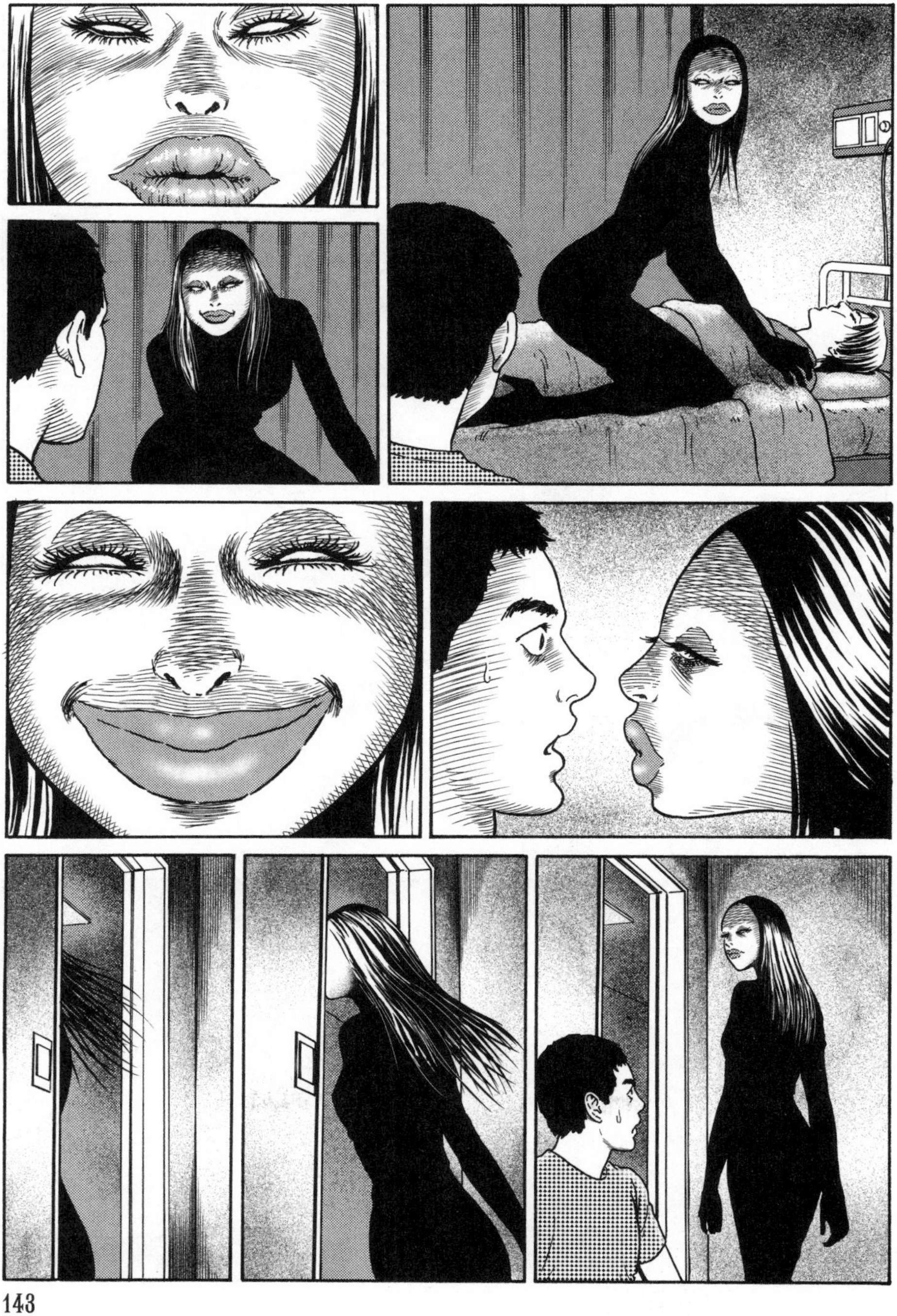

PTT!

H-HEY, MORIGUCHI... WHAT WAS THAT?

MORIGUCHI, SERIOUSLY, WHAT IS THAT?

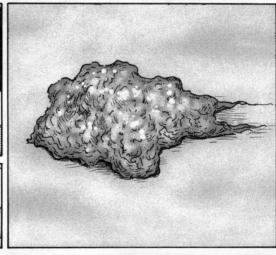

MEAT?

IT'S MEAT...

I'VE BEEN RESCUED... BUT SHE CAME...

SHE CAME AGAIN TONIGHT...

BUT I DON'T NEED THE MEAT ANY-MORE...

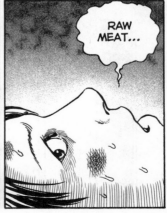

RAW MEAT...

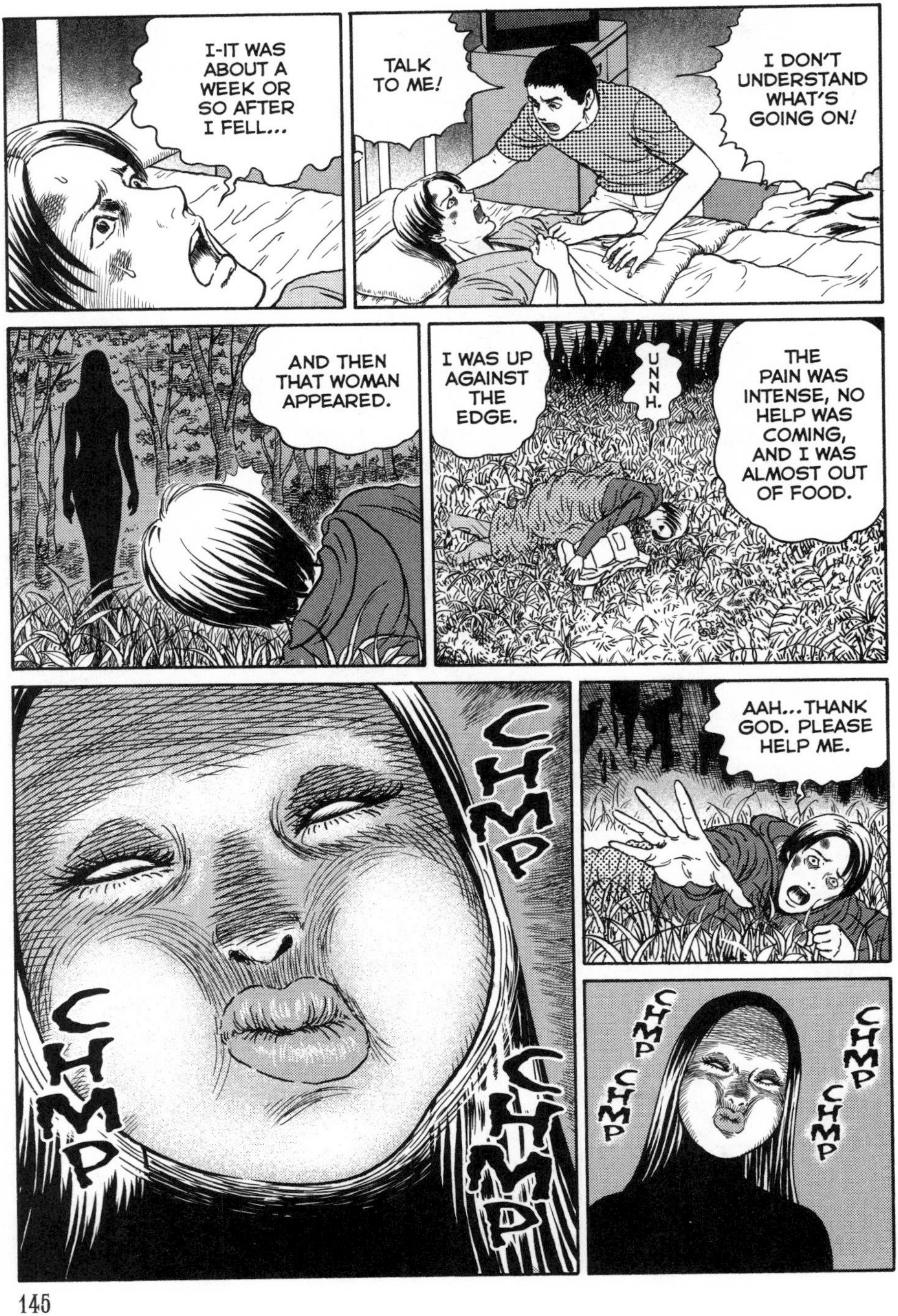
I DON'T UNDERSTAND WHAT'S GOING ON!
TALK TO ME!
I-IT WAS ABOUT A WEEK OR SO AFTER I FELL...
THE PAIN WAS INTENSE, NO HELP WAS COMING, AND I WAS ALMOST OUT OF FOOD.
UNNH.
I WAS UP AGAINST THE EDGE.
AND THEN THAT WOMAN APPEARED.
AAH...THANK GOD. PLEASE HELP ME.
CHMP
CHMP
CHMP
CHMP
CHMP
CHMP
CHMP

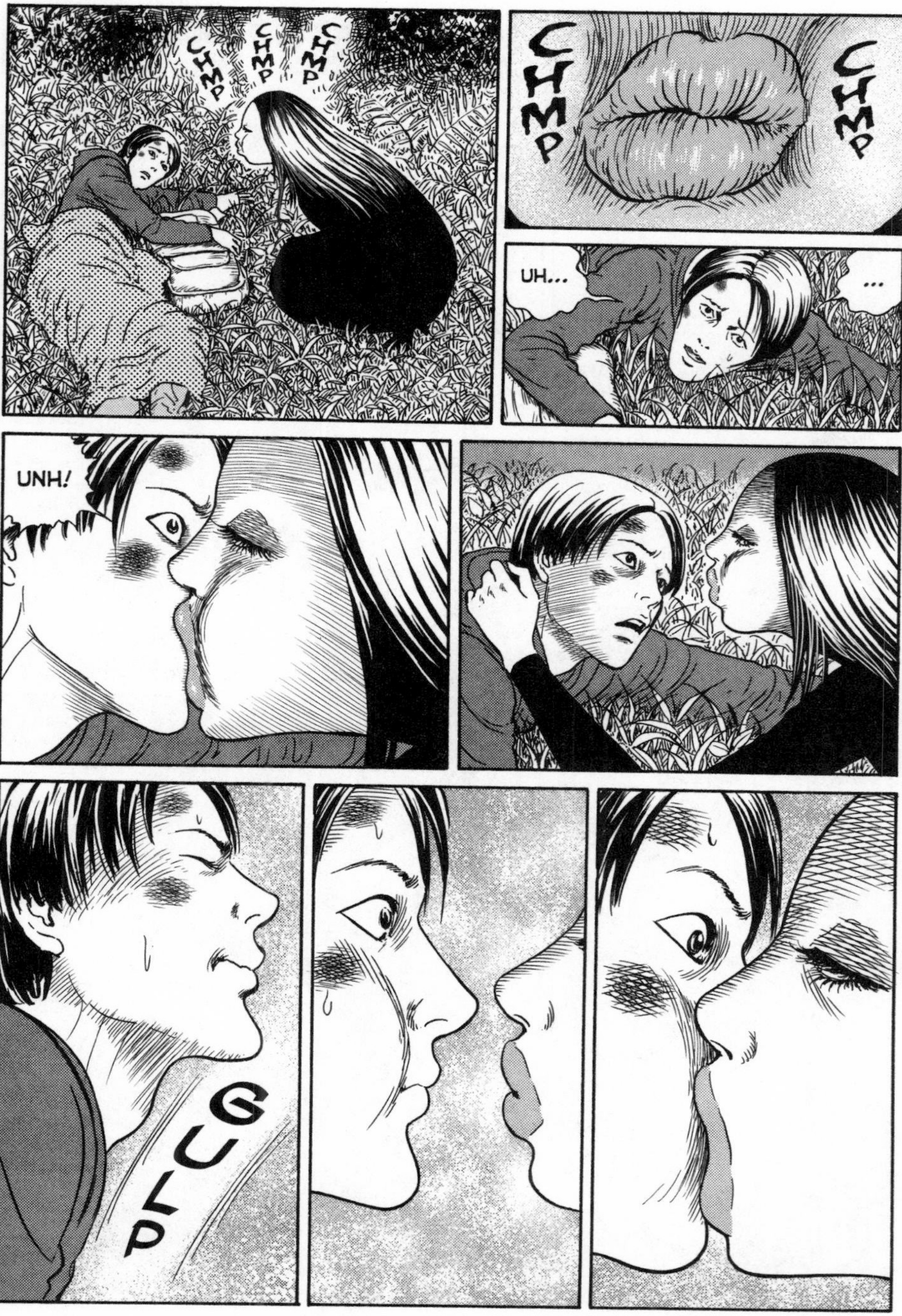
CHMP
CHMP
...
UH...
CHMP
CHMP
CHMP
UNH!
GULP

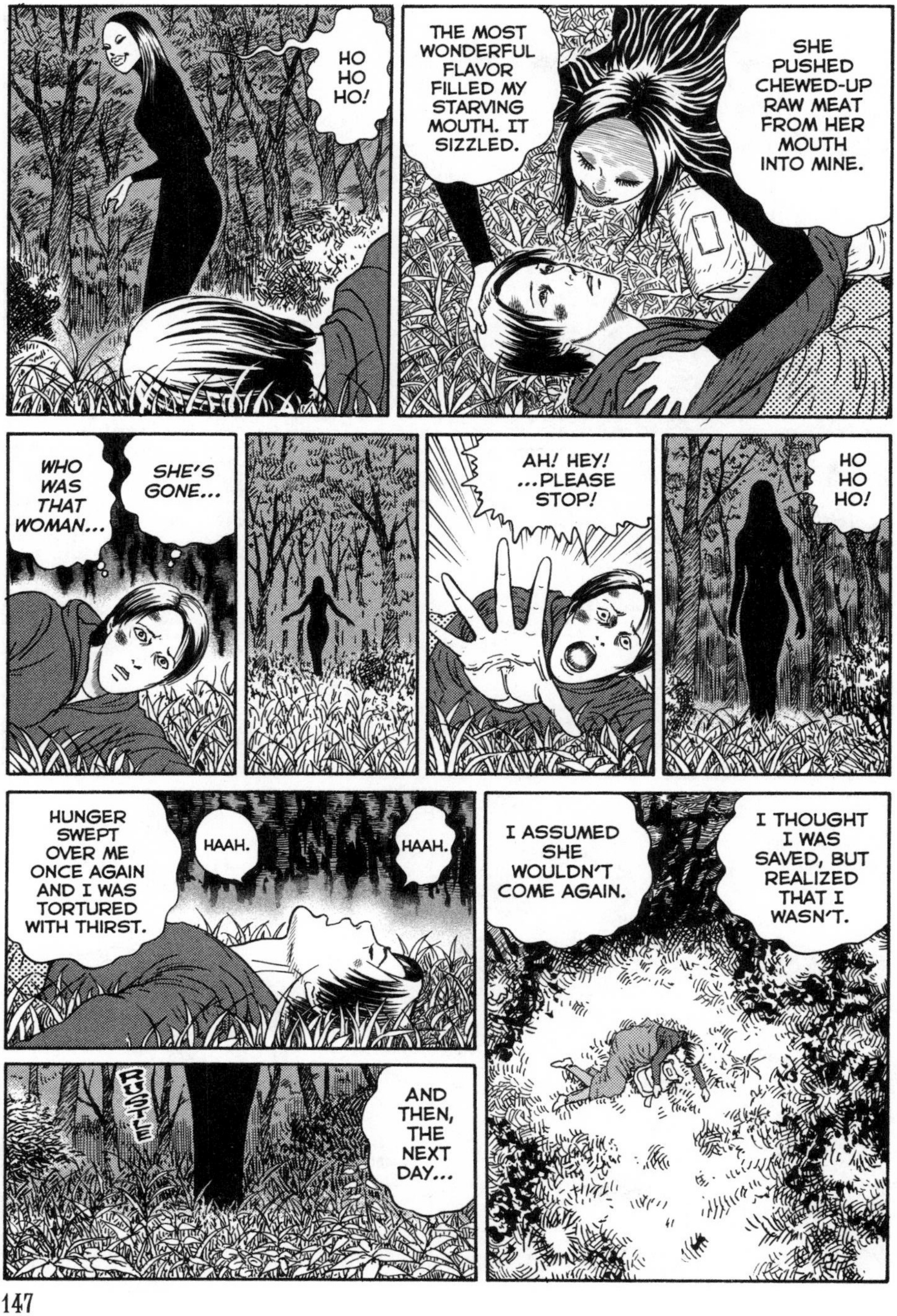
SHE PUSHED CHEWED-UP RAW MEAT FROM HER MOUTH INTO MINE.
THE MOST WONDERFUL FLAVOR FILLED MY STARVING MOUTH. IT SIZZLED.
HO HO HO!
HO HO HO!
AH! HEY! ...PLEASE STOP!
SHE'S GONE...
WHO WAS THAT WOMAN...
I THOUGHT I WAS SAVED, BUT REALIZED THAT I WASN'T.
I ASSUMED SHE WOULDN'T COME AGAIN.
HAAH.
HAAH.
HUNGER SWEPT OVER ME ONCE AGAIN AND I WAS TORTURED WITH THIRST.
AND THEN, THE NEXT DAY...
RUSTLE

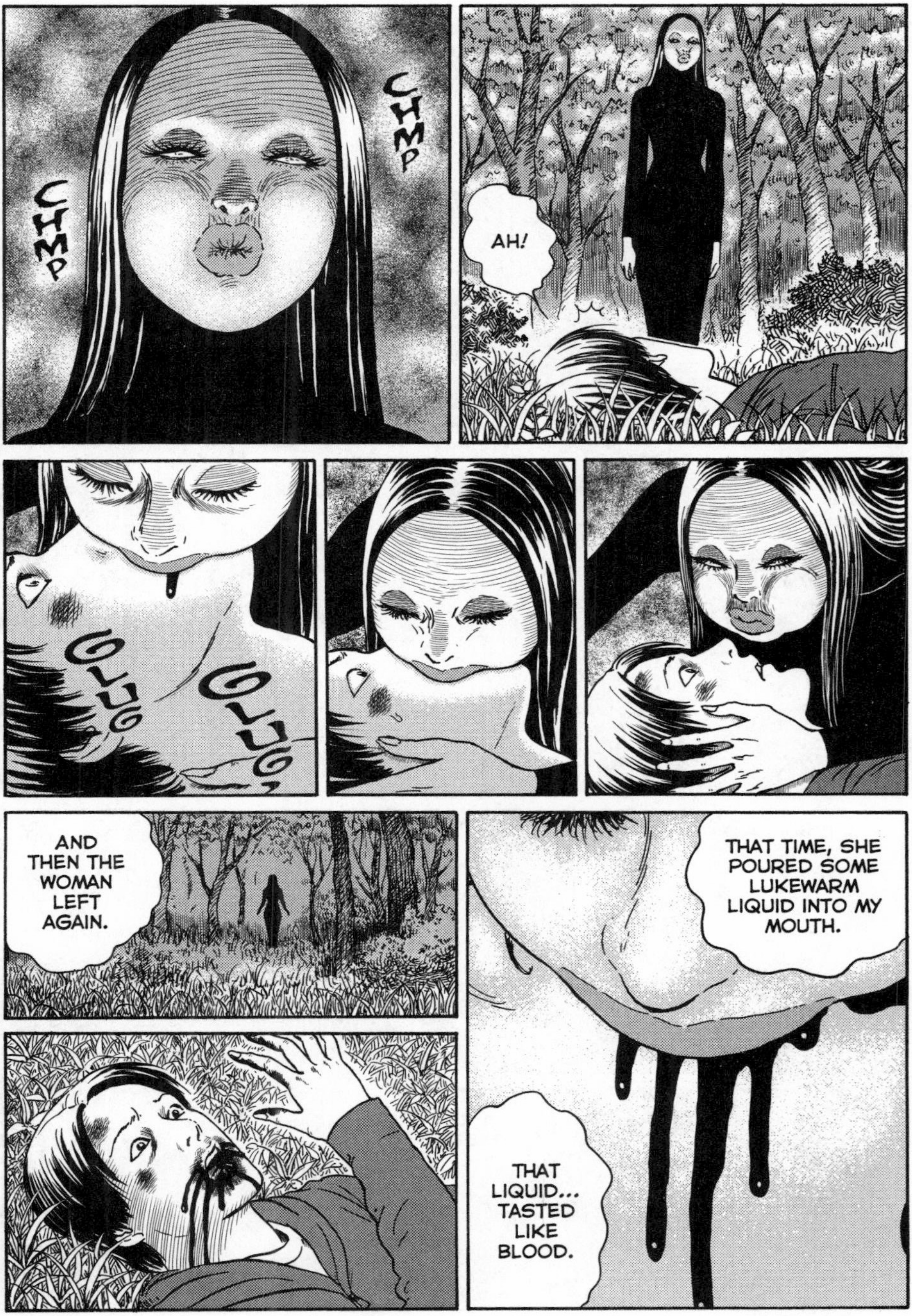
AH!
CHMP
CHMP
GLUG
GLUG
THAT TIME, SHE POURED SOME LUKEWARM LIQUID INTO MY MOUTH.
THAT LIQUID... TASTED LIKE BLOOD.
AND THEN THE WOMAN LEFT AGAIN.

CHMP

CHMP

AH!

GLUG GLUG

AND THEN THE WOMAN LEFT AGAIN.

THAT TIME, SHE POURED SOME LUKEWARM LIQUID INTO MY MOUTH.

THAT LIQUID... TASTED LIKE BLOOD.

HO HO HO!

THE MOST WONDERFUL FLAVOR FILLED MY STARVING MOUTH. IT SIZZLED.

SHE PUSHED CHEWED-UP RAW MEAT FROM HER MOUTH INTO MINE.

WHO WAS THAT WOMAN...

SHE'S GONE...

AH! HEY! ...PLEASE STOP!

HO HO HO!

HUNGER SWEPT OVER ME ONCE AGAIN AND I WAS TORTURED WITH THIRST.

HAAH.

HAAH.

I ASSUMED SHE WOULDN'T COME AGAIN.

I THOUGHT I WAS SAVED, BUT REALIZED THAT I WASN'T.

RUSTLE

AND THEN, THE NEXT DAY...

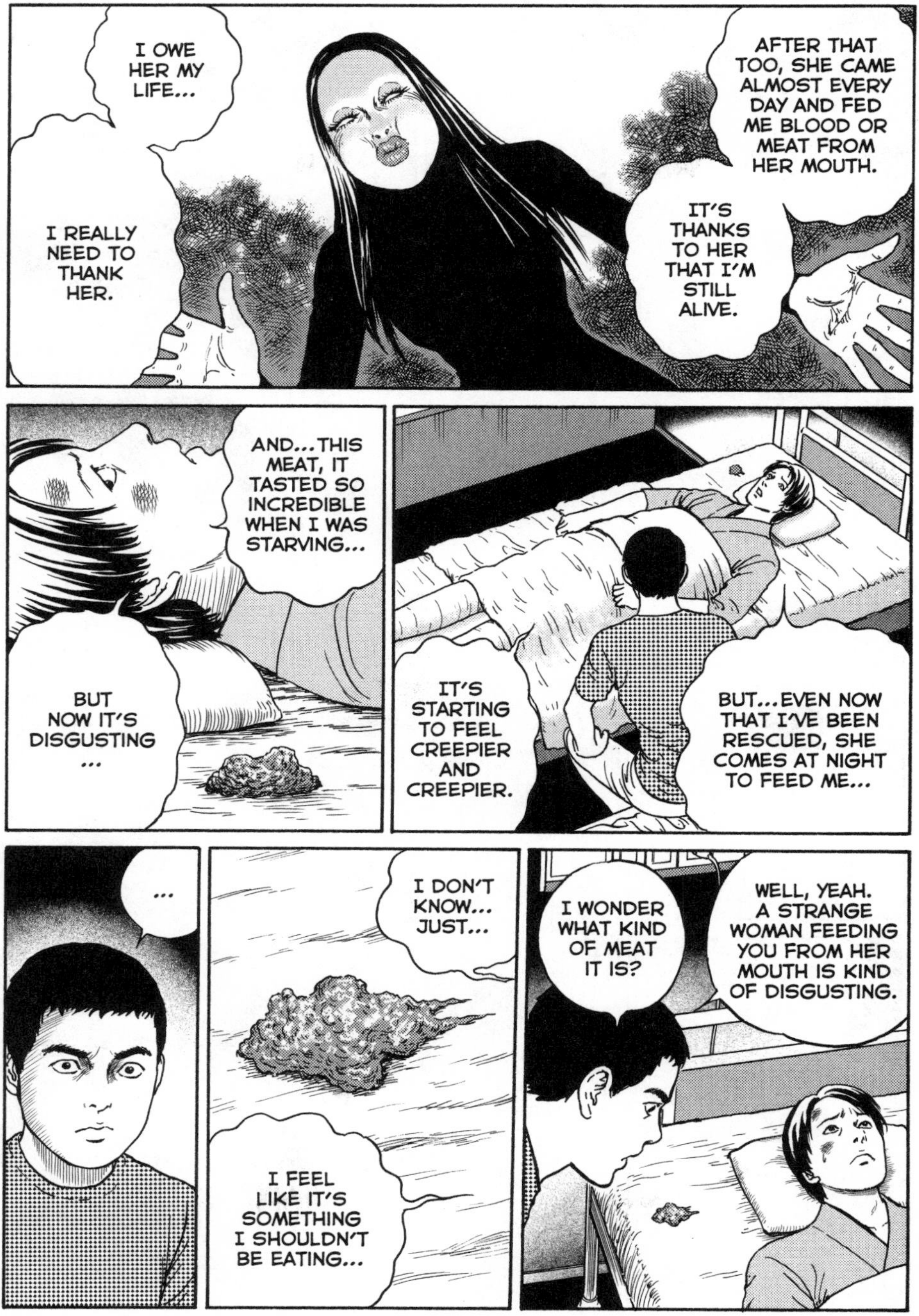
AFTER THAT TOO, SHE CAME ALMOST EVERY DAY AND FED ME BLOOD OR MEAT FROM HER MOUTH.
IT'S THANKS TO HER THAT I'M STILL ALIVE.
I OWE HER MY LIFE...
I REALLY NEED TO THANK HER.
BUT...EVEN NOW THAT I'VE BEEN RESCUED, SHE COMES AT NIGHT TO FEED ME...
IT'S STARTING TO FEEL CREEPIER AND CREEPIER.
AND...THIS MEAT, IT TASTED SO INCREDIBLE WHEN I WAS STARVING...
BUT NOW IT'S DISGUSTING ...
WELL, YEAH. A STRANGE WOMAN FEEDING YOU FROM HER MOUTH IS KIND OF DISGUSTING.
I WONDER WHAT KIND OF MEAT IT IS?
I DON'T KNOW... JUST...
I FEEL LIKE IT'S SOMETHING I SHOULDN'T BE EATING...
...

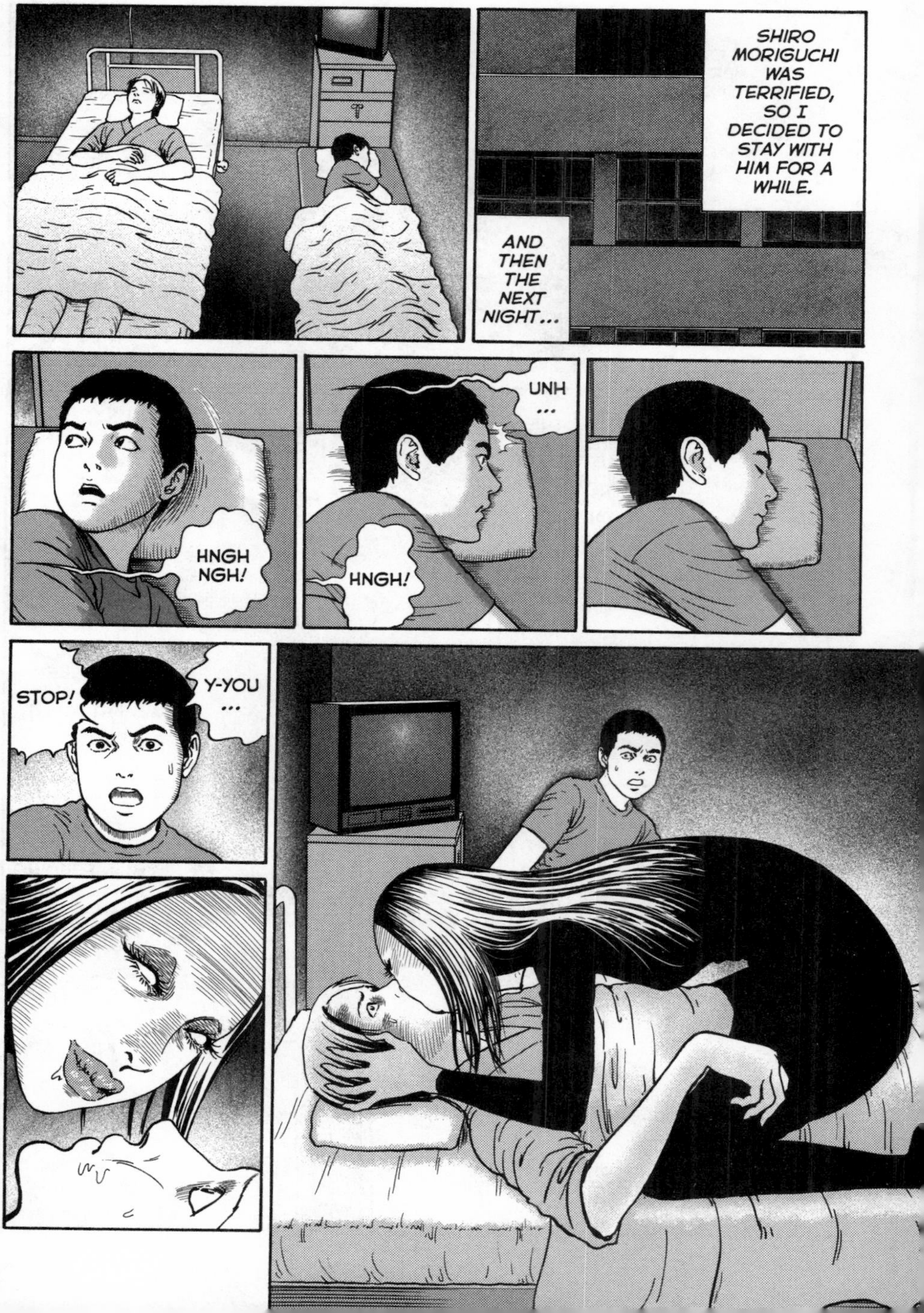

SHIRO MORIGUCHI WAS TERRIFIED, SO I DECIDED TO STAY WITH HIM FOR A WHILE.
AND THEN THE NEXT NIGHT...
UNH ...
HNGH!
HNGH NGH!
Y-YOU ...
STOP!

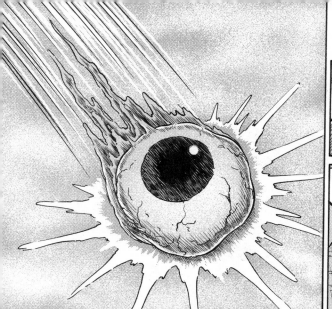

HNGH!

PLEH!

AH! WAIT!

HO HO HO HO!

AAH!

AFTER-HOURS ENTRY

YOU!

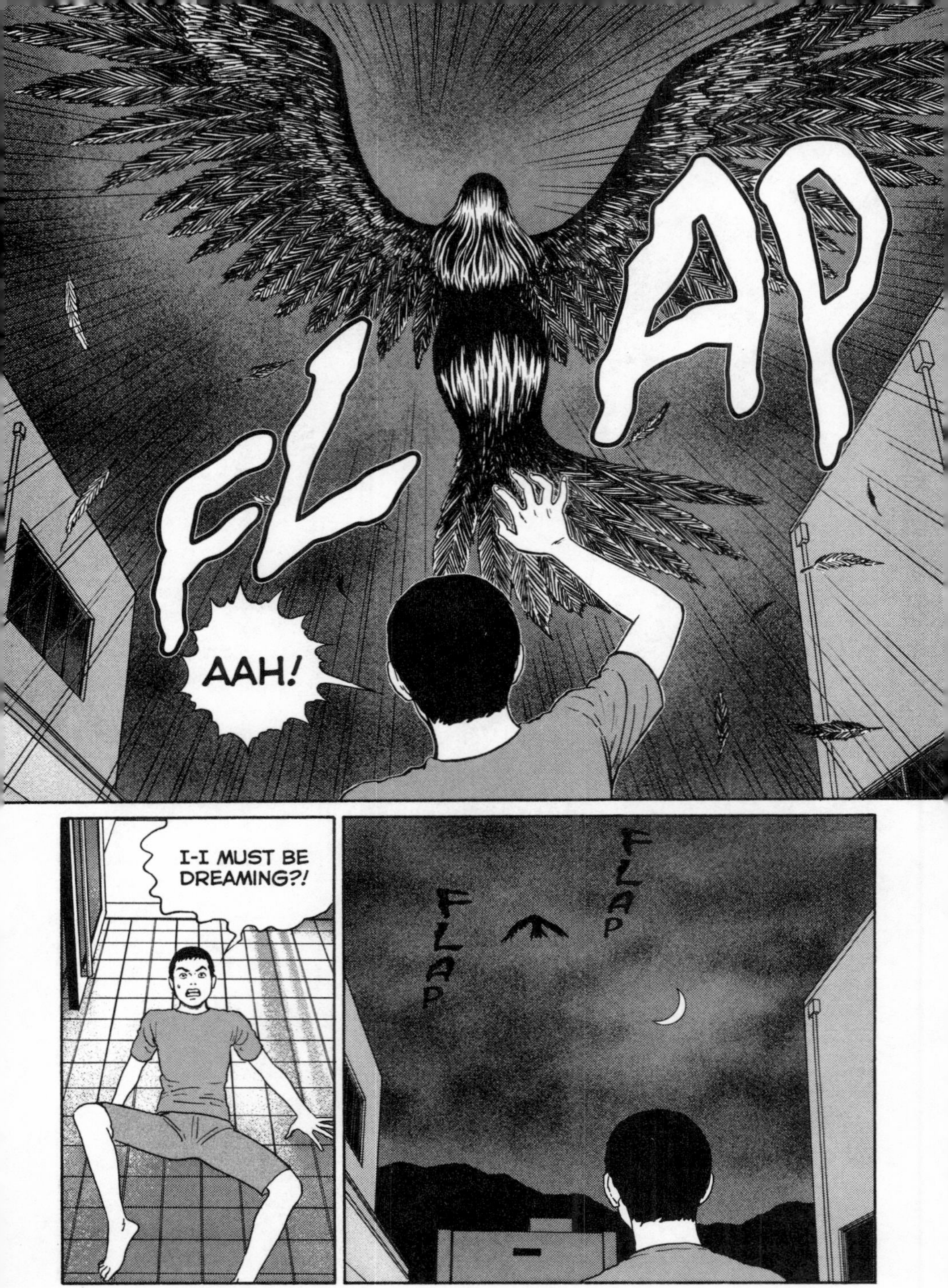
FLAP
AAH!
FLAP
FLAP
I-I MUST BE DREAMING?!

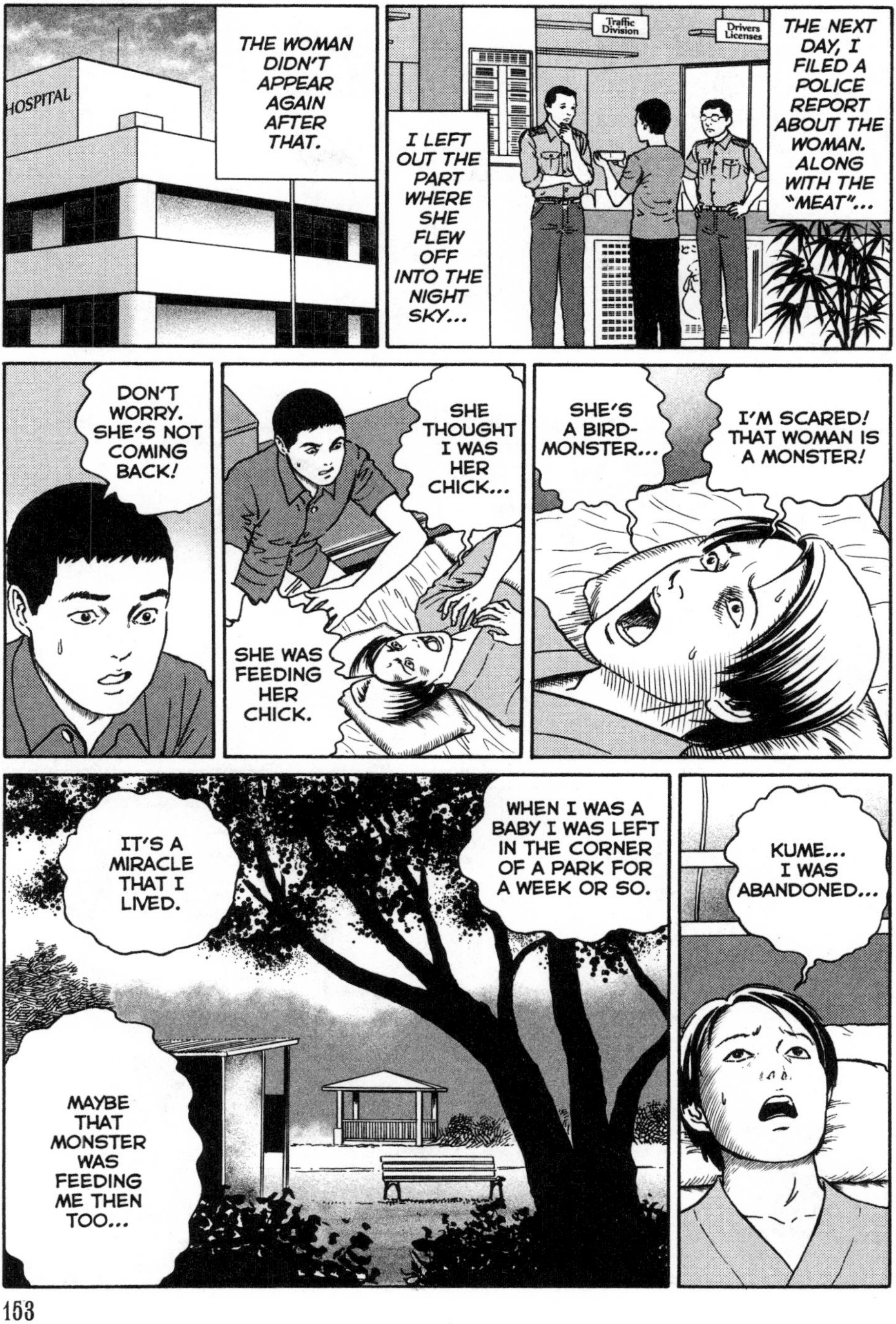
Traffic Division
Drivers Licenses
THE NEXT DAY, I FILED A POLICE REPORT ABOUT THE WOMAN. ALONG WITH THE "MEAT"...
I LEFT OUT THE PART WHERE SHE FLEW OFF INTO THE NIGHT SKY...
HOSPITAL
THE WOMAN DIDN'T APPEAR AGAIN AFTER THAT.
I'M SCARED! THAT WOMAN IS A MONSTER!
SHE'S A BIRD-MONSTER...
SHE THOUGHT I WAS HER CHICK...
SHE WAS FEEDING HER CHICK.
DON'T WORRY. SHE'S NOT COMING BACK!
KUME... I WAS ABANDONED...
WHEN I WAS A BABY I WAS LEFT IN THE CORNER OF A PARK FOR A WEEK OR SO.
IT'S A MIRACLE THAT I LIVED.
MAYBE THAT MONSTER WAS FEEDING ME THEN TOO...

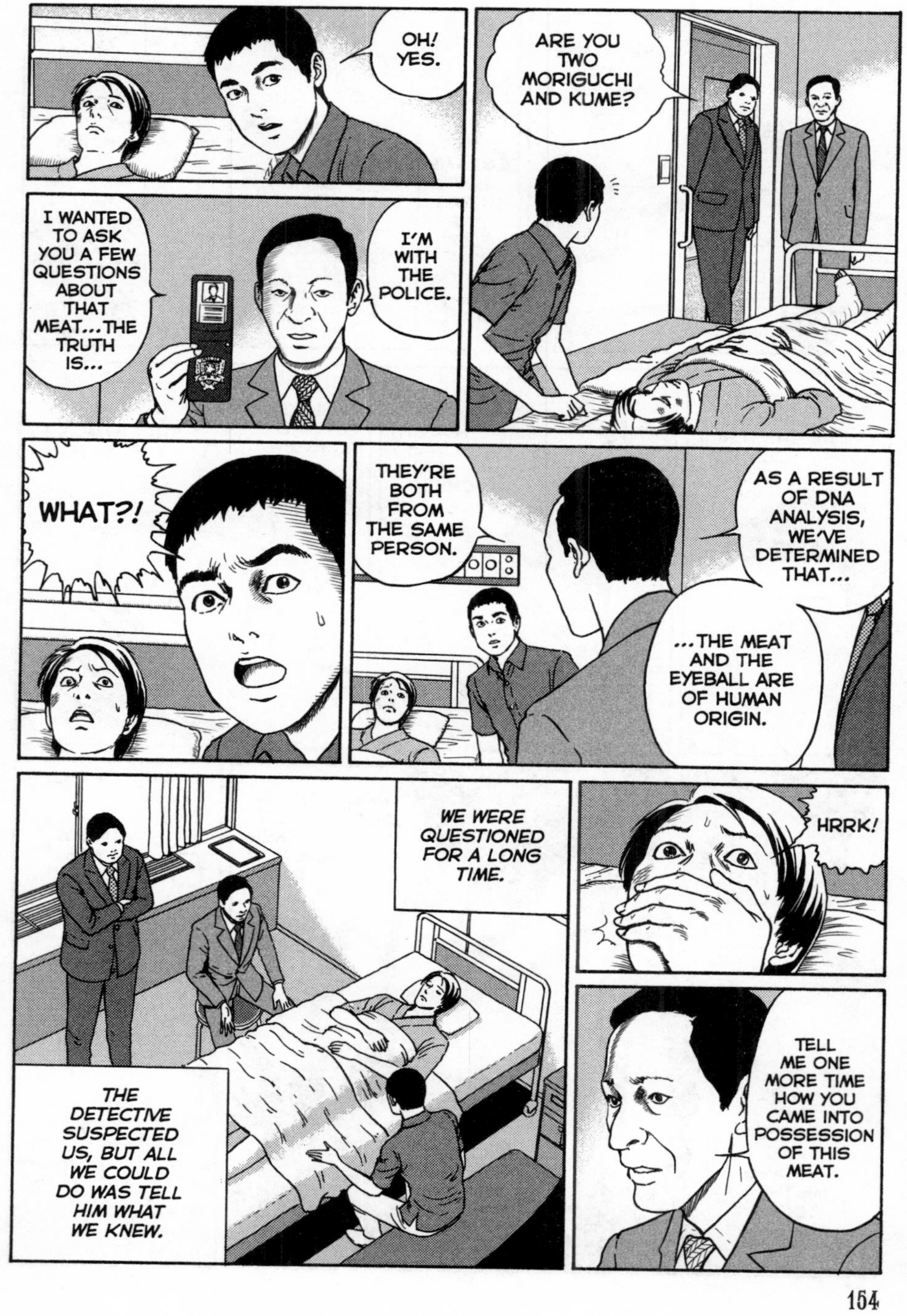
ARE YOU TWO MORIGUCHI AND KUME?
OH! YES.
I'M WITH THE POLICE.
I WANTED TO ASK YOU A FEW QUESTIONS ABOUT THAT MEAT...THE TRUTH IS...
AS A RESULT OF DNA ANALYSIS, WE'VE DETERMINED THAT...
...THE MEAT AND THE EYEBALL ARE OF HUMAN ORIGIN.
THEY'RE BOTH FROM THE SAME PERSON.
WHAT?!
HRRK!
TELL ME ONE MORE TIME HOW YOU CAME INTO POSSESSION OF THIS MEAT.
WE WERE QUESTIONED FOR A LONG TIME.
THE DETECTIVE SUSPECTED US, BUT ALL WE COULD DO WAS TELL HIM WHAT WE KNEW.

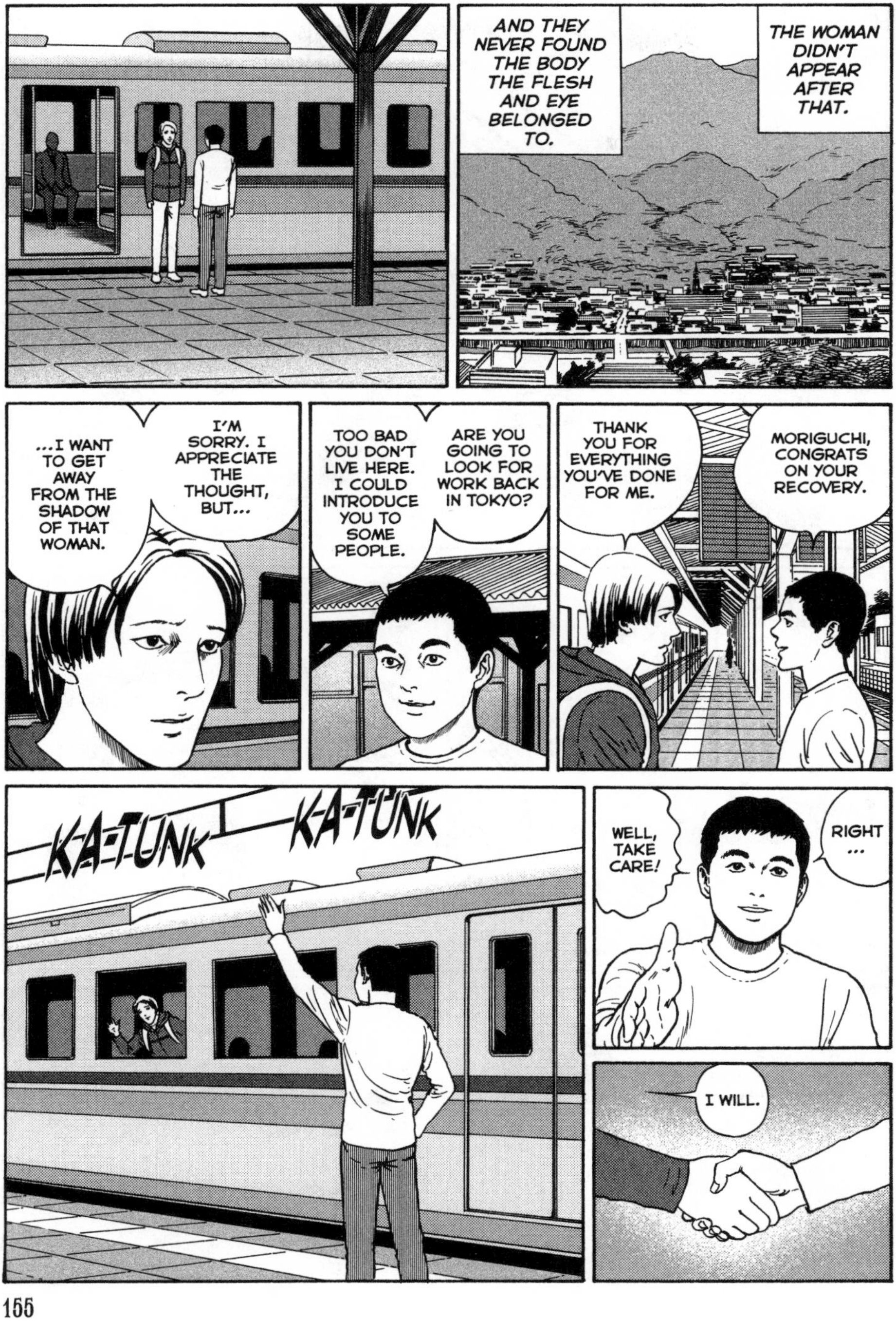
THE WOMAN DIDN'T APPEAR AFTER THAT.
AND THEY NEVER FOUND THE BODY THE FLESH AND EYE BELONGED TO.
MORIGUCHI, CONGRATS ON YOUR RECOVERY.
THANK YOU FOR EVERYTHING YOU'VE DONE FOR ME.
ARE YOU GOING TO LOOK FOR WORK BACK IN TOKYO?
TOO BAD YOU DON'T LIVE HERE. I COULD INTRODUCE YOU TO SOME PEOPLE.
I'M SORRY. I APPRECIATE THE THOUGHT, BUT...
...I WANT TO GET AWAY FROM THE SHADOW OF THAT WOMAN.
RIGHT...
WELL, TAKE CARE!
I WILL.
KA-TUNK
KA-TUNK

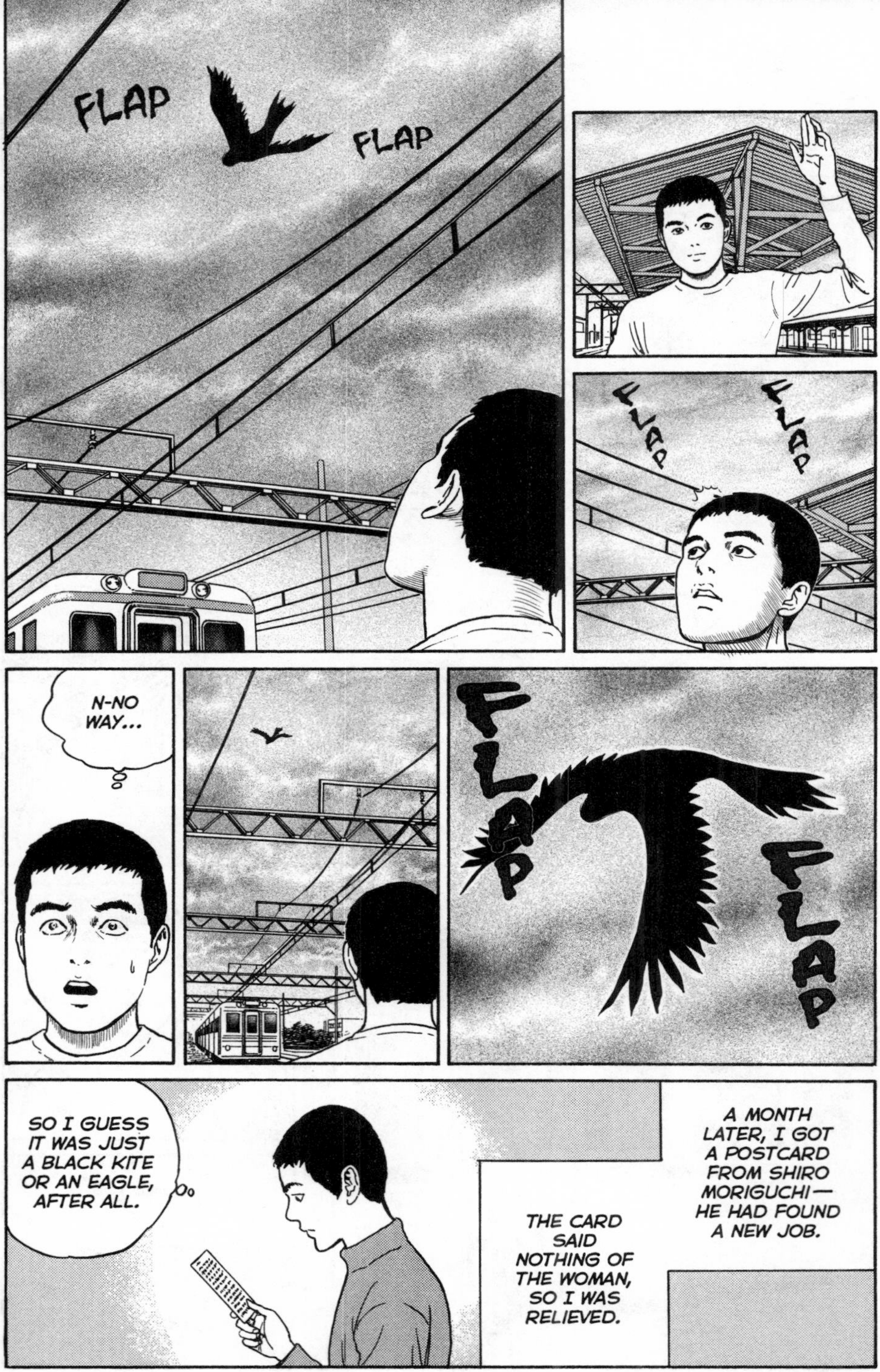
FLAP
FLAP
FLAP
FLAP
FLAP
FLAP
N-NO WAY...
A MONTH LATER, I GOT A POSTCARD FROM SHIRO MORIGUCHI— HE HAD FOUND A NEW JOB.
THE CARD SAID NOTHING OF THE WOMAN, SO I WAS RELIEVED.
SO I GUESS IT WAS JUST A BLACK KITE OR AN EAGLE, AFTER ALL.

A FEW YEARS LATER, SHIRO MORIGUCHI'S CORPSE WAS DISCOVERED...

...IN A FROZEN HOLLOW ON THE SUMMIT OF MOUNT FUJI.

SHIRO'S POSSESSIONS WERE FOUND NEAR THE BODY...

AND DNA TESTING CONFIRMED THAT IT WAS INDEED HIM.

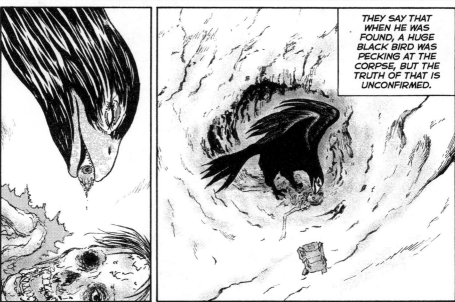

THEY SAY THAT WHEN HE WAS FOUND, A HUGE BLACK BIRD WAS PECKING AT THE CORPSE, BUT THE TRUTH OF THAT IS UNCONFIRMED.

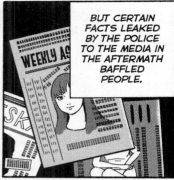

BUT CERTAIN FACTS LEAKED BY THE POLICE TO THE MEDIA IN THE AFTERMATH BAFFLED PEOPLE.
APPARENTLY, THE DNA FROM THE MEAT THE WOMAN HAD FED SHIRO A FEW YEARS EARLIER...
...WAS A PERFECT MATCH FOR SHIRO'S OWN DNA.
HOW ON EARTH COULD THIS BE?
SHIRO WAS FED HIS OWN FLESH.
WHAT FOLLOWS ARE THE FINAL SECTIONS OF THE JOURNAL FOUND AMONG SHIRO'S POSSESSIONS.
Diary
August 8
That woman showed up!
I thought she wouldn't,
and yet...
into my locked room
How?!
in?!
"AUGUST 8. THAT WOMAN SHOWED UP!! I THOUGHT SHE WOULDN'T, AND YET...
"SHE GOT INTO MY LOCKED ROOM.
"HOW ON EARTH DID SHE GET IN?!"

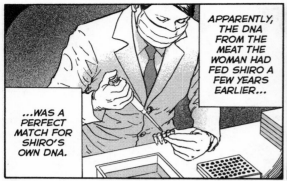

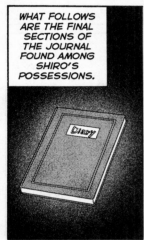

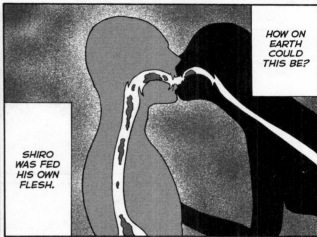

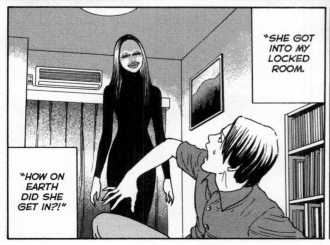

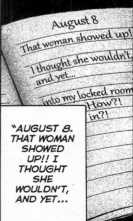

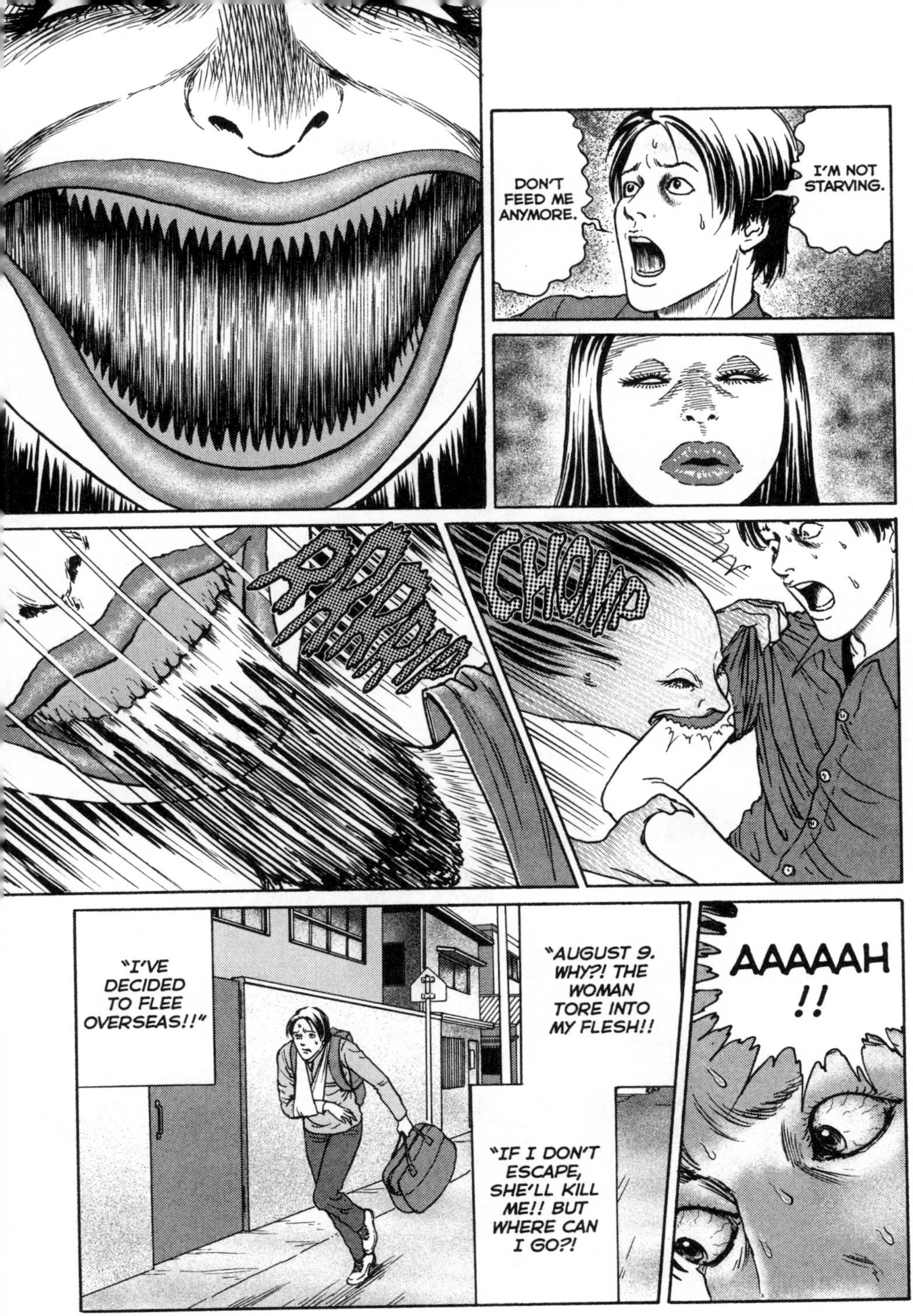
I'M NOT STARVING.
DON'T FEED ME ANYMORE.
CHOMP
AAAAAH !!
"AUGUST 9. WHY?! THE WOMAN TORE INTO MY FLESH!!
"IF I DON'T ESCAPE, SHE'LL KILL ME!! BUT WHERE CAN I GO?!
"I'VE DECIDED TO FLEE OVERSEAS!!"

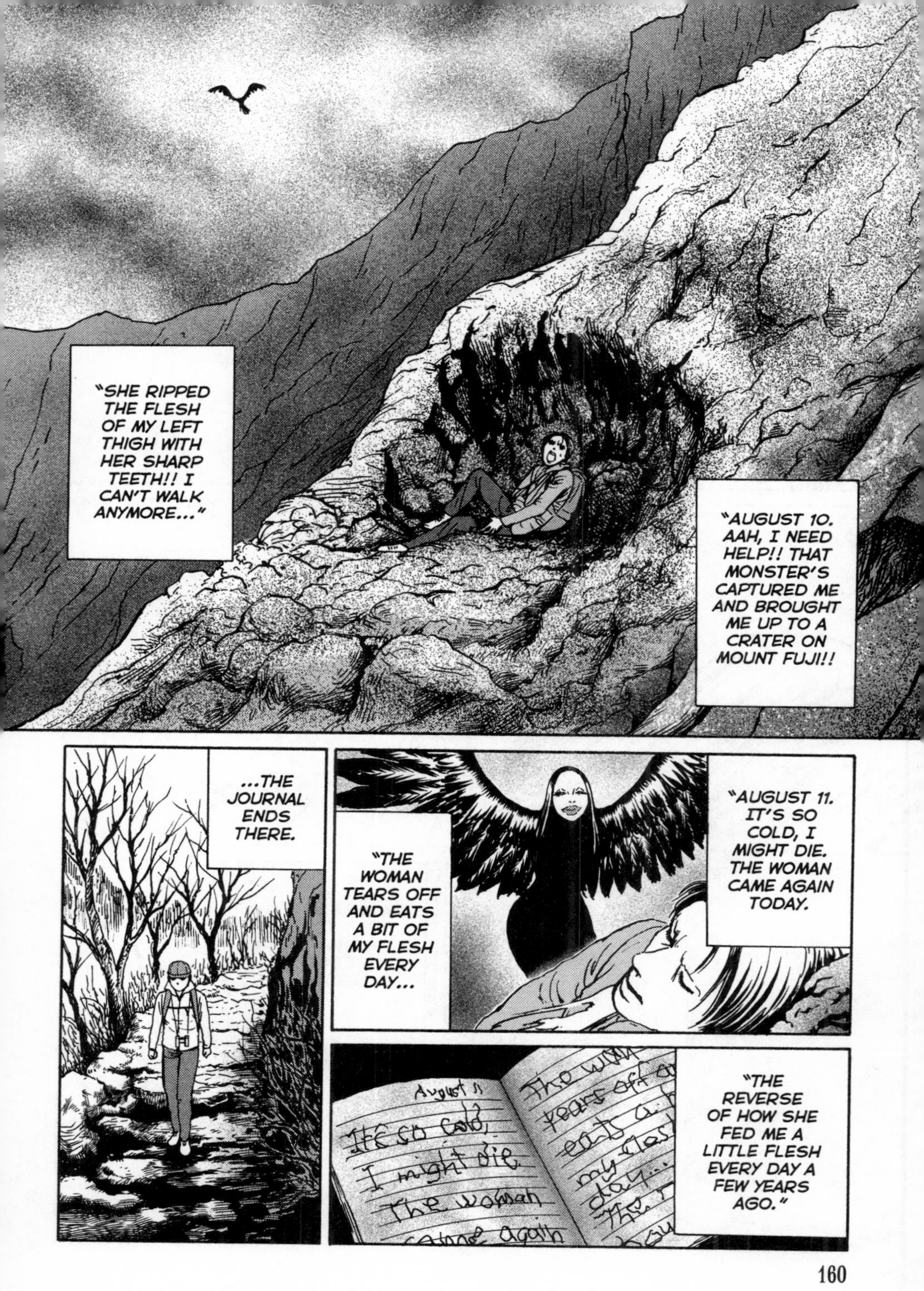
"AUGUST 10. AAH, I NEED HELP!! THAT MONSTER'S CAPTURED ME AND BROUGHT ME UP TO A CRATER ON MOUNT FUJI!!
"SHE RIPPED THE FLESH OF MY LEFT THIGH WITH HER SHARP TEETH!! I CAN'T WALK ANYMORE..."
"AUGUST 11. IT'S SO COLD, I MIGHT DIE. THE WOMAN CAME AGAIN TODAY.
"THE WOMAN TEARS OFF AND EATS A BIT OF MY FLESH EVERY DAY...
"THE REVERSE OF HOW SHE FED ME A LITTLE FLESH EVERY DAY A FEW YEARS AGO."
It's so cold,
I might die
The woman
...THE JOURNAL ENDS THERE.

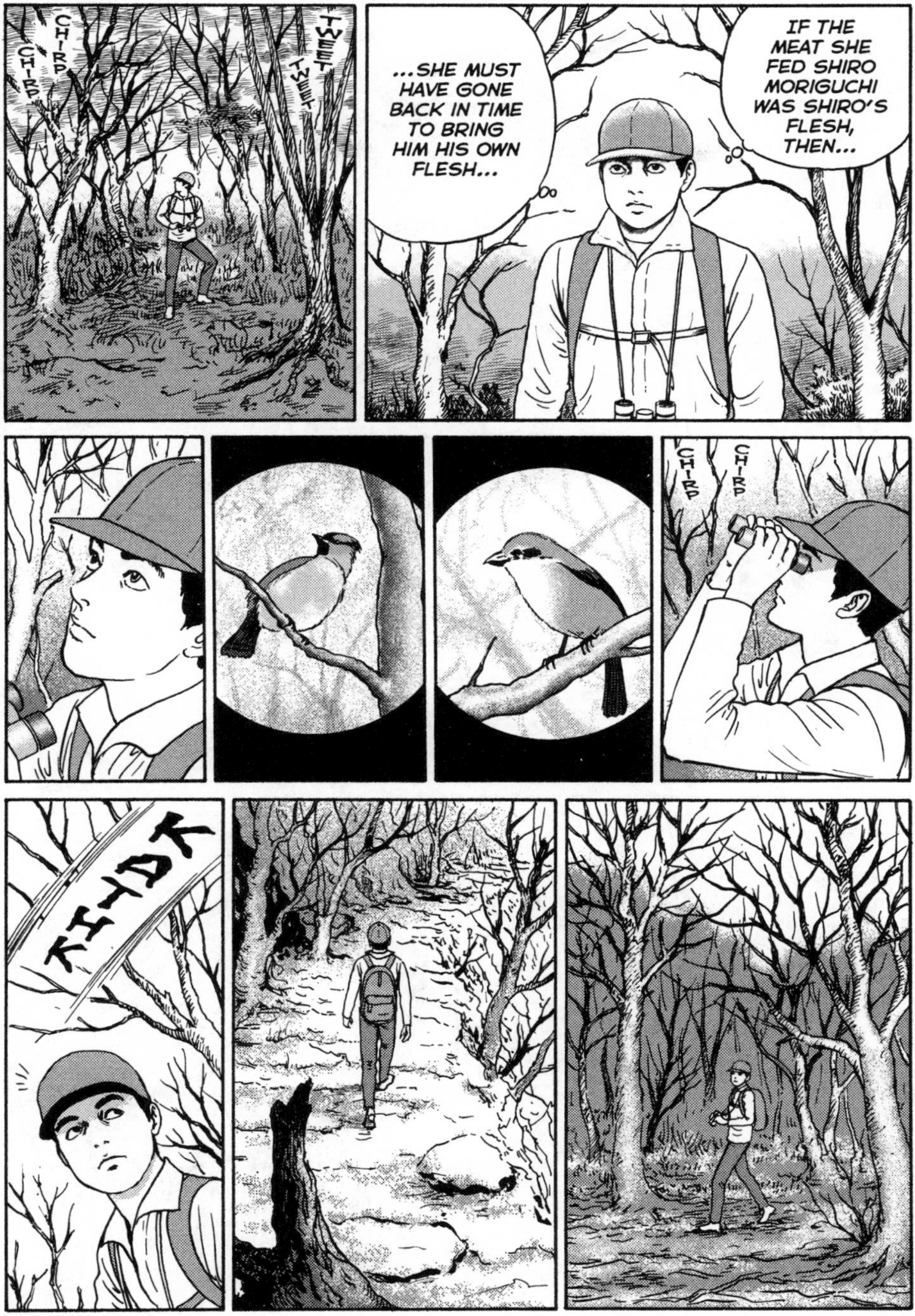
IF THE MEAT SHE FED SHIRO MORIGUCHI WAS SHIRO'S FLESH, THEN...
...SHE MUST HAVE GONE BACK IN TIME TO BRING HIM HIS OWN FLESH...
TWEET TWEET
CHIRP CHIRP
CHIRP CHIRP

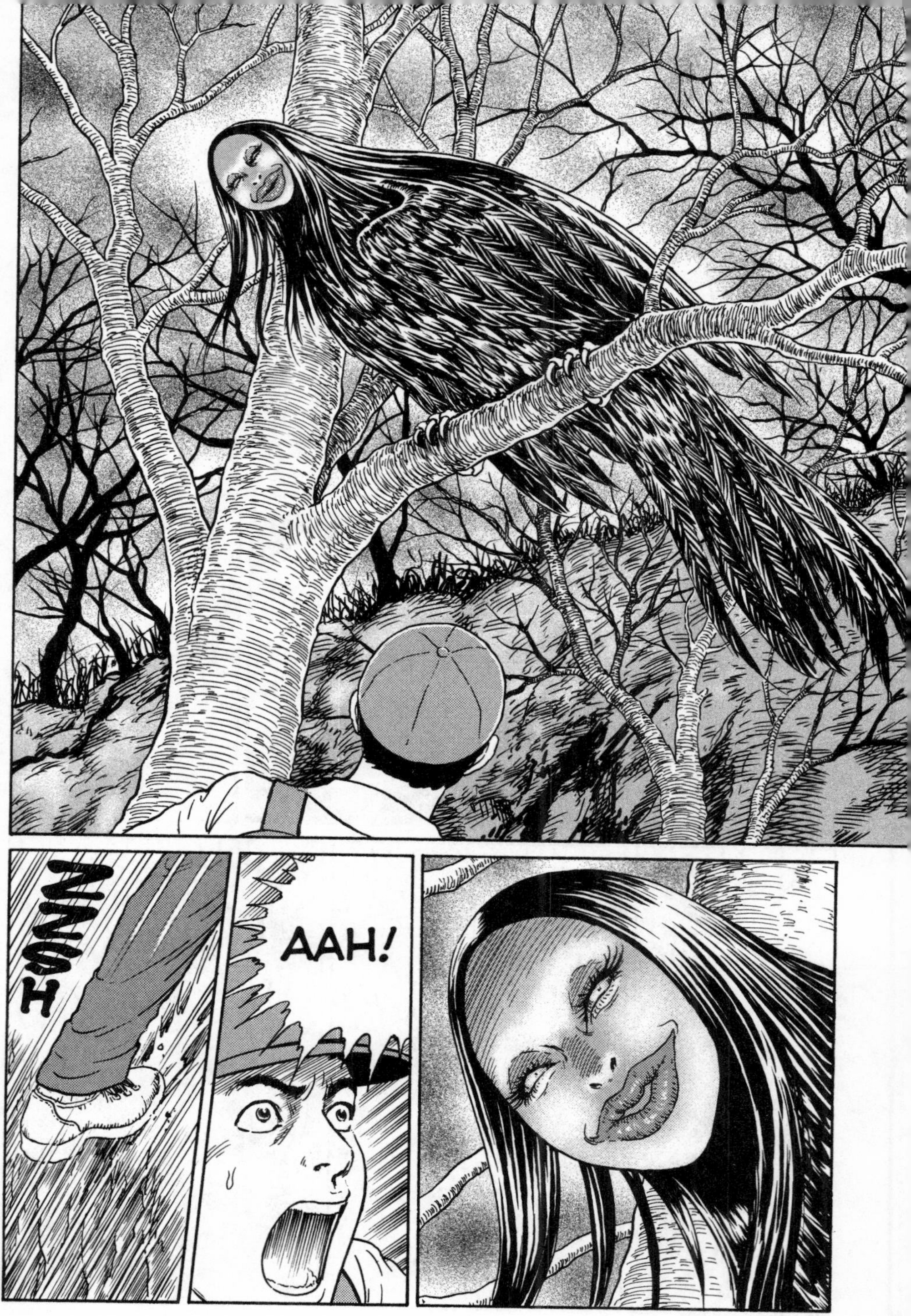
AAH!

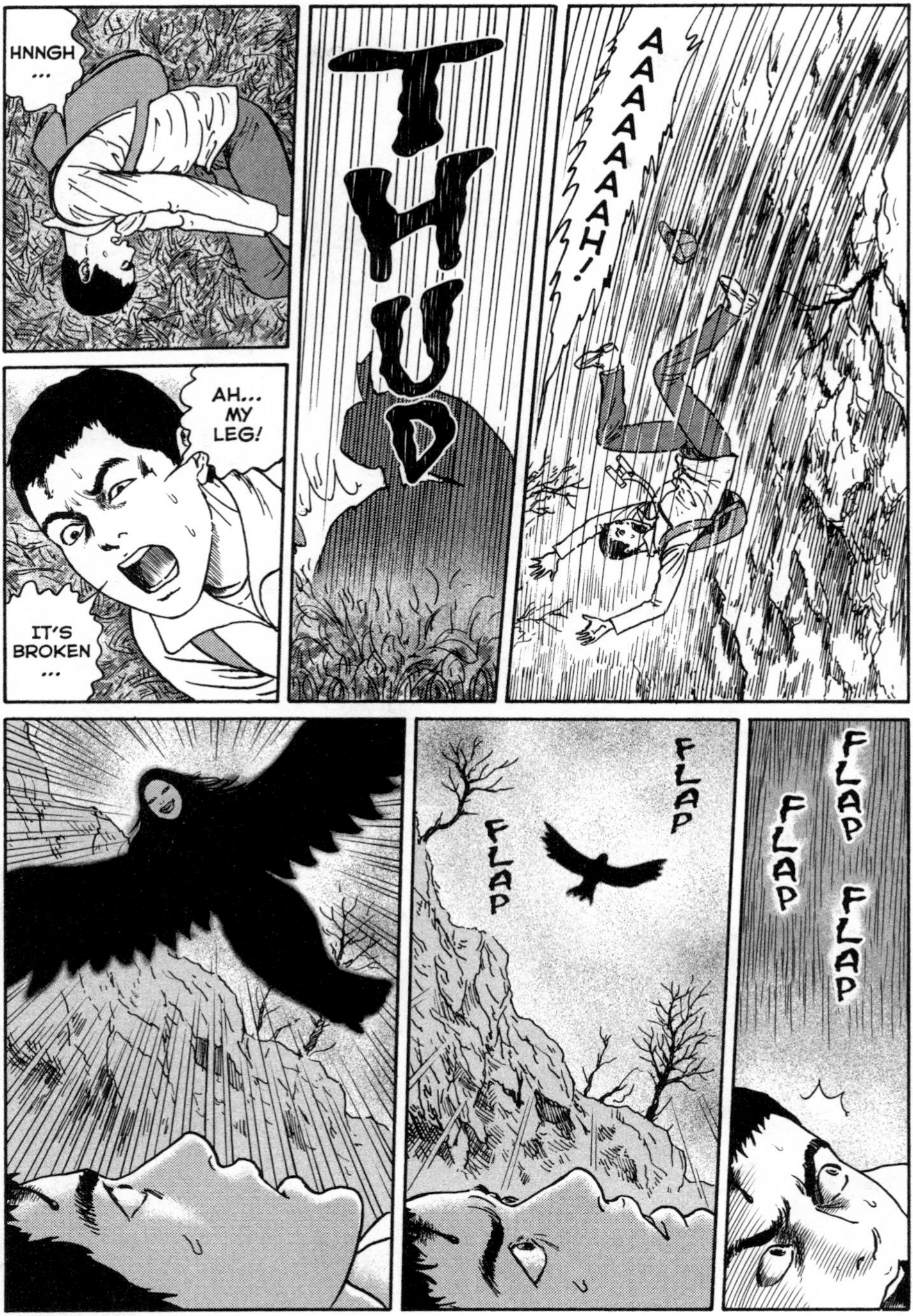
AAAAAAAAH!
THUD
HNNGH...
AH... MY LEG!
IT'S BROKEN...
FLAP FLAP
FLAP FLAP
FLAP
FLAP

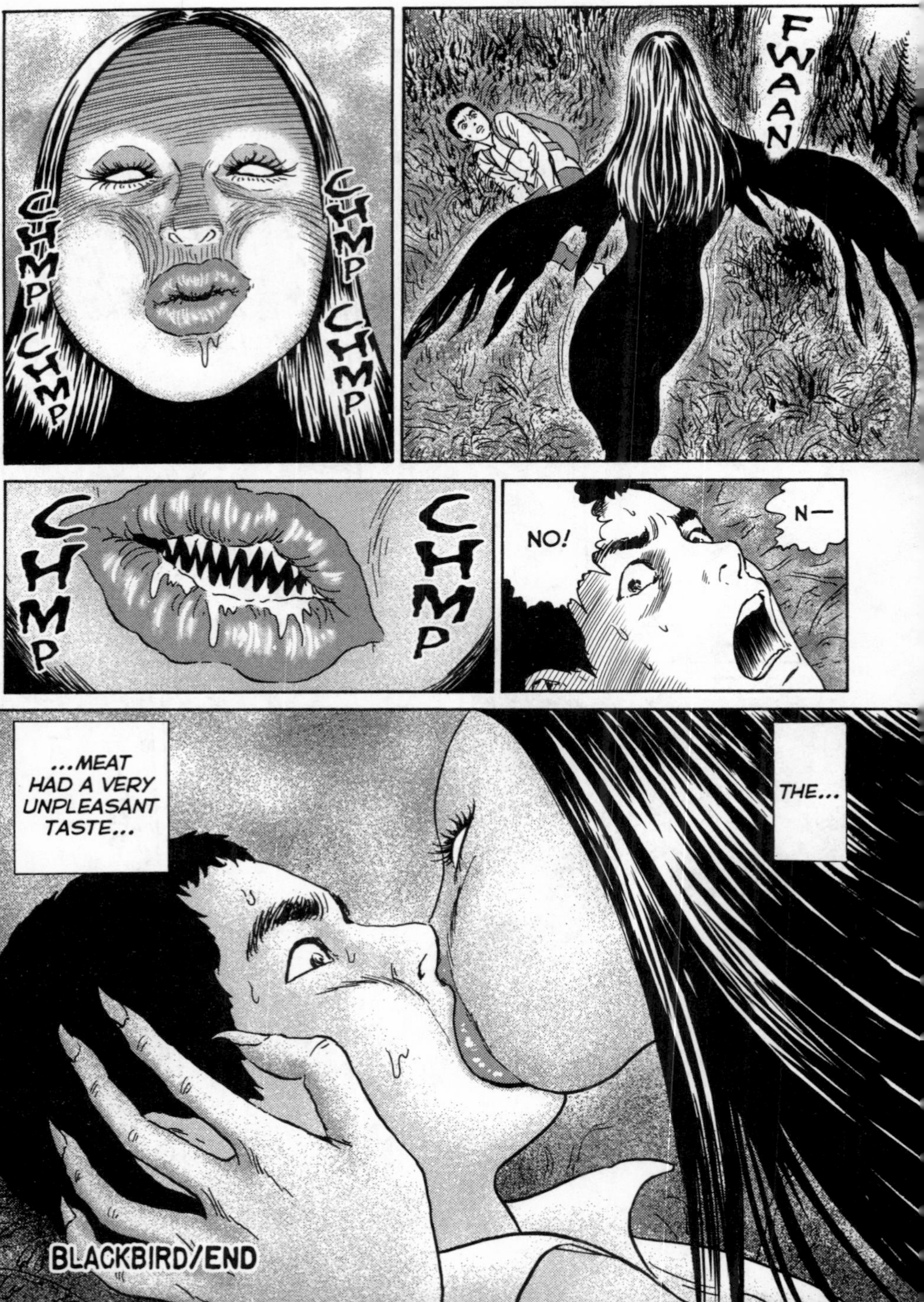
FWAAN
CHMP CHMP
CHMP CHMP
N—
NO!
CHMP
CHMP
THE...
...MEAT HAD A VERY UNPLEASANT TASTE...
BLACKBIRD/END

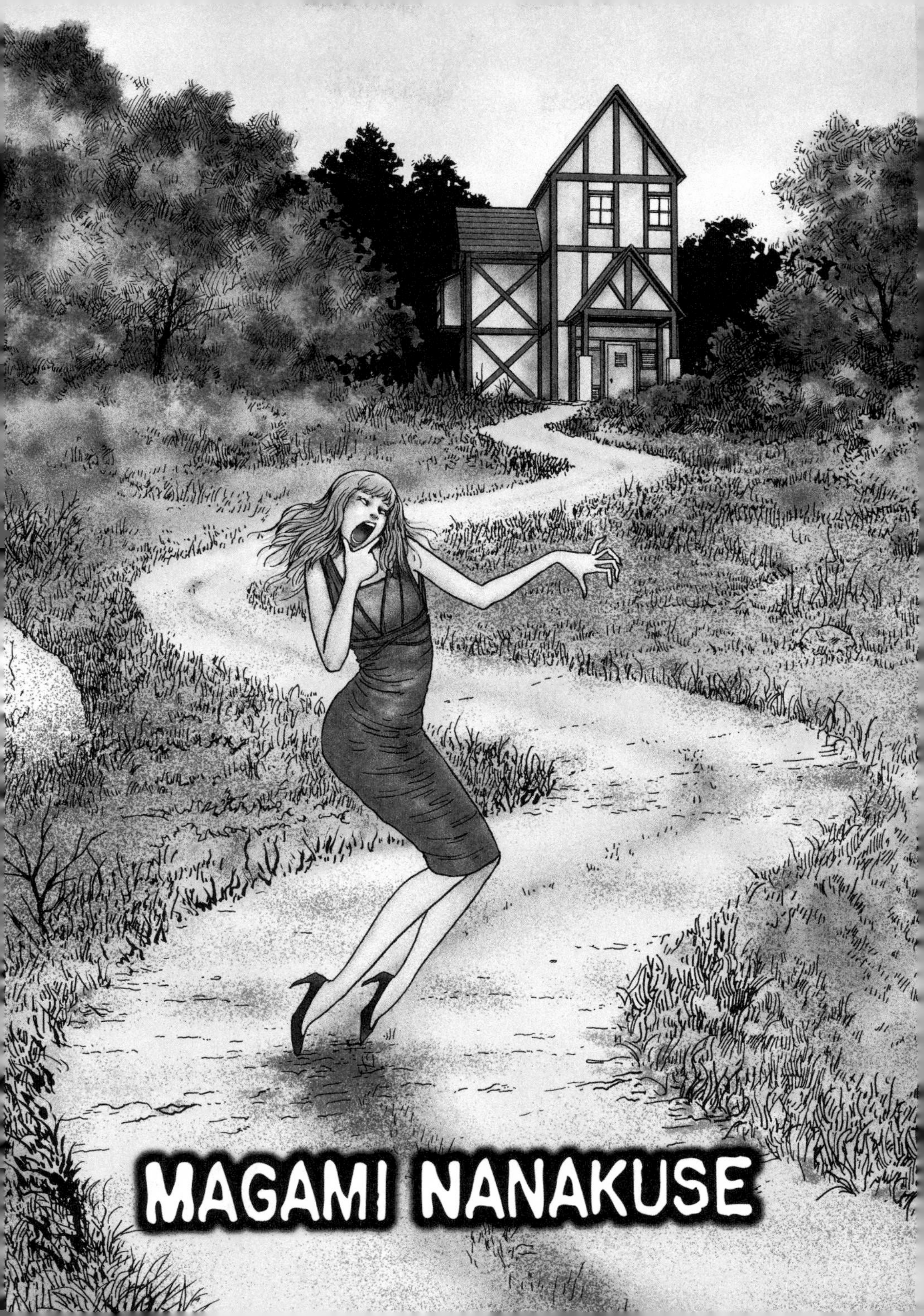
MAGAMI NANAKUSE

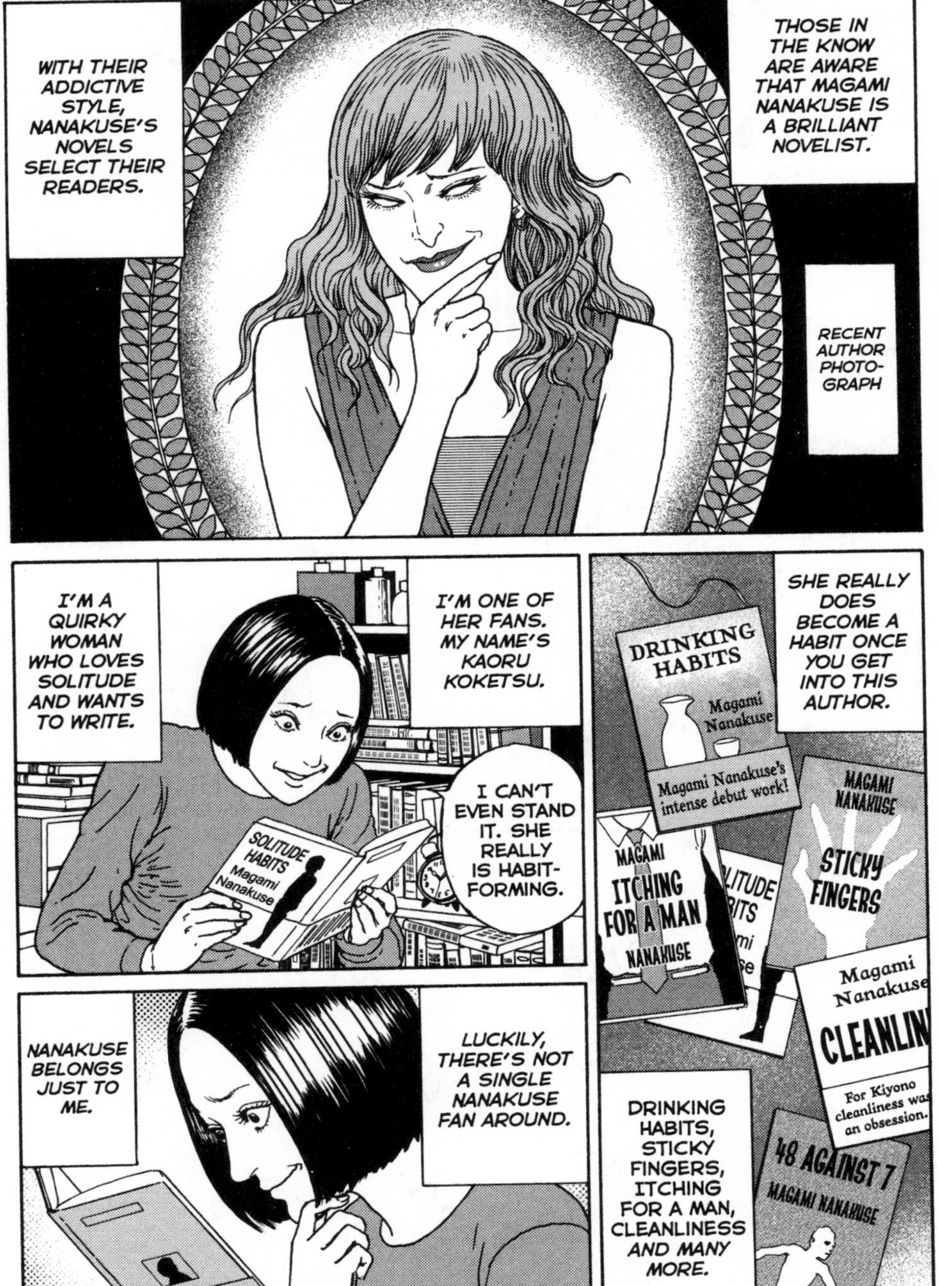
THOSE IN THE KNOW ARE AWARE THAT MAGAMI NANAKUSE IS A BRILLIANT NOVELIST.
WITH THEIR ADDICTIVE STYLE, NANAKUSE'S NOVELS SELECT THEIR READERS.
RECENT AUTHOR PHOTO-GRAPH
SHE REALLY DOES BECOME A HABIT ONCE YOU GET INTO THIS AUTHOR.
DRINKING HABITS
Magami Nanakuse
Magami Nanakuse's intense debut work!
MAGAMI NANAKUSE
STICKY FINGERS
MAGAMI
ITCHING FOR A MAN
NANAKUSE
LITUDE
BITS
mi
se
Magami Nanakuse
CLEANLIN
For Kiyono cleanliness was an obsession.
48 AGAINST 7
MAGAMI NANAKUSE
DRINKING HABITS, STICKY FINGERS, ITCHING FOR A MAN, CLEANLINESS AND MANY MORE.
I'M ONE OF HER FANS. MY NAME'S KAORU KOKETSU.
I'M A QUIRKY WOMAN WHO LOVES SOLITUDE AND WANTS TO WRITE.
I CAN'T EVEN STAND IT. SHE REALLY IS HABIT-FORMING.
SOLITUDE HABITS
Magami Nanakuse
LUCKILY, THERE'S NOT A SINGLE NANAKUSE FAN AROUND.
NANAKUSE BELONGS JUST TO ME.

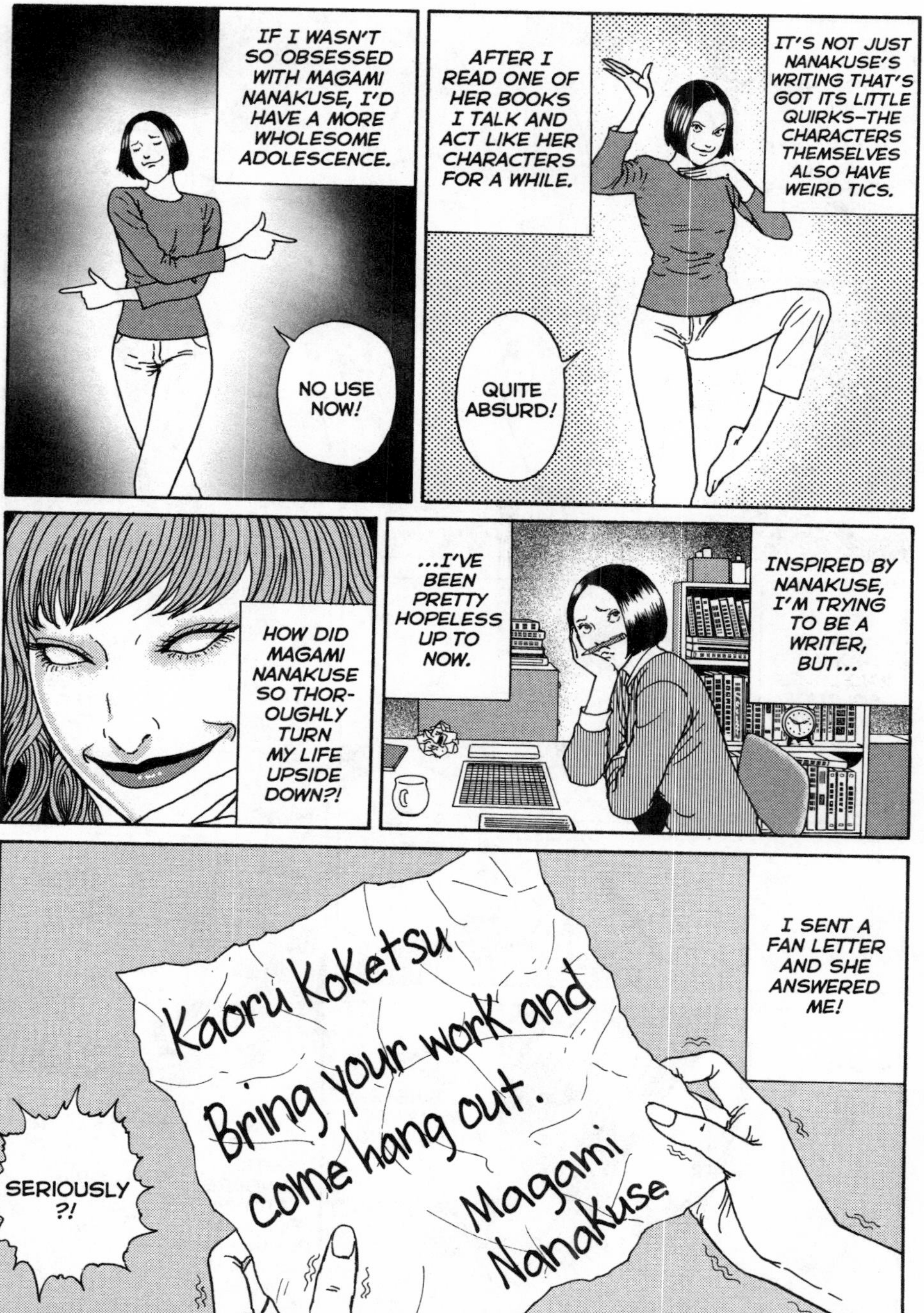
IT'S NOT JUST NANAKUSE'S WRITING THAT'S GOT ITS LITTLE QUIRKS—THE CHARACTERS THEMSELVES ALSO HAVE WEIRD TICS.
AFTER I READ ONE OF HER BOOKS I TALK AND ACT LIKE HER CHARACTERS FOR A WHILE.
QUITE ABSURD!
IF I WASN'T SO OBSESSED WITH MAGAMI NANAKUSE, I'D HAVE A MORE WHOLESOME ADOLESCENCE.
NO USE NOW!
INSPIRED BY NANAKUSE, I'M TRYING TO BE A WRITER, BUT...
...I'VE BEEN PRETTY HOPELESS UP TO NOW.
HOW DID MAGAMI NANAKUSE SO THOR-OUGHLY TURN MY LIFE UPSIDE DOWN?!
I SENT A FAN LETTER AND SHE ANSWERED ME!
Kaoru Koketsu
Bring your work and come hang out.
Magami Nanakuse
SERIOUSLY ?!

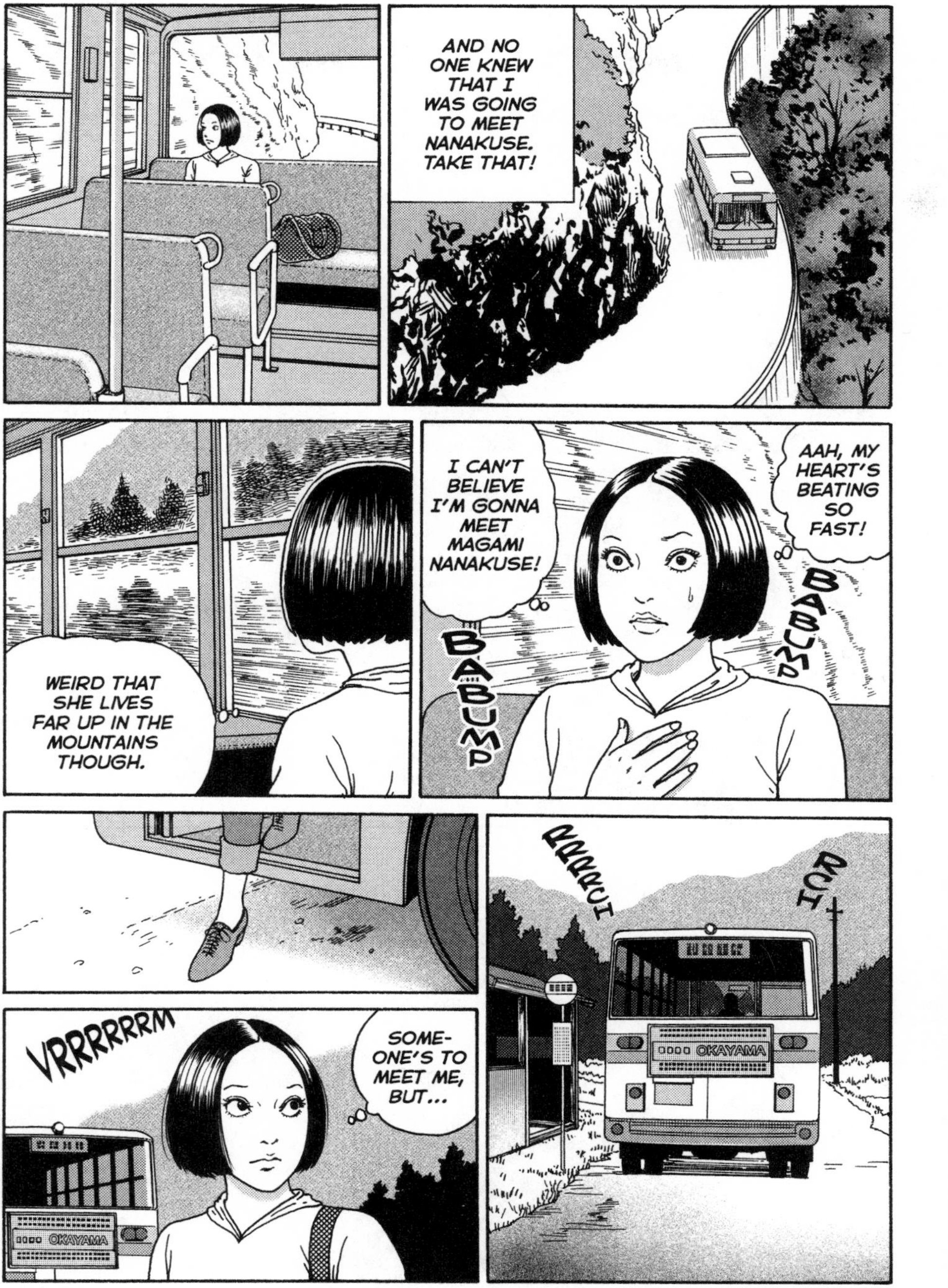
AND NO ONE KNEW THAT I WAS GOING TO MEET NANAKUSE. TAKE THAT!
AAH, MY HEART'S BEATING SO FAST!
I CAN'T BELIEVE I'M GONNA MEET MAGAMI NANAKUSE!
BABUMP
BABUMP
WEIRD THAT SHE LIVES FAR UP IN THE MOUNTAINS THOUGH.
RRRRCH
RCH
OKAYAMA
VRRRRRM
SOME-ONE'S TO MEET ME, BUT...
OKAYAMA

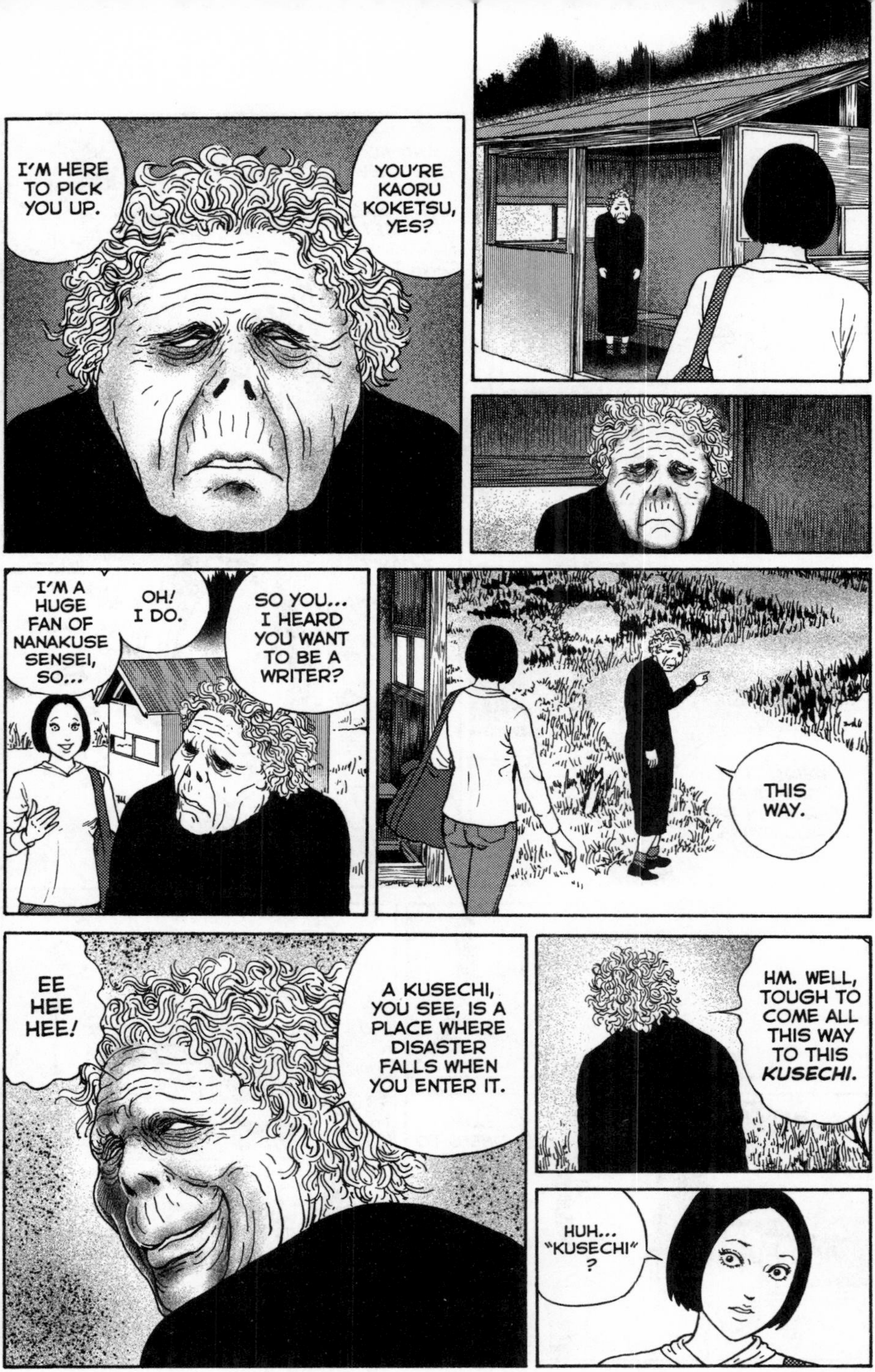
YOU'RE KAORU KOKETSU, YES?
I'M HERE TO PICK YOU UP.
THIS WAY.
SO YOU... I HEARD YOU WANT TO BE A WRITER?
OH! I DO.
I'M A HUGE FAN OF NANAKUSE SENSEI, SO...
HM. WELL, TOUGH TO COME ALL THIS WAY TO THIS *KUSECHI*.
HUH... "KUSECHI"?
A KUSECHI, YOU SEE, IS A PLACE WHERE DISASTER FALLS WHEN YOU ENTER IT.
EE HEE HEE!

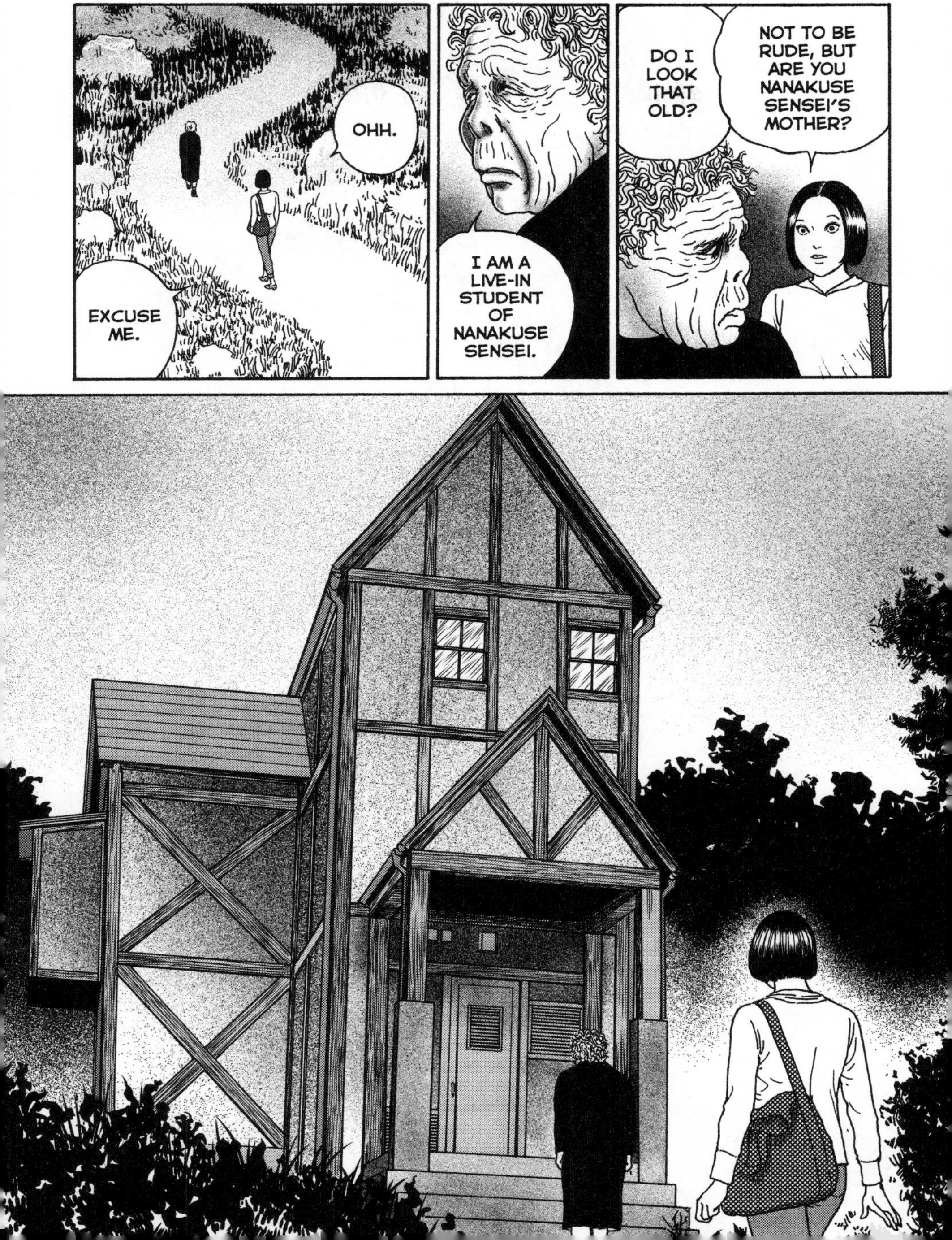
NOT TO BE RUDE, BUT ARE YOU NANAKUSE SENSEI'S MOTHER?
DO I LOOK THAT OLD?
I AM A LIVE-IN STUDENT OF NANAKUSE SENSEI.
OHH.
EXCUSE ME.

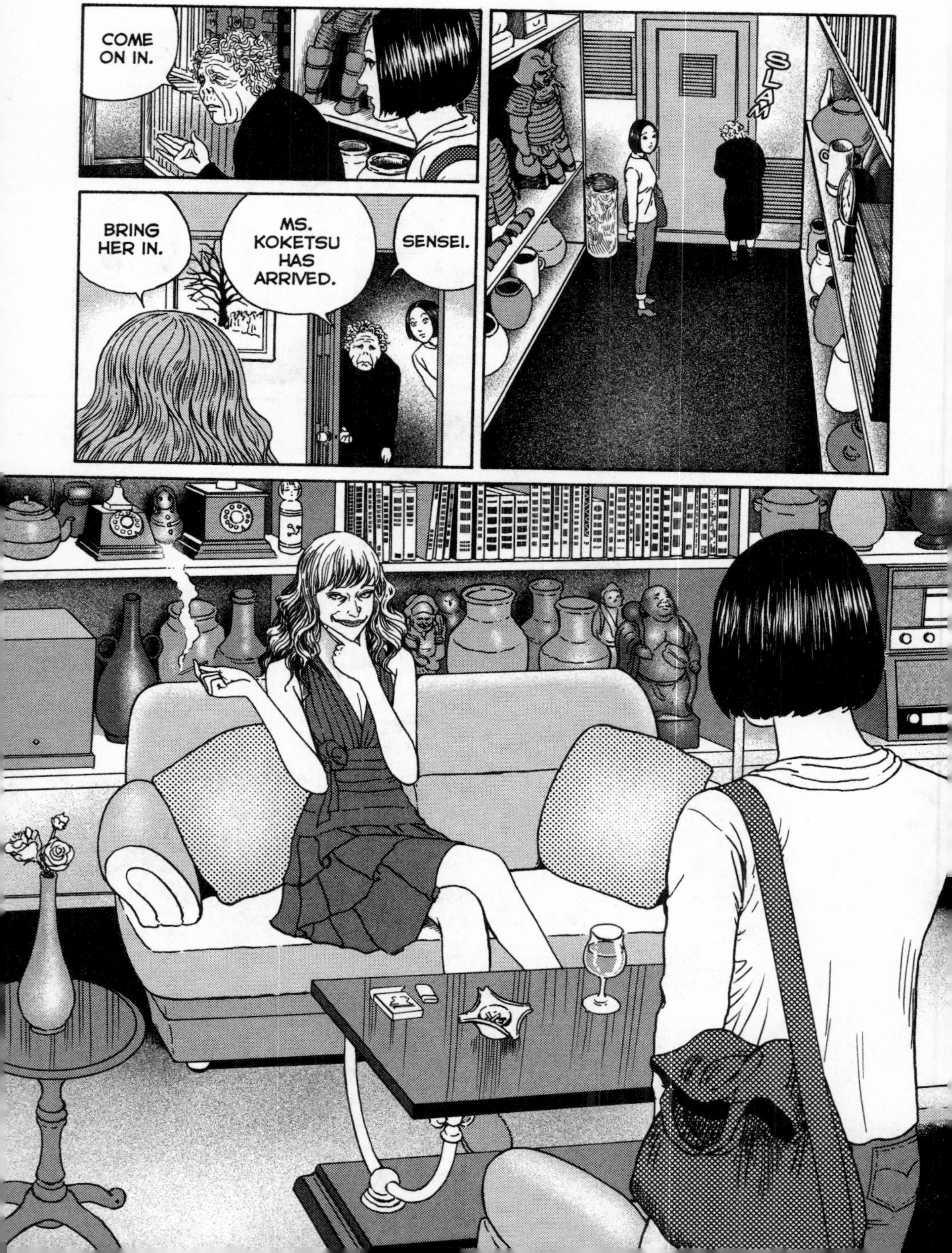
SLAM
COME ON IN.
SENSEI.
MS. KOKETSU HAS ARRIVED.
BRING HER IN.

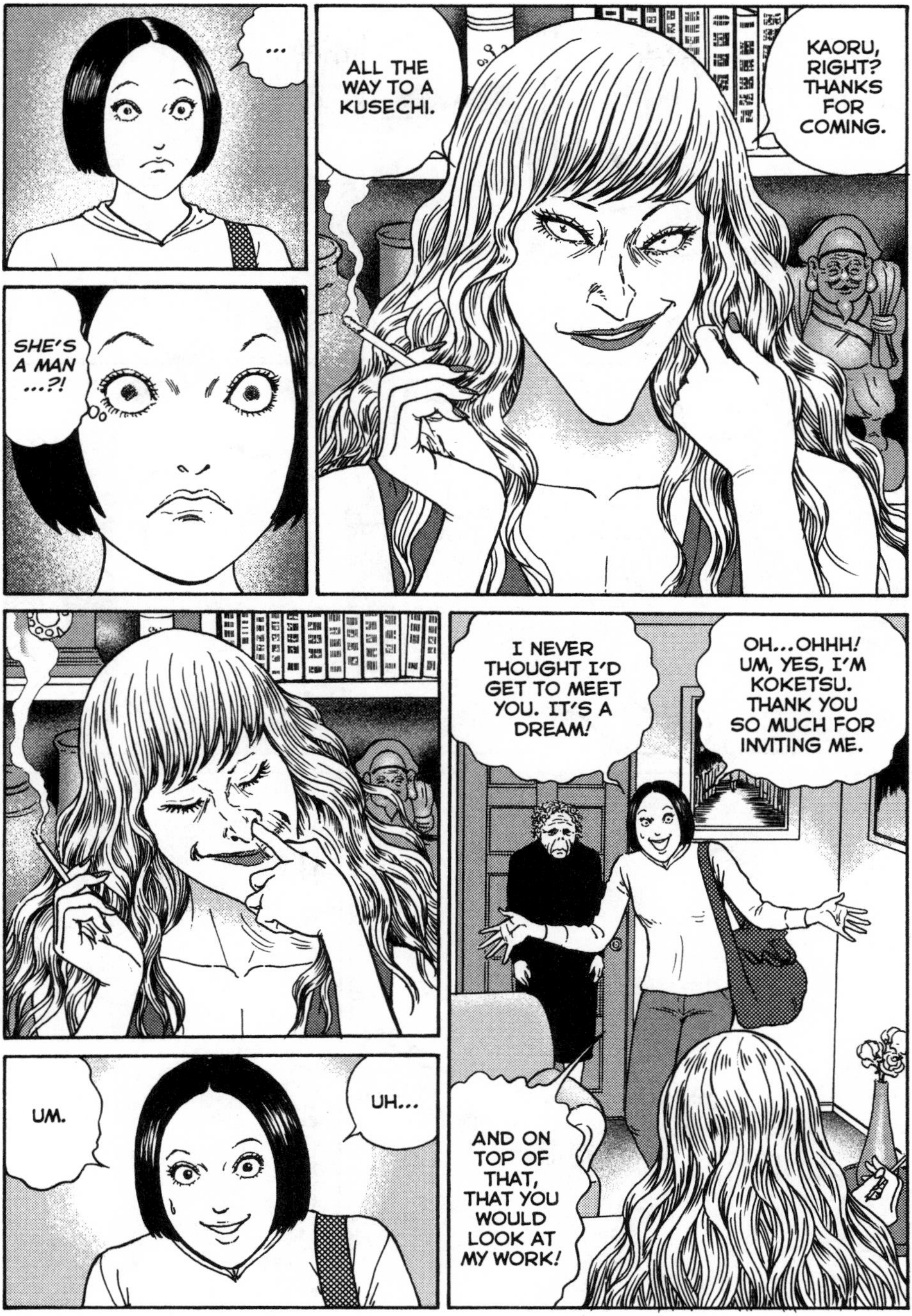
KAORU, RIGHT? THANKS FOR COMING.
ALL THE WAY TO A KUSECHI.
...
SHE'S A MAN ...?!
OH...OHHH! UM, YES, I'M KOKETSU. THANK YOU SO MUCH FOR INVITING ME.
I NEVER THOUGHT I'D GET TO MEET YOU. IT'S A DREAM!
AND ON TOP OF THAT, THAT YOU WOULD LOOK AT MY WORK!
UH...
UM.

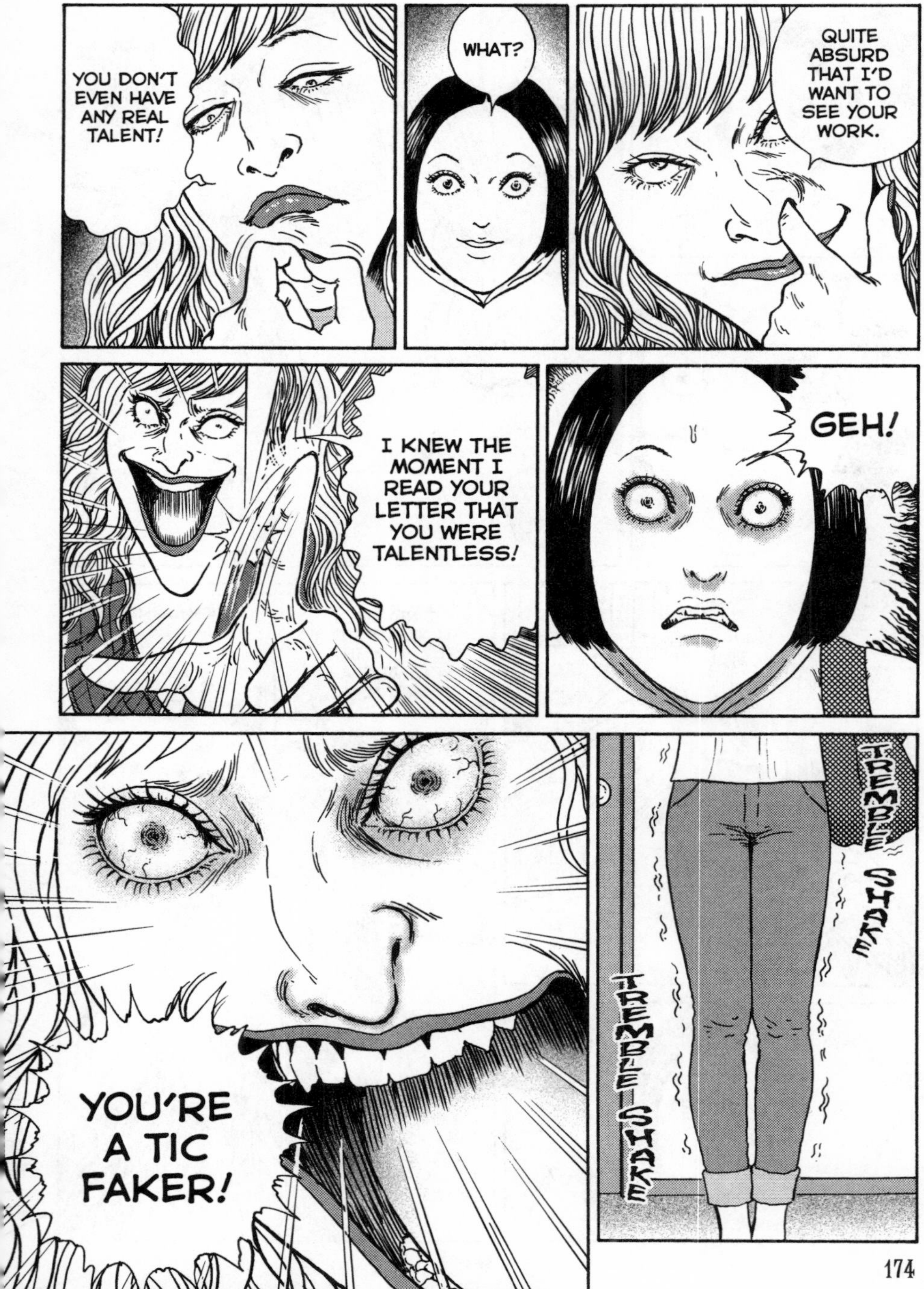
QUITE ABSURD THAT I'D WANT TO SEE YOUR WORK.
WHAT?
YOU DON'T EVEN HAVE ANY REAL TALENT!
GEH!
I KNEW THE MOMENT I READ YOUR LETTER THAT YOU WERE TALENTLESS!
TREMBLE SHAKE
TREMBLE SHAKE
YOU'RE A TIC FAKER!

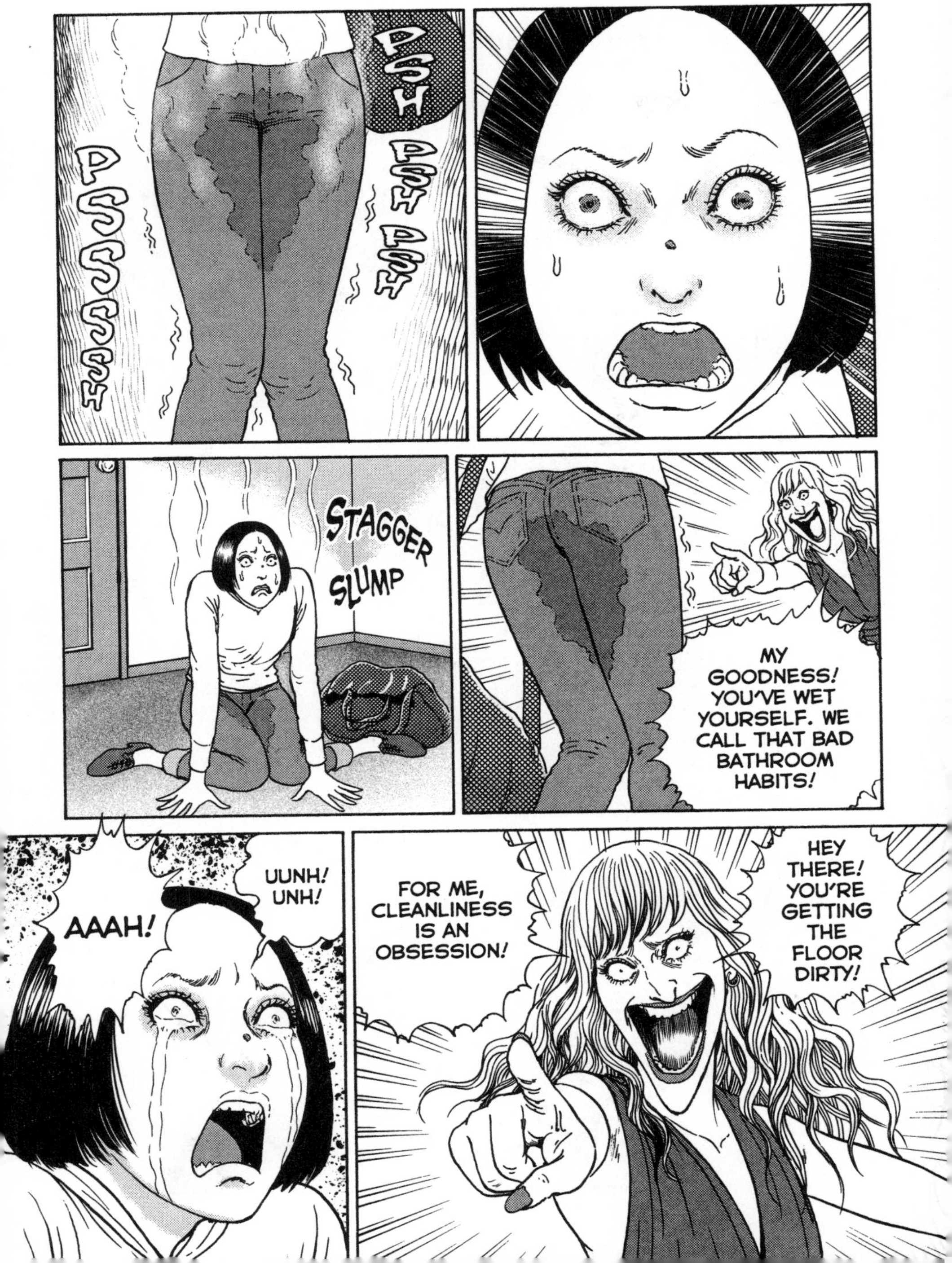
PSH PSH PSH PSH
PSSSSH
MY GOODNESS! YOU'VE WET YOURSELF. WE CALL THAT BAD BATHROOM HABITS!
STAGGER
SLUMP
HEY THERE! YOU'RE GETTING THE FLOOR DIRTY!
FOR ME, CLEANLINESS IS AN OBSESSION!
UUNH! UNH!
AAAH!

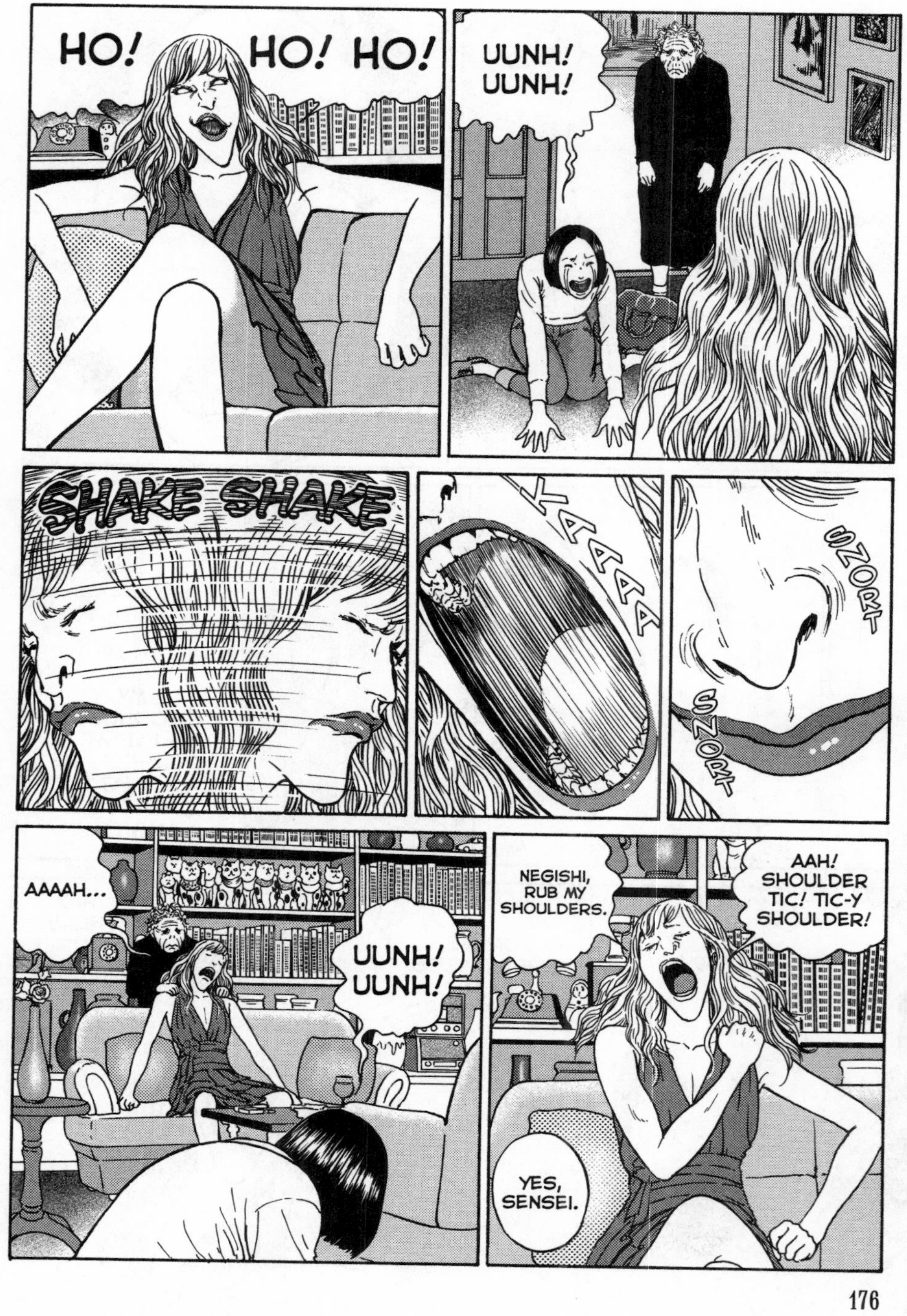
UUNH! UUNH!
HO! HO! HO!
SNORT
SNORT
KAAAAA
SHAKE SHAKE
AAH! SHOULDER TIC! TIC-Y SHOULDER!
NEGISHI, RUB MY SHOULDERS.
YES, SENSEI.
AAAAH...
UUNH! UUNH!

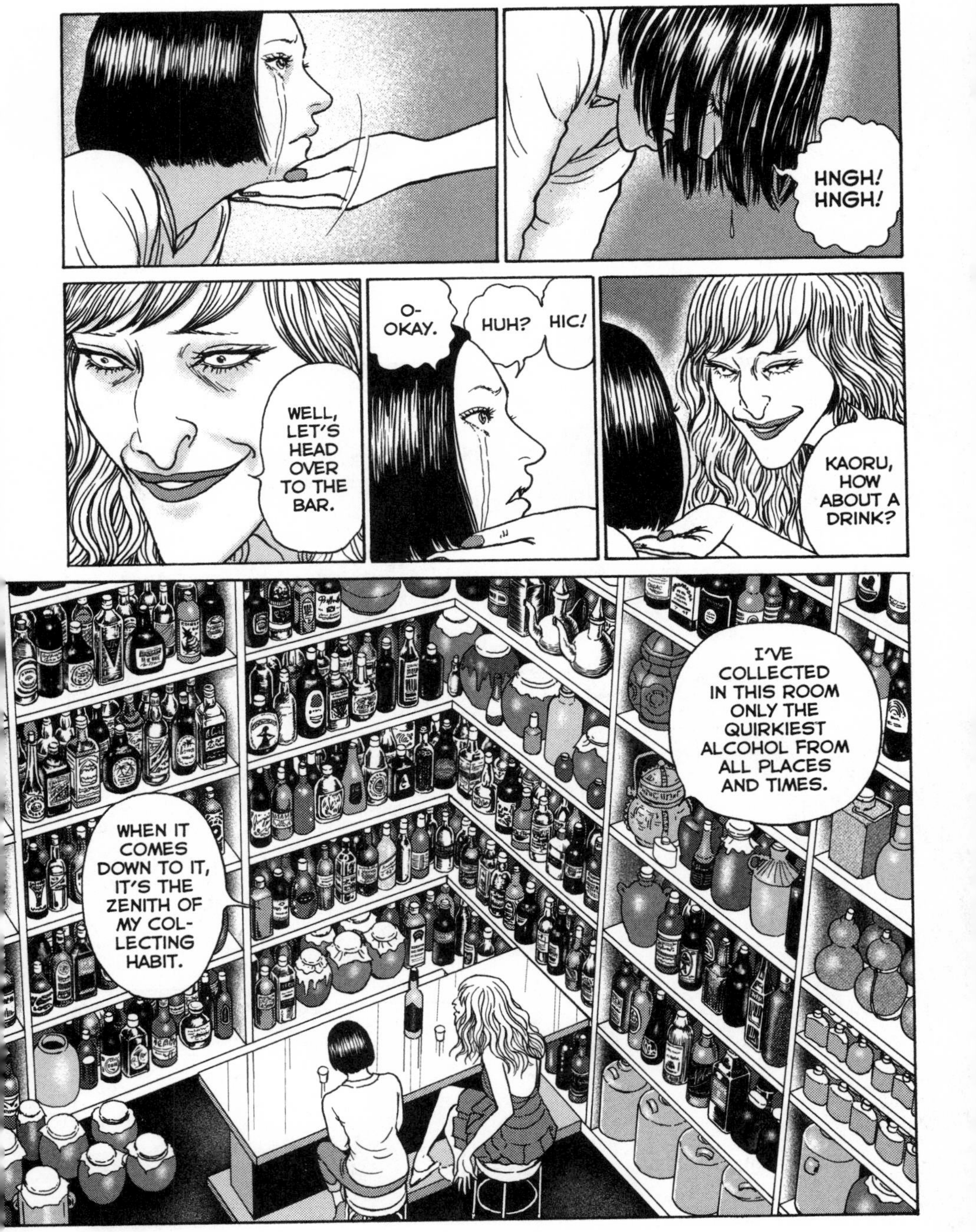
HNGH! HNGH!
KAORU, HOW ABOUT A DRINK?
HIC!
HUH?
O-OKAY.
WELL, LET'S HEAD OVER TO THE BAR.
I'VE COLLECTED IN THIS ROOM ONLY THE QUIRKIEST ALCOHOL FROM ALL PLACES AND TIMES.
WHEN IT COMES DOWN TO IT, IT'S THE ZENITH OF MY COL-LECTING HABIT.

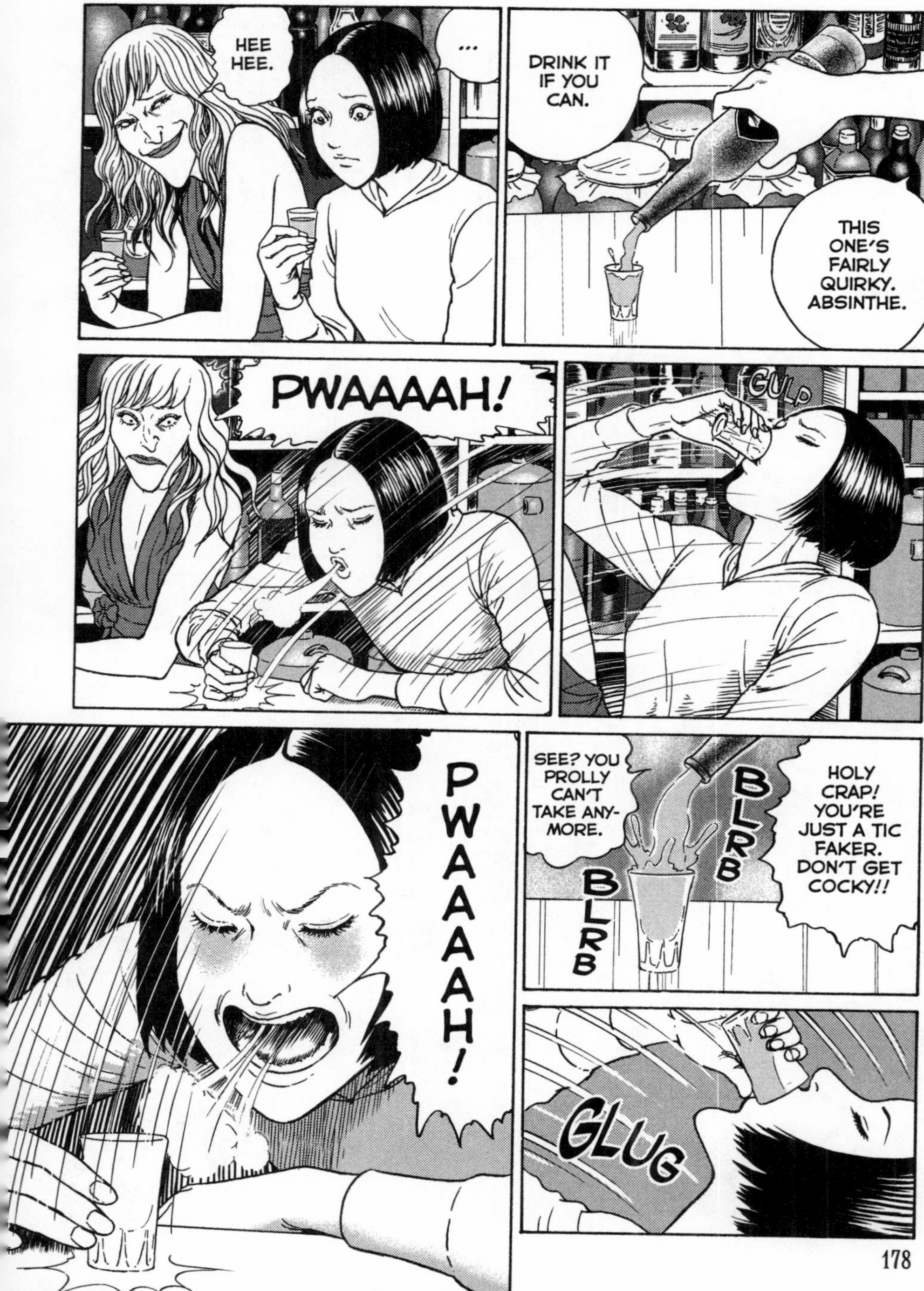
DRINK IT IF YOU CAN.
THIS ONE'S FAIRLY QUIRKY. ABSINTHE.
...
HEE HEE.
GULP
PWAAAAH!
HOLY CRAP! YOU'RE JUST A TIC FAKER. DON'T GET COCKY!!
BLRB
SEE? YOU PROLLY CAN'T TAKE ANY-MORE.
BLRB
GLUG
PWAAAAAH!

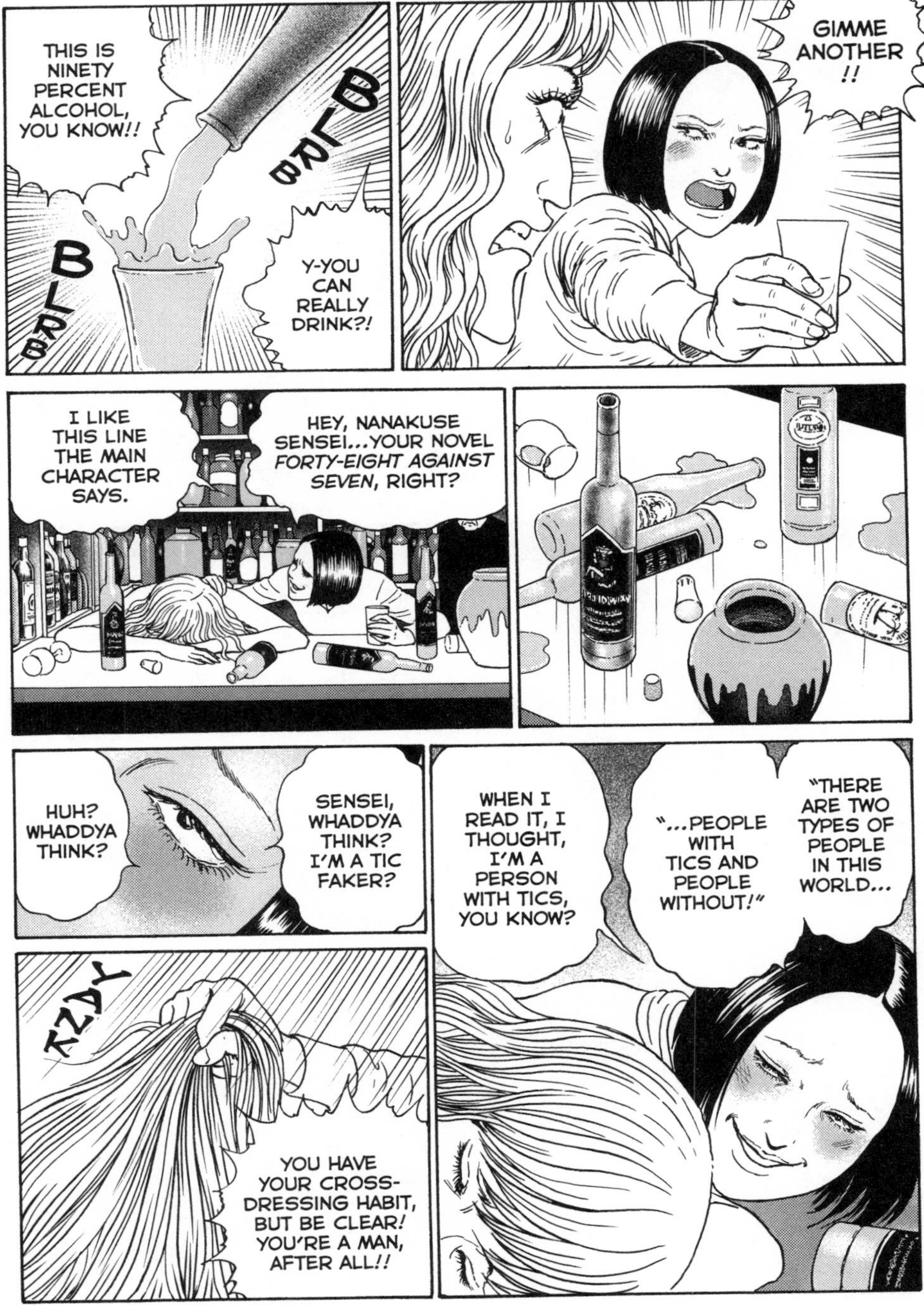
GIMME ANOTHER!!
THIS IS NINETY PERCENT ALCOHOL, YOU KNOW!!
BLRB
Y-YOU CAN REALLY DRINK?!
BLRB
HEY, NANAKUSE SENSEI...YOUR NOVEL *FORTY-EIGHT AGAINST SEVEN*, RIGHT?
I LIKE THIS LINE THE MAIN CHARACTER SAYS.
"THERE ARE TWO TYPES OF PEOPLE IN THIS WORLD...
"...PEOPLE WITH TICS AND PEOPLE WITHOUT!"
WHEN I READ IT, I THOUGHT, I'M A PERSON WITH TICS, YOU KNOW?
SENSEI, WHADDYA THINK? I'M A TIC FAKER?
HUH? WHADDYA THINK?
YOU HAVE YOUR CROSS-DRESSING HABIT, BUT BE CLEAR! YOU'RE A MAN, AFTER ALL!!

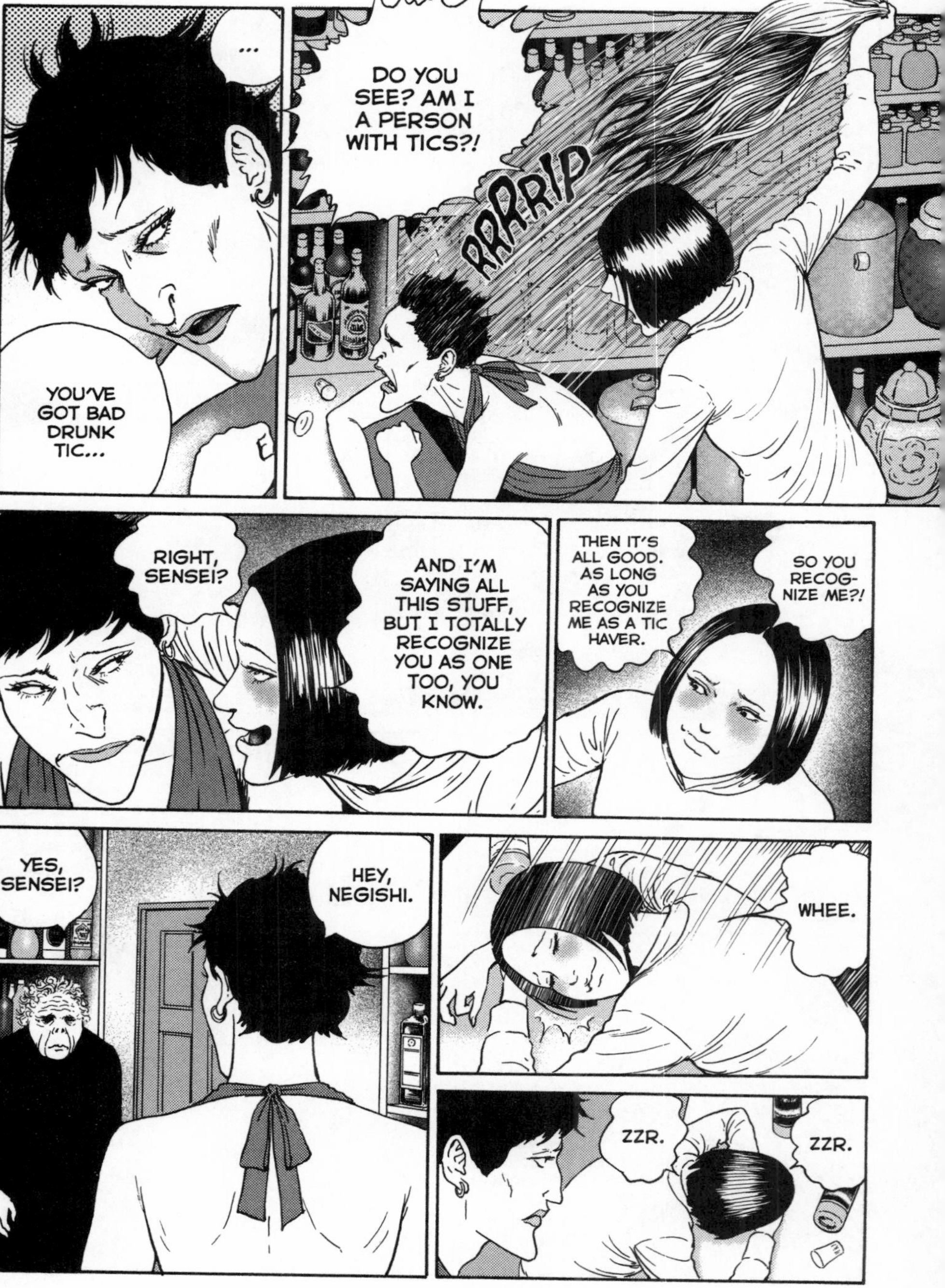
DO YOU SEE? AM I A PERSON WITH TICS?!
RRRRIP
...
YOU'VE GOT BAD DRUNK TIC...
SO YOU RECOG-NIZE ME?!
THEN IT'S ALL GOOD. AS LONG AS YOU RECOGNIZE ME AS A TIC HAVER.
AND I'M SAYING ALL THIS STUFF, BUT I TOTALLY RECOGNIZE YOU AS ONE TOO, YOU KNOW.
RIGHT, SENSEI?
WHEE.
ZZR.
ZZR.
HEY, NEGISHI.
YES, SENSEI?

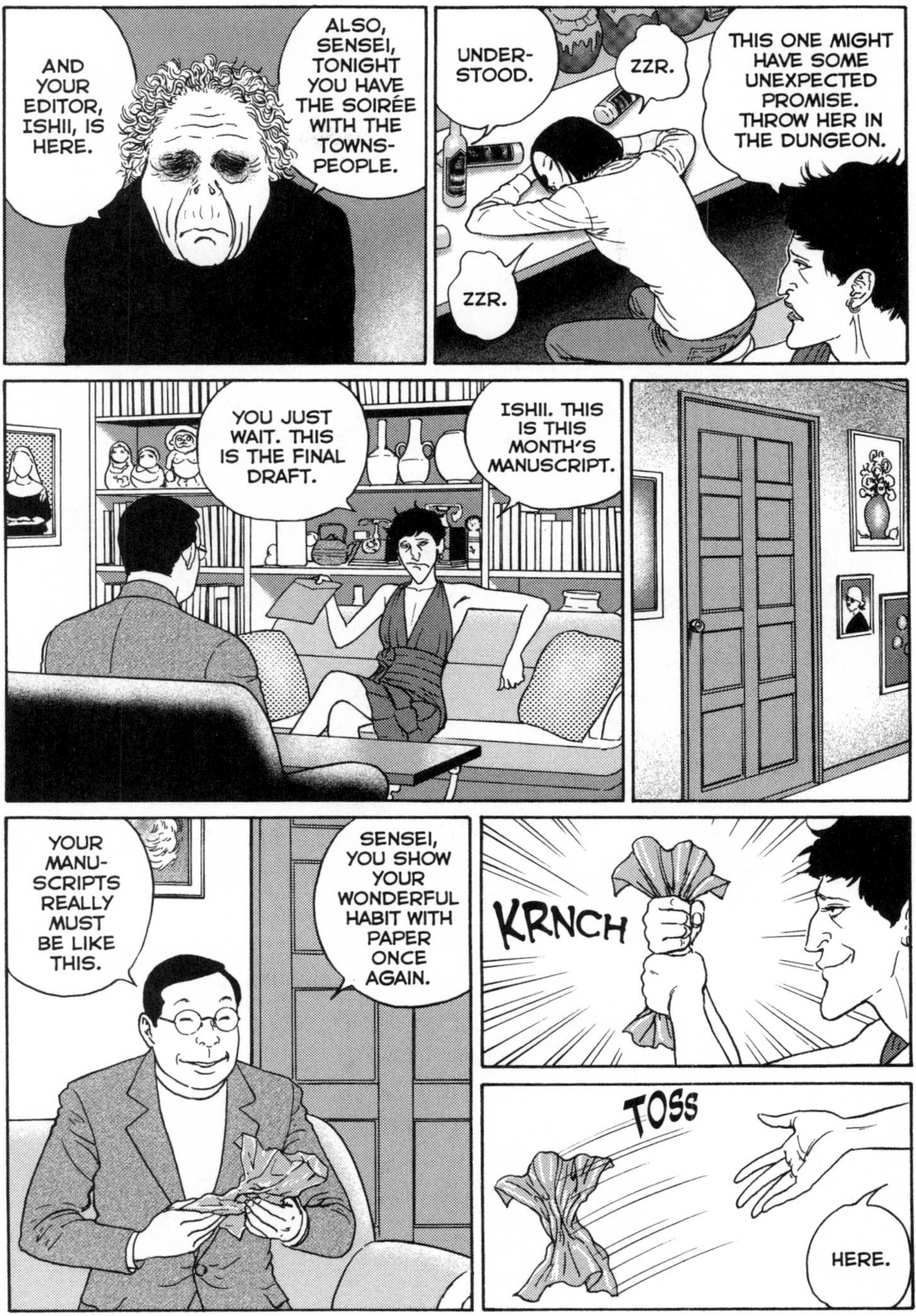
THIS ONE MIGHT HAVE SOME UNEXPECTED PROMISE. THROW HER IN THE DUNGEON.
ZZR.
UNDER-STOOD.
ZZR.
ALSO, SENSEI, TONIGHT YOU HAVE THE SOIRÉE WITH THE TOWNS-PEOPLE.
AND YOUR EDITOR, ISHII, IS HERE.
ISHII. THIS IS THIS MONTH'S MANUSCRIPT.
YOU JUST WAIT. THIS IS THE FINAL DRAFT.
KRNCH
TOSS
HERE.
SENSEI, YOU SHOW YOUR WONDERFUL HABIT WITH PAPER ONCE AGAIN.
YOUR MANU-SCRIPTS REALLY MUST BE LIKE THIS.

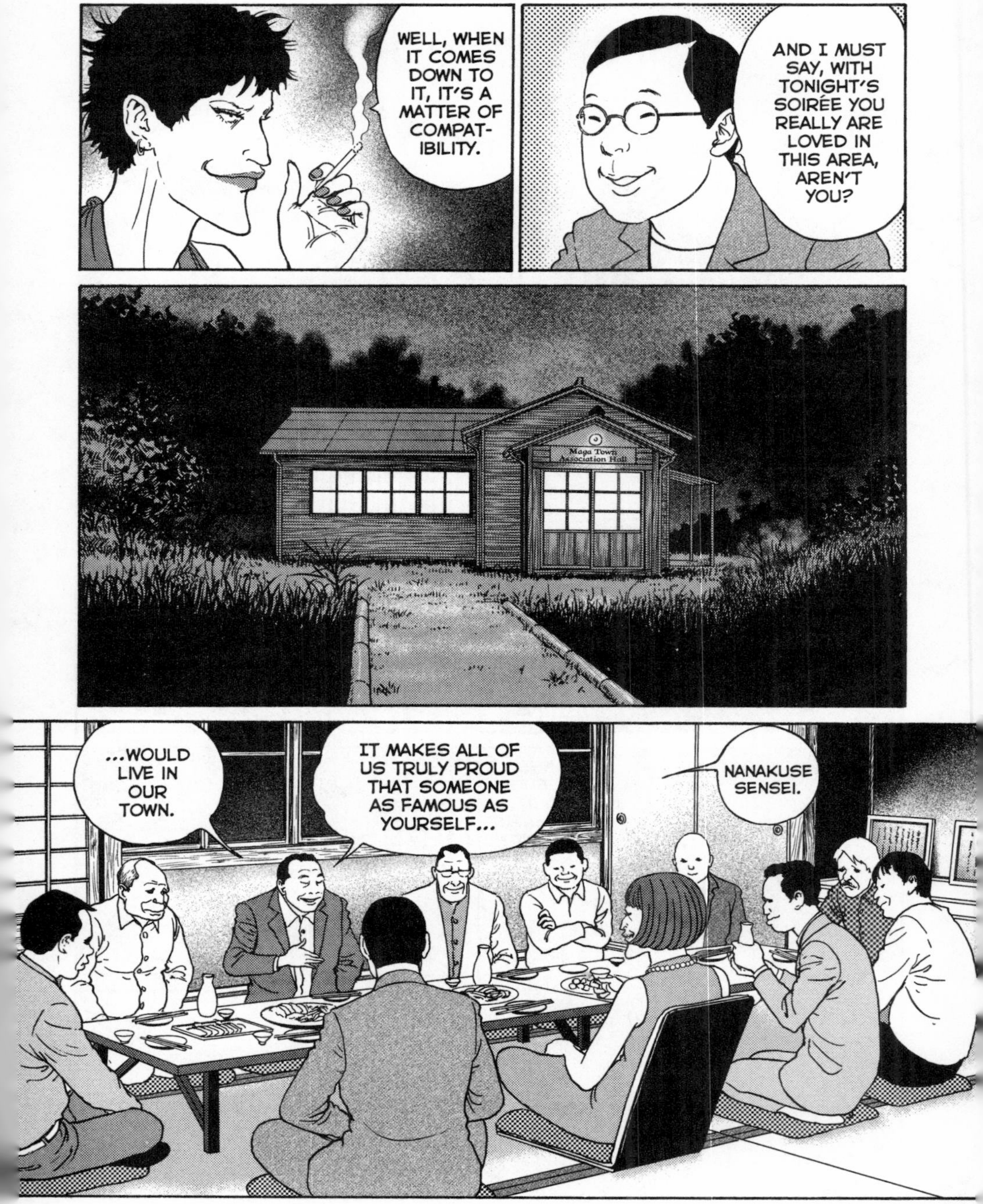
AND I MUST SAY, WITH TONIGHT'S SOIRÉE YOU REALLY ARE LOVED IN THIS AREA, AREN'T YOU?
WELL, WHEN IT COMES DOWN TO IT, IT'S A MATTER OF COMPAT-IBILITY.
Maga Town Association Hall
NANAKUSE SENSEI.
IT MAKES ALL OF US TRULY PROUD THAT SOMEONE AS FAMOUS AS YOURSELF...
...WOULD LIVE IN OUR TOWN.

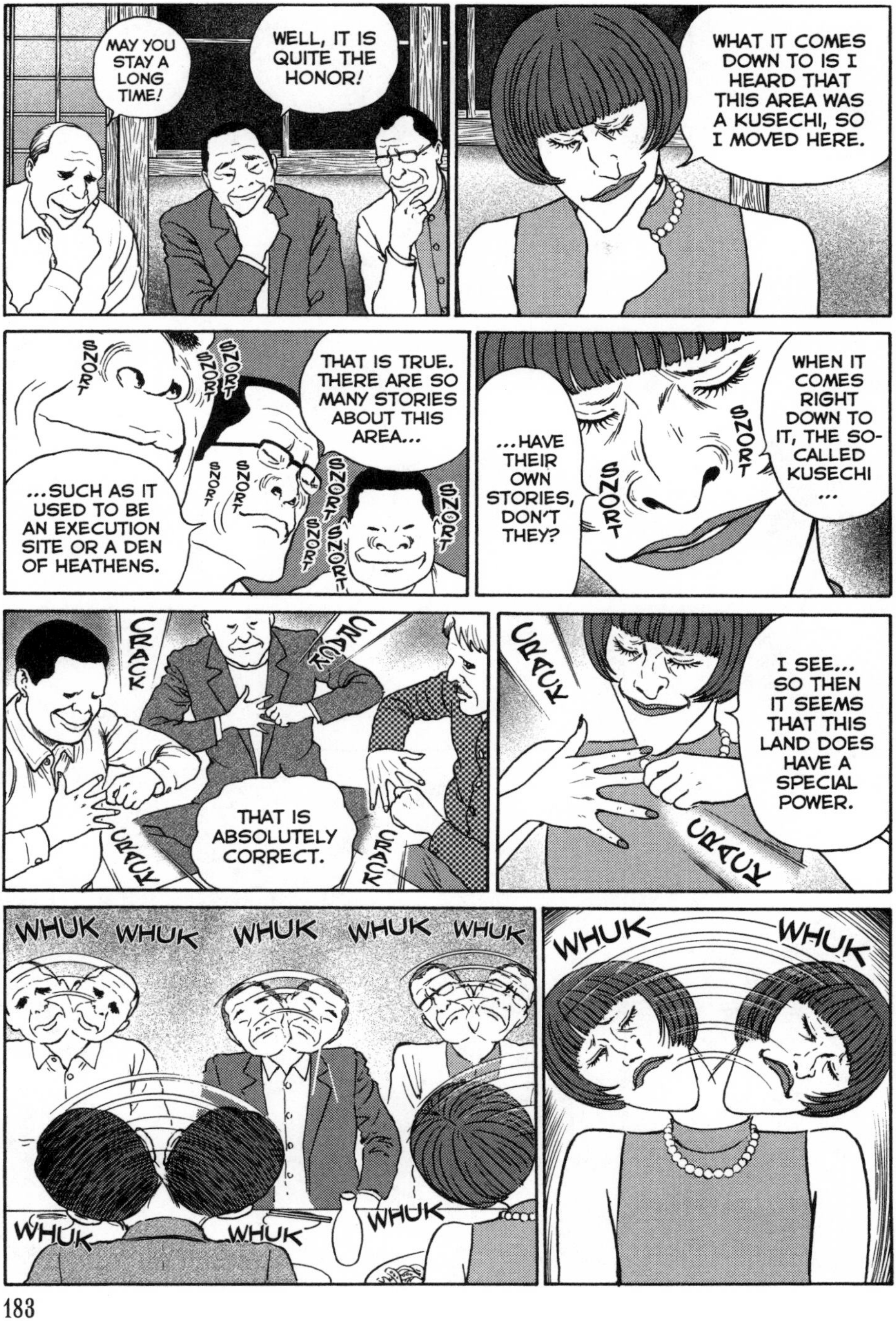
WHAT IT COMES DOWN TO IS I HEARD THAT THIS AREA WAS A KUSECHI, SO I MOVED HERE.
WELL, IT IS QUITE THE HONOR!
MAY YOU STAY A LONG TIME!
WHEN IT COMES RIGHT DOWN TO IT, THE SO-CALLED KUSECHI ...
SNORT
SNORT
...HAVE THEIR OWN STORIES, DON'T THEY?
THAT IS TRUE. THERE ARE SO MANY STORIES ABOUT THIS AREA...
SNORT
SNORT
SNORT
SNORT
SNORT
SNORT
SNORT
SNORT
SNORT
...SUCH AS IT USED TO BE AN EXECUTION SITE OR A DEN OF HEATHENS.
CRACK
I SEE... SO THEN IT SEEMS THAT THIS LAND DOES HAVE A SPECIAL POWER.
CRACK
CRACK
CRACK
THAT IS ABSOLUTELY CORRECT.
CRACK
CRACK
WHUK
WHUK
WHUK
WHUK
WHUK
WHUK
WHUK
WHUK
WHUK
WHUK

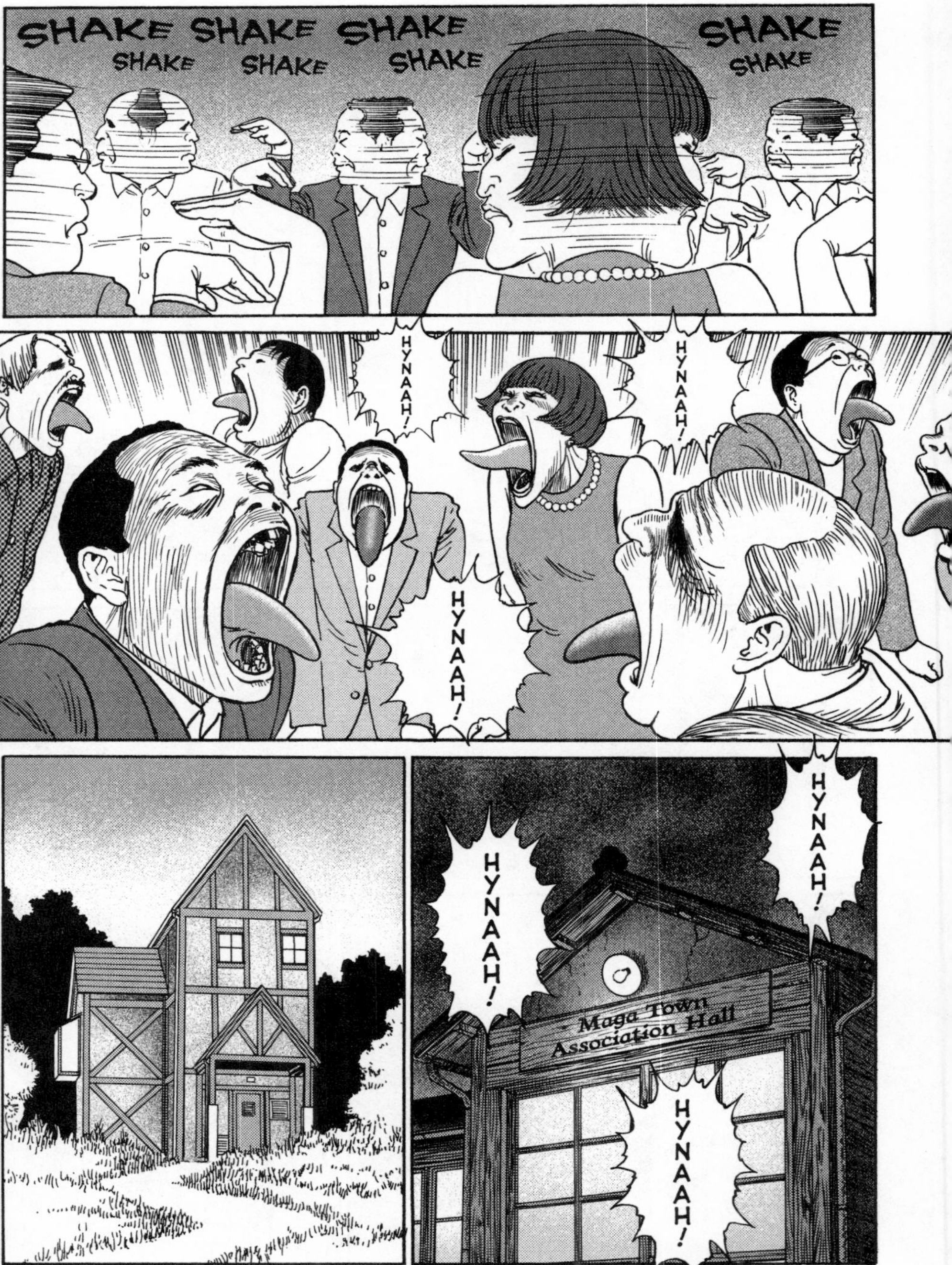
SHAKE
SHAKE
SHAKE
SHAKE
SHAKE
SHAKE
SHAKE
SHAKE
HYNAAH!
HYNAAH!
HYNAAH!
HYNAAH!
HYNAAH!
Maga Town Association Hall
HYNAAH!

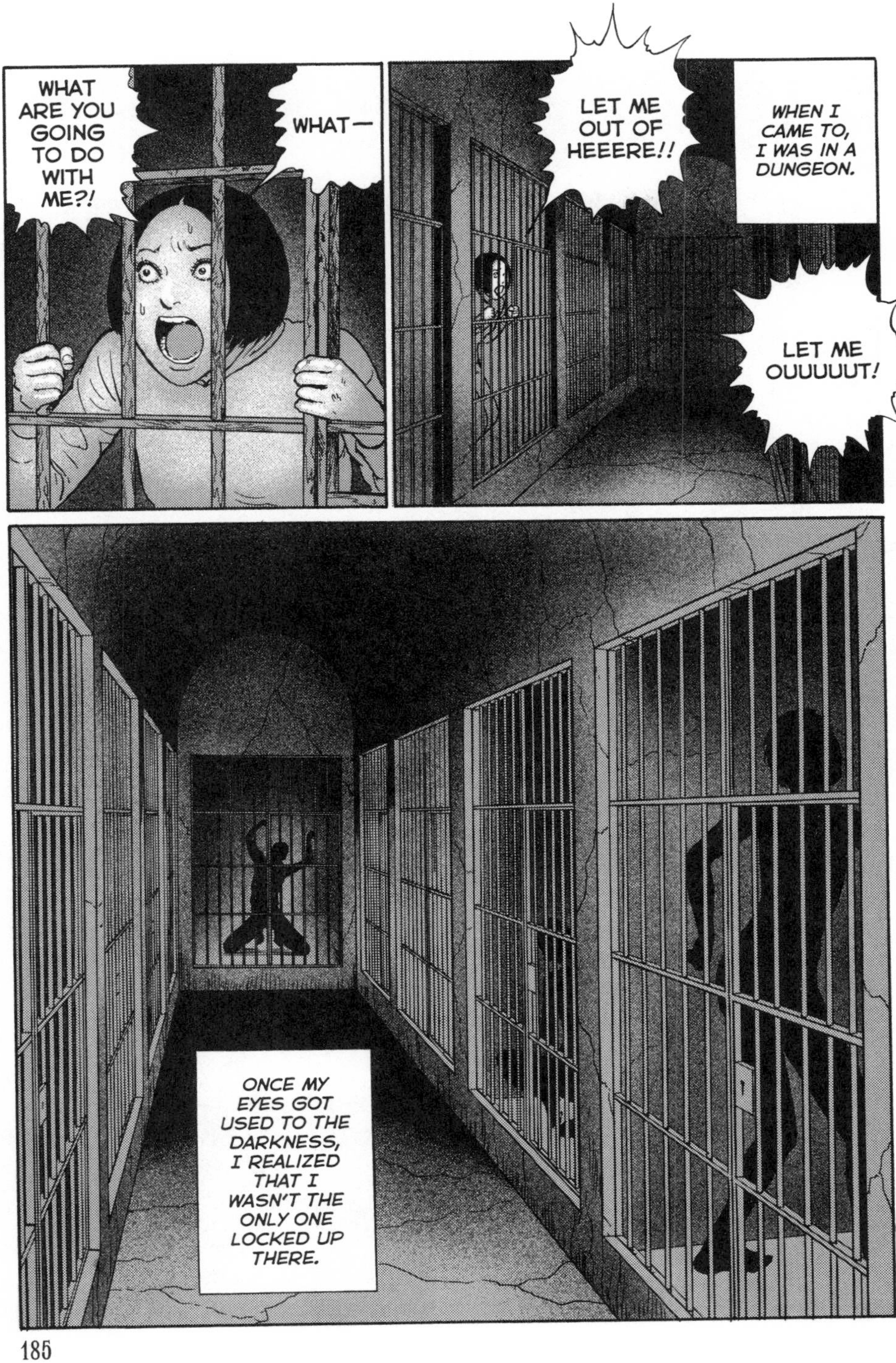
WHEN I CAME TO, I WAS IN A DUNGEON.
LET ME OUT OF HEEERE!!
LET ME OUUUUUT!
WHAT—
WHAT ARE YOU GOING TO DO WITH ME?!
ONCE MY EYES GOT USED TO THE DARKNESS, I REALIZED THAT I WASN'T THE ONLY ONE LOCKED UP THERE.

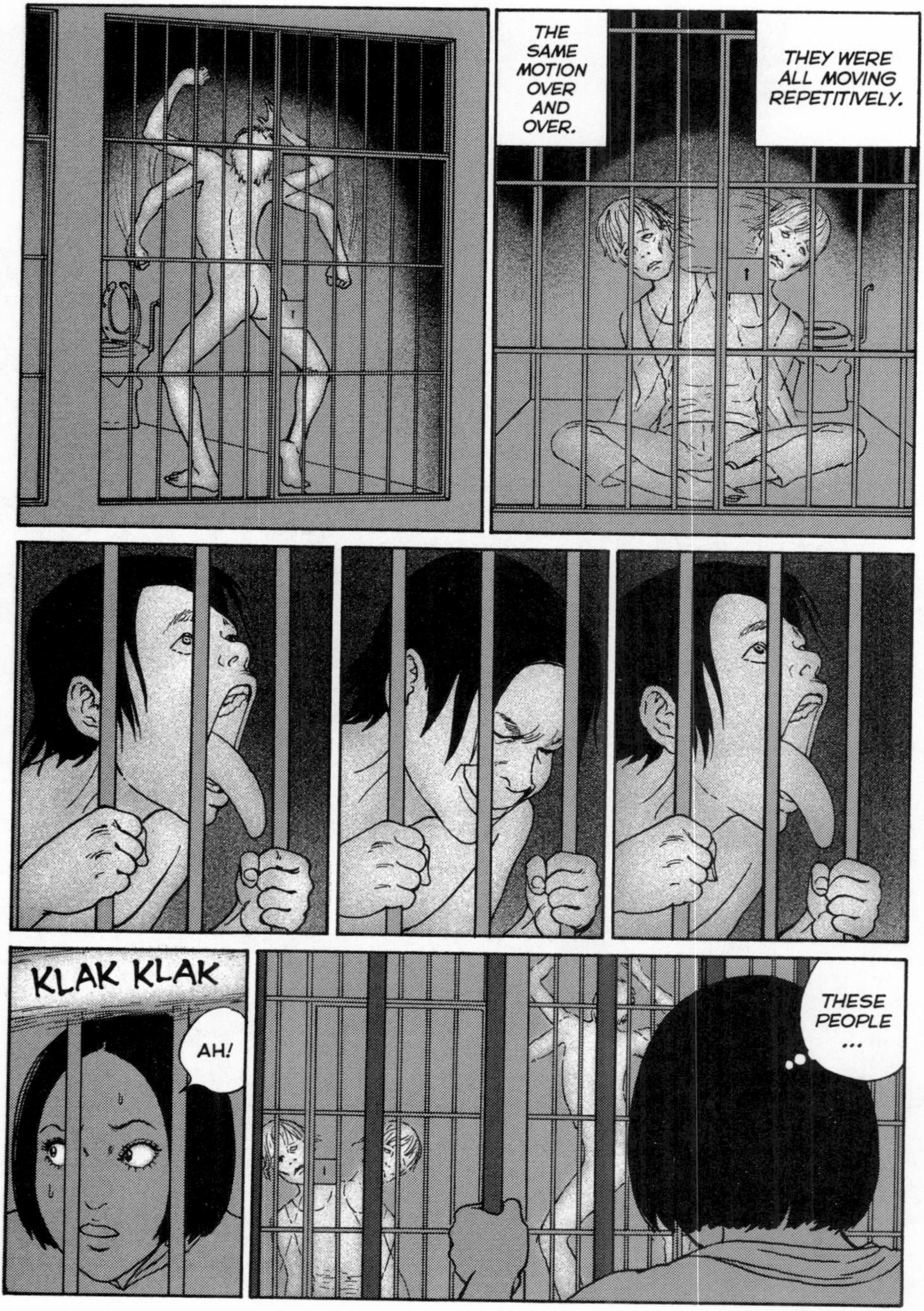
THEY WERE ALL MOVING REPETITIVELY.
THE SAME MOTION OVER AND OVER.
THESE PEOPLE ...
KLAK KLAK
AH!

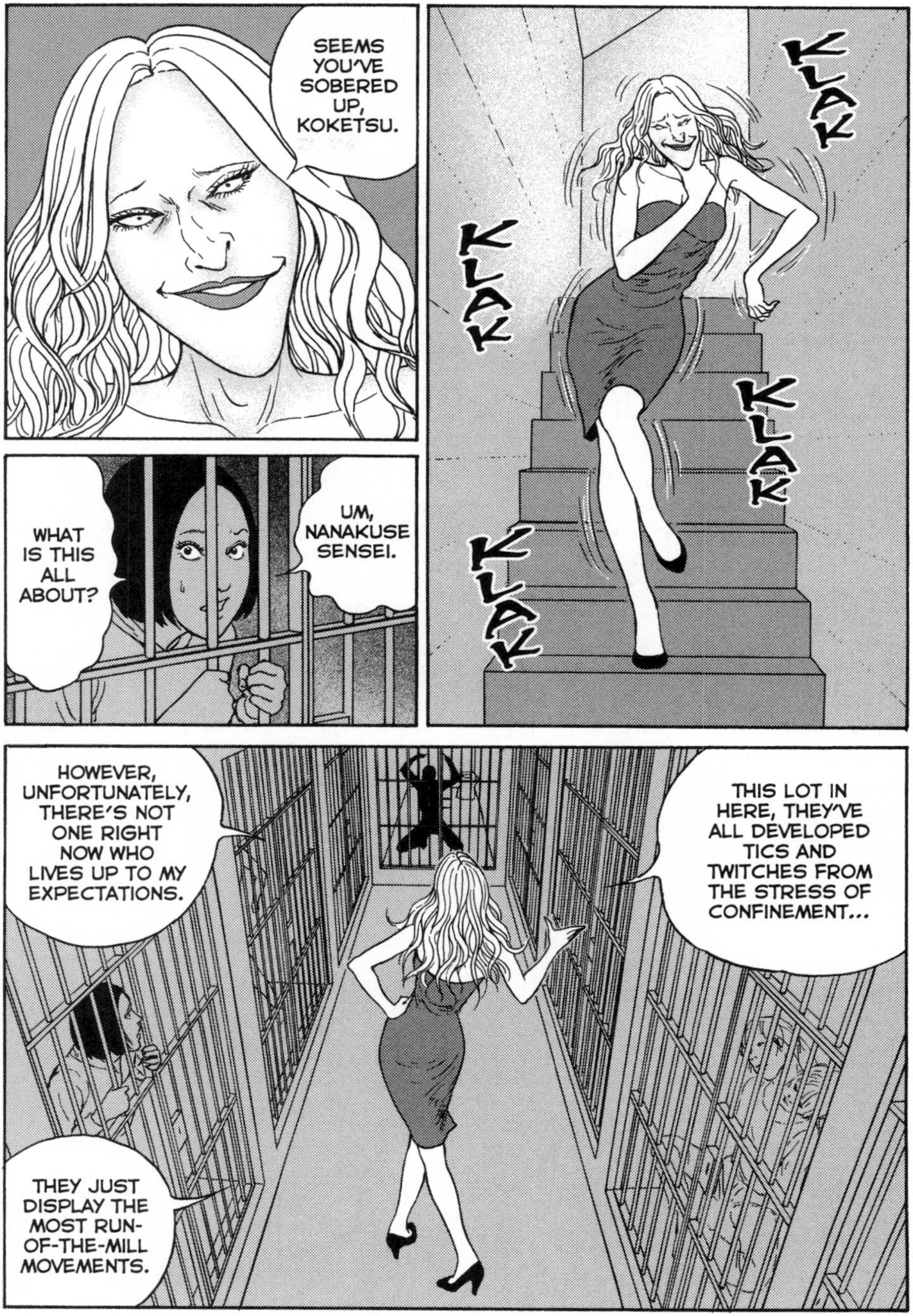
KLAK
KLAK
KLAK
KLAK
SEEMS YOU'VE SOBERED UP, KOKETSU.
UM, NANAKUSE SENSEI.
WHAT IS THIS ALL ABOUT?
THIS LOT IN HERE, THEY'VE ALL DEVELOPED TICS AND TWITCHES FROM THE STRESS OF CONFINEMENT...
HOWEVER, UNFORTUNATELY, THERE'S NOT ONE RIGHT NOW WHO LIVES UP TO MY EXPECTATIONS.
THEY JUST DISPLAY THE MOST RUN-OF-THE-MILL MOVEMENTS.

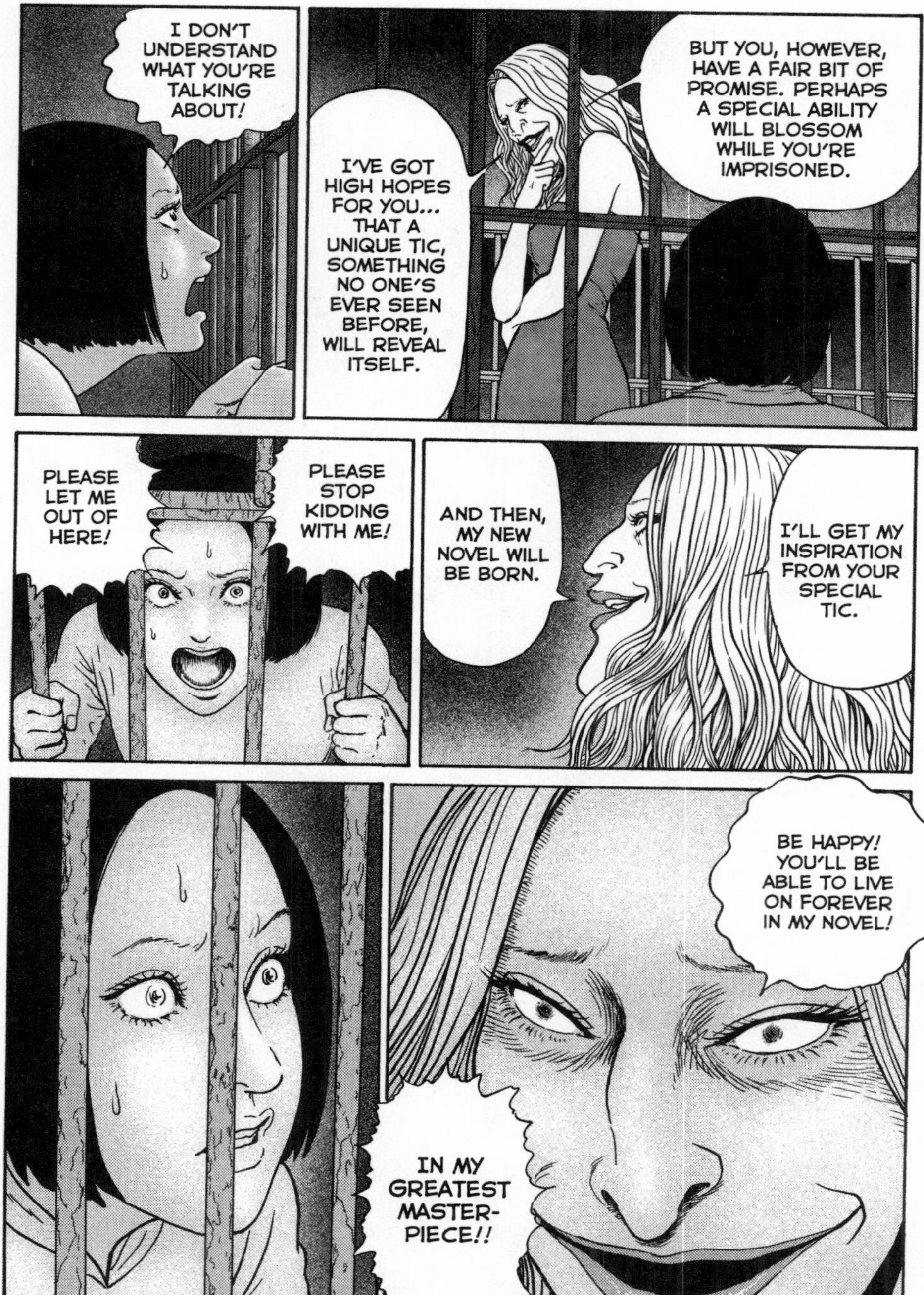
BUT YOU, HOWEVER, HAVE A FAIR BIT OF PROMISE. PERHAPS A SPECIAL ABILITY WILL BLOSSOM WHILE YOU'RE IMPRISONED.
I'VE GOT HIGH HOPES FOR YOU... THAT A UNIQUE TIC, SOMETHING NO ONE'S EVER SEEN BEFORE, WILL REVEAL ITSELF.
I DON'T UNDERSTAND WHAT YOU'RE TALKING ABOUT!
I'LL GET MY INSPIRATION FROM YOUR SPECIAL TIC.
AND THEN, MY NEW NOVEL WILL BE BORN.
PLEASE STOP KIDDING WITH ME!
PLEASE LET ME OUT OF HERE!
BE HAPPY! YOU'LL BE ABLE TO LIVE ON FOREVER IN MY NOVEL!
IN MY GREATEST MASTER-PIECE!!

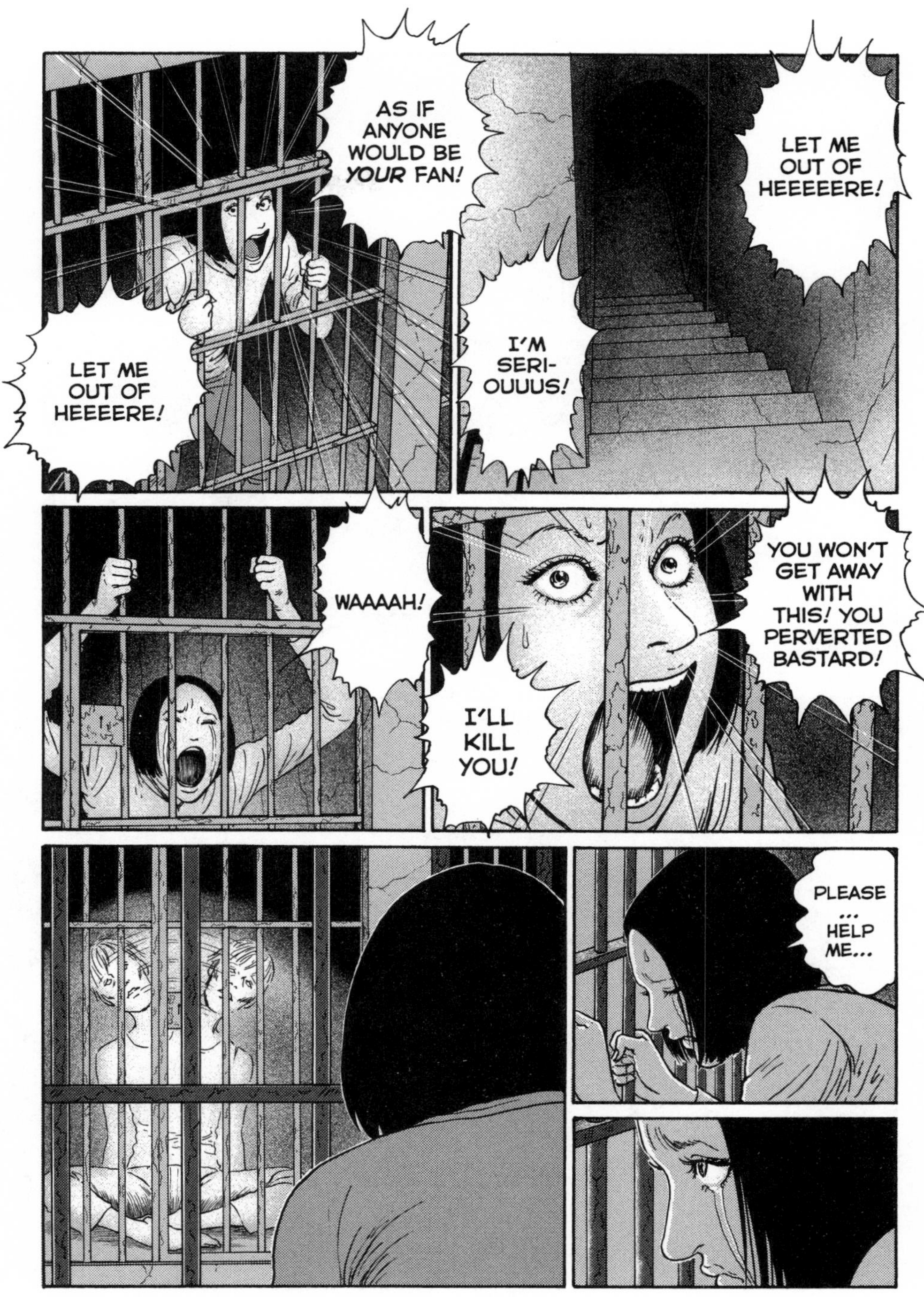
LET ME OUT OF HEEEEERE!
I'M SERI-OUUUS!
AS IF ANYONE WOULD BE *YOUR* FAN!
LET ME OUT OF HEEEERE!
YOU WON'T GET AWAY WITH THIS! YOU PERVERTED BASTARD!
I'LL KILL YOU!
WAAAAH!
PLEASE ... HELP ME...

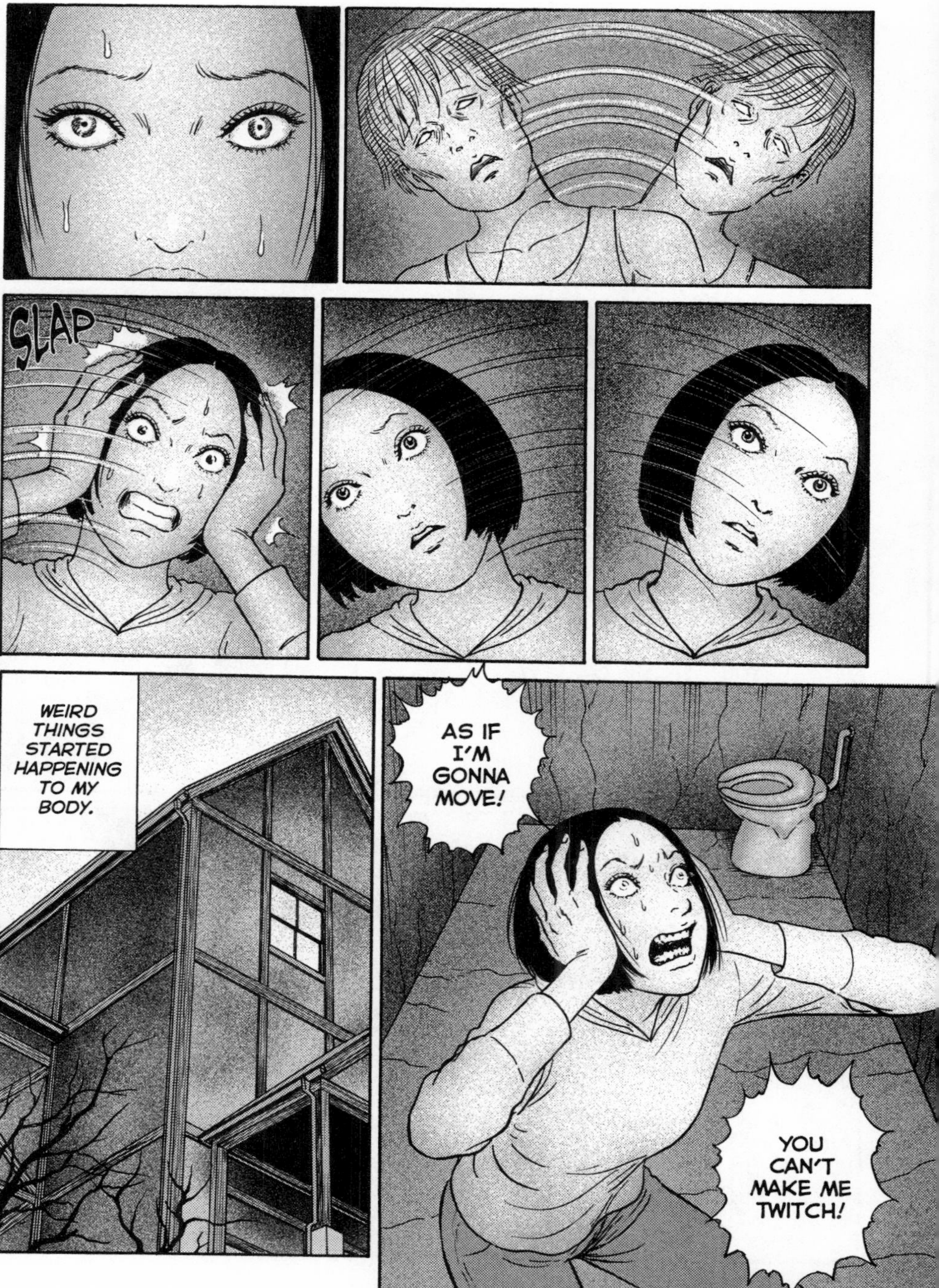
SLAP
AS IF I'M GONNA MOVE!
YOU CAN'T MAKE ME TWITCH!
WEIRD THINGS STARTED HAPPENING TO MY BODY.

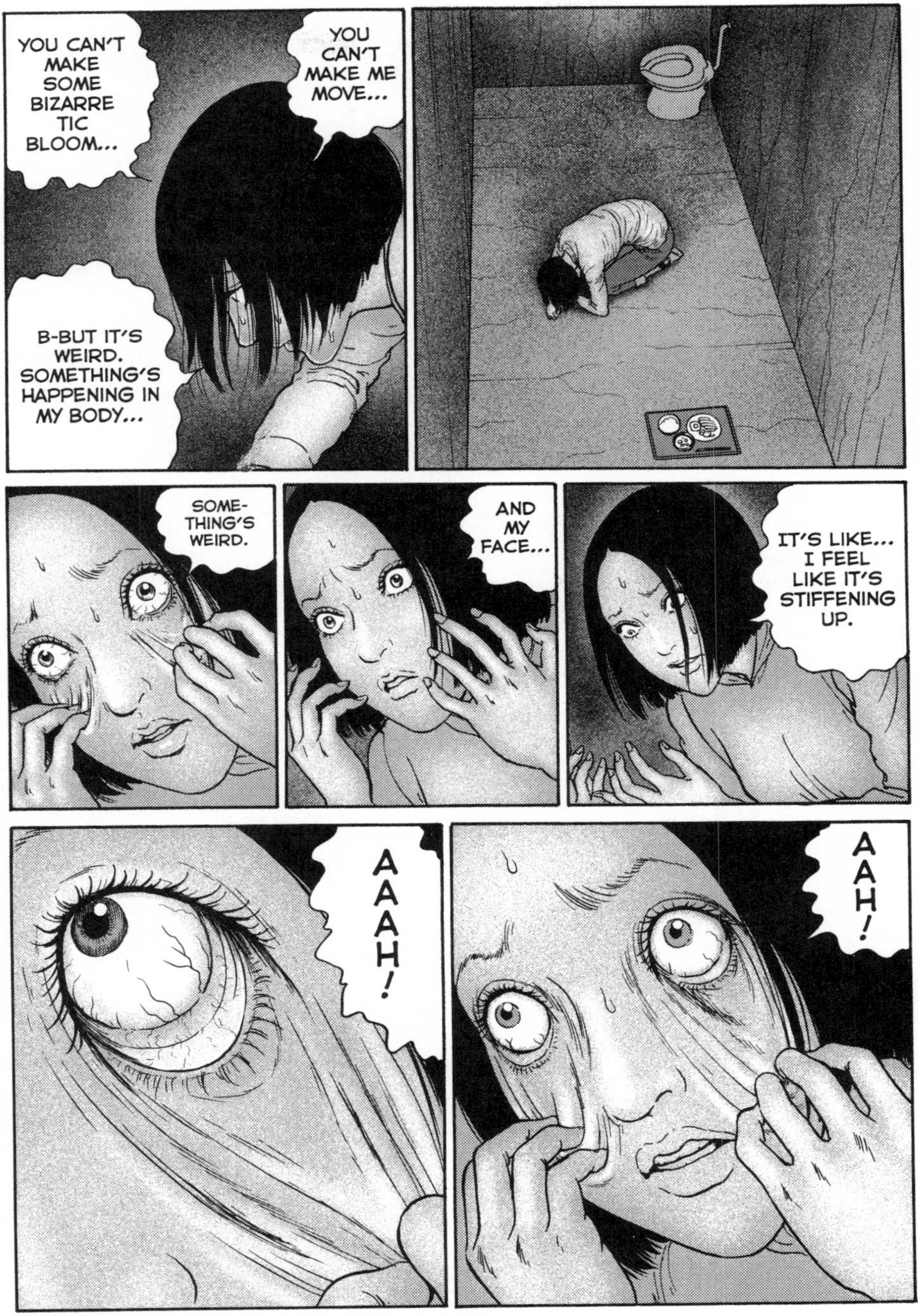
YOU CAN'T MAKE ME MOVE...
YOU CAN'T MAKE SOME BIZARRE TIC BLOOM...
B-BUT IT'S WEIRD. SOMETHING'S HAPPENING IN MY BODY...
IT'S LIKE... I FEEL LIKE IT'S STIFFENING UP.
AND MY FACE...
SOME- THING'S WEIRD.
AAH!
AAAH!

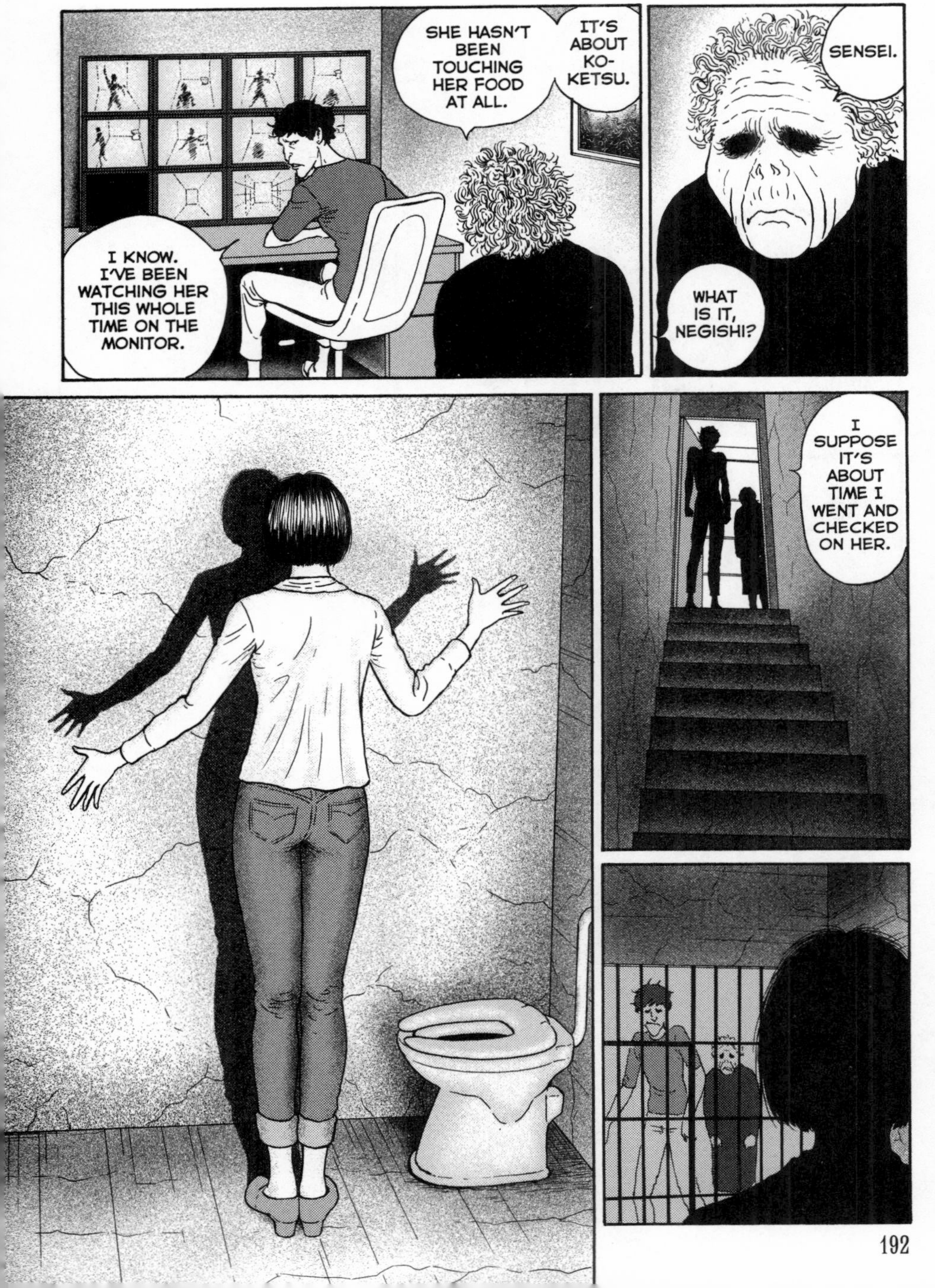
SENSEI.
WHAT IS IT, NEGISHI?
IT'S ABOUT KO-KETSU.
SHE HASN'T BEEN TOUCHING HER FOOD AT ALL.
I KNOW. I'VE BEEN WATCHING HER THIS WHOLE TIME ON THE MONITOR.
I SUPPOSE IT'S ABOUT TIME I WENT AND CHECKED ON HER.

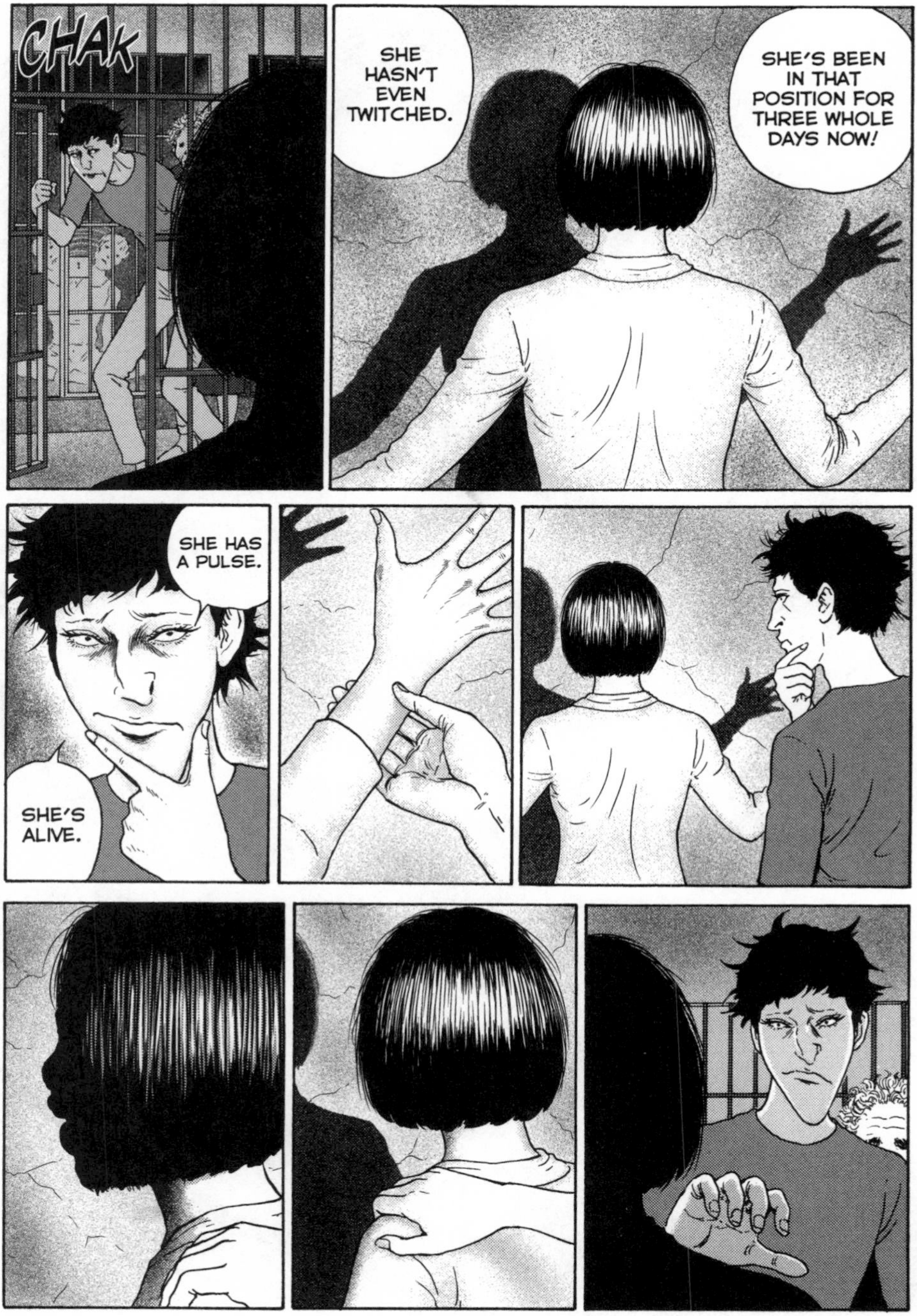
SHE'S BEEN IN THAT POSITION FOR THREE WHOLE DAYS NOW!
SHE HASN'T EVEN TWITCHED.
CHAK
SHE HAS A PULSE.
SHE'S ALIVE.

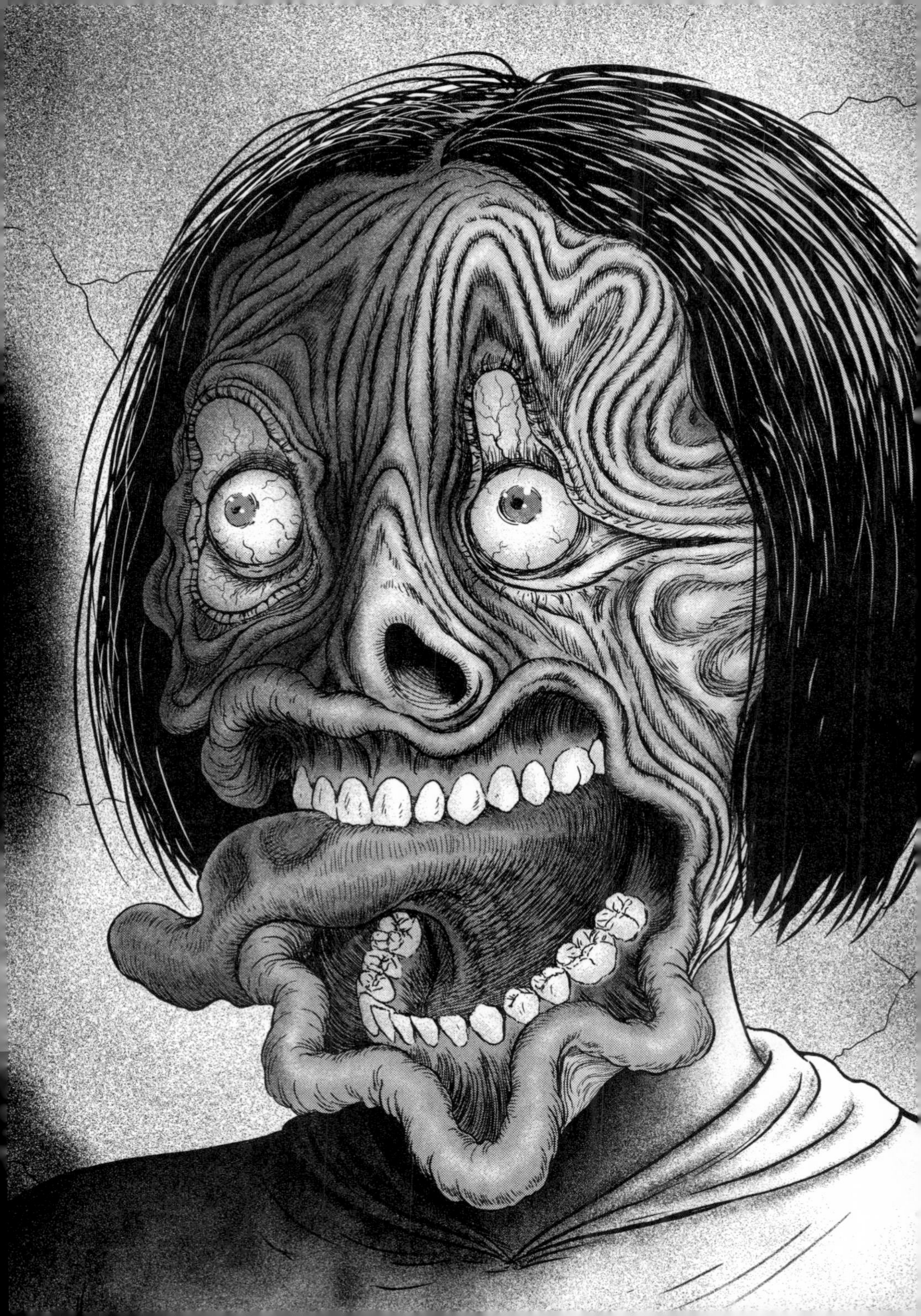

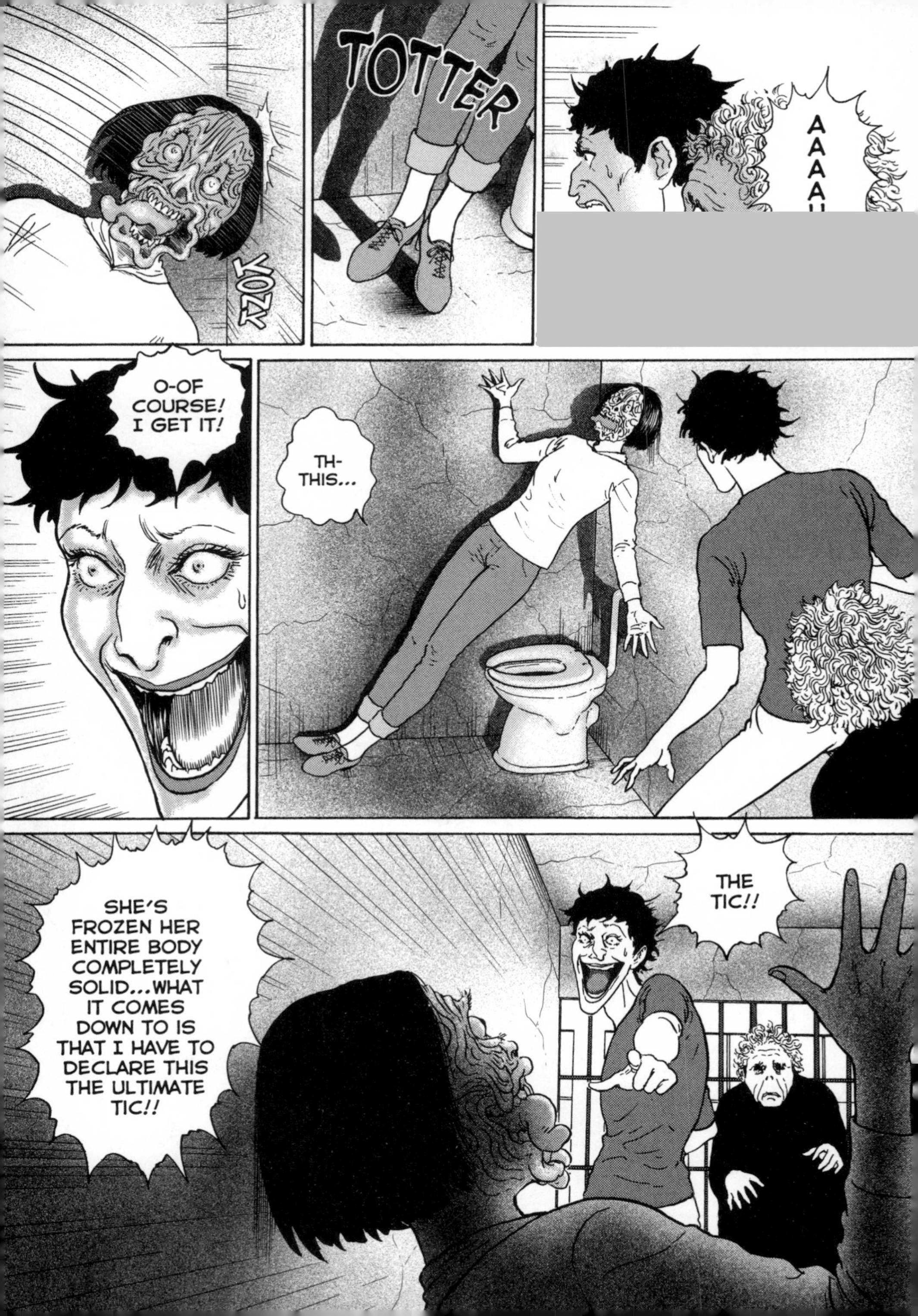
AAAA
TOTTER
YONK
TH- THIS...
O-OF COURSE! I GET IT!
THE TIC!!
SHE'S FROZEN HER ENTIRE BODY COMPLETELY SOLID...WHAT IT COMES DOWN TO IS THAT I HAVE TO DECLARE THIS THE ULTIMATE TIC!!

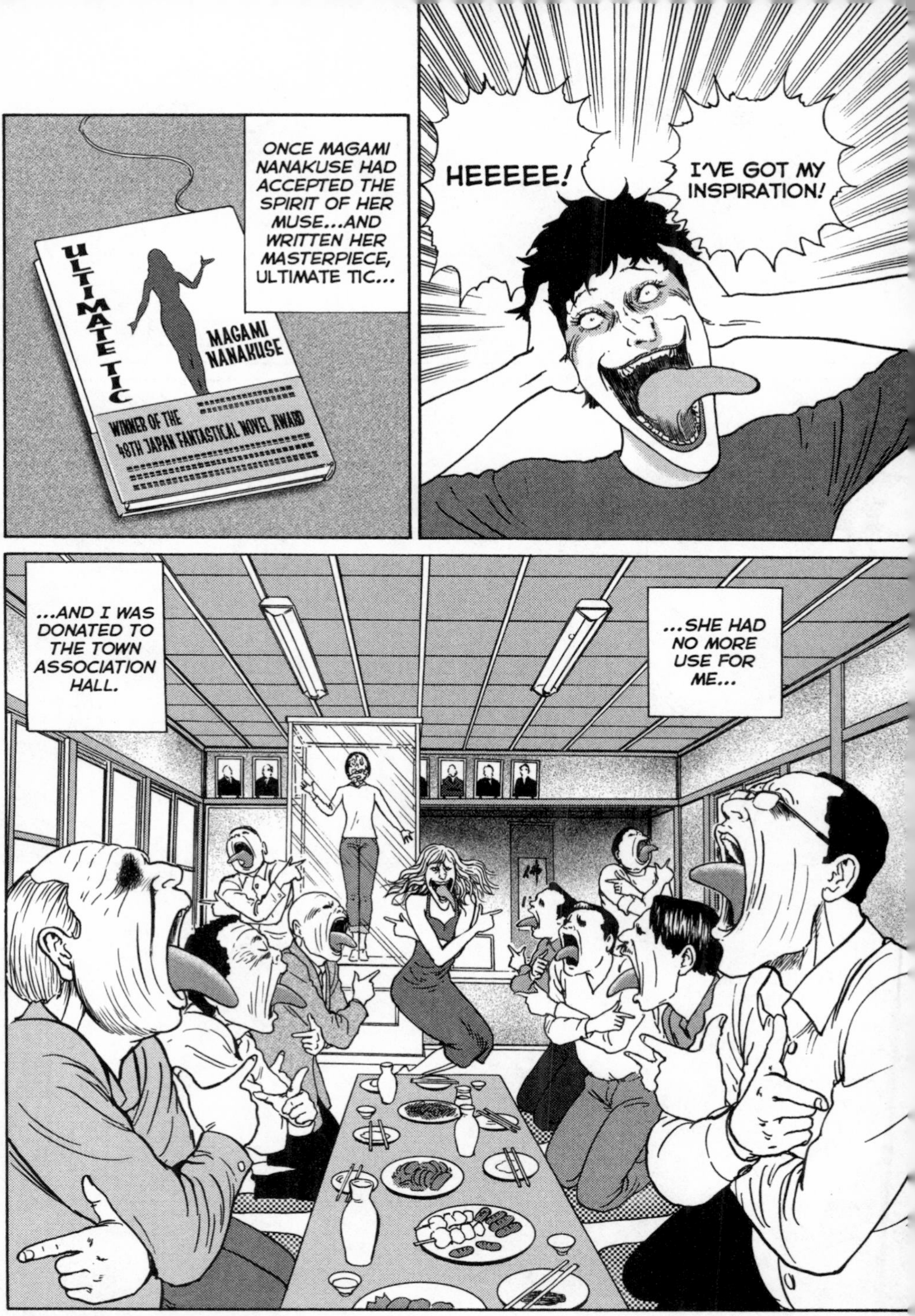
HEEEEE!
I'VE GOT MY INSPIRATION!
ONCE MAGAMI NANAKUSE HAD ACCEPTED THE SPIRIT OF HER MUSE...AND WRITTEN HER MASTERPIECE, ULTIMATE TIC...
ULTIMATE TIC
MAGAMI NANAKUSE
WINNER OF THE 48TH JAPAN FANTASTICAL NOVEL AWARD
...SHE HAD NO MORE USE FOR ME...
...AND I WAS DONATED TO THE TOWN ASSOCIATION HALL.

MAGAMI NANAKUSE/END

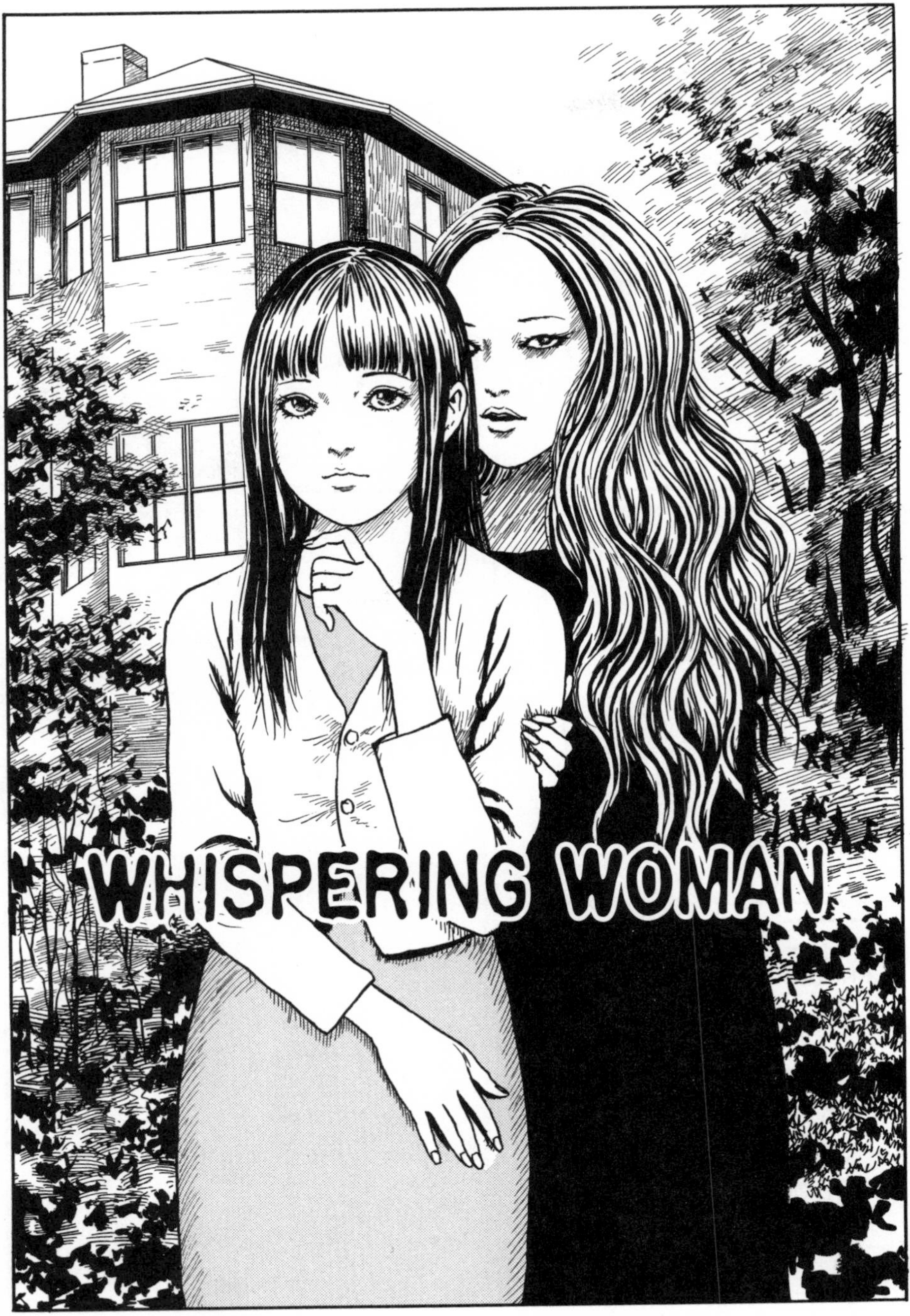
WHISPERING WOMAN

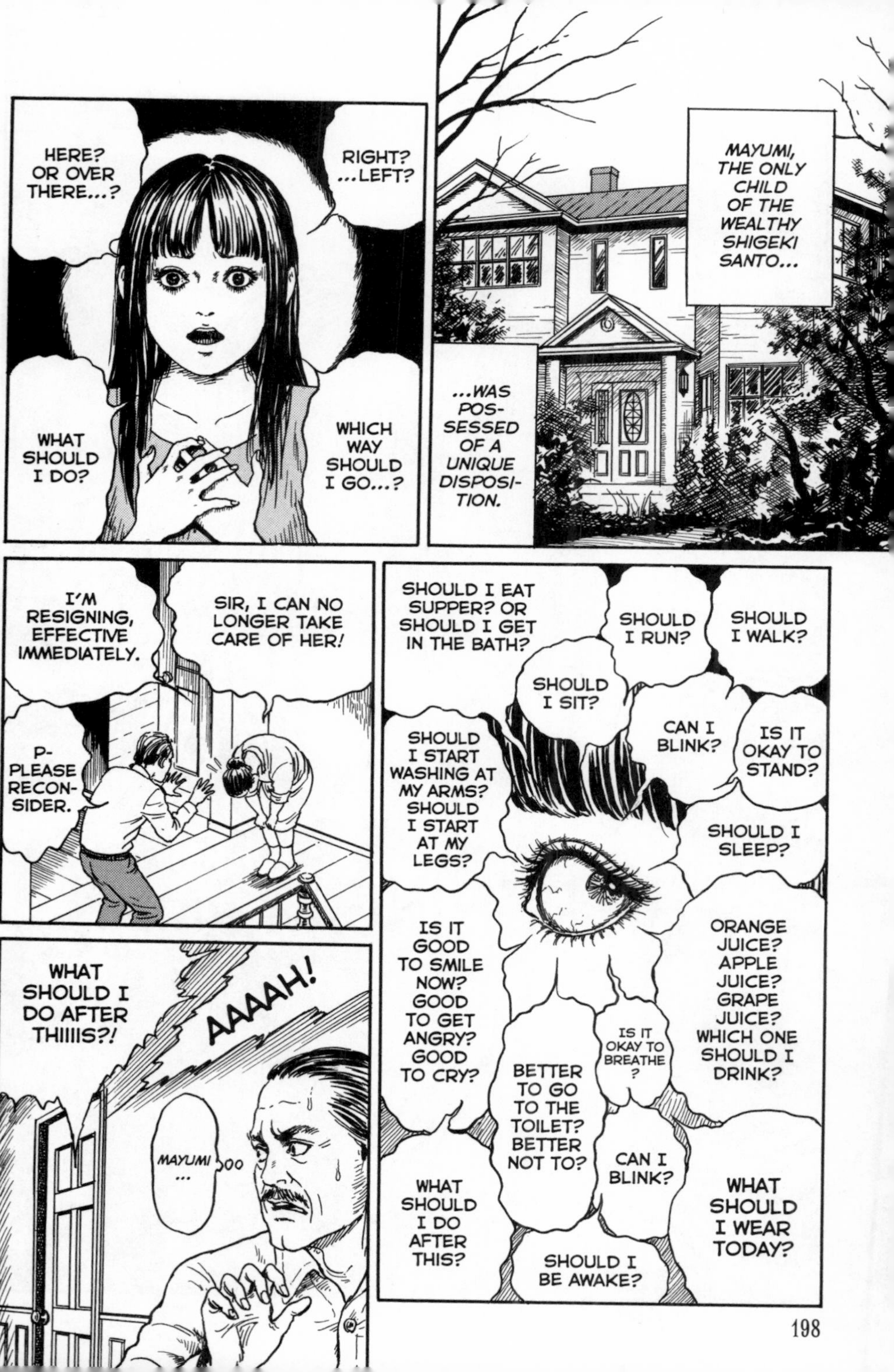
MAYUMI, THE ONLY CHILD OF THE WEALTHY SHIGEKI SANTO...
...WAS POSSESSED OF A UNIQUE DISPOSITION.
RIGHT? ...LEFT?
HERE? OR OVER THERE...?
WHICH WAY SHOULD I GO...?
WHAT SHOULD I DO?
SHOULD I WALK?
SHOULD I RUN?
SHOULD I EAT SUPPER? OR SHOULD I GET IN THE BATH?
SHOULD I SIT?
IS IT OKAY TO STAND?
CAN I BLINK?
SHOULD I START WASHING AT MY ARMS? SHOULD I START AT MY LEGS?
SHOULD I SLEEP?
ORANGE JUICE? APPLE JUICE? GRAPE JUICE? WHICH ONE SHOULD I DRINK?
IS IT GOOD TO SMILE NOW? GOOD TO GET ANGRY? GOOD TO CRY?
IS IT OKAY TO BREATHE?
BETTER TO GO TO THE TOILET? BETTER NOT TO?
WHAT SHOULD I WEAR TODAY?
CAN I BLINK?
WHAT SHOULD I DO AFTER THIS?
SHOULD I BE AWAKE?
SIR, I CAN NO LONGER TAKE CARE OF HER!
I'M RESIGNING, EFFECTIVE IMMEDIATELY.
P-PLEASE RECONSIDER.
AAAAH!
WHAT SHOULD I DO AFTER THIIIIS?!
MAYUMI...

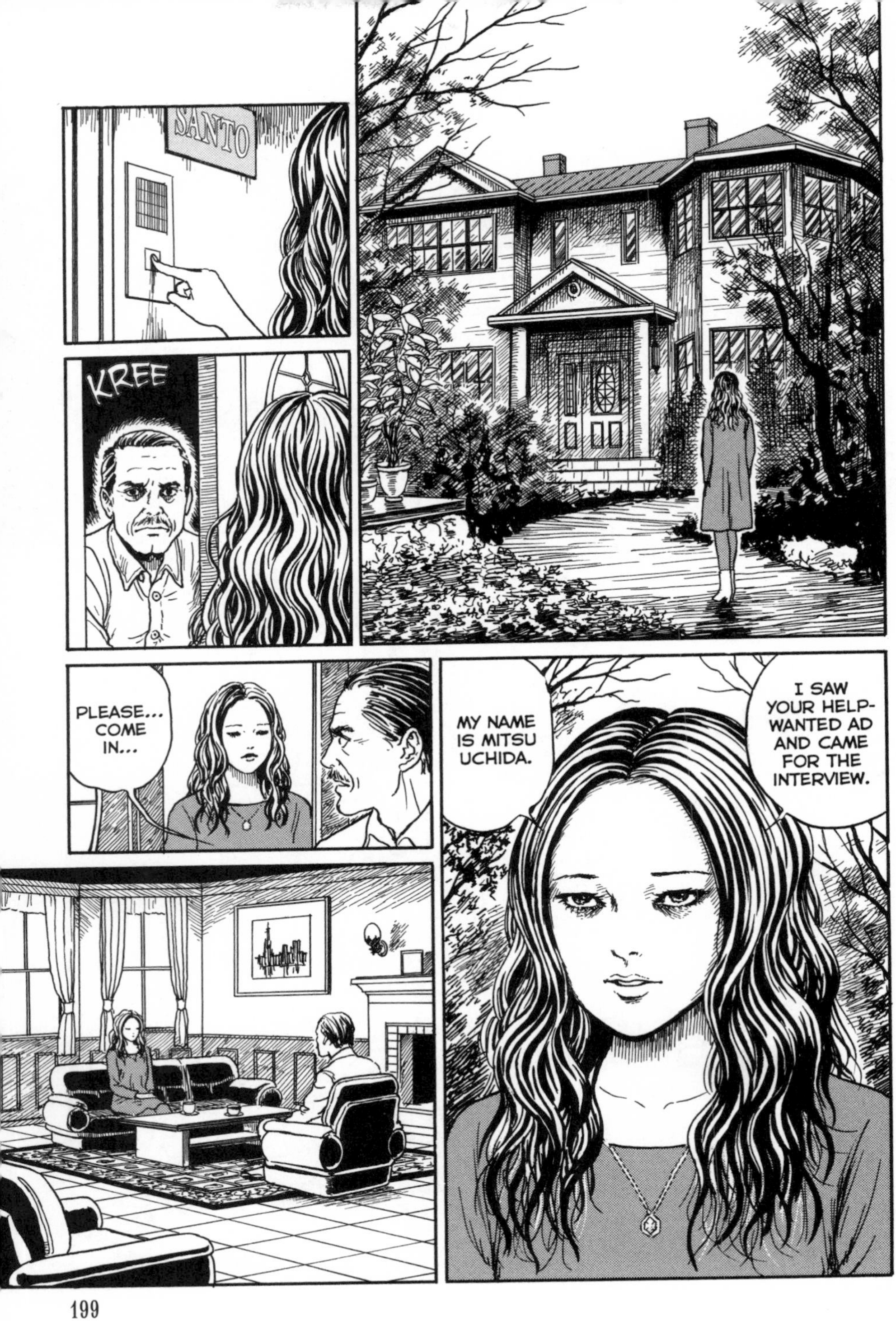
SANTO
KREE
I SAW YOUR HELP-WANTED AD AND CAME FOR THE INTERVIEW.
MY NAME IS MITSU UCHIDA.
PLEASE... COME IN...

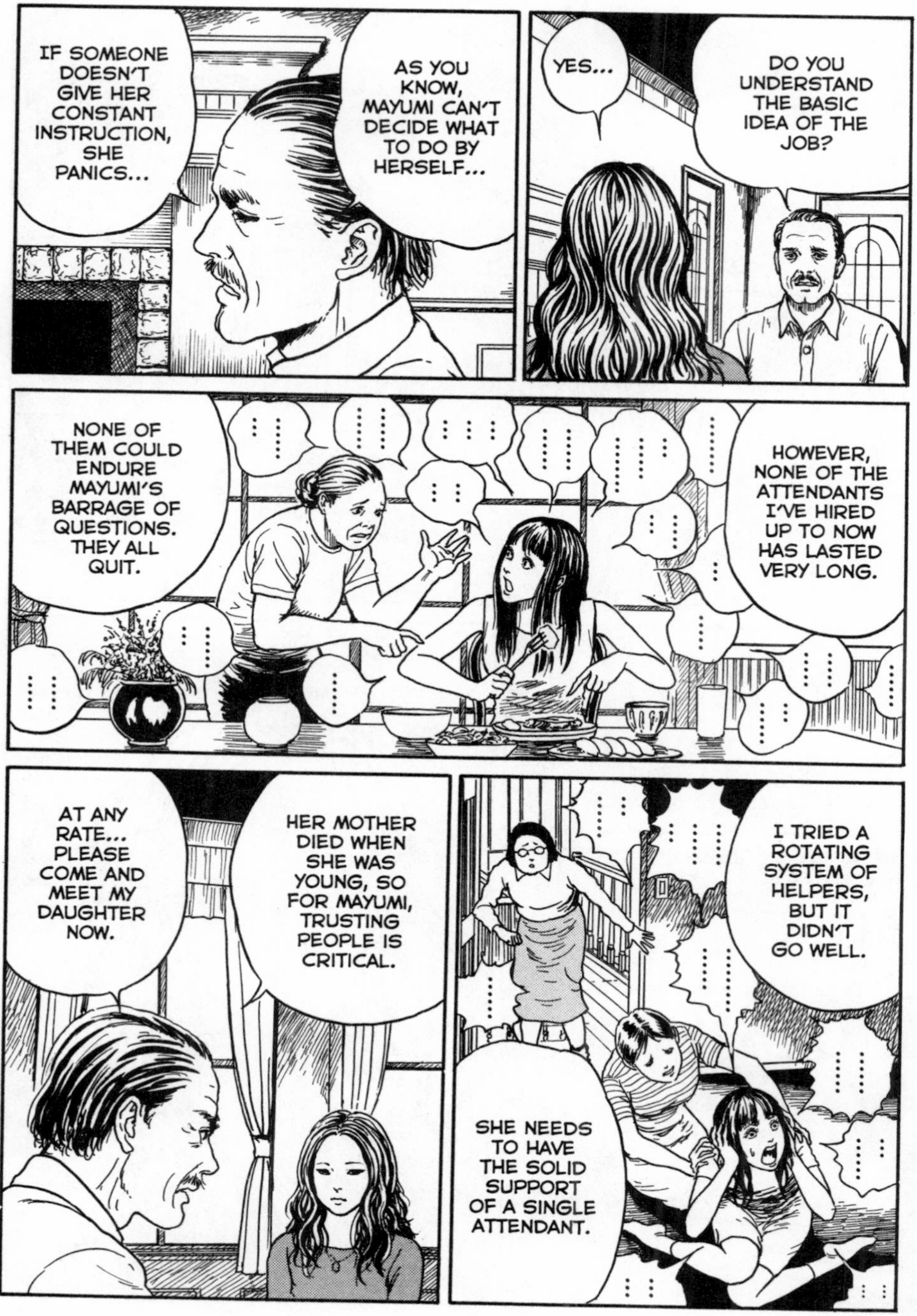
DO YOU UNDERSTAND THE BASIC IDEA OF THE JOB?
YES...
AS YOU KNOW, MAYUMI CAN'T DECIDE WHAT TO DO BY HERSELF...
IF SOMEONE DOESN'T GIVE HER CONSTANT INSTRUCTION, SHE PANICS...
HOWEVER, NONE OF THE ATTENDANTS I'VE HIRED UP TO NOW HAS LASTED VERY LONG.
NONE OF THEM COULD ENDURE MAYUMI'S BARRAGE OF QUESTIONS. THEY ALL QUIT.
I TRIED A ROTATING SYSTEM OF HELPERS, BUT IT DIDN'T GO WELL.
SHE NEEDS TO HAVE THE SOLID SUPPORT OF A SINGLE ATTENDANT.
HER MOTHER DIED WHEN SHE WAS YOUNG, SO FOR MAYUMI, TRUSTING PEOPLE IS CRITICAL.
AT ANY RATE... PLEASE COME AND MEET MY DAUGHTER NOW.

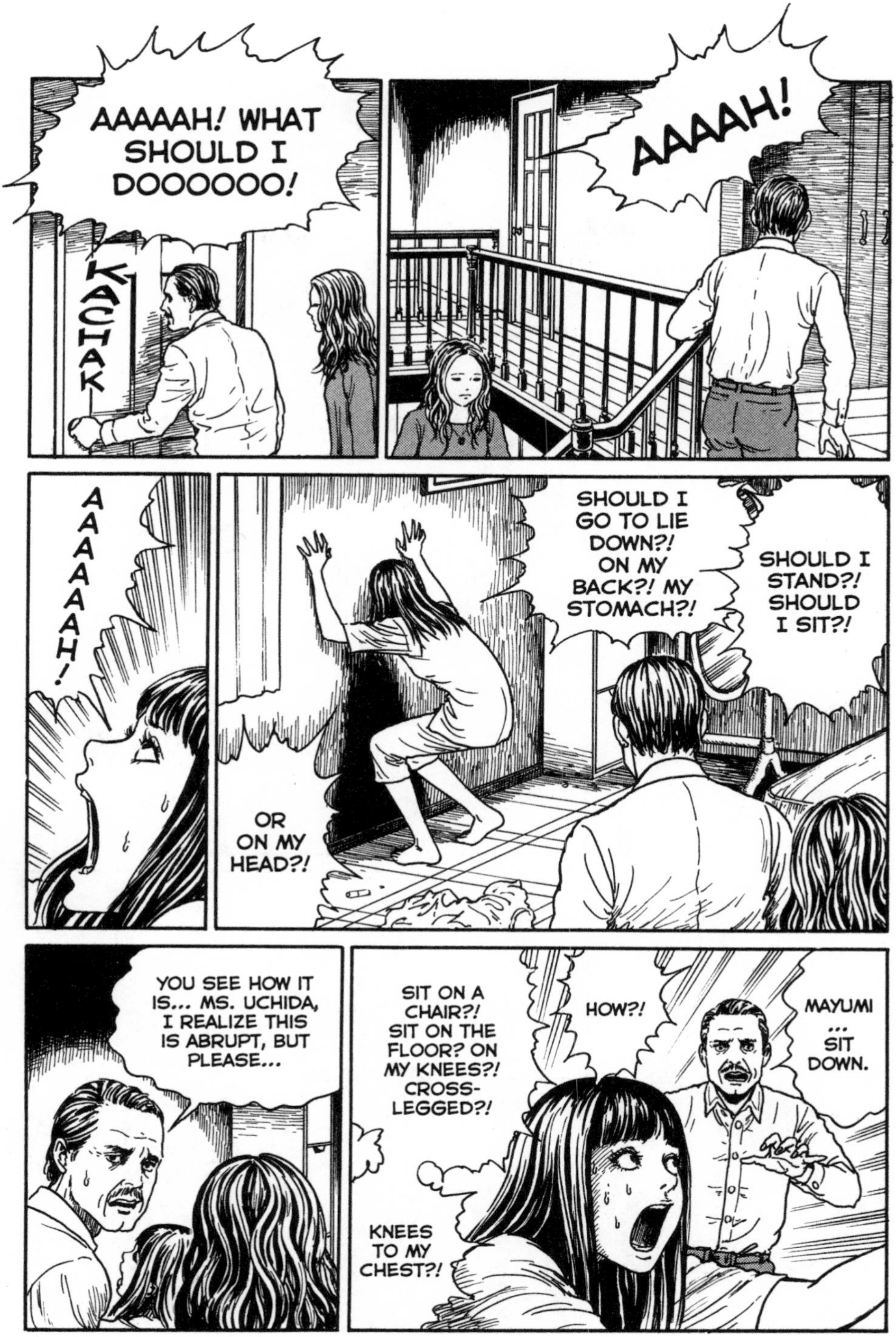
AAAAH!
AAAAAH! WHAT SHOULD I DOOOOOO!
KACHAK
SHOULD I STAND?! SHOULD I SIT?!
SHOULD I GO TO LIE DOWN?! ON MY BACK?! MY STOMACH?!
OR ON MY HEAD?!
AAAAAAH!
MAYUMI ... SIT DOWN.
HOW?!
SIT ON A CHAIR?! SIT ON THE FLOOR? ON MY KNEES?! CROSS-LEGGED?!
KNEES TO MY CHEST?!
YOU SEE HOW IT IS... MS. UCHIDA, I REALIZE THIS IS ABRUPT, BUT PLEASE...

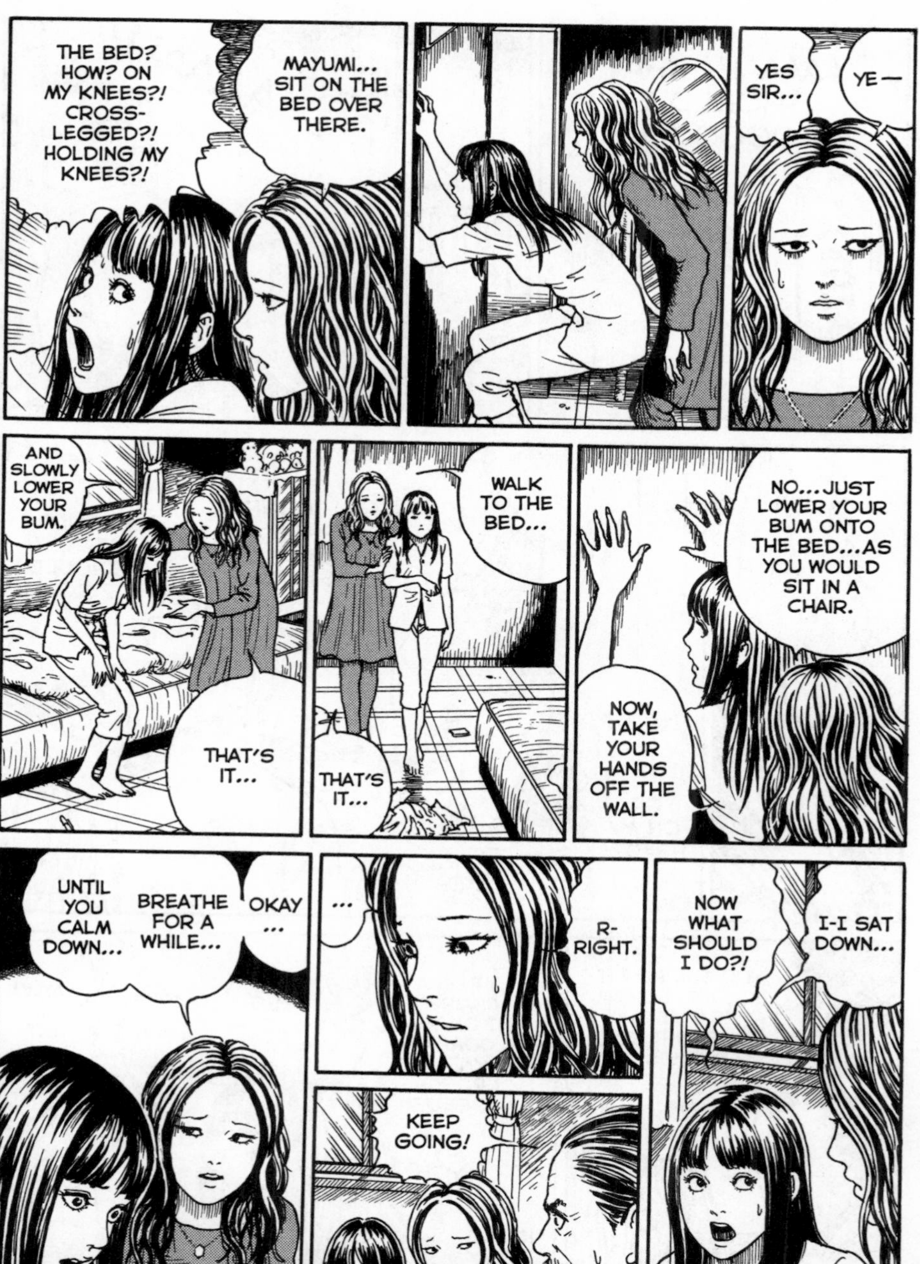
YE—
YES SIR...
MAYUMI... SIT ON THE BED OVER THERE.
THE BED? HOW? ON MY KNEES?! CROSS-LEGGED?! HOLDING MY KNEES?!
NO... JUST LOWER YOUR BUM ONTO THE BED... AS YOU WOULD SIT IN A CHAIR.
NOW, TAKE YOUR HANDS OFF THE WALL.
WALK TO THE BED...
THAT'S IT...
AND SLOWLY LOWER YOUR BUM.
THAT'S IT...
I-I SAT DOWN...
NOW WHAT SHOULD I DO?!
R-RIGHT.
...
KEEP GOING!
OKAY...
BREATHE FOR A WHILE...
UNTIL YOU CALM DOWN...
FOO
HAA

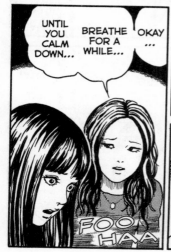

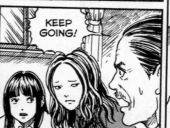

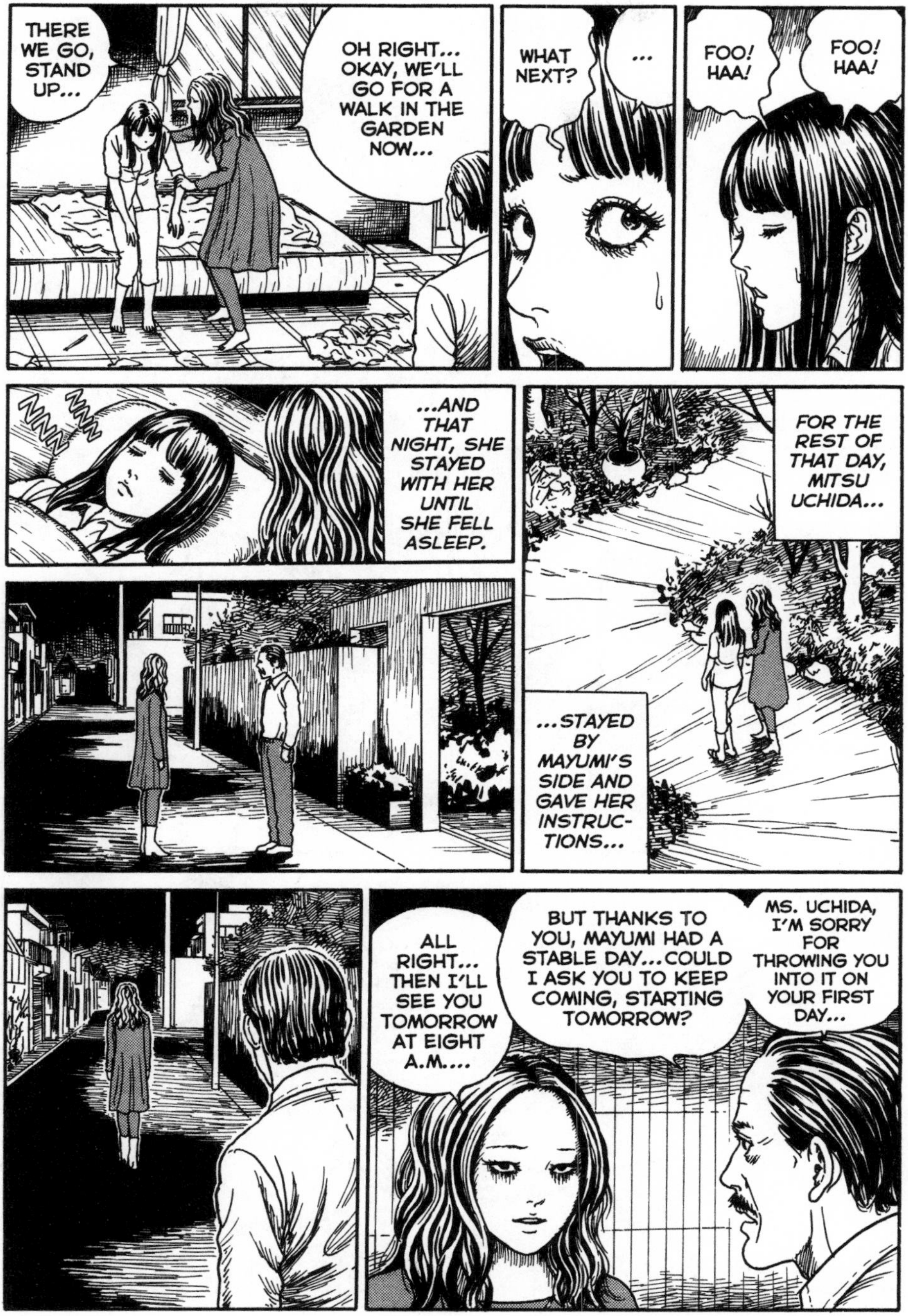
FOO! HAA!
FOO! HAA!
...
WHAT NEXT?
OH RIGHT... OKAY, WE'LL GO FOR A WALK IN THE GARDEN NOW...
THERE WE GO, STAND UP...
FOR THE REST OF THAT DAY, MITSU UCHIDA...
...STAYED BY MAYUMI'S SIDE AND GAVE HER INSTRUCTIONS...
...AND THAT NIGHT, SHE STAYED WITH HER UNTIL SHE FELL ASLEEP.
MS. UCHIDA, I'M SORRY FOR THROWING YOU INTO IT ON YOUR FIRST DAY...
BUT THANKS TO YOU, MAYUMI HAD A STABLE DAY...COULD I ASK YOU TO KEEP COMING, STARTING TOMORROW?
ALL RIGHT... THEN I'LL SEE YOU TOMORROW AT EIGHT A.M....

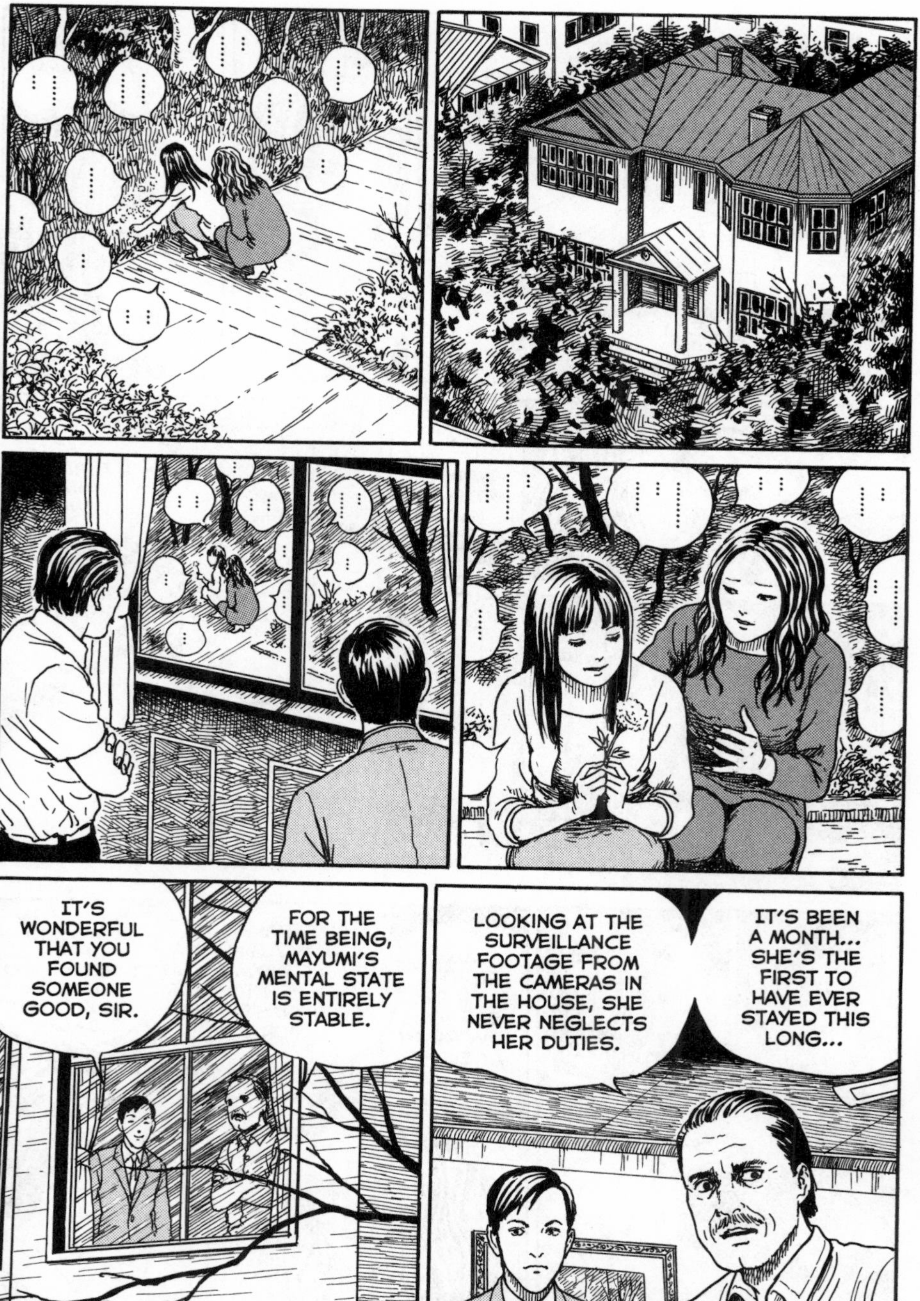
IT'S BEEN A MONTH... SHE'S THE FIRST TO HAVE EVER STAYED THIS LONG...
LOOKING AT THE SURVEILLANCE FOOTAGE FROM THE CAMERAS IN THE HOUSE, SHE NEVER NEGLECTS HER DUTIES.
FOR THE TIME BEING, MAYUMI'S MENTAL STATE IS ENTIRELY STABLE.
IT'S WONDERFUL THAT YOU FOUND SOMEONE GOOD, SIR.

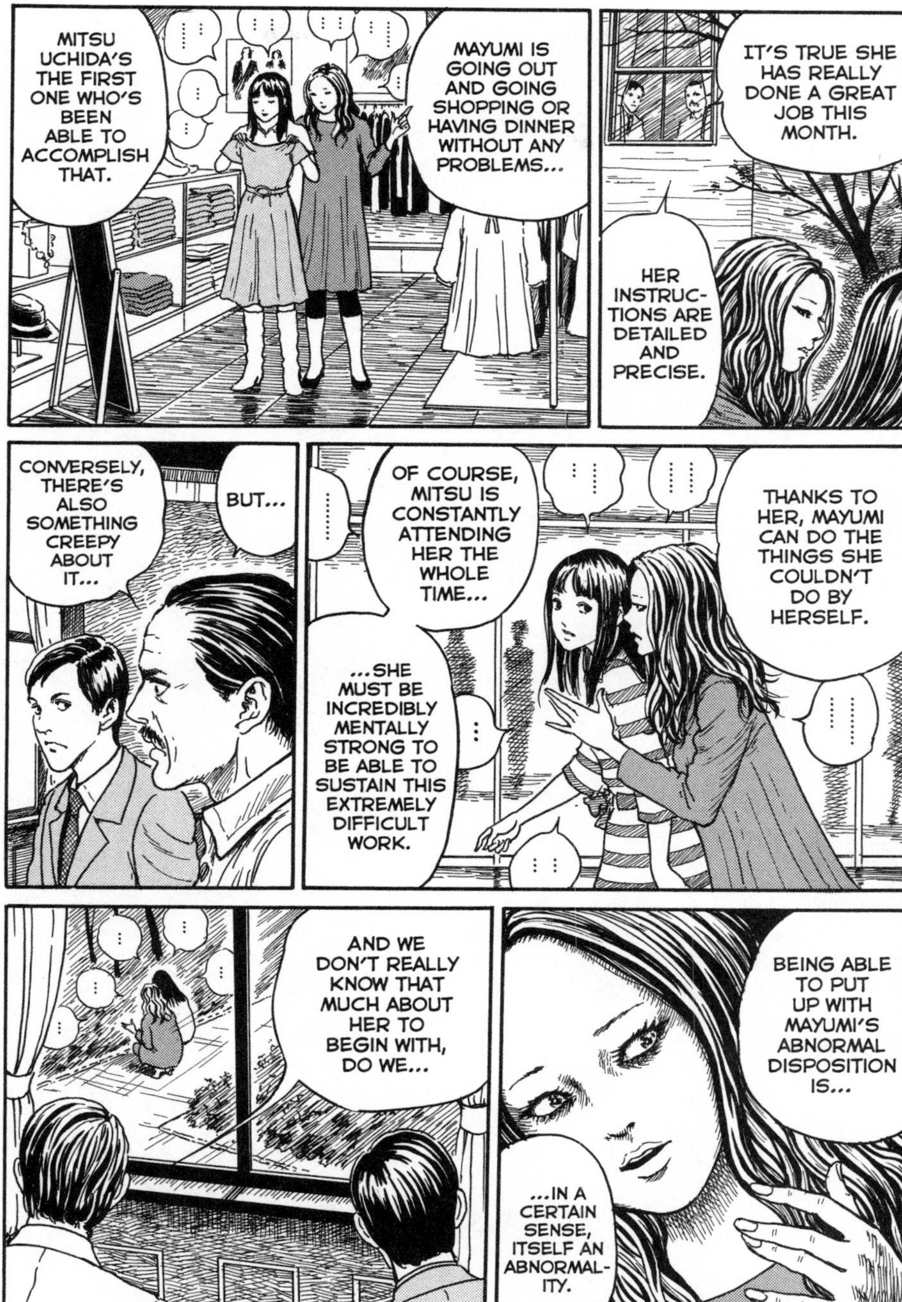
IT'S TRUE SHE HAS REALLY DONE A GREAT JOB THIS MONTH.
HER INSTRUCTIONS ARE DETAILED AND PRECISE.
MAYUMI IS GOING OUT AND GOING SHOPPING OR HAVING DINNER WITHOUT ANY PROBLEMS...
MITSU UCHIDA'S THE FIRST ONE WHO'S BEEN ABLE TO ACCOMPLISH THAT.
THANKS TO HER, MAYUMI CAN DO THE THINGS SHE COULDN'T DO BY HERSELF.
OF COURSE, MITSU IS CONSTANTLY ATTENDING HER THE WHOLE TIME...
...SHE MUST BE INCREDIBLY MENTALLY STRONG TO BE ABLE TO SUSTAIN THIS EXTREMELY DIFFICULT WORK.
BUT...
CONVERSELY, THERE'S ALSO SOMETHING CREEPY ABOUT IT...
BEING ABLE TO PUT UP WITH MAYUMI'S ABNORMAL DISPOSITION IS...
...IN A CERTAIN SENSE, ITSELF AN ABNORMALITY.
AND WE DON'T REALLY KNOW THAT MUCH ABOUT HER TO BEGIN WITH, DO WE...

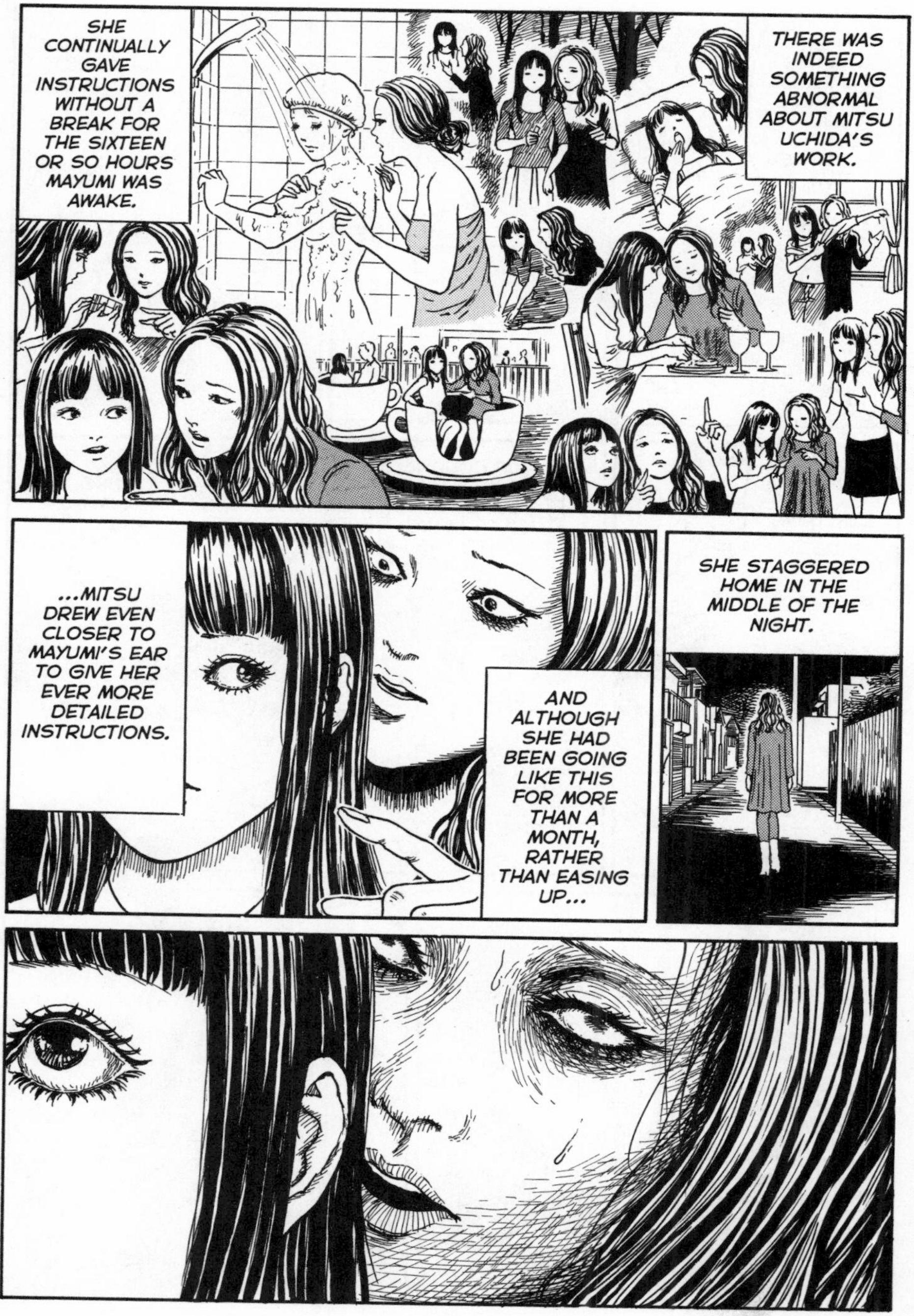
THERE WAS INDEED SOMETHING ABNORMAL ABOUT MITSU UCHIDA'S WORK.
SHE CONTINUALLY GAVE INSTRUCTIONS WITHOUT A BREAK FOR THE SIXTEEN OR SO HOURS MAYUMI WAS AWAKE.
SHE STAGGERED HOME IN THE MIDDLE OF THE NIGHT.
AND ALTHOUGH SHE HAD BEEN GOING LIKE THIS FOR MORE THAN A MONTH, RATHER THAN EASING UP...
...MITSU DREW EVEN CLOSER TO MAYUMI'S EAR TO GIVE HER EVER MORE DETAILED INSTRUCTIONS.

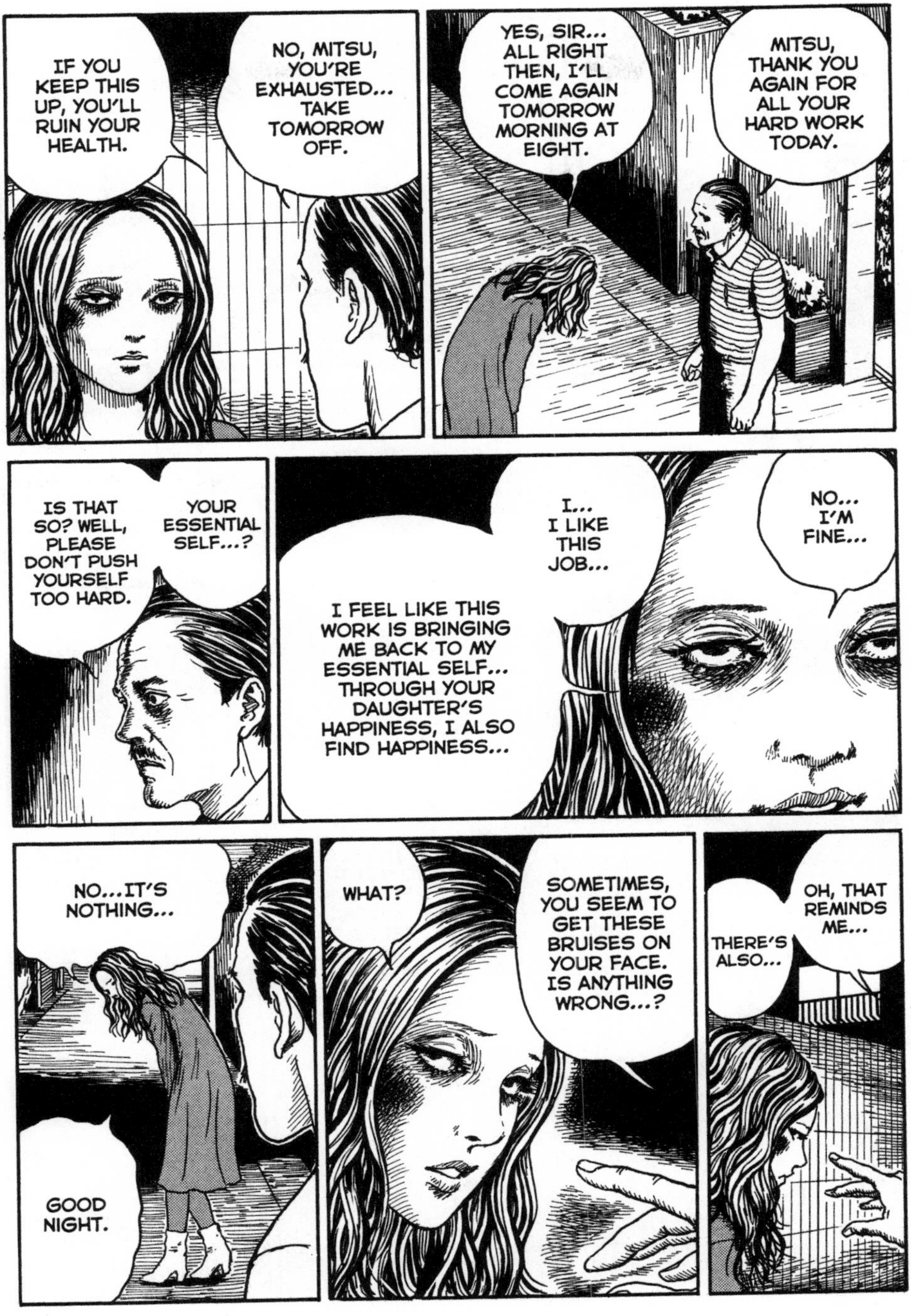
MITSU, THANK YOU AGAIN FOR ALL YOUR HARD WORK TODAY.
YES, SIR... ALL RIGHT THEN, I'LL COME AGAIN TOMORROW MORNING AT EIGHT.
NO, MITSU, YOU'RE EXHAUSTED... TAKE TOMORROW OFF.
IF YOU KEEP THIS UP, YOU'LL RUIN YOUR HEALTH.
NO... I'M FINE...
I... I LIKE THIS JOB...
I FEEL LIKE THIS WORK IS BRINGING ME BACK TO MY ESSENTIAL SELF... THROUGH YOUR DAUGHTER'S HAPPINESS, I ALSO FIND HAPPINESS...
YOUR ESSENTIAL SELF...?
IS THAT SO? WELL, PLEASE DON'T PUSH YOURSELF TOO HARD.
OH, THAT REMINDS ME...
THERE'S ALSO...
SOMETIMES, YOU SEEM TO GET THESE BRUISES ON YOUR FACE. IS ANYTHING WRONG...?
WHAT?
NO...IT'S NOTHING...
GOOD NIGHT.

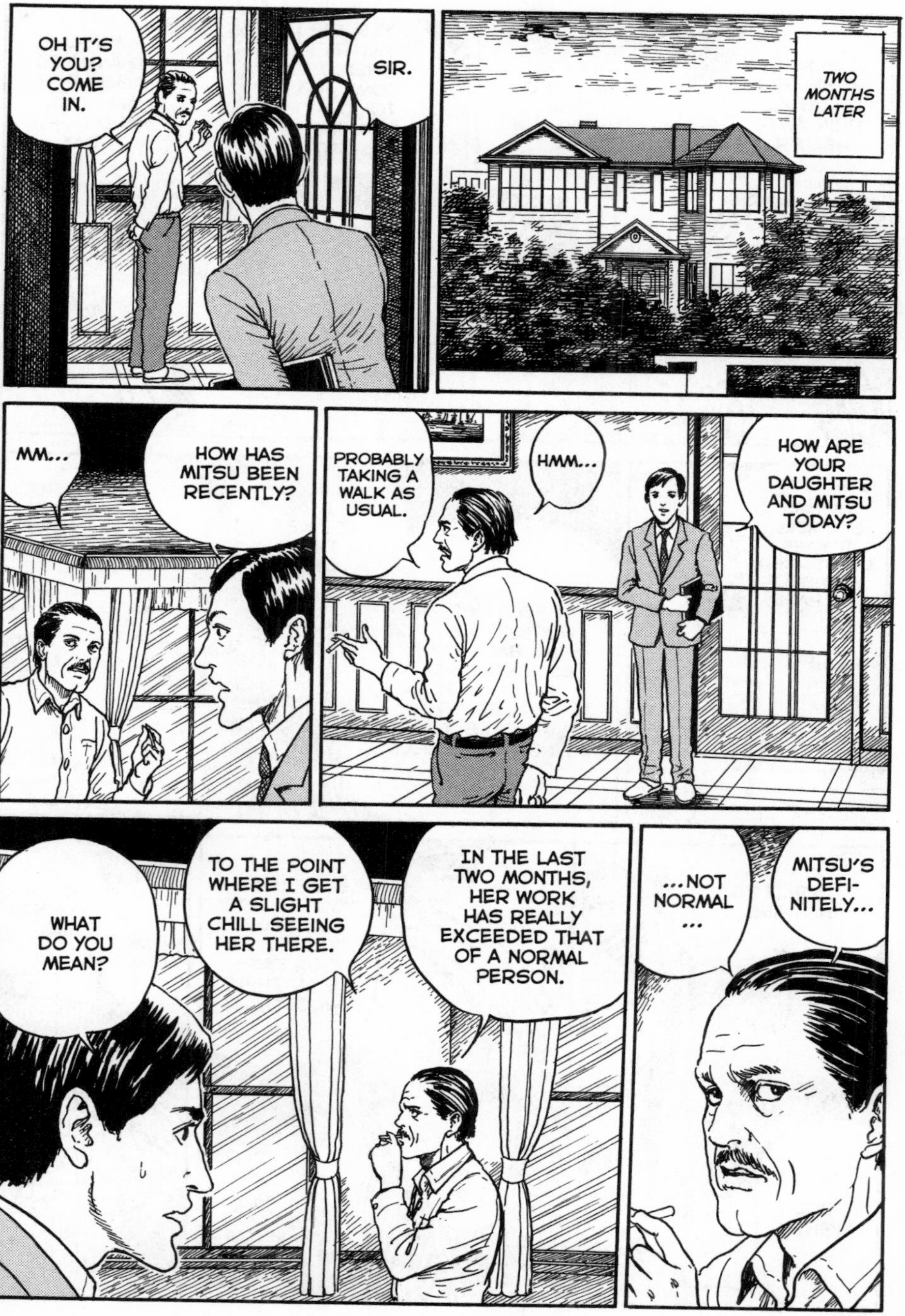
TWO MONTHS LATER
SIR.
OH IT'S YOU? COME IN.
HOW ARE YOUR DAUGHTER AND MITSU TODAY?
HMM...
PROBABLY TAKING A WALK AS USUAL.
HOW HAS MITSU BEEN RECENTLY?
MM...
MITSU'S DEFI-NITELY...
...NOT NORMAL ...
IN THE LAST TWO MONTHS, HER WORK HAS REALLY EXCEEDED THAT OF A NORMAL PERSON.
TO THE POINT WHERE I GET A SLIGHT CHILL SEEING HER THERE.
WHAT DO YOU MEAN?

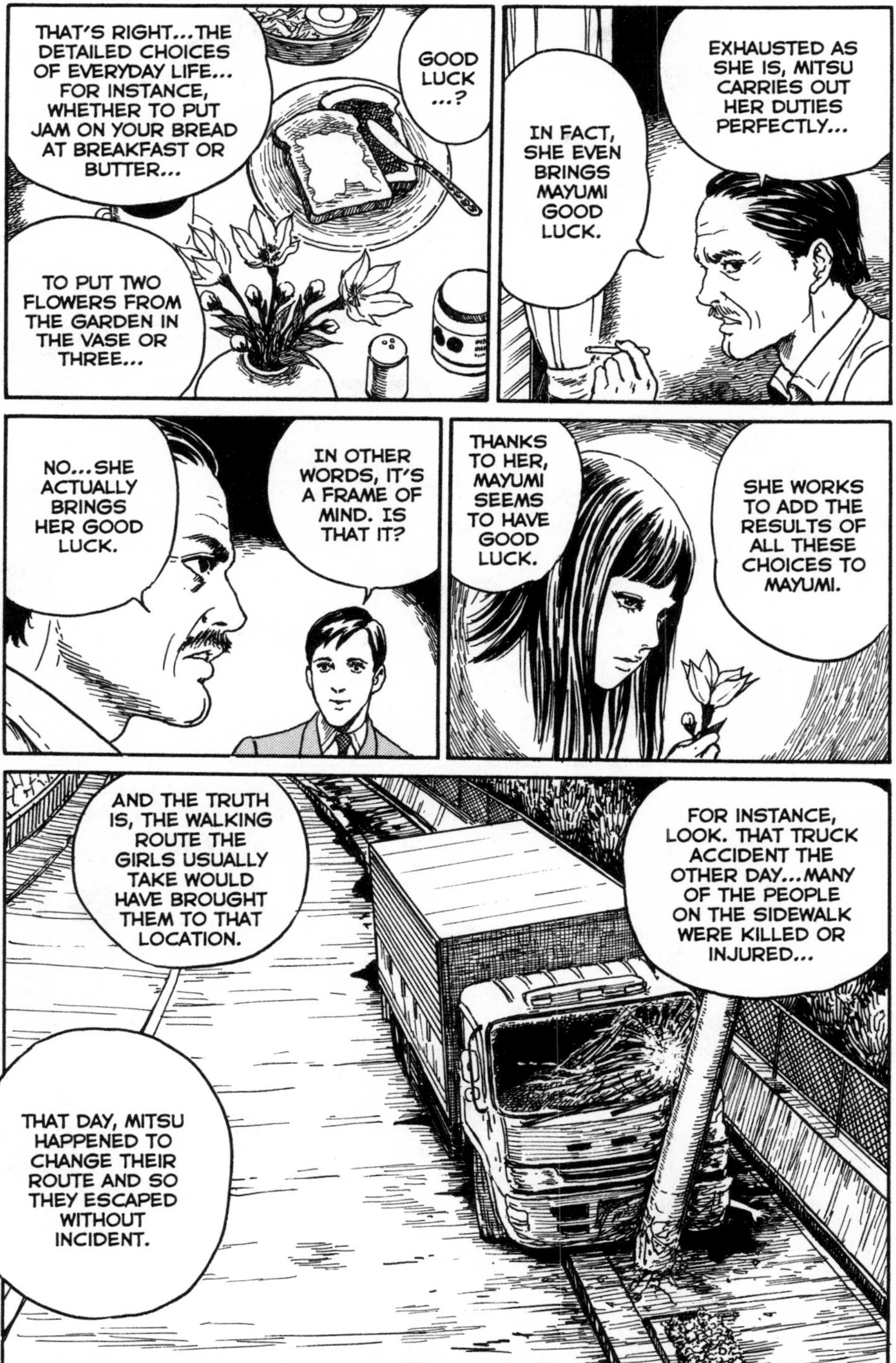
EXHAUSTED AS SHE IS, MITSU CARRIES OUT HER DUTIES PERFECTLY...
IN FACT, SHE EVEN BRINGS MAYUMI GOOD LUCK.
GOOD LUCK ...?
THAT'S RIGHT...THE DETAILED CHOICES OF EVERYDAY LIFE... FOR INSTANCE, WHETHER TO PUT JAM ON YOUR BREAD AT BREAKFAST OR BUTTER...
TO PUT TWO FLOWERS FROM THE GARDEN IN THE VASE OR THREE...
SHE WORKS TO ADD THE RESULTS OF ALL THESE CHOICES TO MAYUMI.
THANKS TO HER, MAYUMI SEEMS TO HAVE GOOD LUCK.
IN OTHER WORDS, IT'S A FRAME OF MIND. IS THAT IT?
NO...SHE ACTUALLY BRINGS HER GOOD LUCK.
FOR INSTANCE, LOOK. THAT TRUCK ACCIDENT THE OTHER DAY...MANY OF THE PEOPLE ON THE SIDEWALK WERE KILLED OR INJURED...
AND THE TRUTH IS, THE WALKING ROUTE THE GIRLS USUALLY TAKE WOULD HAVE BROUGHT THEM TO THAT LOCATION.
THAT DAY, MITSU HAPPENED TO CHANGE THEIR ROUTE AND SO THEY ESCAPED WITHOUT INCIDENT.

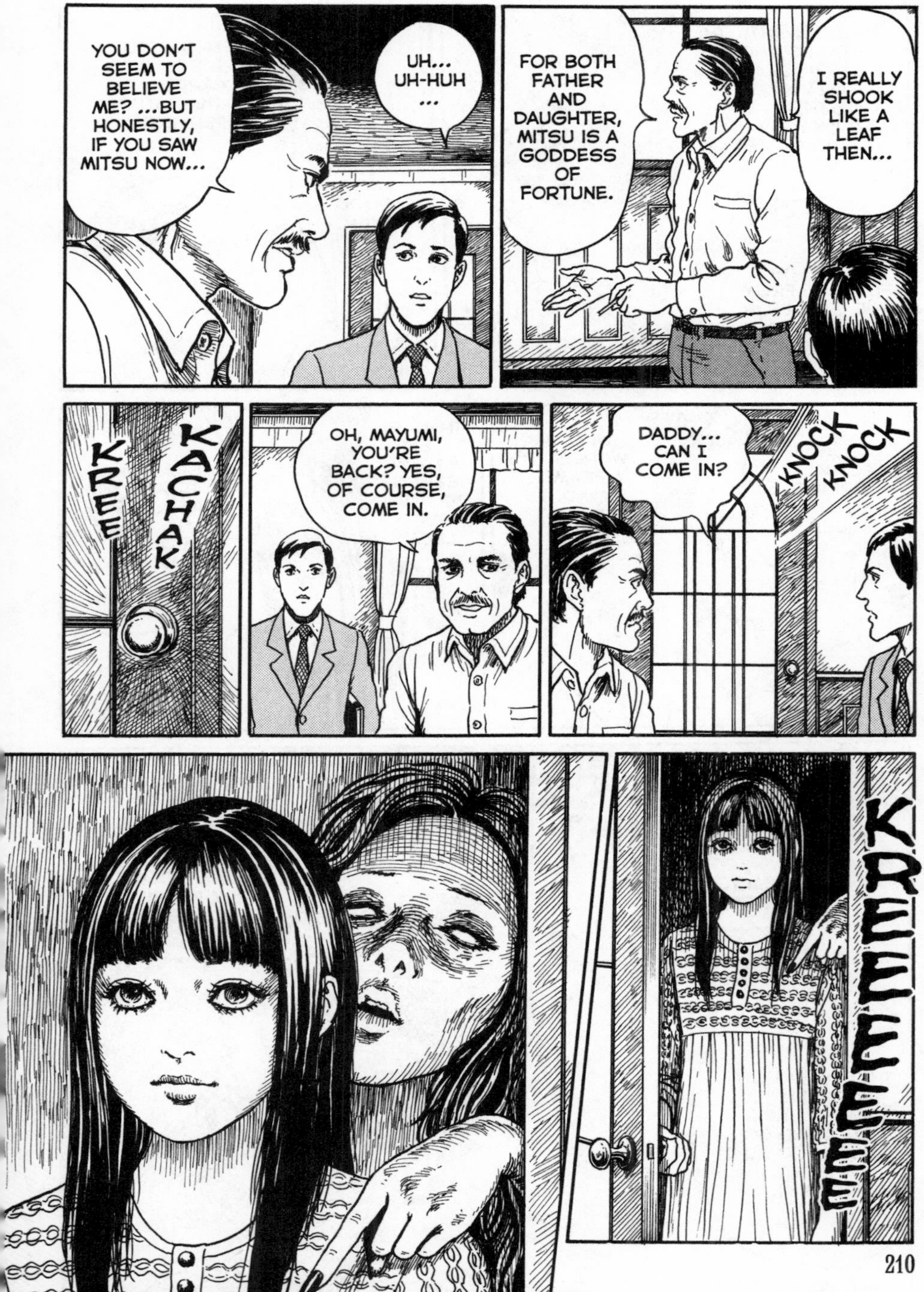
I REALLY SHOOK LIKE A LEAF THEN...
FOR BOTH FATHER AND DAUGHTER, MITSU IS A GODDESS OF FORTUNE.
YOU DON'T SEEM TO BELIEVE ME? ...BUT HONESTLY, IF YOU SAW MITSU NOW...
UH... UH-HUH ...
KNOCK KNOCK
DADDY... CAN I COME IN?
OH, MAYUMI, YOU'RE BACK? YES, OF COURSE, COME IN.
KACHAK
KREE
KREEEEEEE

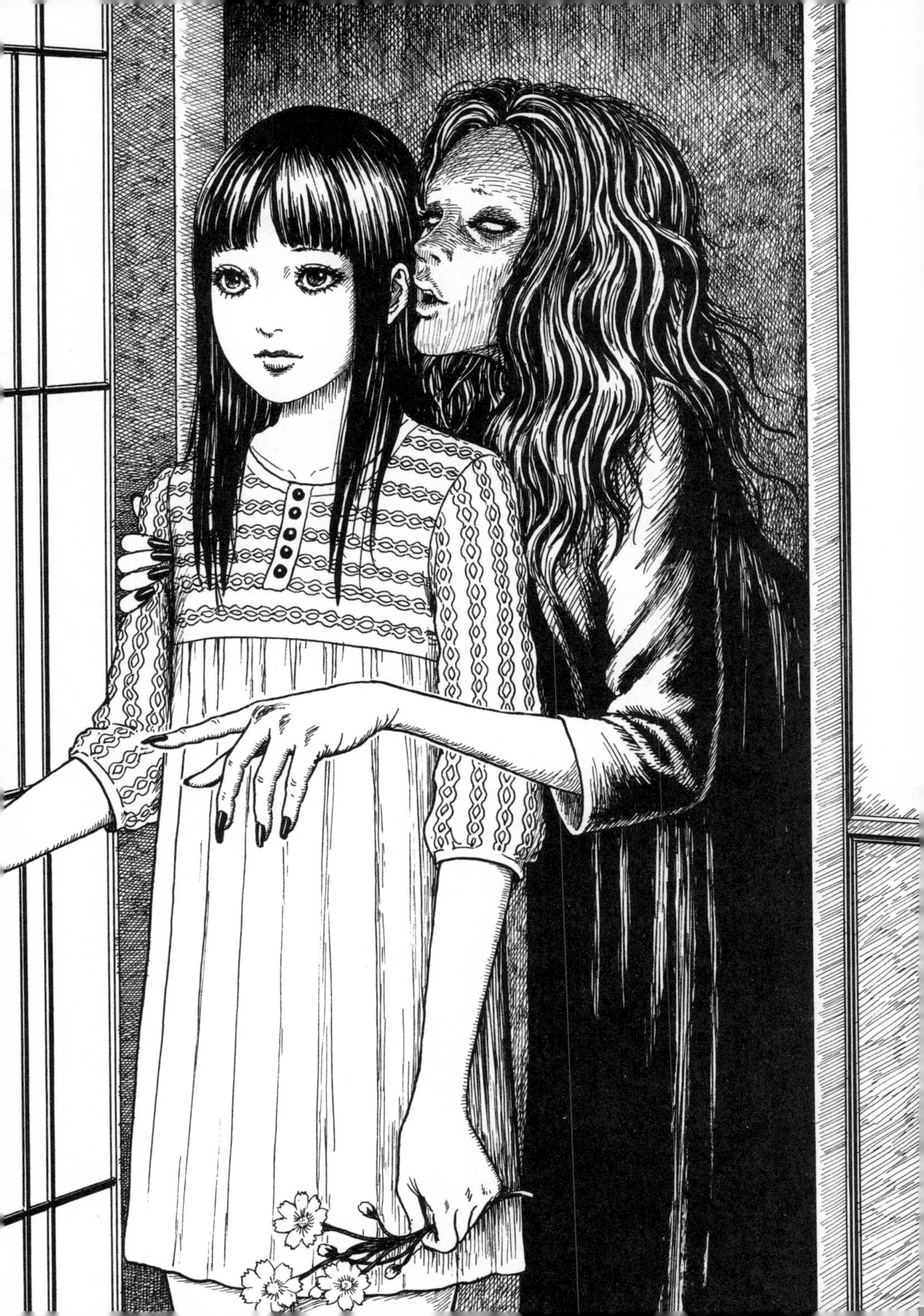

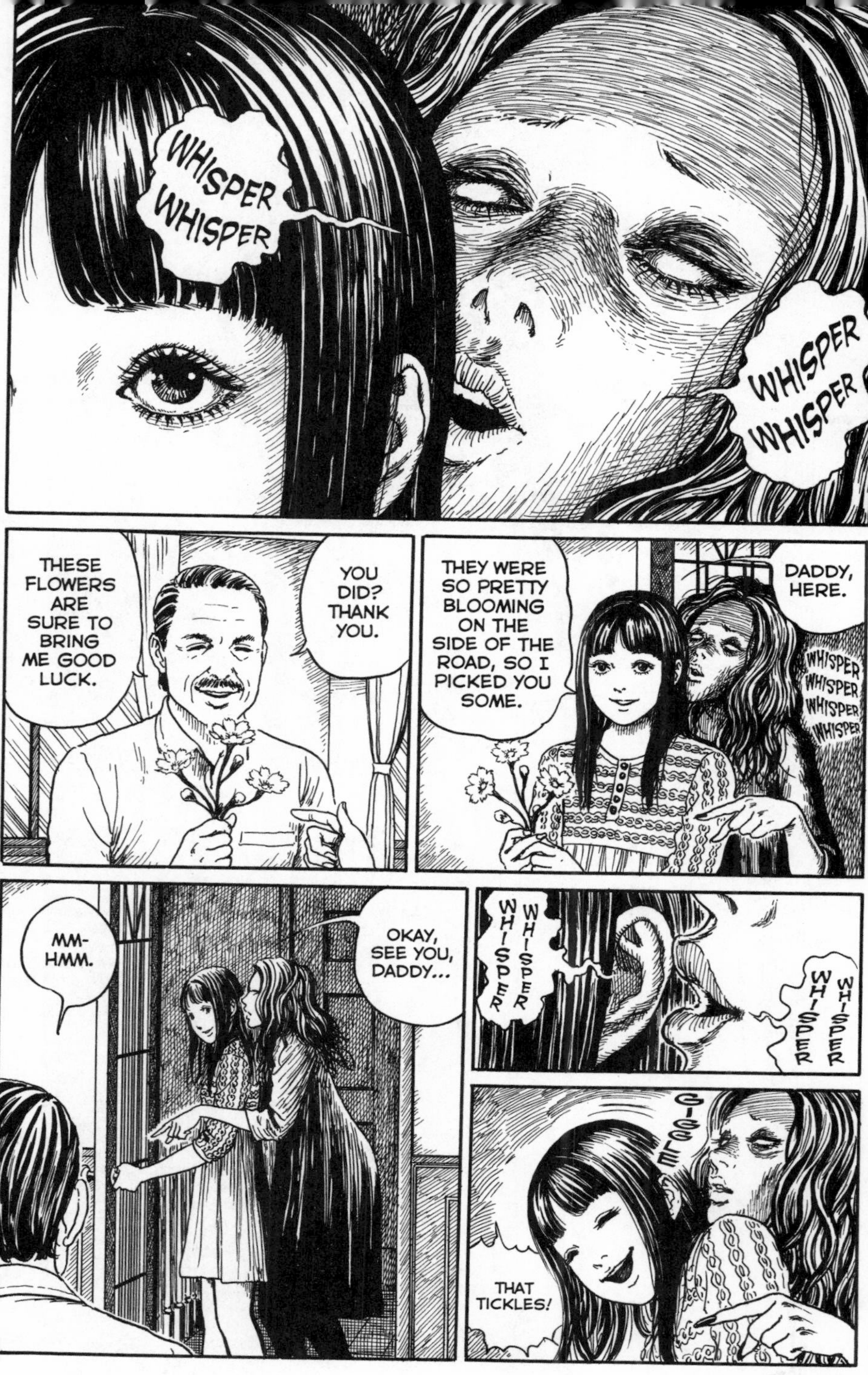
WHISPER WHISPER
WHISPER WHISPER
DADDY, HERE.
THEY WERE SO PRETTY BLOOMING ON THE SIDE OF THE ROAD, SO I PICKED YOU SOME.
WHISPER WHISPER WHISPER WHISPER
YOU DID? THANK YOU.
THESE FLOWERS ARE SURE TO BRING ME GOOD LUCK.
WHISPER WHISPER
WHISPER WHISPER
GIGGLE
THAT TICKLES!
OKAY, SEE YOU, DADDY...
MM-HMM.

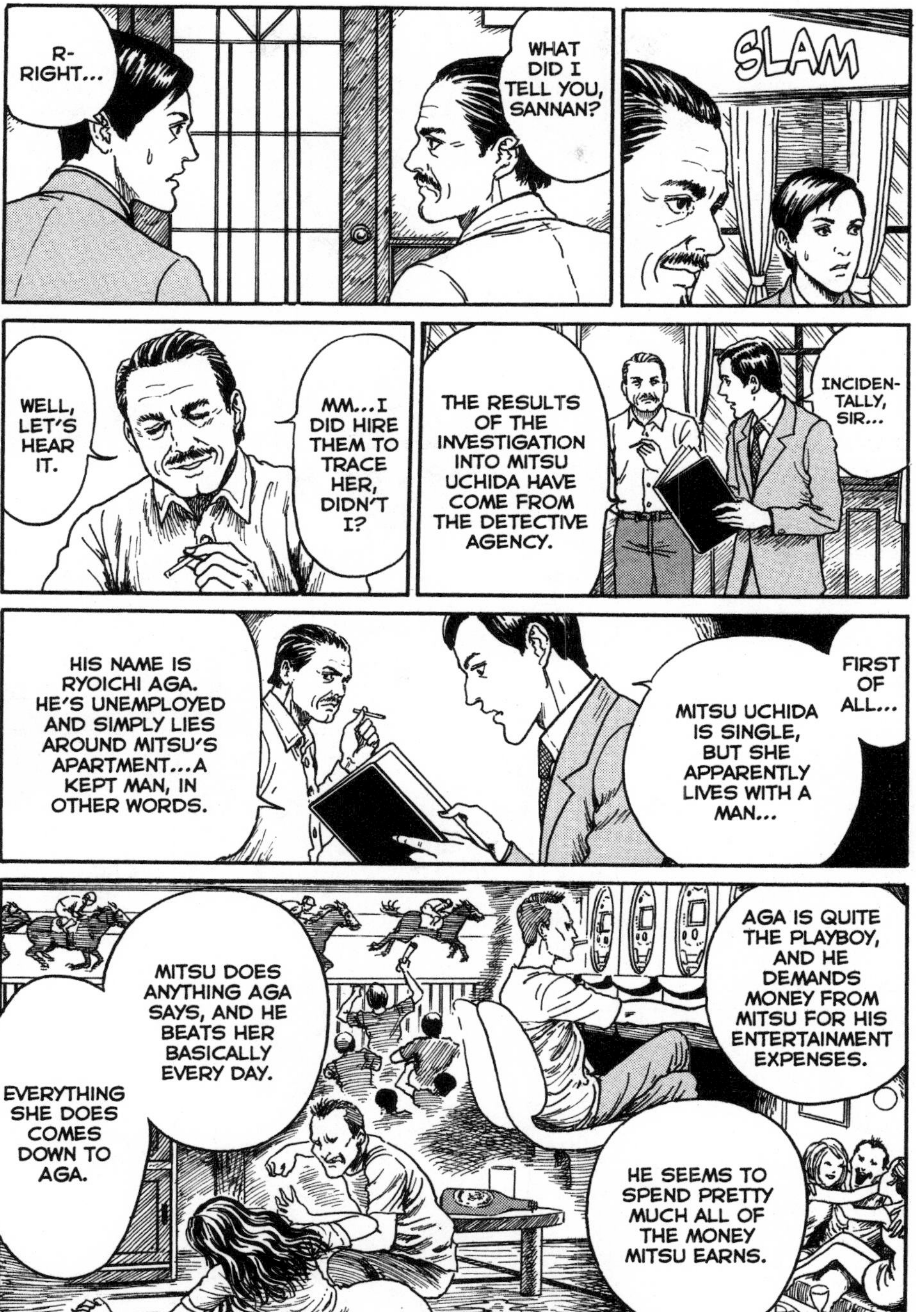
SLAM
WHAT DID I TELL YOU, SANNAN?
R-RIGHT...
INCIDENTALLY, SIR...
THE RESULTS OF THE INVESTIGATION INTO MITSU UCHIDA HAVE COME FROM THE DETECTIVE AGENCY.
MM...I DID HIRE THEM TO TRACE HER, DIDN'T I?
WELL, LET'S HEAR IT.
FIRST OF ALL...
MITSU UCHIDA IS SINGLE, BUT SHE APPARENTLY LIVES WITH A MAN...
HIS NAME IS RYOICHI AGA. HE'S UNEMPLOYED AND SIMPLY LIES AROUND MITSU'S APARTMENT...A KEPT MAN, IN OTHER WORDS.
AGA IS QUITE THE PLAYBOY, AND HE DEMANDS MONEY FROM MITSU FOR HIS ENTERTAINMENT EXPENSES.
MITSU DOES ANYTHING AGA SAYS, AND HE BEATS HER BASICALLY EVERY DAY.
HE SEEMS TO SPEND PRETTY MUCH ALL OF THE MONEY MITSU EARNS.
EVERYTHING SHE DOES COMES DOWN TO AGA.

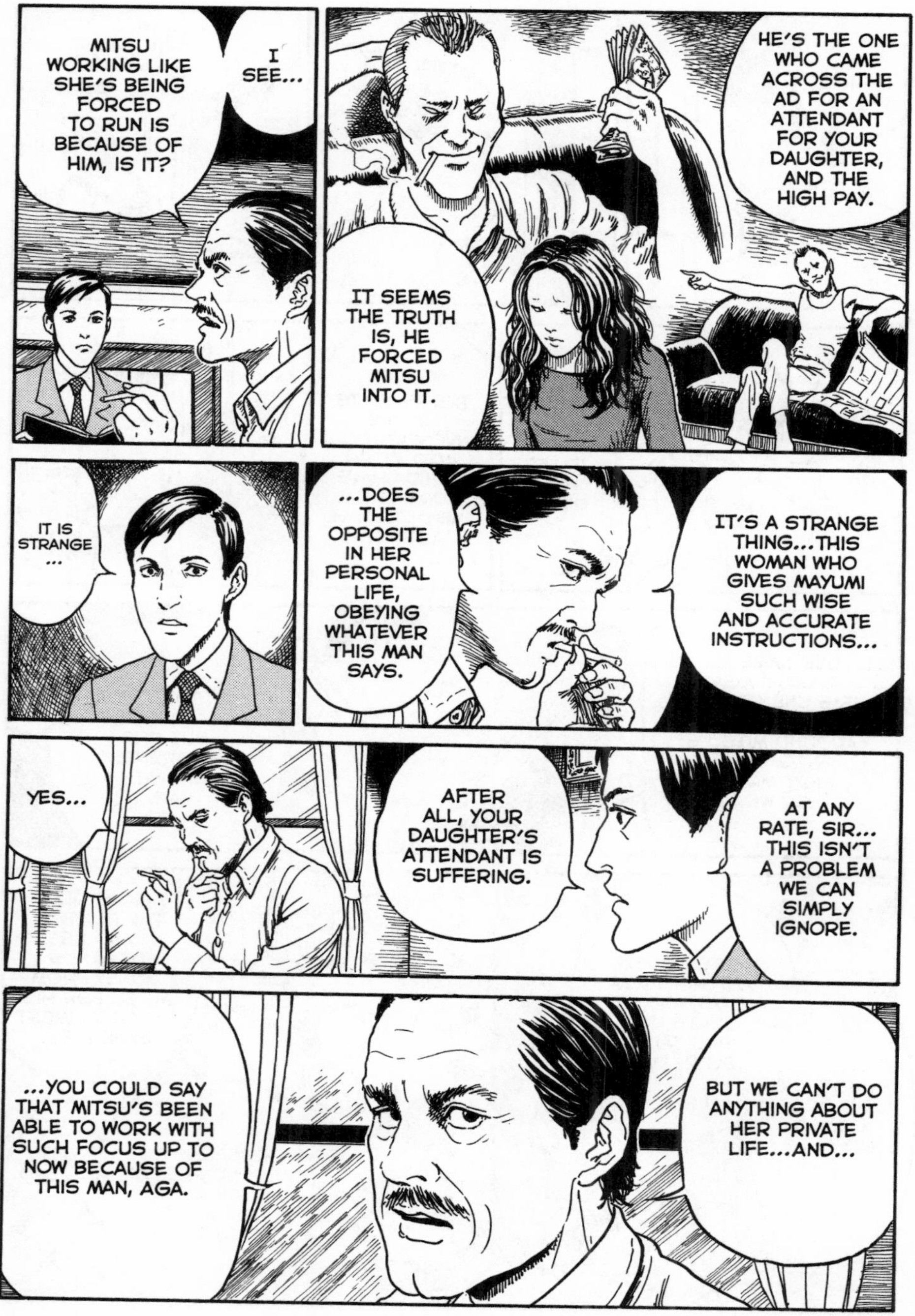
HE'S THE ONE WHO CAME ACROSS THE AD FOR AN ATTENDANT FOR YOUR DAUGHTER, AND THE HIGH PAY.
IT SEEMS THE TRUTH IS, HE FORCED MITSU INTO IT.
I SEE...
MITSU WORKING LIKE SHE'S BEING FORCED TO RUN IS BECAUSE OF HIM, IS IT?
IT'S A STRANGE THING...THIS WOMAN WHO GIVES MAYUMI SUCH WISE AND ACCURATE INSTRUCTIONS...
...DOES THE OPPOSITE IN HER PERSONAL LIFE, OBEYING WHATEVER THIS MAN SAYS.
IT IS STRANGE ...
AT ANY RATE, SIR... THIS ISN'T A PROBLEM WE CAN SIMPLY IGNORE.
AFTER ALL, YOUR DAUGHTER'S ATTENDANT IS SUFFERING.
YES...
BUT WE CAN'T DO ANYTHING ABOUT HER PRIVATE LIFE...AND...
...YOU COULD SAY THAT MITSU'S BEEN ABLE TO WORK WITH SUCH FOCUS UP TO NOW BECAUSE OF THIS MAN, AGA.

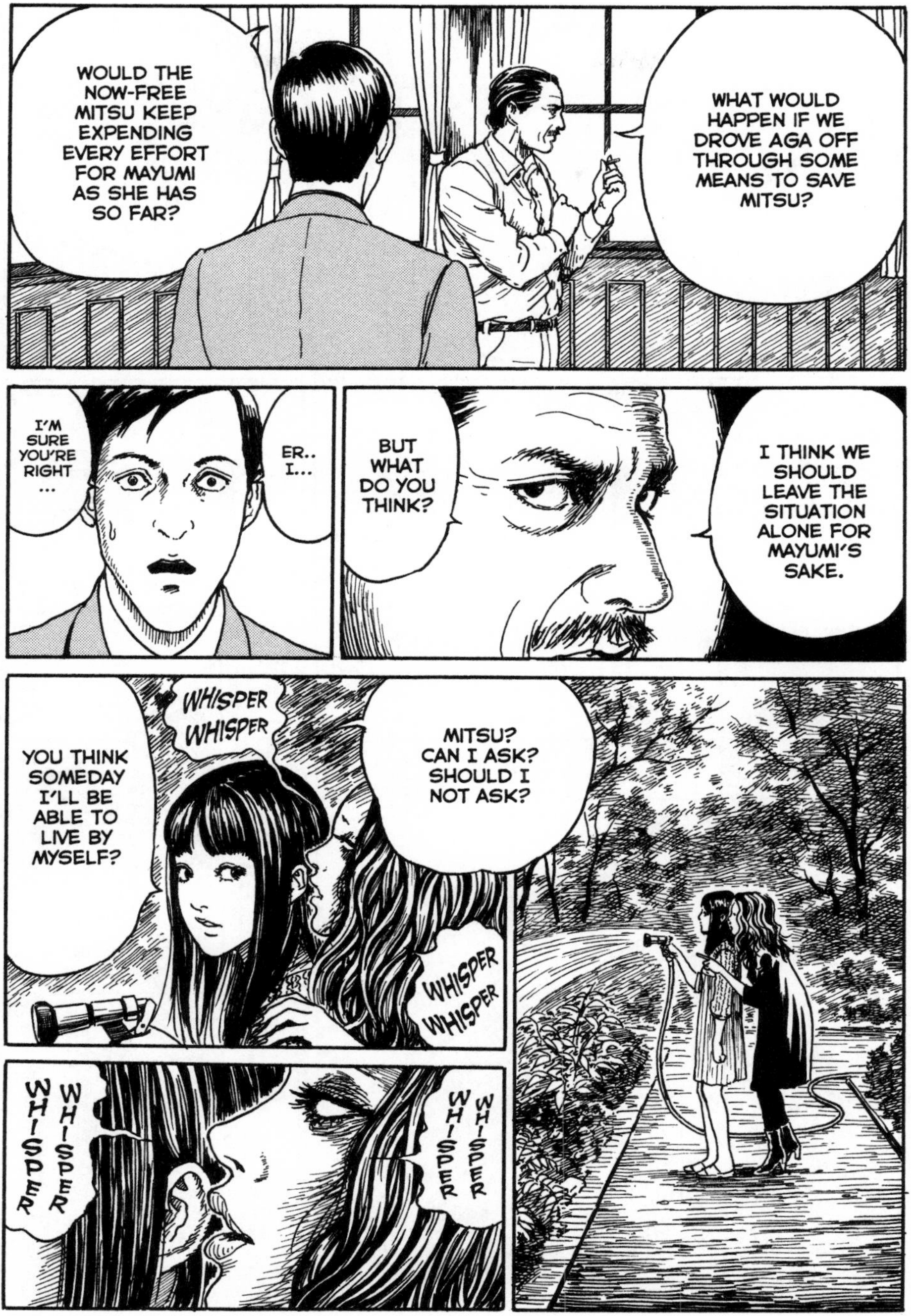
WHAT WOULD HAPPEN IF WE DROVE AGA OFF THROUGH SOME MEANS TO SAVE MITSU?
WOULD THE NOW-FREE MITSU KEEP EXPENDING EVERY EFFORT FOR MAYUMI AS SHE HAS SO FAR?
I THINK WE SHOULD LEAVE THE SITUATION ALONE FOR MAYUMI'S SAKE.
BUT WHAT DO YOU THINK?
ER.. I...
I'M SURE YOU'RE RIGHT ...
MITSU? CAN I ASK? SHOULD I NOT ASK?
WHISPER WHISPER
YOU THINK SOMEDAY I'LL BE ABLE TO LIVE BY MYSELF?
WHISPER WHISPER
WHISPER WHISPER
WHISPER WHISPER

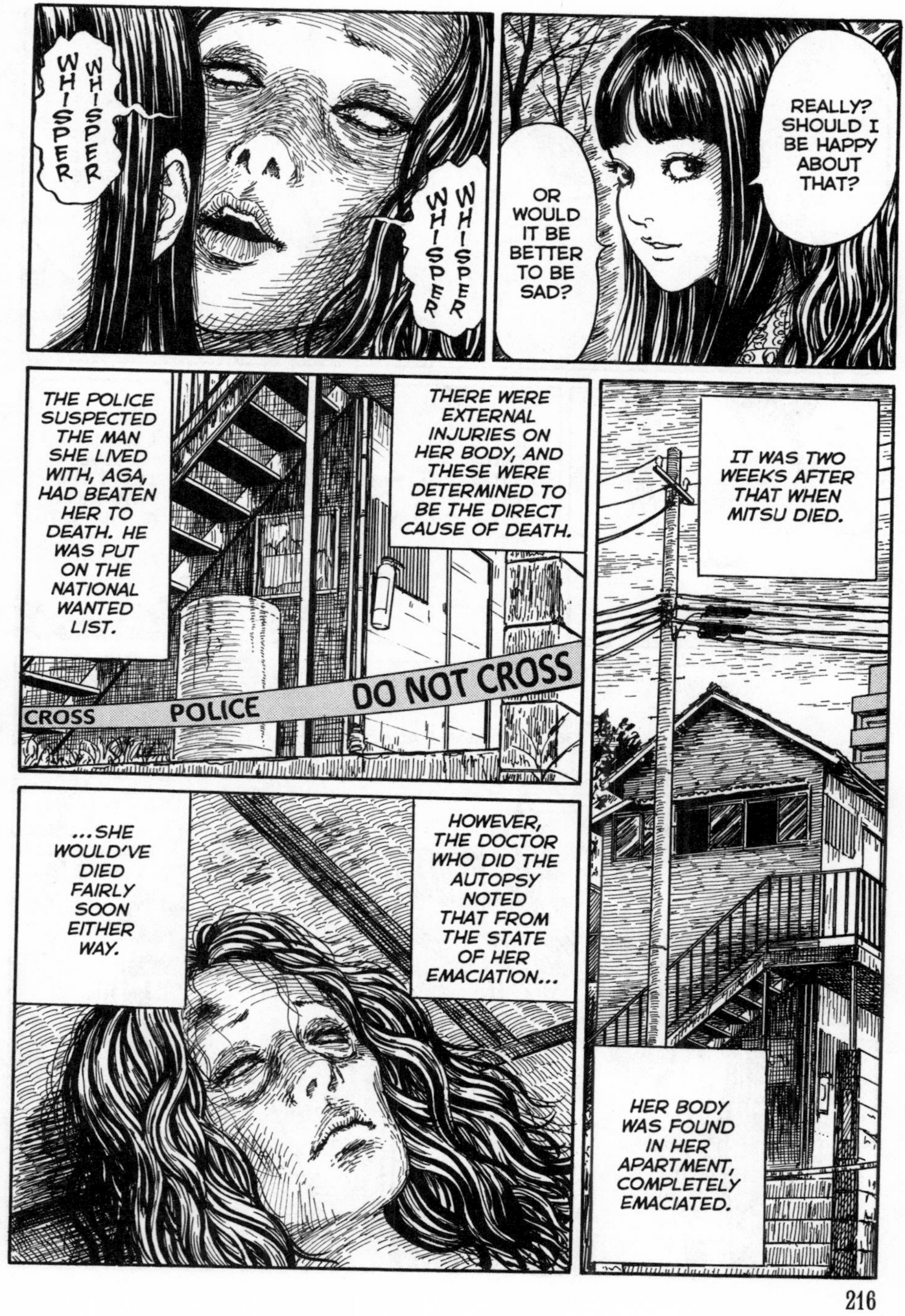
REALLY? SHOULD I BE HAPPY ABOUT THAT?
OR WOULD IT BE BETTER TO BE SAD?
WHISPER WHISPER
WHISPER WHISPER
IT WAS TWO WEEKS AFTER THAT WHEN MITSU DIED.
HER BODY WAS FOUND IN HER APARTMENT, COMPLETELY EMACIATED.
THERE WERE EXTERNAL INJURIES ON HER BODY, AND THESE WERE DETERMINED TO BE THE DIRECT CAUSE OF DEATH.
THE POLICE SUSPECTED THE MAN SHE LIVED WITH, AGA, HAD BEATEN HER TO DEATH. HE WAS PUT ON THE NATIONAL WANTED LIST.
DO NOT CROSS
POLICE
CROSS
HOWEVER, THE DOCTOR WHO DID THE AUTOPSY NOTED THAT FROM THE STATE OF HER EMACIATION...
...SHE WOULD'VE DIED FAIRLY SOON EITHER WAY.

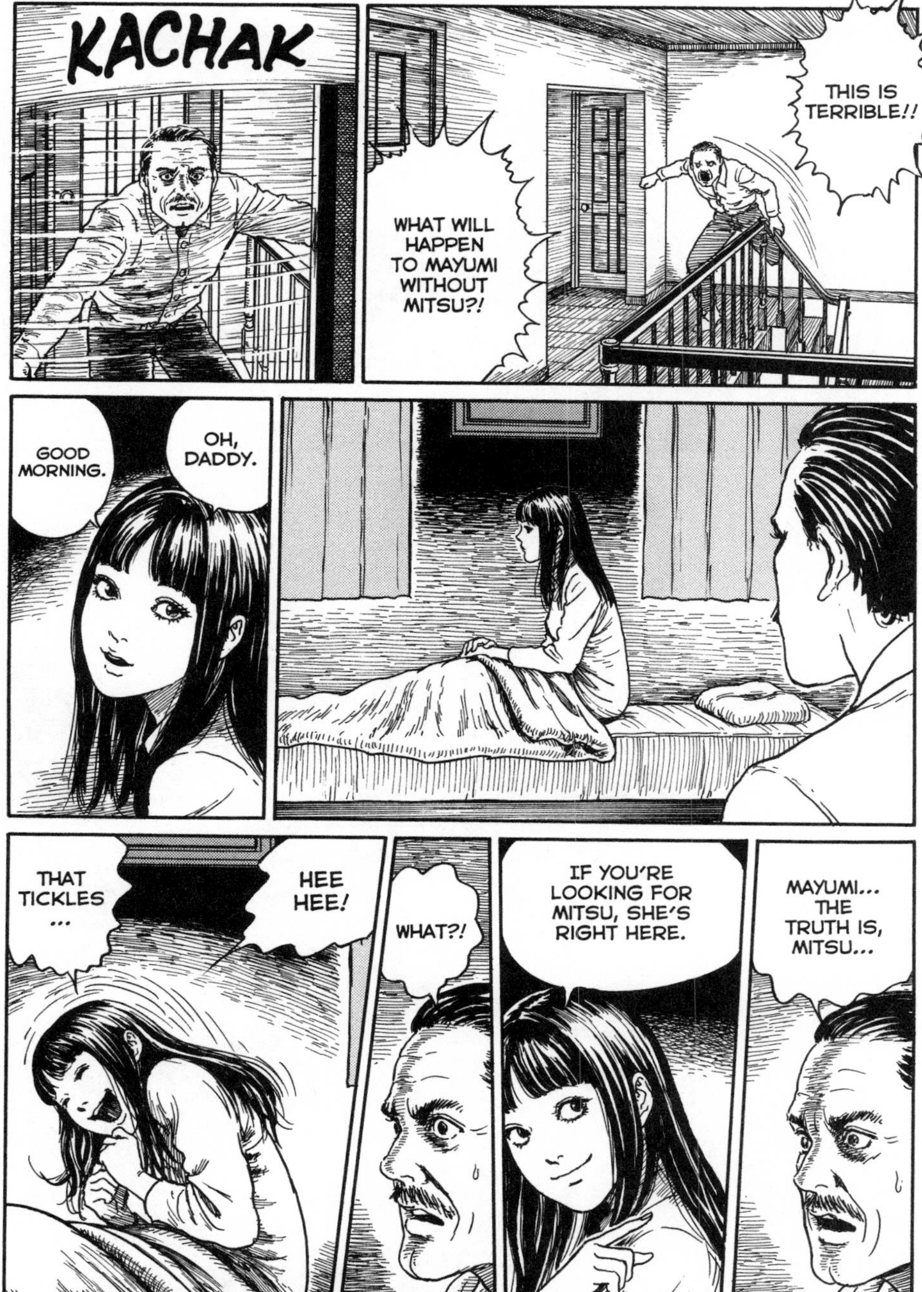
THIS IS TERRIBLE!!
WHAT WILL HAPPEN TO MAYUMI WITHOUT MITSU?!
KACHAK
OH, DADDY.
GOOD MORNING.
MAYUMI... THE TRUTH IS, MITSU...
IF YOU'RE LOOKING FOR MITSU, SHE'S RIGHT HERE.
WHAT?!
HEE HEE!
THAT TICKLES ...

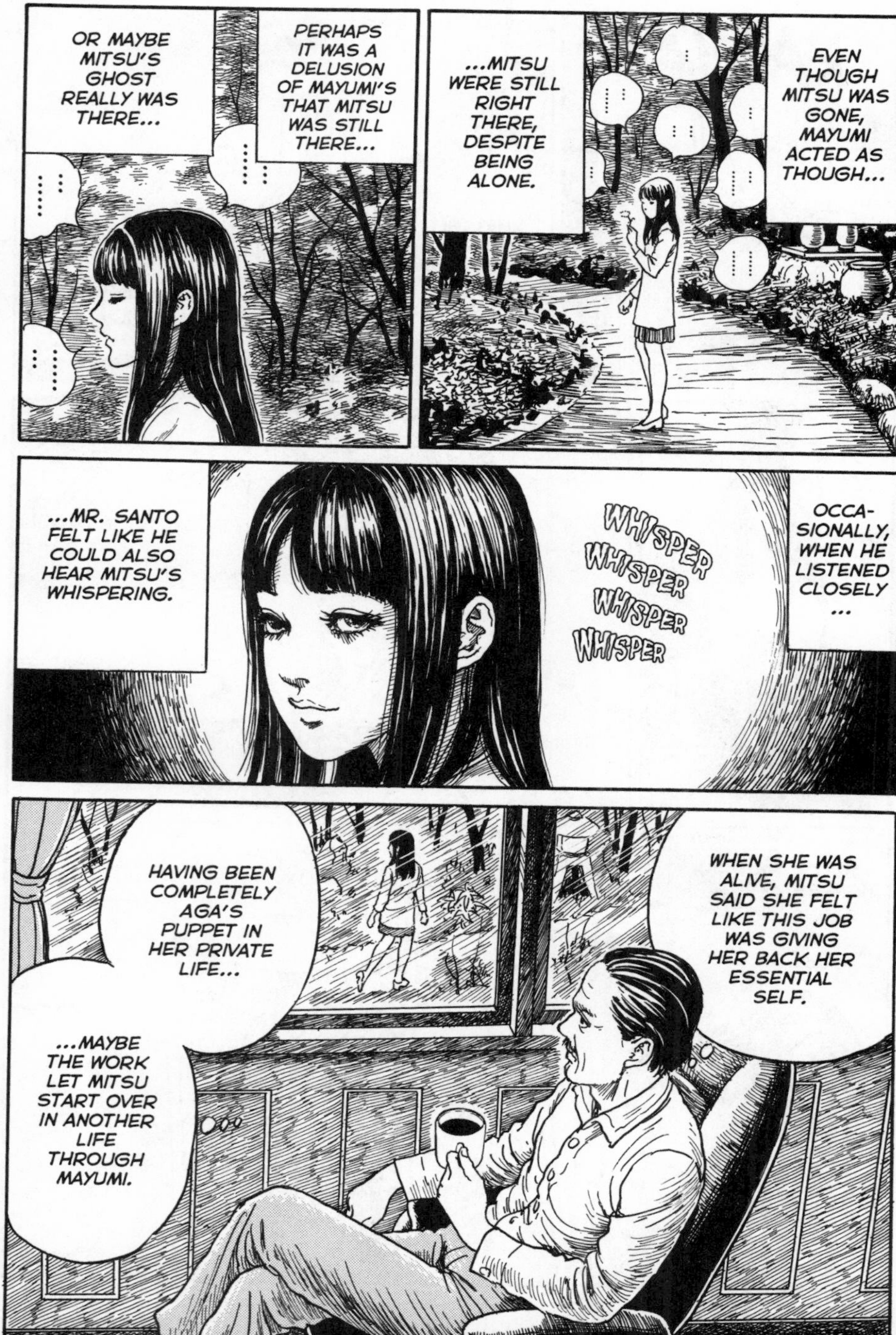
EVEN THOUGH MITSU WAS GONE, MAYUMI ACTED AS THOUGH...
...MITSU WERE STILL RIGHT THERE, DESPITE BEING ALONE.
PERHAPS IT WAS A DELUSION OF MAYUMI'S THAT MITSU WAS STILL THERE...
OR MAYBE MITSU'S GHOST REALLY WAS THERE...
OCCASIONALLY, WHEN HE LISTENED CLOSELY...
WHISPER
WHISPER
WHISPER
WHISPER
...MR. SANTO FELT LIKE HE COULD ALSO HEAR MITSU'S WHISPERING.
WHEN SHE WAS ALIVE, MITSU SAID SHE FELT LIKE THIS JOB WAS GIVING HER BACK HER ESSENTIAL SELF.
HAVING BEEN COMPLETELY AGA'S PUPPET IN HER PRIVATE LIFE...
...MAYBE THE WORK LET MITSU START OVER IN ANOTHER LIFE THROUGH MAYUMI.

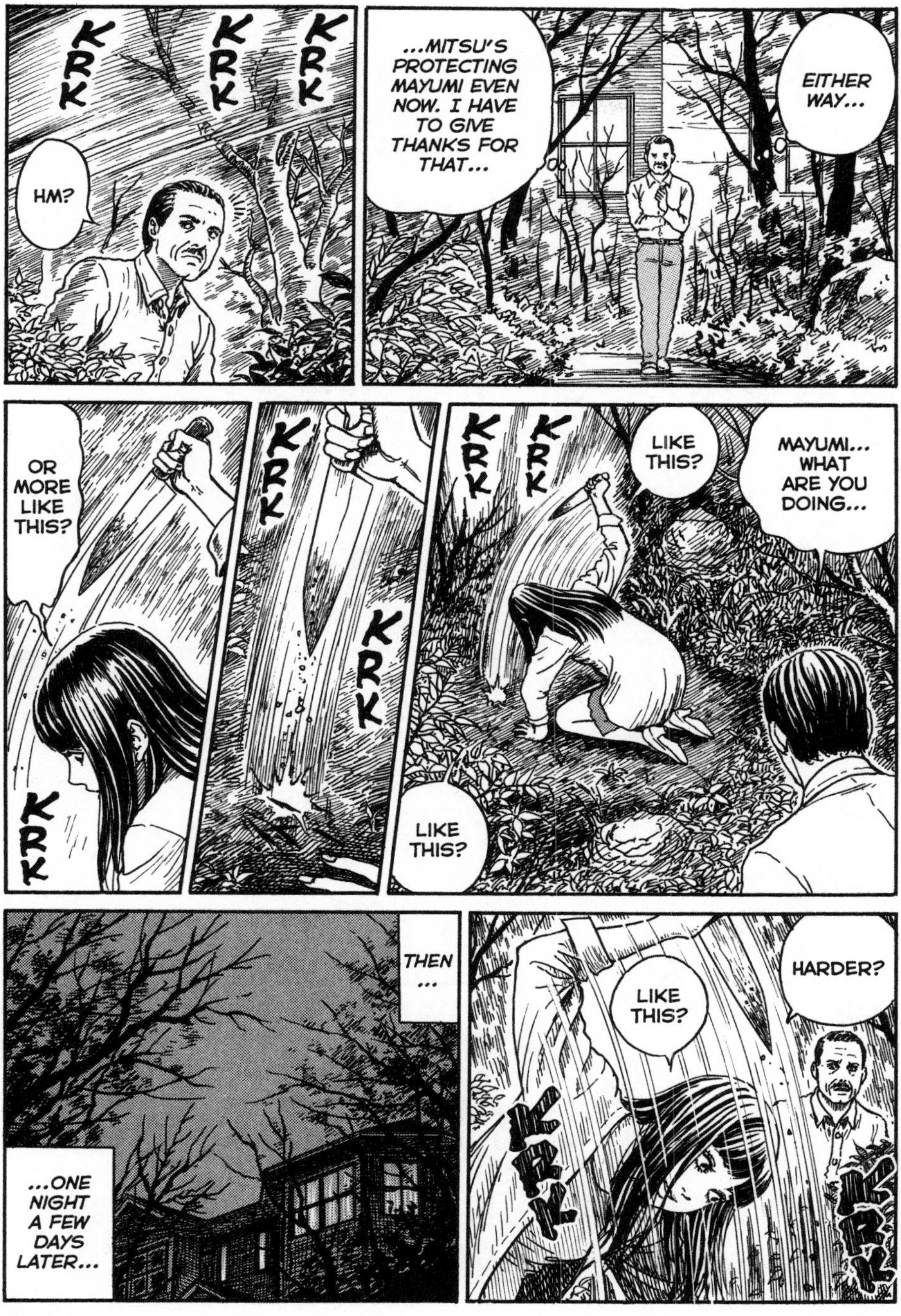
EITHER WAY...
...MITSU'S PROTECTING MAYUMI EVEN NOW. I HAVE TO GIVE THANKS FOR THAT...
KRK KRK KRK
HM?
MAYUMI... WHAT ARE YOU DOING...
LIKE THIS?
KRK KRK
LIKE THIS?
KRK KRK
OR MORE LIKE THIS?
KRK
HARDER?
LIKE THIS?
THEN...
...ONE NIGHT A FEW DAYS LATER...

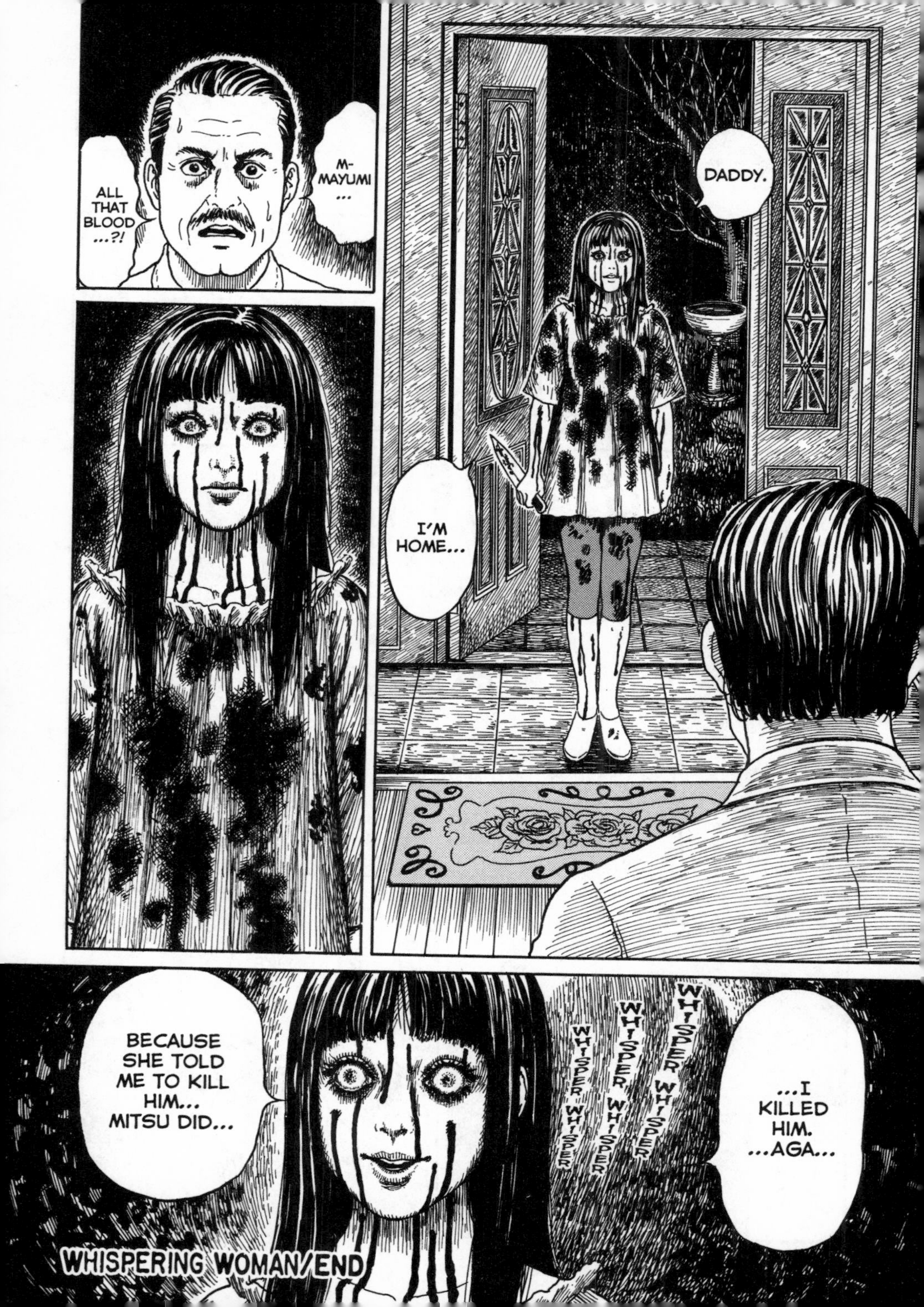
DADDY.
I'M HOME...
M-MAYUMI...
ALL THAT BLOOD...?!
...I KILLED HIM. ...AGA...
WHISPER WHISPER
WHISPER WHISPER
WHISPER WHISPER
BECAUSE SHE TOLD ME TO KILL HIM... MITSU DID...
WHISPERING WOMAN/END

AFTERWORD

SO THIS IS MY FIRST COLLECTION OF HORROR STORIES IN EIGHT YEARS. EVER SINCE I PUT OUT *SHIN YAMI NO KOE KAIDAN* IN 2006.

DURING THOSE EIGHT YEARS, I WAS DOING PLENTY OF WORK ON ILLUSTRATIONS AND MANGA ABOUT CATS OR ABOUT SOCIETY, BUT EVEN TAKING THAT INTO ACCOUNT, THE TIME SEEMS TOO EMPTY SOMEHOW. WHAT ON EARTH WAS I DOING ALL THAT TIME? WELL, I DO REMEMBER A BUNCH OF THINGS—LIKE SOME REALLY DETAILED WORK AND A BUSY PRIVATE LIFE—BUT EVEN STILL, EIGHT YEARS?! IT IS TRUE THAT I'M NOT AS STRONG AS I USED TO BE AND I COULDN'T WORK ANY FASTER THAN I WAS, BUT I FEEL LIKE I WASTED A WHOLE LOT OF TIME. DURING THIS PERIOD, MR. TOSHIYASU HARADA, MY EDITOR, A MAN WHO HAD BEEN SO GOOD TO ME FOR SO MANY YEARS AT ASAHI SONORAMA, PASSED AWAY. I HAD WANTED TO WORK WITH MR. HARADA AGAIN, SO WHEN HE PASSED AWAY, HE LEFT A GAPING HOLE IN MY HEART. OH, AND A FEW HOURS AFTER MR. HARADA LEFT US, OUR CAT YONSUKE ALSO DIED (THE MODEL FOR THE MONSTER CAT YON THAT SHOWS UP IN MY CAT MANGA). IT MIGHT BE A COINCIDENCE, BUT I EXPERIENCED IT AS A MYSTERIOUS SORT OF CONNECTION.

AND SO, A COLLECTION OF HORROR STORIES AFTER EIGHT YEARS. WHEN HE SAW MY FIRST STORYBOARD FOR THE FIRST STORY, "FUTON," MY EDITOR MR. YOSHIDA GOT WORRIED AND CALLED ME. HE FELT THAT MY INSTINCTS FOR HORROR HADN'T RETURNED. I DON'T KNOW IF IT WAS BECAUSE I HADN'T DRAWN HORROR IN SUCH A LONG TIME, BUT IT WAS INDEED A SUBPAR STORYBOARD. I REDID THE WHOLE THING, BUT IT STILL DIDN'T QUITE COME TOGETHER FOR ME; IT WAS A RELUCTANT START TO MY FIRST HORROR SERIALIZATION IN SOME TIME. I WENT ON TO DRAW SIX MORE STORIES AFTER THAT, SO MAYBE IN THE END MY HORROR INSTINCTS HAVE RETURNED...?

AT ANY RATE, I'M VERY HAPPY TO HAVE THIS COLLECTION PUBLISHED. I WANT TO OFFER MY SINCEREST GRATITUDE TO EVERYONE IN THE *NEMUKI+* EDITORIAL DIVISION WHO GAVE ME THIS OPPORTUNITY, STARTING WITH MY EDITORS MIKIO YOSHIDA AND MAKIKO HARA, AND TO KEISUKE MINOHARA OF ROCKET BOMB WHO DID THE COVER DESIGN.

JUNJI ITO
APRIL 30, 2014

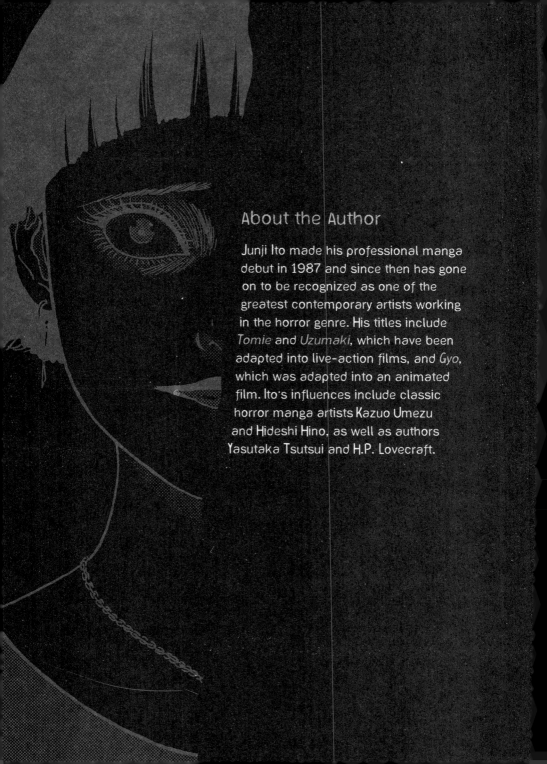

About the Author

Junji Ito made his professional manga
debut in 1987 and since then has gone
on to be recognized as one of the
greatest contemporary artists working
in the horror genre. His titles include
Tomie and *Uzumaki*, which have been
adapted into live-action films, and *Gyo*,
which was adapted into an animated
film. Ito's influences include classic
horror manga artists Kazuo Umezu
and Hideshi Hino, as well as authors
Yasutaka Tsutsui and H.P. Lovecraft.

FraGments of Horror

Fragments of Horror
VIZ Signature Edition

Story & Art by Junji Ito

Translation & Adaptation/Jocelyne Allen
Touch-up Art & Lettering/Eric Erbes
Cover & Graphic Design/Sam Elzway
Editors/Masumi Washington, Nick Mamatas

Fragments of Horror
©Junji Ito 2014
Originally published in Japan in 2014 by Asahi Shimbun Publications Inc., Japan.
English translation rights arranged with Asahi Shimbun Publications Inc., Japan
through TOHAN CORPORATION, Tokyo.

Printed in the U.S.A.

Published by VIZ Media, LLC
P.O. Box 77010
San Francisco, CA 94107

10 9 8 7 6 5
First printing, June 2015
Fifth printing, April 2019

VIZ SIGNATURE